Strategic Integration of Social Media into Project Management Practice

Gilbert Silvius
LOI University of Applied Sciences, The Netherlands & University of Johannesburg, South Africa

A volume in the Advances in IT Personnel and Project Management (AITPPM) Book Series

BUSINESS SCIENCE Reference
An Imprint of IGI Global

Published in the United States of America by
Business Science Reference (an imprint of IGI Global)
701 E. Chocolate Avenue
Hershey PA, USA 17033
Tel: 717-533-8845
Fax: 717-533-8661
E-mail: cust@igi-global.com
Web site: http://www.igi-global.com

Library of Congress Cataloging-in-Publication Data

Names: Silvius, Gilbert, editor.
Title: Strategic integration of social media into project management practice / Gilbert Silvius, editor.
Description: Hershey : Business Science Reference, 2016. | Includes bibliographical references and index.
Identifiers: LCCN 2015046859| ISBN 9781466698673 (hardcover : alk. paper) | ISBN 9781466698680 (ebook)
Subjects: LCSH: Project management. | Management--Technological innovations. | Online social networks in business. | Communication in management.
Classification: LCC HD69.P75 S7647 2016 | DDC 658.4/04--dc23 LC record available at http://lccn.loc.gov/2015046859

This book is published in the IGI Global book series Advances in IT Personnel and Project Management (AITPPM) (ISSN: 2331-768X; eISSN: 2331-7698)

British Cataloguing in Publication Data
A Cataloguing in Publication record for this book is available from the British Library.

Advances in IT Personnel and Project Management (AITPPM) Book Series

Sanjay Misra
Covenant University, OTA, Nigeria
Ricardo Colomo-Palacios
Østfold University College, Norway

ISSN: 2331-768X
EISSN: 2331-7698

Mission

Technology has become an integral part of organizations in every sector, contributing to the way in which large enterprises, small businesses, government agencies, and non-profit organizations operate. In the midst of this revolution, it is essential that these organizations have a thorough knowledge of how to implement and manage IT projects as well as an understanding of how to attract and supervise the employees associated with these projects.

The **Advances in IT Personnel and Project Management (AITPPM)** book series aims to provide current research on all facets of IT Project Management including factors to consider when managing and working with IT personnel. Books within the AITPPM book series will provide managers, IT professionals, business leaders, and upper-level students with the latest trends, applications, methodologies, and literature available in this field.

Coverage

- IT Personnel Management
- Requirements Management
- Performance Evaluation
- Agile Project Management
- Cost-Effective Methods for Project Management
- IT Entrepreneurship
- Measuring Project Success
- IT Strategy
- Project Management Software
- Project Sponsorship

IGI Global is currently accepting manuscripts for publication within this series. To submit a proposal for a volume in this series, please contact our Acquisition Editors at Acquisitions@igi-global.com or visit: http://www.igi-global.com/publish/.

The Advances in IT Personnel and Project Management (AITPPM) Book Series (ISSN 2331-768X) is published by IGI Global, 701 E. Chocolate Avenue, Hershey, PA 17033-1240, USA, www.igi-global.com. This series is composed of titles available for purchase individually; each title is edited to be contextually exclusive from any other title within the series. For pricing and ordering information please visit http://www.igi-global.com/book-series/advances-personnel-project-management/77666. Postmaster: Send all address changes to above address.

Titles in this Series

For a list of additional titles in this series, please visit: www.igi-global.com

Modern Techniques for Successful IT Project Management
Shang Gao (Zhongnan University of Economics and Law, China) and Lazar Rusu (Stockholm University, Sweden)
Business Science Reference • copyright 2015 • 374pp • H/C (ISBN: 9781466674738) • US $225.00 (our price)

Handbook of Research on Effective Project Management through the Integration of Knowledge and Innovation
George Leal Jamil (Informações em Rede, Brazil) Sérgio Maravilhas Lopes (CETAC.MEDIA - Porto and Aveiro Universities, Portugal) Armando Malheiro da Silva (Porto University, Portugal) and Fernanda Ribeiro (Porto University, Portugal)
Business Science Reference • copyright 2015 • 602pp • H/C (ISBN: 9781466675360) • US $285.00 (our price)

Handbook of Research on Technology Project Management, Planning, and Operations
Terry T. Kidd (Texas A&M University, USA)
Information Science Reference • copyright 2009 • 610pp • H/C (ISBN: 9781605664002) • US $265.00 (our price)

Managing Very Large IT Projects in Businesses and Organizations
Matthew Guah (Erasmus University Rotterdam, The Netherlands)
Information Science Reference • copyright 2009 • 358pp • H/C (ISBN: 9781599045467) • US $165.00 (our price)

Editorial Advisory Board

Table of Contents

Detailed Table of Contents

With growing maturity of social media over the last few years, many companies started using these tools to interact with customers and employees. Business functions such as Sales, Marketing and Human Resources have innovatively embedded these technologies to support their processes and became, as such, an instrument for renewal. The use of social media in Project Management, however, seems to be very limited. The profession lags behind having difficulty keeping pace with the rapidly evolving web 2.0 driven technological innovations which are delivering on their promise to foster collaboration. The paper discusses the potential of social media in the project management practice. As the move towards harnessing the power of social media within the Project Management framework requires adequate organizational change, the study also addresses the implications of such an initiative on structure, culture, and control.

This chapter provides insight into the effects of social media on (the execution of) project management. Billions of people nowadays make daily use of social media. This phenomenon also gradually found its way to the business world. With projects being an essential element of many organizations, project managers must be aware what social media is all about and how it can strengthen their projects. The time is right for project managers to explore and embrace social media as an additional tool to be used for managing projects more effectively. This chapter tries to bridge an existing knowledge gap within organizations about how to make effective use of social media within projects. It is described how the functionalities of social media may be used within project management. Moreover, several overall effects of social media on project management are illuminated. And finally, four barriers for social media use within project management are captured.

Email is standard way of communication in our daily life and in projects. But email traffic becomes more and more cumbersome. More than 25 percent of a working day is spend on email related tasks. Email is misused, and can create crisis in project teams. Nowadays the current generation of project team members is more used to using social media and social collaboration to communicate. To take advantage of that and to limit the use of email, the Zero email program was introduced within Atos. Limiting the use of emails with project teams can be achieved by introducing the right set of tools, a thorough management of change program, using early adaptors, starting small and acting – as a project manager – as a good example. Completely get rid of all email is still not possible; only when all parties are working with the same social media and collaboration tooling, a 80% result can be achieved. But in the current global world of project management with all its different stakeholders and parties, there is still a long way to go.

This chapter examines the introduction and implementation of the pilot project Twitcident in an emergency response room setting. Twitcident is a web-based system for filtering, searching and analyzing data on real-world incidents or crises. Social media data is seen as important for emergency response operations: it can be used as an 'early warning monitoring system' to detect social unrest, and for improving common operational pictures (COPs). This chapter shows that the expectations on the functioning of the tool were not fully met: first it was hard for the response room professionals to make sense of the data and second, the management did not develop a proper project planning. The recommendations are twofold. On the one hand, the professionals who work with Twitcident must invest in developing new information management routines. On the other hand, the response room management needs to create a much more inclusive project learning strategy.

This chapter presents an insight into a pilot project which took place at a UK higher education institution which used Twitter as a social media tool for engaging industry managers and students in sharing knowledge and collaborating on problem solving in the field of project management. Project management education

popular social media platforms, as well as a robust virtual community. Through social media, PMI creates an environment in which project practitioners create, curate, and share strong value-added content, take part in well-informed discussions, and collaborate to seek effective solutions.

Preface

The last 10 to 12 years has seen the spectacular rise of social media and online social networks, such as Twitter, Facebook, YouTube, Yammer, Google+ and LinkedIn. The use of these media is not only growing in terms of active users, but also in intensity of use. Especially since the introduction of smartphones and other mobile internet devices, using the social media is literally a 'finger tap' away. And although concerns about privacy and misuse of personal data may discourage certain users to engage in these media, the largest social media (Facebook, QQ and WhatsApp) are reporting active users numbers of between 700 and 1.400 million people. That is almost 1/5th of world population and roughly half of all people with an internet connection.

The role social media play in the social life of their users can hardly be overestimated. The way people express and present themselves on social media may be considered an inseparable part of their lifestyle and existence. Also in the professional context, the use of social media is developing. The ease of use of social media, their rapidly developing functionality and their mobile accessibility, make them an efficient tool for team communication and collaboration. Some organizations even redesigned their corporate intranets and knowledge sharing systems as social media. In part replacing top-down structuring of information by bottom up inputs, discussion, personal profiling and ad-hoc collaboration.

Given the importance of (team) collaboration and (stakeholder) communication in projects, it can be expected that social media also provide good opportunities for application in project teams and project management. However, the availability of documented experiences, research and 'best practices' of the use of social media in projects, is still quite limited. This book aims to contribute to the deliberate and effective use of social media in project management, by presenting the opportunities, barriers, technologies, limitations and experiences of social media in projects. The different chapters provide a diverse coverage of studies and applications from Europe, North America, South America, Africa and Asia.

READERSHIP

This book addresses first and foremost project management professionals that are responsible for organizing the communication within project teams and/or with external stakeholders. It is this group that is faced with the task to create an effective and efficient communication infrastructure for the projects they are involved with.

The responsibility for an effective communication infrastructure, however, also rests with project sponsors, PMO leaders and other stakeholders in the context of projects. The book therefore also aims to address these managers and executives.

The third group this book addresses are educators and students in the field of business and project management. In order to prepare for the management of projects, students should already get accustomed to the communication infrastructure and tooling they will work with in their (future) profession.

Organization

This book is structured in four sections, with the following themes:

1. **The Opportunity of Social Media**
   In this section, four research based chapters will explore how the functionality offered by social media can be applied in project management processes and practices.
2. **The Human Factor and Social Media**
   In this section, three chapters present the effect of social media on (virtual) teams and teamwork.
3. **Tools and Technologies of Social Media**
   This section presents, in four chapters, an overview of technologies that can be applied to facilitate stakeholder communication and team collaboration in projects.
4. **Cases and Applications**
   This section presents, in five chapters, a range of empirical studies of projects that applied social media in their communication strategy and discusses the experiences in these cases.
5. **Conclusion**
   This section presents an overall reflection on the content of the chapters of the book by the editor. A second epilogue is provided by the Project Management Institute and describes the social media infrastructure that project management professionals can utilize to stay in touch with their peers and with the profession.

The next paragraphs provide a short introduction to each chapter.

Overview

As the book presents a diverse set of contributions, developed by almost 30 project management professionals and academics, it is felt necessary to provide a bird's eye view of the contents of the chapters.

Section 1: The Opportunity of Social Media

Chapter 1: "Project Management 2.0: Towards the Renewal of the Discipline". In this chapter, the author addresses the question why project managers would integrate social media in the communication in and around their projects. One the 'why' is clear, he describes a number of social media types that can be applied in projects and provides a roadmap for the integration of social media in project management.

Chapter 2: "Effects of Social Media on Project Management". In this chapter, the author reports an explorative study into the potential application areas of social media within the project management subject groups of the ISO 21500 guideline. Next to the potential application areas, the author also explored the perceived barriers to social media use.

Chapter 3: "Social Media Use in Managing Project Communication". In this chapter, the authors develop a framework that project managers can use in order to apply in social media to projects. The chapter concludes that social media can improve organizational communications, especially so in the context of project management, and has an impact on the costs of a project. Important success factors in the use of social media are: affordability, trust and ease-of-use. If these factors have been met than social media technologies can provide a self-organization information network were workers can have: peer-to-peer sharing, content evaluation and push nature.

Chapter 4: "Social Media for Project Management". In this chapter, the author explores how project managers can use social media tools. He describes a range of social media tools that can provide value in projects and provides practical implications and recommendations. The author concludes that "social media is here to stay" and that project managers should carefully research social media tools to determine their fit into the project and the organization itself.

Section 2: The Human Factor and Social Media

Chapter 5: "The Influence of Social Media on Teamwork Aspects". This chapter reports a study into the perceived effect of the functionalities of social media on quality of teamwork. The author concludes that the use of social media has the potential to have a positive influence on the quality of teamwork in projects.

Chapter 6: "Investigating the Intention To Use Social Media Tools Within Virtual Project Teams". In this chapter, the author reports a study into the intention to use social media within virtual project teams, using the Unified Theory of Acceptance and Use of Technology (UTAUT) model. The findings validate the findings of previous studies using the model and indicate the models suitability for further refinement in the virtual project team area and in virtual teams in general.

Chapter 7: "Barriers to Social Media Adoption on Projects". In this chapter, the author, having authored a frequently cited book on social media in project management before, explores the reasons behind the lack of adoption of social media tools in a project environment. She discusses how project practitioners can overcome concerns about the lack of overall strategy, lack of senior management sponsorship, lack of a proven business case, security issues, information overload and the blurring of lines between professional and personal data online in order to realize the benefits of social and collaboration tools. The chapter concludes that social tools are a fundamental part of the current and future project management landscape and that 'social' should be intelligently incorporated into working practices in order to meet a need instead of being a response to outside trends.

Section 3: Tools and Technologies of Social Media

Chapter 8: "Analyzing the Landscape of Social Media". This chapter describes the 'landscape' of social media and discusses the landscape from the perspectives of functionality, social media size and growth, geographical market position, generational differences and gender differences.

Chapter 9: "Social Media Use Within Project Teams". This chapter gives practical recommendations about the social media tools and applications for use on projects. It introduces the reader to the most popular and widely used social media tools and provides considerations for the selection of the best tools to integrate in projects.

Chapter 10: "An Integrated Approach to Collaborative Learning in Projects". In this chapter, the authors develop a social media and web 2.0 based architecture for knowledge management in order to analyze how the web 2.0 technologies can support capturing, sharing and disseminating lessons learned in project management.

Chapter 11: "'Smart' Project Management: Smartphone Apps for Project Management". This chapter reports an explorative study into the functionality of project management apps in the Google Play and Apple App stores. The authors analyze the apps according to type of functionality, project management processes supported, methodology/standard supported, topics covered, website support, languages supported, project roles supported, number of team members supported and number of projects supported.

Section 4: Cases and Applications

Chapter 12: "Developing a Social Media Communication Plan: A Case Study of the Quicker Steps Project". Based upon the theories of communication, this chapter describes the development of a social media communications plan for the Quicker Steps project in Finland. The Quicker Steps project aimed to disseminate knowledge and best practices of the diverse cooperation and partnership solutions between higher education institutions and working life in Finland, Luxemburg, Austria and the United Kingdom. Next to describing the plan, this chapter also presents the result of a study into the effectiveness of the different communication channels.

Chapter 13: "Projects Without Email, Is That Possible?" This chapter describes the case of how ATOS designed and implemented a landscape of project communication that eliminated email and replaced it with unified communications and social media. The authors share their view on the implementation steps, experiences, change aspects and lessons learned.

Chapter 14: "From Reactive to Proactive Use of Social Media in Emergency Response: A Critical Discussion of the Twitcident Project". This chapter reports a pilot project on the use of social media in the public safety sector. The authors discuss how social media, and in particular Twitter, could be used in the response room setting. The study concludes that the centralists had a hard time interpreting and validating social media data and linking them to other sources of information. This finding, however, does not mean that the use of social media data has to be abandoned. The authors conclude that the effective use of social media data requires a learning process.

Chapter 15: "Using Twitter for Collaborative Student and Project Manager Learning". In this chapter, the authors discuss the evolving nature of project management education and in particular the development towards collaborative learning in order to enhance both the employability of students, and enabling managers to reflect on their own practice and understanding. They report their experiences in using Twitter in order to support for collaborative learning. The authors discuss their reflections and perspectives of the value and challenges in using Twitter for this type of endeavor, and present their view on the future implications for adopting the use of Twitter, and social media more broadly, for project teams.

Chapter 16: "Social Media Applications Promote Constituent Involvement in Government Management". This chapter explores the use by local governments of social media applications to communicate with constituents and promote involvement in policy and project management activities. The authors provide a variety of examples from the local government context and discuss suggestions for the use of social media in government.

Section 5: Conclusion

Chapter 17: "Social Project Management?" In this conclusion, the editor of this book reflects upon the lessons that may be learned from this book. In three concise paragraphs, it discusses the common ground amongst the different contributions, the 'takeaways' from the book and the concept of 'social project management' as the future outlook on social media in project management.

Chapter 18: "Inside the Project Management Institute: Setting up Change Makers for Success Based on Social Connection". In this contribution the authors, both employed the Project Management Institute (PMI), present how PMI utilizes popular social media platforms in order to better support project management practitioners, as well as create a robust virtual community. Through social media, PMI aims to create an environment in which project practitioners create, curate, and share strong value-added content, take part in well-informed discussions, and collaborate to seek effective solutions.

Gilbert Silvius
LOI University of Applied Sciences, The Netherlands & University of Johannesburg, South Africa

Acknowledgement

The editor would like to express their gratitude to all the people who contributed to the book as authors, advisors, reviewers, and developers. It is only because of their support and contributions that a publication such as this can develop. I am happy and grateful that so many colleagues, from many different backgrounds and regions, were enthusiastic about the idea to develop this book.

I would also like to thank the team at IGI Global. Their professionalism, and sometimes patience, was an important condition for the development of this book.

I am proud of the result of our joint efforts and hope that it will make a meaningful contribution to the further professionalization of 'the art of' project management.

Gilbert Silvius
LOI University of Applied Sciences, the Netherlands & University of Johannesburg, South Africa

Section 1
The Opportunity of Social Media

Chapter 1
Project Management 2.0: Towards the Renewal of the Discipline

Hamid Nach
Université de Québec à Rimouski, Canada

ABSTRACT

With growing maturity of social media over the last few years, many companies started using these tools to interact with customers and employees. Business functions such as Sales, Marketing and Human Resources have innovatively embedded these technologies to support their processes and became, as such, an instrument for renewal. The use of social media in Project Management, however, seems to be very limited. The profession lags behind having difficulty keeping pace with the rapidly evolving web 2.0 driven technological innovations which are delivering on their promise to foster collaboration. The paper discusses the potential of social media in the project management practice. As the move towards harnessing the power of social media within the Project Management framework requires adequate organizational change, the study also addresses the implications of such an initiative on structure, culture, and control.

INTRODUCTION

With growing maturity of social media over the last few years, many companies considered using these tools to interact with customers and employees. Business functions such as sales, marketing, human resources and public relations have innovatively embedded these technologies to support their processes and became, as such, an instrument for renewal. The use of social media in project management, however, seems to be very limited. The profession lags behind having difficulty keeping pace with the rapidly evolving web 2.0 driven technological advances which, notably, are delivering on their promise to foster collaboration and communication.

In the meantime, todays' projects are becoming ever more complex and dynamic (Kerzner, 2015). Their success rate may provide some cold comfort. Indeed, in a recent study, the Standish Group (2013) showed that the projects that are considered successful (i.e. delivered on time, on budget, with the required quality) are barely above the third of all projects: 39%; 43% were challenged (i.e. late, over budget, and/

DOI: 10.4018/978-1-4666-9867-3.ch001

or with low quality); and 18% literally failed (i.e. cancelled or not used). The report highlights, markedly, that these numbers represent an uptick in the success rates in comparison to the year 2009 in which, 32% are delivered; 44% had quality, deadline or cost problem and 24% failed. Despite the favorable slight increase in success, the project management landscape may still seem bleak. The discipline has not renewed itself in regards to the state-of-the-art advances in technology and information flow, which hinders the proper development of the discipline.

Furthermore, information-based business models are now providing organizations with capabilities to respond rapidly to customers' demands and to the changing ecosystem's conditions (Bharadwaj, El Sawy, Pavlou, & Venkatraman, 2013). Furthermore, Web 2.0 and social based technologies have reached the maturity stage and have become real Weapons of Mass "Collaboration" (McAfee, 2009). Mobile technologies, too, have become an integral part in organizational life (Nicol, 2013). Smartphones and tablets for example have open up new venues as to how information is created, accessed and shared in real-time. They also created an unprecedented level of connectivity to resources and communities. In addition, social media platforms have enhanced the quality and quantity of data generated and accelerated the pace of the information workflow (Bharadwaj et al., 2013). Also, cloud computing is shifting the paradigm of data an information management by moving IT services to the internet, adding a new level of efficiency and economy. Along with these advances, a new generation of young workers who have a great comfort using modern technologies are joining project teams. They are joining the workforce with expectations that are different from those of their managers. Unless these expectations are tackled accordingly, tapping into potentially talent people and turning them into assets may be significantly hindered.

In view of these recent and rapid developments, it is almost obvious that the traditional project management practices and techniques are rendered ineffective for most of today's projects (Levitt, 2011). Notwithstanding the contribution of ground-breaking works that led to tools that are widely used today such as Gantt, PERT and critical path. These tools, however, are many decades old and are merely suitable for the changing requirements of the 21st century business practices (Harrin, 2010). For example, Gantt diagramming is undoubtedly one of the most popular methods of project scheduling – and probably there are still good days ahead for it –, yet it rarely gets through one's head that the diagram was developed by Henry Gantt back in 1910, that is more than a century old, and it was mostly used in the construction projects (Lavender, 2014). However, competing on today's digital age requires organizations to reinvent their tools and processes as the projects they manage are increasingly complex and dynamic, many of which are implemented concurrently. The integration of new knowledge, the velocity of change, the need for innovation and speeding time-to market all add to the complexity and require new means for communicating and coordinating projects. Real-time information and services have become the norm, not the exception in an increasingly global and networked society.

While there are cutting-edge technological advances that drive change in different organizational domains, it is disappointing to realize that there are barely few daring innovations that punctuated the modern project management landscape. Hence, we concur with authors such as Kerzner (2015), Nicoletti (2012) and Harrin (2010) who argue it is time for a renewal of project management. The discipline has much to catch up with the ever burgeoning progresses in technologies that have stormed other fields. For today's project manager, it is an opportunity and a challenge to go beyond using conventional tools such as email, shared folders and repositories, and to learn harnessing the power of social media within the project management practice.

So, how project management, as a discipline, can renew itself in regards to the recent advances in social computing? This book chapter addresses this very question. It offers an updated perspective of project management that considers recent trends in social-based and web 2 technologies. Particularly, it presents what every project manager should embrace to take advantage of social media tools. This document is organized as follows. Firstly, we discuss why using social media is vital for project management and why rethinking the practice of project management is a timely issue. After that, we outline some of the main social media tools that can valuable for project management. Finally we discuss the challenges of integrating social media by addressing the implications of such an initiative on structure, culture, and control.

WHY USE SOCIAL MEDIA IN PROJECT MANAGEMENT?

Project management (PM) has traditionally adopted a top-down approach of coordination and communication (Levine, 2014). First, senior levels of management set a pool of projects to be developed (Kerzner, 2015). After that, they assign a manager to each project and expect having it delivered with respect to the predefined quality, budget and schedule. Undertaking the endeavor requires the project manager to develop a project plan, build a team, set requirements and deadlines, and assign tasks and resources (Ollus, Jansson, Karvonen, Uoti, & Riikonen, 2009). Moving forward also involves ensuring support and coordination between the stakeholders and tracking and reporting progress, usually using an upward flow of communication (Klynstra, 2012).

However, because traditional PM tools are complex and somewhat rigid and often lack real-time communication and collaboration capabilities, — which may be striking by the standards of today's connected world — project managers heavily use the *email* as a communication tool. In this sense, it is not surprising to figure out that, in 2014, the majority of email traffic worldwide which accounts for about 191.4 billion emails per day, comes from the business space, that is 108.8 billion emails per day (The Radicati Group, 2013). By considering the email as the predominant form of communication, project managers add to the traffic by sending and receiving documents such as memos, reminders, specifications, assignments, meeting minutes, reports, etc. The downside of email, however, is that it is not a convenient space to foster collaboration nor to build a sense community. Having documents of different types "attached" to emails also hinders team members from retrieving and disseminating knowledge and does not add to the bottom line.

Furthermore, traditional PM tools and procedures promote a centralized type of control and a localized access to information (Kerzner, 2015). Typically, project managers work according to an hourglass model. The top of the hourglass is the upper management while the bottom is the project team. Being at the center of the hourglass, project managers strive to ensure that information flows between the two parts. However, this model faces a true challenge as the volume, the variety and the velocity of information to be transited increase. Processing and transiting information in a single-tunnel system, weakened by the extensive use of email, may become overwhelming which, eventually, can compromise projects' outcomes.

Communication and collaboration drive projects. It is in this fact that lay the promise of social media and web based collaboration tools. On one hand, social media connects people and gives a voice not only to the project manager but to all the stakeholders. They allow to tap into the intelligence of the team members which can enhance the success rate of projects. In the other hand, web-based collaboration tools are generally easy to deploy and use. They provide a much better user experience comparatively to classical tools. Together, they offer the ability to create a distributed collaboration environment where the team can share ideas, collaborate, communicate, and pool resources regardless of geographical constraints. In this regards, Levine argues, "with traditional project management the processes were designed for the managers who were managing the inputs and out- puts of one project, with the goal of scheduling. Now the focus is on managing the processes and on the project participants, where the real goal is collaboration. Social networking enables this collaboration, which often starts from the bottom up. Project management is an inherently social activity, and social networking tools have evolved into useful project management tools precisely because they enable us to work more naturally" (Levine, 2014, p. 431)

We concur with Coleman (2008) as he argues that using social media in project management is essentially driven by four key factors. Firstly, projects are in essence "social", thus the integration of social networking tools becomes inevitable if one cares to leverage the social experience of a project. Secondly, there is a need to support both linear and nonlinear project activities. Indeed, emergence is inherent to most projects, yet it is barely supported by traditional approaches of managing projects. There is a need to adopt tools and processes that embrace emergence and change. Thirdly, it is critical to rethink project management practices due to the high level of failure of many projects. And finally, there is a need to overcome the complexity of classical PM platforms by adopting tools that are easy to use and are accessible to all the projects' stakeholders.

USING SOCIAL MEDIA IN PROJECT MANAGEMENT

In this section, we will look at different social media tools that can be used by project managers to foster communication and collaboration. But first, what do we mean by social media? Social media is an umbrella term encompassing all the web-based applications that let individuals generate and author content (Waters & Lester, 2010). Social media turns people into active participants in the generation and exchange of information. In this study, we will place a focus on the following tools: social networks, blogs, microblogs, social bookmarks, social tags, wikis, syndication, image and video sharing, and social-based collaboration. We will not necessarily provide names of social media vendors. In fact, the social media landscape evolves rapidly, and any list will always seem partial. We suggest to refer to other studies that provide an up-to-date overview of the social media providers. We also recommend that, at the stage of integrating a social media platform, every project manager should evaluate and benchmark current technologies and select those that best fit the needs of the project.

Social Networks

Social networks have become an integral part of many individuals' daily internet routine (Melendez, Wolfson, Adjouadi, & Rishe, 2010). A social network is online group that is designed to bring people with common interest together (Harrin, 2010). Particularly, it allow an individual to create a personal or a professional profile, follow or link to other people, author content and share it. Members can post updates, upload pictures and videos, send and receive messages from other members of the network. Most of social networking sites provide integrated and accessible tools for fast and easy information publication.

Social networking can be very useful for project management. Actually, it can bring a true refinement to the traditional email-based communication model. Before all else, the manager and the project participants can use a social network as a place to discuss about all the project's related topics, keeping, thus, everyone on the same page, literally. The common place facilitated by the social network can help build trust and reinforce the sense of community which is essential for practically all projects.

Particularly, a social network can serve to publish updates such as announcements, status, milestones, specifications, reports, slides, events, polls, etc. These updates can be displayed on the participant's profiles, notified via automatic alerts or possibly emailed. The team members can comment or reply directly on the content page. It is worth noting that most of social networks platforms organize conversations into threads which help users appreciate the overall structure of a conversation and keep relevant discussions connected. The threaded and archived conversation can reveal interesting patterns of communication and events and can act as a reference for future evaluations and decisions.

By using a social network, a project manager can cut down emails and literally transform the way a project team share information. Communication transforms from a one-to-many to a many-to-many communication model. Besides, project resources, such as documents, audio and videos, status and reports become accessible not only to project team, but also to other external stakeholders, if needed. Some social networking systems have capabilities to suggest content or people who may be of interest, based on the content users view, post and comment or based on the people to whom they are connected (Levine, 2014). This functionality can be useful, for example, in a large organization where the social network may suggest an expert who may have a relevant input in the project.

In order to illustrate the use of social networks within project management, consider the case of the Tessitura Network (Levine, 2014). The non-for-profit organization used social networking capabilities to develop a customer relationship management system. Social networking have become a critical element in the project as the team members were geographically dispersed. The social platform allowed the project's participants to be on the same page, reinforcing thus cohesion and commitment. The platform also played a key role keeping everyone at all levels informed and involved in the project every step of the way (Levine, 2014). Lockheed Martin is another company that uses social media, particularly social networking, to transform the way employees collaborate and share knowledge (Walker, 2009). Lockheed's social computing platform, called *Project Unity*[1], allowed the teams to set up a profile (including a biography, experience, education, and interests), create and follow individual or group interests, share and comment on content. The social network was valuable to the company as it was driving conversation and allowed to tap into the power of collaboration between employees.

Blogs

While social networks are about building communities, a blog is essentially about publishing an individual's thoughts and ideas. A blog is a type of shared online journal where an individual express his views and the readers leave responses and comments (Waters & Lester, 2010). A blog can be considered as a set of an easy-to-edit webpages where the blogger can embed resources such as photos, videos, slides, maps, etc. Editing is possible through a lightweight word processor.

For project management, a blog may have benefits in multiple ways. The project sponsor can use a blog to communicate the organization's position or demonstrate commitment to the project. The project manager may use one to communicate weekly updates or changes in the scope or in the requirements of the project for example, allowing thus, to store relevant announcements in a single space. For the project team, a blog can be a good place to share expertise and give feedback. Members can report new experiences or put questions and receive answers from others. That being said, having a blogging platform not only serves as a useful communication tool that link members of project teams, it also provides an advantage to all project members of having references and materials that can be returned to, and searched in the future (). It is also worth noting that project members can subscribe to the blog, which means that every time there is a new entry, the blog subscribers will get notified ().

To illustrate the use of blogs in the context of project management, consider the case of Bell Canada. IT managers at the company used a blogging platform, mainly, to brainstorm ideas (Lynch, 2008). Blogs allowed projects teams to express ideas such as requests for features and provide commons and feedback directly to the expressed ideas. The most voted ideas were reviewed and implemented. BASF, a chemical company headquartered in Germany, illustrates another instance of using blogs in the context of managing a project. To overcome the time difference hurdle — as the team was widely dispersed at a continental scale — managers used blogs to streamline communication. Blogs were used, for example, to make updates about a project status and give assignments for the next tasks to be considered. Blogs were also used by project champions to show support and engagement. Overall, BASF's social tools helped the company move from hierarchies to a fully connected workspace. It particularly helped reduce e-mail load, value existing knowledge and better align with young workers (Hinchcliffe, 2012).

Microblogs

Microblogging, as the name suggests, is like blogging, only the messages are shorter (usually up to 140 characters). The short messages can be set to be viewed by anyone or by a restricted group that can be chosen by the user. Microblogging can be particularly useful for quick communications between team members (Maltzman & Shirley, 2012). They can also help recipients to catch news and updates very quickly (Turban & King, 2012).

Project managers can use microblogging, for example, to send reminders and updates, communicate assignments or inform stakeholders. Likewise, team members may use the platform to report tasks status for example. If a milestone is reached, a task or a timeline is completed, a member can send a short message about it (Hollingsworth, 2010). Microblogs can also help track of colleagues, see what they are working on and better understand what they do. They can also serve as a messaging tool to quickly communicate with multiple contacts (Turban & King, 2012)

Short messages in a microblog, usually include a hashtag. A Hashtag is keyword that describe the content of the message, they are usually preceded by the pound symbol (#). Hashtags can be used to index and filter topics. Clicking on a hashtag brings all the messages that are related to it. This would allow a project team to organize content and track discussion topics based on those keywords. For example, if the team uses the hashtag "#kickoff" to designate messages about the kickoff meeting, then clicking or searching for that hashtag would bring all the kickoff-meeting related messages, allowing the team members to track the conversation.

The case of the Kennedy Center is a good example of how microblogging can be useful for project management. The team members, who were mandated to develop a customer relationship management system, used microblogging as a communication platform. They could send status updates, share new insights, and identify challenges. As Levine points out (2014).The short messages were "monitored by the whole team and everyone was constantly aware of where things are in virtually real-time [...]. The ease of use, lack of formality, and 140-character limitation all combine to remove past barriers and reluctance to take the time and effort to share the information" (p.437). The author adds that "staff members who in the past were reserved and quiet became much more vocal through the online tools. All of this has resulted in Project Management morphing into an integral part of everyone's existence, rather than a separate discipline imposed on the project. This has streamlined operations, and made projects more predictable and repeatable" (Levine, 2014. p. 437).

Social Bookmarks and Social Tags

Bookmarking consists of saving the address of a web page so that one can easily return to it later (Waters & Lester, 2010). Social bookmarking adds a social and a collaborative layer to this feature. Instead of being stored locally, social bookmarks are stored and organized on the web. They can be accessed from any computer connected to the web and can be shared with other users which would allow to access to the favorites of other users. When adding a new social bookmark, a user is usually prompted to assign one or more tags that best describe the content of the web link. A tag, generally, is a keyword that is chosen by a user that describes a web resource. The tagged web content is not restricted to a social bookmark, but can also be a blog post, an article, a photo, a video, or a website. The collection of tags becomes folksonomies (from folk and taxonomy) which are informal, user-generated systems of classification that works to organize web content (Turban & King, 2012).

Social bookmarking and social tagging can be a versatile and a useful mechanism that can help team members to classify and categorize content. For example, they would help build and organize a knowledge reference for projects that requires to be highly informed about a subject or a situation. The most commonly used tags and categories may reveal a trending topic that may be of interest for a project team. Tags can simply work as a thematic search mechanism, as clicking on a tag — let's say "quality control" — will bring all the resources and conversations that are related to this topic.

Wikis

A wiki is a website that allow multiple users to freely create, edit, remove and comment on its content. As outlined by Murugesan (2009, p.10). It is "a simple yet powerful web-based collaborative authoring (or content-management) system for creating and editing content. It lets anyone add a new article or revise an existing article through a Web browser." The term wiki is derived from the Hawaiian word *wikiwiki*, which means fast or quick. It also stands for "What I Know Is" as to convey the sharing mindset of the tool. The content of a wiki is typically a set of web pages that are collectively written and edited by authorized users. Documents on a wiki can be edited rapidly, using a light word processor.

Most wikis provide a way to keep track of changes and incorporate comprehensive versioning and change control for their content, and all changes are archived in a history file (Louridas, 2006). Web pages can be recovered in case of errors, and compared to more recent versions. Wikis fit in the social media landscape because of the opportunity they offer to author content collectively, and build a community. Wikis are flexible and easy to deploy and use. Others benefits of wikis are presented by Murugesan (2007) as follows:

- Asynchronous contribution by a distributed team of people, experts, peers, and employees.
- Sharing of ideas or viewpoints by a group or a project team.
- Collective intelligence, which exploit the power of various individuals to create collaborative work.

Using a wiki in project management may have multiple instances. For example, a project team can use a wiki for setting meeting agenda and keeping meeting minutes. It can also be a place for managing notes, team agendas, project calendar, tasks and documentation. Instead of exchanging e-mails soliciting input and comments and then trying to merge everybody's views, a wiki users can work together on private web pages in near real time (Gholami & Murugesan, 2011). Early in the project life cycle, wikis can serve as a repository of specific customer requirements or functional specifications. In the final stages of the project, wikis can be the store for quality control tests and customers' acceptance (Nicoletti, 2012).

As an example of using wiki in a project management setting, a Dutch transport company used a wiki within a project of development of a municipal traffic and transport plan (Hout, Vrancken, & Schrijnen, 2010). The wiki proved to be helpful throughout the development process. It also provided a number of practical functions as it stimulated peer-to-peer, communication which, before, was hampered by place and time dependency (Hout et al., 2010). Similarly, TD industries used a wiki platform within construction project teams who were geographically dispersed. Team members could quickly author and review content, such best practices within the system. The company's partners also had the opportunity to author content within the wiki or to comment on existing content. The system had the benefit of increasing the accuracy and velocity of information flow within the organization.

Syndication

Syndication, which is also called a "feed", or RSS (really simple syndication) is special format document that is used to publish content, which are frequently updated, like blogs, microblogs or wikis (Kresimir, Vrecko, & Zlatk, 2013). RSS feeds allow informing on the activity of a website in an automatic way — push rather than pull — (Nicoletti, 2012). In other words, the information is sent to the user rather than requested by the user. Syndication allows to subscribe to updates. So every time a new content is posted, the feed is updated automatically for the subscriber (Harrin, 2010). Project teams may use syndication to subscribe to multiple information resources that are used in the context of the project. Consequently, they would be able to stay informed about the project using a single access point: the RSS aggregator tool.

Photo and Video Sharing

Photos and videos can deliver material in an engaging way comparing to text. They can enrich the experience of social networking which could be particularly useful for distributed teams (Waters & Lester, 2010). There are several ways to use videos to enhance project communications. One way is to use videos of the project to track its progress. If it happens to be a product development project, it would be appropriate to post a video, on the social network or the blog, as a milestone is achieved, a new feature is implemented or as prototype becomes technologically advanced (Maltzman & Shirley, 2012). In this case, using a video will surpass traditional mean of communication to pass on the information (Maltzman & Shirley, 2012). Another example of using videos is viewing a meeting presentation where the team members can later view, voice an opinion, or express an idea. Photos and images too, can be used to support a collaborative work. They can be created, edited and annotated collaboratively, which can bring a significant support to requirements elicitation and prototyping.

Social-Based Collaboration

There exists a wide array of collaboration tools ranging from open source to expensive, and from one tool to integrated sets (Brown, Huettner, & James-Tanny, 2007). However, the new generation project management tools let organizational actors extent their collaboration to the web (Bradley & McDonald, 2013). Web-based technologies and applications which have emerged into prominence in the last years present new opportunities to support project management activities, collaborate and share information (Gholami & Murugesan, 2011). Web-based technologies are easy to implement and use. Their friendly and responsive user interface makes them more attractive to use (Gholami & Murugesan, 2011).

Web-based technologies provide an important advantage as they only require a browser to be used. They are also flexible and generally lead to high level of user involvement. Examples of social-based collaboration driven by web technologies are note taking, collaborative mind mapping, web based project management systems, online boards, documents and spreadsheets editing, social brainstorming, collaborative annotating, web based application sharing, online voting and polling, etc. Combining social media with web based collaboration tools would provide rich experience for project stakeholders

In addition to the social-based tools that are driving collaboration in the digital age, mobility, too, is tapping into the social web tools to meet the project manager's social media use needs. Most of the capabilities are discussed above are increasingly available for mobile devices. The combination of mobile access to an ever-expanding Internet has created a high level of connectivity to information (Kerzner, 2015). Mobile devices enable project teams to become increasingly flexible and productive.

INTEGRATING SOCIAL MEDIA

The Roadmap

It is worth noting that social media is not only about the technology, it is also about people and processes. Integrating social media within the project management framework requires adequate organizational changes to ensure the longevity of integration. For project managers who see an advantage in social media and decide to integrate the tools in project management, we suggest a road map that we delineate in four stages as outlined in the Figure 1.

1. **Evaluate**: The first step towards integrating social media in project management consists of evaluating the landscape of the available social media tools. A throughout assessment of their capability, compatibility and flexibility should be carried out. More importantly, because not all the social media tools would be necessarily suitable for a particular context, it is essential to select the social

Figure 1. A roadmap for social media integration in project management

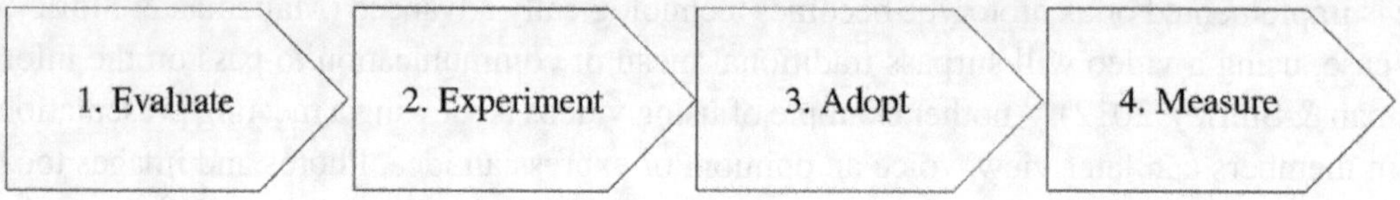

platform that would most fulfill the need of a specific project. Indeed, any technology, including social media technologies, should ultimately contribute to the project's bottom line. At this stage, an evaluation of the opportunities, the costs and the risks — be it either organizational or technological risks — should be undertaken.

2. **Experiment:** After recognizing the social platform's features and capabilities, a project manager may consider experimenting with the selected social media technologies at a small scale. The underlying idea is to conduct a pilot project to explore and get familiarized to the tools and evaluate how they would be of a value for the project's needs. Proceeding this way give an opportunity to retrospect on the experience. At this stage, managers may ensure that they have the support of upper management. Motivating and training team members to use the social media technology in a proper manner in line with project objectives and needs is indispensable for efficient use of the technologies. Besides, there may be an opportunity to customize the tool in a way to respond best to the projects' tasks. So, creative project managers may consider putting the effort to set usage guidelines, to leverage the functionality of tools and to discuss ways to improve its usage within the project context.
3. **Adopt:** At this stage, the adoption of social media as part of project management practices can be at a wider scale. However, project managers who are enthusiastic about the pilote project should not succumb to the idea that "*we built it, they will come*". Project managers must use the lessons learned in the pilote project to scale up the social media platform to others projects and teams. Managers should continue giving a clear forward momentum to the social media initiative. They may promote the success stories of adaptation lead by examples, and start showing the benefits of social media to employees and encourage them to use it by conducting seminars and training classes, for example (Gholami & Murugesan, 2011). Managers should also be patient as the move from old-fashioned technologies to web based tools may require some time to settle. More considerations should addressed at this stage concerning structure and control as we will discuss below.
4. **Measure:** It essential at his stage to measure the impact of the social media integration on the projects and organization's performances. Managers need to assess the impact of using these tools on the teams' performance and members' collaboration by quantitative or qualitative measurements (Gholami & Murugesan, 2011). Like in any IT spending, achieving a Return on Investment (ROI) is a critical factor in evaluating social media technologies, however, assessing Return on Collaboration (ROC) is of a great importance too. Return on Collaboration as suggested by Green (2010) allows to quantifiably measure the gains achieved by collaboration technologies such as the ones describe in this study.

Managerial Considerations

It is widely accepted that changing technological tools in a work setting requires changes in processes, structure and culture. Social media are no exception. With the integration of social media, some project management practices will have to go through some change. At least the process of communication will undergo a shift from one-to-many to a many-to-many communication model. Besides, there would be many project management activities that can be performed collaboratively. Hence, in order to tap into the power of social tools within project management, managers should anticipate changes at the organizational culture and structure.

In a traditional project management approach, project planning falls in the realm of the project manager. Baselines, resources and tasks are set in the early stages of the project leaving, very often, little room for change. Project requirements are also typically well-defined and known in advance (Kerzner, 2015). However, integrating social media requires a move from an extensive-control and authoritarian style of leadership to a rather participative and a collaborative management style. Collaboration remains most effective in organizations that are open, with a decentralized decision-making structure (Green, 2010). In essence, social media technologies may have an impact only if they are integrated in working environment where collaboration is fully integrated into structure. Also, there should be a healthy balance between "well-defined planning" and "emergence". Emergent structures help to turn separate strategic plans, project plans, and daily to-do lists of team members into one business development master plan and many-to-many hierarchies (Filve, 2008). In other words, there should be room for the plans and the task to evolve organically along the project (Ollus et al., 2009).

Making a successful transition to managing project with the help of social media also requires changes in culture and a shift in how team participants engage. It is essential that the team members be sensitized to reaching a balanced between the "need to know" and the "need to share". A social network, for instance, lives and sustains only by the contributions and the conversation held by its members. Some young project teams who may be comfortable with the sharing mindset of social media, may be encouraged to show the example and drive the conversation. It is also important that the project leader redefines his role from project manager to a facilitator of collaboration amongst all project members and between the project and its stakeholders.

At the financial firm Grant Thornton, for example, the integration of social as collaborative tools required that the company's corporate culture changes from one of control and risk-aversion, to one of participation and collaboration (Flinders, 2014). The CIO reported that the initiative benefited from throughout support from the board of directors and all service lines. In his terms, Grant Thornton created an "enabling culture by developing practical rules, simple guidelines. Because some managers were scared of using the social collaboration platform – Grant Thornton did some reverse mentoring, with youngsters teaching older members of staff to do things like blogging (Flinders, 2014). In this view, it is also vital that executive managers show support and engagement toward a social media initiative.

Integrating social media may also require changes in the execution of key project processes to achieve flexibility and embrace change. The term "agile" may best describe this project management paradigm. Agile project management consists of "a set of principles, whose goal is to render the process of project management simpler, more flexible and iterative in order to achieve better performance (cost, time and quality), with less management effort and higher levels of innovation and added value for the customer" (Conforto, Salum, Amaral, da Silva, & de Almeida, 2014). Some of the distinctive features of the agile project management trend are self-directed teams, team autonomy to make decisions, limited planning, minimal scope, small projects, emphasis on speed, performance measuring, iterations, collaborative work and customer involvement (Conforto et al., 2014).

Integrating social media into project management is not without risks. Slippage, confidentiality and privacy may pose issues that need to be addressed. It is important that the project managers develop a social media policy with established comprehensive, written rules that addresses the guidelines as how project members use social technologies. The social media policy should be comprehensive, clear and well communicated. Project managers should establish best social media practices, including a code of ethics (Keyes, 2012). Some basic guidelines might be thought of a social media etiquette is required around topics like deleting and modifying the contributions of others or posting on the blog or the social network (Waters & Lester, 2010).

Finally it is worth noting that there is no "one size fits all" approach towards introducing social media within the project management framework. It is important to acknowledge that every organization is unique, and so are projects. Project managers should examine the broad range of possibilities of social media to enhance collaboration and explore how different approaches can be used under different circumstances.

CONCLUSION

Social media is not just another buzzword for project management. Organizations that are using social media and social based collaboration tools within project management are reaping significant benefits (Gholami & Murugesan, 2011). We believe it is a timely issue to leverage social media and web driven collaboration technologies as an instrument for renewal of the project management discipline. Social media offers a great opportunity for project managers to enhance their practice. Depending on how they're integrated and used, social media technologies, such as the ones presented in this study can be powerful tools for collaboration. Perhaps the main challenge of project managers is to create the appropriate working environment for the project participants to promote the interaction, the participation and the proactive collaboration. Social media may be even more critical for large projects involving a lot of people from different specialties, organizations and physical work places (Barroso, Ricciardi & Azevedo, 2013).

Finally, as there is still a small body of literature on the use of social media within the project management context, future work may develop sound and fine-tuned frameworks on social media evaluation and deployment within project teams. The drivers and the barriers of social media adoption and integration may also be further investigated. Developing key performance indicators and dashboards about social media within the project management is certainly an area where future research is encouraged. The challenges and the impact of using social media and web-based collaborative on individuals, groups and organizations also offer fertile ground for future enquiries. We consider this book as a stepping stone for more investigations on this under-researched area and we hope that the book will inspire the project management community, researchers and practitioners alike, to step up their collaborative efforts to renew the project management field. It is an exciting area whose time has come.

REFERENCES

Barroso, A., Ricciardi, R., & Azevedo, J. (2013). Web 2.0 and project management: reviewing the change path and discussing a Few Cases. In I. R. Management Association (Ed.), Enterprise Resource Planning: Concepts, Methodologies, Tools, and Applications. IGI Global.

Bharadwaj, A., El Sawy, O., Pavlou, P., & Venkatraman, N. (2013). Digital business strategy: Toward a next generation of insights. *Management Information Systems Quarterly*, *37*(2), 471–482.

Bradley, A., & McDonald, M. (2013). *The Social Organization: How to Use Social Media to Tap the Collective Genius of Your Customers and Employees*. Harvard Business Press.

Coleman, D. (2008). Social Project Management *Agile Product & Project Management Executive Reports, 8*(5).

Conforto, E. C., Salum, F., Amaral, D. C., da Silva, S. L., & de Almeida, L. F. M. (2014). Can Agile Project Management Be Adopted by Industries Other than Software Development? *Project Management Journal*, *45*(3), 21–34. doi:10.1002/pmj.21410

Filve, A. (2008). Discovering the benefits of project management 2.0. *Cutter IT Journal*, *21*(5), 40–45.

Flinders, K. (2014). Social media for communication inside the enterprise. Retrieved from http://www.computerweekly.com/feature/Social-media-for-communication-inside-the-enterprise

Gholami, B., & Murugesan, S. (2011). Global IT Project Management Using Web 2.0. *International Journal of Information Technology Project Management*, *2*(3), 30–52. doi:10.4018/jitpm.2011070103

Green, B. (2010). Realizing returns on collaboration in an IP-enabled world. *NetworkWorld Asia*, *6*(1), 24–26.

Harrin, H. (2010). *Social media for project managers*. Project Management Institute.

Hinchcliffe, D. (2012). Enterprise 2.0 success: BASF. Retrieved from: http://www.zdnet.com/article/enterprise-2-0-success-basf/

Hollingsworth, C. (2010). PMPs on FB? OMG. *PM NETWORK*, *24*(3), 40–46.

Hout, R., Vrancken, J., & Schrijnen, P. (2010). Wiki-Based Knowledge Management in a Transport Consultancy, a Case Study. *The Electronic Journal Information Systems Evaluation*, *13*(2), 133–142.

Kerzner, R. (2015). *Project Management 2.0*. Wiley.

Keyes, J. (2012). *Enterprise 2.0: Social Networking Tools to Transform Your Organization*. Boca Raton, FL: CRC Press. doi:10.1201/b12532

Klynstra, M. (2012). Retrieved from http://www.enterpriseappstoday.com/social-media/social-media-meets-project-management.html

Kresimir, J., Vrecko, I. V., & Zlatk, B. (2013). Web 2.0 Technologies Supporting Project Management Needs. *Interdisciplinary Management Research*, *9*, 219–226.

Lavender, S. (2014). *Management for the Construction Industry*. Routledge.

Levine, A. (2014). Social Networking Tools: An Introduction to Their Role in Project Management. In P. Dinsmore & J. Cabanis-brewin (Eds.), The AMA Handbook of Project Management (4th edition ed.): American management Association.

Levitt, R. (2011). Towards project management 2.0. *Engineering Project Organization Journal*, *1-3*(3), 197–210. doi:10.1080/21573727.2011.609558

Louridas, P. (2006). Using wikis in software development. *IEEE Software*, *23*(2), 88–91. doi:10.1109/MS.2006.62

Lynch, C. (2008). Blogs Clean Up Project Management Messes. Retrieved from http://www.cio.com/article/163250

Maltzman, R., & Shirley, D. (2012). *Green Project Management*. CRC Press.

McAfee, A. (2009). *Enterprise 2.0: New Collaborative Tools for Your Organization's Toughest Challenges*. Harvard Business Press.

Melendez, L., Wolfson, O., Adjouadi, M., & Rishe, N. (2010). Qualitative Analysis of Commercial Social Neworks Profiles. In B. Furht (Ed.), *Handbook of Social Network Technologies and Applications*. Springer Science & Business Media. doi:10.1007/978-1-4419-7142-5_5

Murugesan, S. (2007). Business uses of Web 2.0, potentials and prospects. *Business-IT Strategies*, *10*(1), 1–28.

Murugesan, S. (2009). Web X.0: A Road Map. In M. San (Ed.), *Handbook of Research on Web 2.0, 3.0, and X.0: Technologies, Business, and Social Applications: Technologies, Business, and Social Applications*. IGI Global.

Nicol, D. (2013). *Mobile Strategy: How Your Company Can Win by Embracing Mobile Technologies*. IBM Press.

Nicoletti, B. (2012). *Lean and Digitize: An Integrated Approach to Process Improvement*. Gower Publishing, Ltd.

Ollus, M., Jansson, K., Karvonen, I., Uoti, M., & Riikonen, H. (2009). On Services for Collaborative Project Management. In L. Camarinha-Matos, I. Paraskakis, & H. Afsarmanesh (Eds.), *Leveraging Knowledge for Innovation in Collaborative Networks* (Vol. 307, pp. 451–462). Springer Berlin Heidelberg. doi:10.1007/978-3-642-04568-4_47

The Radicati Group. (2013). Email Statistics Report, 2013-2017.

The Standish Group. (2013). *CHAOS Manifesto 2013: Think Big*. Act Small.

Turban, E., & King, D. (2012). *Electronic Commerce 2012: Managerial and Social Networks Perspectives* (7th ed.). Prentice Hall.

Walker, R. (2009). Social-networking tools fuel collaboration. *GCN.com*. Retrieved from http://gcn.com/Articles/2009/06/10/Social-networking-tools-fuel-collaboration.aspx

Waters, J., & Lester, L. (2010). *The Everything Guide to Social Media: All you need to know about participating in today's most popular online communities*. Karen Cooper.

KEY TERMS AND DEFINITIONS

Blog: A type of shared online journal where an individual express his views and the readers leave responses and comments.

Project Management 2.0: A set processes for managing project using web 2.0 and social-based collaborative tools.

Social Media: Social media is an umbrella term encompassing all the web-based applications that let individuals generate and author content.

Social Network: Online group that is designed to bring people with common interest together.

Wiki: A website that allow multiple users to freely create, edit, remove and comment on its content.

ENDNOTES

1. Lockheed Martin released the code source of its social media framework using an open source software license under the name *Eureka streams*.

Chapter 2
Effects of Social Media on Project Management

Mark Sponselee
Van Aetsveld, The Netherlands

ABSTRACT

This chapter provides insight into the effects of social media on (the execution of) project management. Billions of people nowadays make daily use of social media. This phenomenon also gradually found its way to the business world. With projects being an essential element of many organizations, project managers must be aware what social media is all about and how it can strengthen their projects. The time is right for project managers to explore and embrace social media as an additional tool to be used for managing projects more effectively. This chapter tries to bridge an existing knowledge gap within organizations about how to make effective use of social media within projects. It is described how the functionalities of social media may be used within project management. Moreover, several overall effects of social media on project management are illuminated. And finally, four barriers for social media use within project management are captured.

INTRODUCTION

Many people, including project team members and stakeholders around you, nowadays make daily use of social media. For instance, in 2013, there were more than 1.3 billion registered users on Facebook and more than 340 million tweets a day on Twitter (KPMG, 2013). More and more communication takes place online. Social media provide a platform to individuals, communities and organizations to interact digitally and to be involved with people all over the world. Social media give people the option to finally have a say in things they are interested in, resulting in an increased level of involvement and a sense of society.

It is a new and easy to use way of interacting and working which gradually has found its way to the business world. "This represents an enormous challenge for firms, as many established management methods are ill-suited to deal with customers who no longer want to be talked at; instead, customers want firms to listen, appropriately engage, and respond" (Kietzmann et al., 2010, pp. 250).

DOI: 10.4018/978-1-4666-9867-3.ch002

The International Standardization Organization (ISO) 21500 Guideline, introduced in 2012, provides insight into the complexity of projects. No less than ten subject groups, such as stakeholder management, scope management, resource management and risk management, are to be managed during the project (ISO, 2012). Projects are an essential part of organizations. Therefore, executives and project managers must be aware what social media is all about and how it can strengthen their projects. Project managers must adopt, adapt and work the way others work. "After all, even if you feel it's a waste of time, you won't personally make social media tools go away just by ignoring them" (Herrin, 2010, pp. 13).

The pace of change within the project management discipline is however relatively slow when compared to the evolvement of social media. Through the years, the number of available tools and techniques designed for use within project management did not increase significantly. An all-embracing project management tool that covers and supports all knowledge areas of project management is still lacking. The search for a more complete and flexible tool for use in projects would make the control and management of projects much easier.

Many projects (about 70%) still fail to deliver on time and within budget. Bad communication is considered a major problem (Standish Group International, 1999). Teun van Aken (1995) states that a project manager increases his chances of delivering a successful project through good communication with project stakeholders and by being informed on time on project issues.

With that in mind, one would think that the level of collaboration required between project team members and with stakeholders and the collaborative capabilities offered by social media would result in a perfect match. Social media exhibit all characteristics of a project collaboration tool. Elizabeth Herrin (2010) rightfully endorses this by stating that "Project managers are primarily focused on creating participation in projects, and because of this, it is important to know how to engage people. Harnessing the power of social media technologies is one way to do this" (p. 5). Another clear advantage of social media applications compared to traditional applications is that these are often free of charge or at least very inexpensive (Kangas et al., 2008, pp. 54). This fact makes social media even more attractive.

The time is right for executives and project managers to explore and embrace social media as an additional tool to be used for managing projects more effectively. "Projects that want to be understood by their environments, cannot withhold themselves from using social media" (King, 2010, pp. 4). Kaplan and Haenlein (2010) confirm that many business executives, decision makers and consultants are already identifying ways to make profitable use of social media platforms. For most firms, however, it is still unclear how to use social media effectively and what should be avoided (Mustonen, 2009). This knowledge gap must be resolved. Deployment of social media in a project environment would mean the introduction of a tool that has already been tried and tested in other environments and that project team members and stakeholders will likely be familiar with. "Social media are a solution. They exist in many forms, possess diverse functionalities and are versatile, fast and cheap to use" (King, 2010, pp. 21).

The aim of this chapter is to bridge the existing knowledge gap within organizations about how to make effective use of social media within projects. The high amount of people that daily use social media indicates that social media care several interesting functionalities. What exactly are those social media functionalities? And in what way can these functionalities be used for managing the project management subject groups of the ISO 21500 guideline? Wat are those usage areas? In order to be able to answer those questions, in the background section of this chapter, the social media functionalities together with a brief introduction into the project management subject groups are demonstrated. A thorough understanding of the functionalities and the project management subject groups helps managers in discovering additional ways to manage projects by using social media.

The main focus of this chapter provides insight into three topics. First of all, usage areas of the social media functionalities within the project management subject groups of the ISO 21500 guideline is explored. Secondly, several overall effects of social media on project management is illustrated. And thirdly, some barriers for using social media within project management are mentioned. In this way, the relationship between social media and improving the execution and control of projects is discussed. In such cases, social media contribute to the successful completion of projects.

BACKGROUND

Social Media

In the 21 century, the phenomenon social media has become a daily part of life of many people. For instance, Facebook has more than 1.3 billion registered users and there are 340 million tweets a day on Twitter (KPMG, 2013). Every day, more than 100 million videos are watched on video sharing site YouTube (Kaplan & Haenlein, 2010) and over 1 million US dollars are spent in the virtual world of Second Life each day (Mayfield, 2008). Moreover, in 2014, Facebook took over WhatsApp for no less than 19 billion US dollars (NRC, 2014)!

Above numbers and examples demonstrate the magnitude of social media, which is still growing exponentially. Antony Mayfield (2008, pp. 4) correctly states that "Social computing is not a fad, nor is it something that will pass you or your company by. Gradually, social computing will impact almost every role, at every kind of company, in all parts of the world".

Although billions of people make use of social media, there seems to be limited understanding of what the term 'social media' exactly means. Before exploring its functionalities, it is necessary to first clarify what is meant by social media. Social media build on the World Wide Web 2.0 platforms, in which content and applications are no longer created and published by individuals, but instead are continuously modified by all users in a participatory and collaborative fashion (Kaplan & Haenlein, 2010; King, 2010; Mustonen, 2009). In his e-book 'What is social media?', Antony Mayfield (2008) mentions that most or practically all social media share several characteristics, namely participation, openness, conversation, communication and connectedness. Consumers utilize social media as a new communication landscape for creating, modifying, sharing, distributing and discussing internet content and for finding information, inspiration and like-minded people (Mayfield, 2008, pp. 7). Evans (2008) emphasizes that by sharing thoughts, experiences and information on social media people are better able to make more-informed choices (p. 31). The social aspect is related to the high level of interaction between users (Kaplan & Haenlein, 2010). Social media give power to the people. As a result, new ideas, services, business models and technologies emerge and evolve at dizzying speed in social media (Mayfield, 2008, pp. 7).

An enormous amount of social media platforms and applications exist. Several researchers (for instance Mayfield, 2008; Mustonen, 2009; Kaplan & Haenlein, 2010) tried to categorize social media applications. Although name differences occur in their categorizations, and probably new variants may develop in upcoming years, they all agree on the existence of six social media categories: collaborative projects (also referred to as wikis), blogs (including microblogging), content communities (including and referred to as photo-, audio- and video-sharing and discussion forums), social networking sites, virtual game worlds and virtual social worlds. Collaborative projects, such as Projectplace and Wikipedia, enable the joint and simultaneous creation of content by many end-users (Kaplan & Haenlein, 2010, pp.

62). Blogs, such as Blogger, Blogspot.com and Twitter (microblogging), are special types of websites that usually display date-stamped entries in reverse chronological order (OECD, 2007). Content communities, such as YouTube, Spotify and Instagram, offer users the opportunity to share media content, ranging from text and photos, to videos and music. While content communities are primarily organized around interests, social networking sites mainly focus on people. People joining social networking sites, such as Facebook and LinkedIn, usually create personal information profiles and then build a network by connecting to friends and colleagues, or by inviting real-world contacts to join the social networking site (Mayfield, 2008; Kaplan & Haenlein, 2010). Virtual worlds, such as Second Life and World of Warcraft, are computer based simulated environments inhabited by three-dimensional avatars (Kaplan & Haenlein, 2010, pp. 60).

Based on above features, Kietzmann et al. (2011) provide a comprehensive definition of social media: "Social media employ mobile and web-based technologies to create highly interactive platforms via which individuals and communities share, co-create, discuss and modify user-generated content" (p. 241).

Social Media Functionality

Kietzmann et al. (2011) introduced a sophisticated and all-embracing framework that further defines social media by using seven functional building blocks: identity, conversations, sharing, presence, relationships, reputation and groups. Kietzmann et al. (2011) illustrate and define the functionalities of social media in the honeycomb of social media, which is displayed in Figure 1.

Each building block in the honeycomb unpacks a specific facet of social media experience. The building blocks of social media functionalities help people make sense of the social media ecology and its possibilities. The building blocks are not mutually exclusive and do not all have to be present in a social media activity. Rather, social media applications differ in the extent to which they focus on some

Figure 1. The honeycomb of social media functionality (Kietzmann et al, 2011)

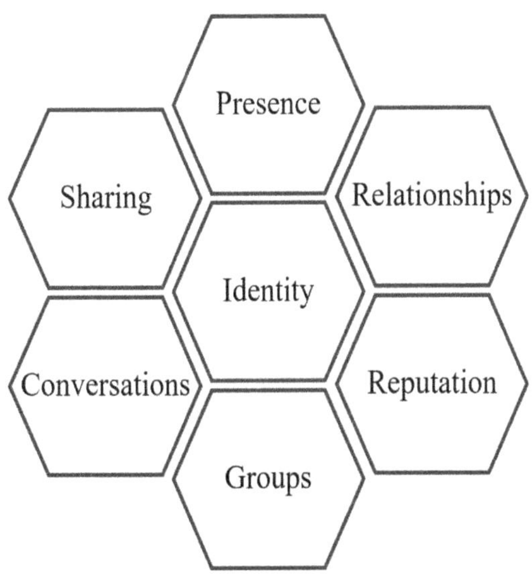

or all of the functional building blocks. Some focus more on identity, relationships and reputation, others more on conversations and sharing, and so on. "Each social media application has its own character" (King, 2010, pp. 15).

Social Media Functionality 1: Identity

The first social media functionality 'identity' represents the extent to which users reveal their identities in a social media setting. This usually includes disclosing objective information such as name, age, gender, profession, and the like. Kaplan and Haenlein (2010) complement that a user's identity may also occur through the conscious or unconscious self-disclosure of subjective information such as thoughts, feelings, likes, etc. Setting up personal profiles to create an identity is a requirement in many social media platforms, such as LinkedIn and Facebook. A major concern of available identity data on social media for firms is privacy protection and control.

Social Media Functionality 2: Conversations

The second functionality of social media is 'conversation'. This represents the extent to which users communicate with other users in a social media setting. Many social media applications, such as WhatsApp, Twitter and Facebook, are designed primarily to facilitate 'digital' conversations among individuals and groups. Such conversations can be started for all kind of reasons, for instance to make oneself heard, to meet like-minded people or to be on the cutting edge of new ideas or trending topics.

Social Media Functionality 3: Sharing

The third social media functionality is 'sharing'. It represents the extent to which users exchange, distribute, and receive content. The content that is shared can take many forms, such as text, video, links and pictures. Snapchat and Instagram are examples of social media platforms that are built around sharing pictures. YouTube is well known for sharing videos.

Social Media Functionality 4: Presence

The fourth social media functionality is 'presence'. Presence represents the extent to which users can know if other users are accessible. This includes knowing where other people are and whether they are available or online, in the real world or in the virtual world. This often implies that social media platforms offer an indication of presence or a status line indicator. The honeycomb of presence is linked to the traits of other functional blocks in the honeycomb, including relationships and conversations.

Social Media Functionality 5: Relationships

The fifth functionality of social media is 'relationships' and represents the extent to which users can be related to other users. By 'relate' is meant that two or more users have some form of association that leads them to converse, share objects of sociality, meet up, or simply just list each other as friend. Consequently, the way users are related often determines the what-and-how of information exchange.

There is a strong link between the 'identity' and 'relationships' functionalities. Kietzmann et al. (2010) state that: 'The general rule is that social media communities which don't value identity highly, also don't value relationships highly' (p.246).

Social Media Functionality 6: Reputation

'Reputation' is the sixth functionality of social media. It represents the extent to which users can identify the standing of others, including themselves, in a social media setting. Reputation of social media users is mainly based on the trust in that person and the content of people on the social media platform. Examples of popular metrics that are used to scale reputation are the amount of followers on Twitter, the amount of likes on Facebook and the total view counts of videos on YouTube.

Social Media Functionality 7: Groups

The seventh social media functionality is 'groups'. It represents the extent to which users can form communities and sub-communities. Two types of groups exist. The first variant concerns the sorting and placing of contacts by individuals into self-created groups. The second variant are online groups similar to clubs in the offline world. Those groups can be open to anyone, closed (approval required), or secret (by invitation only). Flickr, LinkedIn and Facebook, for instance, all provide the option to form groups with administrators who manage the groups, approve applicants, and invite others to join.

Modern Project Management: ISO 21500 Guideline

Two well-known project management associations are the International Project Management Association (IPMA) and the Project Management Institution (PMI). Both have developed a widespread used framework for project management, with a list of project management areas of attention. PMI introduced the Project Management Body of Knowledge (PMBoK) (Project Management Institute, 2008), while IPMA is well-known for its International Competence Baseline 3 (ICB 3) (IPMA, 2006). Both project management organizations recently united their project management knowledge. They worked together in the development of a project management guideline that provides adequate guidance for the project manager of today. This joint effort resulted in the widely accepted ISO 21500 Guideline (ISO, 2012), which was officially published on September 1, 2012. Silvius rightly (Zandhuis et al., 2012, pp. 5) appoints the guideline as the fundament for the further development of current and future standards in the project management profession. It is a worldwide standard that prescribes how people can best work together in projects. The ISO 21500 is developed to finally create a uniform language for the project management profession (Zandhuis et al., 2012, pp. 35).

ISO 21500 consists of general principles and unambiguous descriptions of project management processes and functions as an umbrella for all methods, models and best practices of project management. In addition to the high-level description of concepts and processes in the ISO 21500, other existing project management frameworks such as PMBOK, ICB3 and PRINCE2 (Office of Government Commerce, 2009) provide more detailed information on how to execute projects. ISO 21500 is a worldwide common reference for project management, whereby everyone has the right for its own method or approach (Zandhuis et al., 2012, pp. 45).

According to the ISO 21500 *"projects consist of a unique set of processes consisting of coordinated and controlled activities with start and end dates, performed to achieve project objectives. Achievement of project objectives requires the provision of deliverables conforming to specific requirements. A project may be subject to multiple constraints."* (ISO 21500, 2012). The ISO 21500 guideline is developed for any type of project, irrespective of complexity, size or duration. During a project five process groups are passed: initiating, planning, implementing, controlling and closing.

Project Management Subject Groups

The ISO 21500 guideline recognizes ten project management subject groups: integration, stakeholder, scope, resource, time, cost, risk, quality, procurement and communication. The subject groups are defined in Table 1.

Each subject group consists of several project management processes that must be executed and which contribute to successfully completing the project. ISO 21500 has 39 project management processes in total. Not all project management processes must be identically executed in all projects. It is up to the project manager to decide what processes are relevant and how strict the processes are applied. It may be necessary to repeat some processes in order to reach agreement on the project goals and to fully define and satisfy all stakeholder requirements. In Table 2 it is listed and cross-referenced for each process group and subject group what project management processes may be executed. The table illustrates which project management processes correspond with which subject group and in what process group it is executed.

In the next section of this chapter it will be described how the social media functionalities can be used within project management. The usage areas, overall effects and barriers are the outcomes of a research conducted in the context of a master thesis for the master project management at the Hogeschool Utrecht. The first part of this research consisted of an extensive literature study, in which the social media functionalities and the project management subject groups were illuminated. Another part of the

Table 1. Project management subject groups (International Organization for Standardization), 2012)

Subject Group	Definition Subject Group
Integration	The processes required to identify, define, combine, unify, coordinate, control and close the various activities and processes related to the project.
Stakeholder	The processes required to identify and manage the project sponsor, customers and other stakeholders.
Scope	The processes required to identify and define the work and deliverables, and only the work and deliverables required.
Resource	The processes required to identify and acquire adequate project resources such as people, facilities, equipment, materials, infrastructure and tools.
Time	The processes required to schedule the project activities and to monitor progress to control the schedule.
Cost	The processes required to develop the budget and to monitor progress to control costs.
Risk	The processes required to identify and manage threats and opportunities.
Quality	The processes required to plan and establish quality assurance and control.
Procurement	The processes required to plan and acquire products, services or results, and to manage supplier relationships.
Communication	The processes required to plan, manage and distribute information relevant to the project.

Table 2. Project management processes cross-referenced on the process groups and subject groups (International Organization for Standardization, 2012)

Subject\Process	Initiating	Planning	Implementing	Controlling	Closing
Integration	Develop project charter	Develop project plans	Direct project work	Control project work Control changes	Close project phase or project Collect lessons learned
Stakeholder	Identify stakeholder		Manage stakeholders		
Scope		Define scope Create work breakdown structure Define activities		Control scope	
Resource	Establish project team	Estimate resources Define project organization	Develop project team	Control resources Manage project team	
Time		Sequence activities Estimate activity durations Develop schedule		Control schedule	
Cost		Estimate costs Develop budget		Control costs	
Risk		Identify risks Assess risks	Treat risks	Control risks	
Quality		Plan quality	Perform quality assurance	Perform quality control	
Procurement		Plan procurements	Select suppliers	Administer procurements	
Communication		Plan communications	Distribute information	Manage communications	

research was reserved for interviewing experiences project managers and social media experts. In those interviews the usage areas of the social media functionalities in the project management subject groups, the overall effects of social media on project management and the barriers for using social media in project management were discussed.

USING SOCIAL MEDIA FUNCTIONALITY IN PROJECT MANAGEMENT

In this paragraph it is explained how the seven social media functionalities can be used for managing projects and the ten project management subject groups of the ISO 21500 Guideline. For each social media functionality, several usage areas are acknowledged.

Social Media Functionality 1: Identity

The first social media functionality identity refers to the extent to which users reveal themselves. This functionality is useful in project management because it allows the setup of profile pages on social media, it helps with recruiting project resources and it is employable for background research on (potential) stakeholders and suppliers.

Usage Area 1: Profile Pages on Social Media

The identity functionality provides people with the opportunity to set up detailed profile pages on social network sites. When project team members fill in profile pages on social media applications such as Yammer and LinkedIn, they provide insight into their personality and skills to colleagues. Project resources and stakeholders can introduce themselves to other project team members and stakeholders by referring to their names, location, pictures, project roles, experience and competences (Rai, 2012). Not only is it good to know the backgrounds and competences of project team members, it is also very important to know who is responsible for what within the project. As a result of this, it will be easier to contact the (right) person. This usage area may contribute to executing the project management processes 'define project organization' and 'identify stakeholder'.

Usage Area 2: Recruiting Project Resources

Although an identity on social media can be limited to basic information such as name, age, and hometown, far more detailed information can be enlightened as well. LinkedIn, for instance allows people to fully reveal their personal profile, working career, knowledge areas and educational history (Mayfield, 2008, 14). This is very useful information when projects are searching for a competent specialist during the recruitment process. This usage area may take place in the project management processes 'establish project team' and 'estimate resources'.

Usage Area 3: Research on (Potential) Stakeholders and Suppliers

Social media allow people to execute background research on people and companies. For instance, the backgrounds, roles and responsibilities of stakeholders can be retrieved. Such information can be utilized for communication purposes, for reaching stakeholders faster and for reducing the distance between the project and its stakeholders. Moreover, it is possible to determine the identity of (potential) suppliers, which is valuable information during public tenders and supplier selection processes. This usage area may take place in the project management processes 'identify stakeholders' and 'select suppliers'.

Social Media Functionality 2: Conversations

The second social media functionality conversations relates to the extent to which users communicate with each other. This functionality can very well be used in project management for short (video) chats, content related discussions and online solicitations.

Usage Area 4: Short (Video) Chats

Whether individuals or a group of people must be informed, the conversation possibilities offered by social media are plenty. WhatsApp, Google Chat, Microsoft Lync, Yammer, Projectplace and Communicator are well known examples of social media applications that allow 24/7 chat communication between project team members and stakeholders, independent of the location of people. Besides informing people, with conversations it is also possible to receive answers on questions. Social media applications are well suited for starting discussions with project team members. Furthermore, applications such as Skype and FaceTime allow the possibility for video chats. In case of occurring risks, scope issues or quality issues project team members can be alerted via social media applications so that can be started with a fast response to the problem. Although the communication subject group benefits most, this usage area can be used in many more project management processes.

Usage Area 5: Content Related Discussions

Social media provide a platform for content related discussions around certain topics, such as mitigation measures for project risks or the desired design of a product. Such discussions can either be executed with the help of the social media chat boxes (more suited for short and quick discussions between two people) or on discussions walls, such as the walls available on Facebook and Yammer (more suited for intensive discussions with more people) (Mayfield, 2008). This usage area supports many subject groups and project management processes.

Usage Area 6: Online Solicitations

Video chat applications allow the possibility for online solicitations, for instance with people from another country. Despite the distance, people are still able to see each other when talking. This is perceived as valuable information. Online solicitations save time and travel costs. This usage area may take place in the project management processes 'establish project team' and 'estimate resources'.

Social Media Functionality 3: Sharing

The third social media functionality sharing is concerned with the extent to which users exchange, distribute and receive content. This functionality allows project content and project status updates to be shared at one central location, enables product and document reviews and uses the knowledge of the crowd.

Usage Area 7: Project Content and Status Updates at one Central Location

Project content and status updates can be shared with project team members and stakeholders on social media. Social media is a fast and efficient information device for projects (King, 2010). Documents, presentations, photos, figures, etc. can be exchanged, distributed and received 24/7 on social media so that team members can work together, even when they are separated by location, in the development of project deliverables (Mustonen, 2009). It is the central place where project team members and stakeholders stay up-to-date on progress, project issues and achievements and which is always accessible. This usage area may take place in the project management process 'direct project work'.

Usage Area 8: Product and Document Reviews

Within several social media applications it is possible to work together when drafting documentation. People can co-produce and review each other's products and documents. This usage area may contribute to the project management processes 'perform quality assurance' and 'perform quality control'.

Usage Area 9: Knowledge of the Crowd

With the help of social media it is possible to use the full 'thinking power' of all project team members. For instance, when (occurring) project risks and quality issues are shared on social media applications such as Yammer, the knowledge of the crowd can be used for working out solutions for mitigating the risks or resolving quality issues. This usage area may for instance take place in the project management processes 'define scope' or 'treat risks'.

Social Media Functionality 4: Presence

The fourth social media functionality presence is related to the extent to which users know if others are available. This functionality can be used for retrieving and utilizing the availability and location of resources and for working independent of time, location and device.

Usage Area 10: Retrieving and Utilizing the Availability and Location of Resources

In projects it is relevant to know if and when project team members are available and where they are located. In case of questions, project risks and quality concerns it is important to know who can be contacted and when and where that person can be contacted. Most social media applications, such as WhatsApp, Facebook and Yammer indicate whether people are currently online or when they were online for the last time, so that a conversation can be started immediately. The choice than remains whether to start a conversation directly via social media, or to walk by and start face-to-face communication. Some social media applications, like Foursquare, also indicate where the person is located. Such information is helpful when direct contact with a project team member is necessary. This usage area may take place in the project management process 'distribute information'.

Usage Area 11: Working Remotely, Independent of Time, Location and Device

Social media applications can bring people together despite of the geographical distribution of project team members and stakeholders and support working remotely. With social media people can be available 24/7, in case of project emergencies. Even when they are at home, in the train or on vacation. Communication can now take place at the moment that suits a person best. This usage area may take place in the project management process 'develop schedule'.

Social Media Functionality 5: Relationships

The fifth social media functionality is relationships. It refers to the extent to which users relate to each other. It helps project managers in gathering insight into existing relationships and for engaging stakeholders with the project.

Usage Area 12: Insight into Relationships

The networks of project team members are often used to lay contact with (new or existing) project stakeholders, for instance with decision makers. Therefore, for the project manager, it is valuable to know who is related to who. Relationships can be either internal (between project resources) or external to the project team (with project stakeholders). LinkedIn, Facebook and Yammer are examples of social media applications that provides detailed insight into which project team member is closely related to a (potential) client, stakeholder or supplier. That person might therefore be asked to lay contact or improve the relationship with that particular client, stakeholder or supplier. There is no better acquaintance than an introduction by a shared friend. This usage area may take place in the project management process 'manage stakeholders'.

Usage Area 13: Engaging Stakeholders

Project information, progress and delivered products or prototypes can be shared on social media. This makes it possible for project stakeholders to stay informed about the current status of the project. Sometimes, stakeholders are asked to think with the project on developing (parts of) the project deliverables. They co-create the project results. Besides using the knowledge of the crowd, such actions increase stakeholder engagement. Goodwill and support from resources and stakeholders have to be ensured as it will improve the chance for project success. Just like the previous usage area, this usage area may contribute to the project management process 'manage stakeholders'.

Social Media Functionality 6: Reputation

The sixth social media functionality reputation refers to the extent to which users know the social standing of others and content. Examples of uses of this functionality are the creation of project pages and the nomination of project ambassadors.

Usage Area 14: Project Pages

Just like people having personal profile pages, it is also advisable to introduce project pages on social media (walls). The project page is than the communication platform where the project is brought to the spotlight. This will contribute to a more positive image and atmosphere surrounding the project. Applications such as LinkedIn, Facebook, Yammer, Projectplace, Twitter, Sharepoint, etc. are good platforms for installing project pages. Inter alia, relevant project information and delivered products can be communicated and distributed on such project pages. Tell the world about the project. What are you working on (and what not), what are you delivering, and when? This usage area for instance may take place in 'manage communications', 'manage stakeholders' or 'distribute information'.

Usage Area 15: Project Ambassadors

People can act as project ambassadors. Especially people with many endorsements, likes, followers, recommendations, and the like, on social media can reach many people. When they say positive things about the project, this will help in the project promotion. This usage area may take place in 'manage stakeholders', 'develop project resources' and 'distribute information'.

Social Media Functionality 7: Groups

The seventh social media functionality is groups. It is related to the extent to which users are ordered or form communities. Two examples of the usefulness of this functionality are the possibility for more targeted communication and cooperation between project resources.

Usage Area 16: Targeted Communication

Stakeholder groups can be formed and reached with the help of social media. Stakeholder groups can for instance be formed around products or subjects. Examples of social media applications that allow the creation of groups are Yammer, WhatsApp, LinkedIn, Facebook, SharePoint and Projectplace. It is important to decide on which application(s) to use for group communication. It is preferable to use applications where the stakeholders that must be reached are already familiar with. The message sent for communication purposes can be differentiated and adapted per group. This usage area may contribute to the project management process 'plan communications' 'manage stakeholders' and 'distribute information'.

Usage Area 17: Cooperation between Project Team Members

Most social media applications, such as Facebook, Yammer, LinkedIn, WhatsApp and many more, allow users to form communities or (sub-)groups. The groups can be open to anyone, closed (approval required), or secret (by invitation only). Within such groups, members built and share documentation, share status updates and start discussions around certain topics such as project progress, results, risks, quality and even scoping issues. The group members will react to each other and will thrive the project forward. This usage area may take place in 'direct project work', 'define project organization' and 'develop project team'.

All mentioned usage areas of the social media functionalities in project management are summed up in Table 3.

EFFECTS OF SOCIAL MEDIA ON PROJECT MANAGEMENT

While the previous paragraph described possibilities for using the social media functionalities within projects, this paragraph lists several (overall) effects of social media for the project management profession.

Effect 1: Social media enable real time project information

Table 3. Usage areas of social media functionalities in project management

Social Media Functionality	Usage Area
Identity	1. Profile pages on social media 2. Recruiting project resources 3. Research on (potential) stakeholders and suppliers
Conversations	4. Short (video) chats 5. Content related discussions 6. Online solicitations
Sharing	7. Project content and status updates at one central location 8. Product and document reviews 9. Knowledge of the crowd
Presence	10. Retrieving and utilizing the availability and location of others 11. Working remotely, independent of time, location and device
Relationship	12. Insight into relationships 13. Engaging stakeholders
Reputation	14. Project pages 15. Project ambassadors
Groups	16. Targeted communication 17. Cooperation between project team members

Social media are primarily used for conversations between people and for sharing information, documents, etc. with people. When used in projects, social media herewith enable the provision of real time project information to project team members and stakeholders. Within projects, social media is often applied for distributing project status updates, starting (short) discussions with people or sharing (new versions of) documents or other content with a person or a group of people. Social media allow a timely delivery of information to others, what can be used for making accurate decisions on how to proceed with the project.

Effect 2: Social media support iterative and incremental project management

During recent years, incremental project management methods, such as Agile, are gaining ground within the project management profession. Social media support those incremental project management methods, in which (parts of) deliverables are submitted in short sprints. Social media applications, such as WhatsApp, Google Chat, Microsoft Lync, Facebook, Yammer, Projectplace, Twitter, and many more all allow users to start chats with each other so that quick choices, decisions and alterations can be made on what to deliver and how to proceed in the short and iterative sprints.

Effect 3: Social media improve project efficiency

Another effect is that social media improve the efficiency of projects. Most social media facilitate the creation of (separated) groups and communities, where people are offered a central place to discuss, share and build information, documents, profiles, risks, planning and the like together. This is the place where the latest information is retrieved, project documents are build or where content related discussions start. Such discussions, or information provision in general, may also be executed with chat applications. Social media offer people to react quicker and more easily than ever before.

Effect 4: Social media simplify remote working

Social media simplify remote working, a trend within organizations that allows and facilitates employees to do their work at home, using a device that is connected to the computer system at the office. Because social media allow people to access information at all times, independent of time and place it herewith contributes to providing employees the possibility to do more work from home, instead of coming to the office at times that best suit them.

Effect 5: Social media facilitate project and personal branding

Social media applications provide a platform to people for their personal branding. It also facilitates the branding of projects. Personal pages, project pages and even organization pages on social media applications are very common. Project pages, on applications such as Yammer, LinkedIn, Facebook, Twitter and Projectplace, are actively used to inform project team members and stakeholders on matters like the project scope and goals, project team members, current project status, occurring project risks, delivered results, upcoming events, and all other information that is considered relevant to distribute. With its enormous reach for project communication, social media can increase the project visibility and may contribute to a positive project reputation.

Effect 6: Social media stimulate content related discussions

The sixth effect of social media on project management is that it stimulates content related discussions within projects. Social media stimulate the sharing of knowledge and experience between users. Social media applications facilitate people to start conversations and discussions and to ask (open) questions, on which people react whenever they have something to add. An outcome of this is that the knowledge of the crowd is used, instead of only the limited knowledge of one person. The use of knowledge of other people may involve people from outside the project as well.

The six overall effects of social media on project management are listed below:

1. Social media enable real time project information
2. Social media support iterative and incremental project management
3. Social media improve project efficiency
4. Social media simplify remote working
5. Social media facilitate project and personal branding
6. Social media stimulate content related discussions

Above effects indicate that social media is useful both inside the project (between project team members) and outside the project (with project stakeholders). While all seven effects provide an added value on the collaboration between project team members, effects 1, 4, 5 and 6 also make it easier to involve and inform project stakeholders from outside the project.

BARRIERS FOR SOCIAL MEDIA USE IN PROJECT MANAGEMENT

Several factors exist that withhold project managers from making use of social media within the project management profession. Some important barriers are listed below:

Barrier 1: Overwhelming number of social media applications

The (exponentially growing) number of social media applications available is perceived as a barrier for using it. It is not possible, nor desirable, to use all of them. Otherwise, it will become time-consuming to check all applications for updates. And efficiency gains will be lost. Therefore, it is advised to invest some time up front and choose and confirm with each other what social media applications to use (for the project). It is suggested to choose applications that are already used by and common to project team members and stakeholders.

Barrier 2: Negative publicity can reach many people

With the help of social media, an individual can reach many people with an opinion or statement. A negative comment on the project or the organization can reach hundreds, thousands or even millions of people in the country or around the world, which may have a disastrous effect on the project. The best way to mitigate the risk of negative comments is to build a positive project reputation by means of project branding, which eventually may contribute to less damage.

Barrier 3: Fading dividing line between work and private

The third barrier concerns the fading dividing line between work and private. The pitfall is that people start working 24/7 at 'strange' times and that work related use of social media mixes with private use of social media. Employees are also worried that with social media, (project) managers are better able to see what they are doing (also outside working hours). Most people however have already 'accepted' the fact that the dividing line between work and private has faded to some extent. For employees, the advice is to rethink what (personal) information to provide on social media and to understand that all messages can be seen and found by everyone else in the world. For managers, it is recommended that if they want to secure employee involvement in the use of social media they may not abuse information gathered from social media.

Barrier 4: Data security on social media

The last barrier relates to data security on social media. When using social media, much (company) secret or valuable information is shared in open space where it may get in the hands of people that should not know about it. Organizations rather want to secure their information. Therefore, it is proposed to (project) organizations to write social media protocols on what may and what may not be shared on social media and to think about how to keep outsiders away.

The identified four barriers for using social media within project management are listed below:

1. Overwhelming number of social media applications
2. Negative publicity can reach many people
3. Fading dividing line between work and private
4. Data security on social media

FUTURE RESEARCH DIRECTIONS

The amount of articles and books written on the relationship between social media and project management is limited. Therefore, I would like to advise to start more research on the effects and application possibilities of social media within projects. The social media functionalities are a good starting point for this matter. The functionalities indicate the added value of social media. In this chapter, I tried to explicit how project management benefits from those functionalities. The added value of each of the seven functionalities for project management can be explored in more detail. Furthermore, it is also desirable and possible to zoom in on each of the ten project management subject groups. (More) examples can be collected on how the subject groups benefit from the social media functionalities.

Several overall effects of social media on project management have been found. It is to be investigated whether these social media effects also exist in other professions than project management, such as agriculture, finance or information technology. The retrieved barriers can also be investigated further. How can these barriers (best) be lowered? And do the barriers also exist in other professions?

Although examples were provided about which social media applications can be used to accomplish an effect with social media on a project management subject group, more research is to be executed on what social media application to use (best) for which project management subject group. Moreover, is to be research in what project situations the introduction of social media is most desired. For instance, the introduction of social media in projects with people at disperse geographical locations or projects that expect a fast response time could be more desirable than in other type of projects.

And finally, as indicated in the results section, social media are of added value both inside the project (the project team) and outside of the project (the project stakeholders). The most suitable social media application for both groups may however differ. Therefore, it is to be researched what social media can best be used internally and which are preferred externally.

CONCLUSION

This chapter tries to bridge an existing knowledge gap within (project) organizations about how to make effective use of social media within projects. This is done by demonstrating its application possibilities. The Honeycomb of Social Media of Kietzmann et al. (2011) with its seven social media functionalities were introduced for this matter. The seven social media functionalities are: identity, conversations, sharing, presence, relationships, reputation and groups. Examples have been provided how each of the social media functionalities can be used for managing the project management processes and ten project management subject groups of the ISO 21500 guideline: integration, stakeholder, scope, resource, time, cost, risk, quality, procurement and communication (ISO, 2012).

For each social media functionality two or three usage areas have been described. The social media functionality identity may be used for profile pages on social media, recruiting project resources and research on (potential) stakeholders and suppliers. The usage areas of the social media functionality conversations are short (video) chats, content related discussions and online solicitations. Project content and status updates at one central location, product and document reviews and knowledge of the crowd are the usage areas of the social media functionality sharing. The social media functionality is linked with the usage areas retrieving and utilizing the availability and location of others and working remotely, independent of time, location and device. Insight into relationships and engaging stakeholders are the usage areas of the social media functionality relationships. The usage areas of the social media functionality reputation are project pages and project ambassadors. Finally, the usage areas of the social media functionality groups are targeted communication and cooperation between project team members.

The chapter also provides insight into the (overall) effects of social media for the project management profession. The following six (overall) effects were distinguished:

Effect 1: Social media enable real time project information
Effect 2: Social media support iterative and incremental project management
Effect 3: Social media improve project efficiency
Effect 4: Social media simplify remote working
Effect 5: Social media facilitate project and personal branding
Effect 6: Social media stimulate content related discussions

Another goal was to retrieve factors that withhold project managers from making use of social media within the project management profession. The following barriers were mentioned:

Barrier 1: Overwhelming number of social media applications
Barrier 2: Negative publicity can reach many people
Barrier 3: Fading dividing line between work and private
Barrier 4: Data security on social media

The large amount of application possibilities of the social media functionalities and the overall effects of social media indicate that social media can very well be utilized as an additional tool within projects. Therefore, I would like to invite project managers and their companies to embrace the results of this chapter and to apply social media deliberately with the aim of improving the execution and control of the project management subject groups. A deliberate application of social media includes taking time to think carefully about the barriers for social media use within project management. For instance, the number of available social media applications is overwhelming, and moreover still growing exponentially. Therefore, I advise to invest some time up front and choose and confirm with each other what social media applications to use (for the project).

REFERENCES

Evans, D. (2008). *Social Media Marketing: An hour a day*. Indianapolis: Wiley Publishing Inc.

Herrin, E. (2010). *Social Media for Project Managers.* PMI.

IPMA (2006). *International Competence Baseline Version 3.0.* Nijkerk.

ISO. (2012). ISO 21500: Guidance on Project Management. Geneva, Switzerland.

Kangas, P., Toivonen, A. & Back, A. (2008). *Ads by Google and other social media models.* VTT research notes 2384.

Kaplan, A. M., & Haenlein, M. (2010). Users of the world unite! The challenges and opportunities of Social Media. *Business Horizons, 53*(1), 59–68. doi:10.1016/j.bushor.2009.09.003

Kietzmann, J. H., & Angell, I. (2010). Panopticon revisited. *Communications of the ACM, 53*(6), 135–138. doi:10.1145/1743546.1743582

Kietzmann, J. H., Hermkens, K., McCarthy, I. P., & Silvestre, B. S. (2010). Social Media? Get serious! Understanding the functional building blocks of social media. *Business Horizons, 2011*(54), 241–251.

King (2010). Social Media and Infrastructural projects. Retrieved from http://www.kennisinhetgroot.nl/upload/documents/produkten/King%20social%20Media_totaal.pdf

KPMG. (2013). *Social Media – Het speelkwartier is voorbij: Time to talk business.* Retrieved from http://secure.kpmg.com/NL/nl/IssuesAndInsights/ArticlesPublications/Documents/PDF/Management-Consulting/Social-media-het-speelkwartier-is-voorbij.pdf

Mayfield, A. (2008). What is Social Media? Retrieved from http://www.icrossing.co.uk/fileadmin/uploads/ebooks/what_is_social_media_icrossing_ebook.pdf

Mustonen, P. (2009). Social Media – a new way to success? *Turku School of Economics. Uniprint, Turku.* Retrieved from http://info.tse.fi/julkaisut/kr/KRe1_2009

NRC. (2014). Facebook buys WhatsApp for 16 billion dollar. Retrieved from http://www.nrc.nl/nieuws/2014/02/19/facebook-koopt-whatsapp-voor-16-miljard-dollar/

OECD. (2007). *Participative web and user-created content: Web 2.0, wikis, and social networking*. Paris: Organisation for Economic Co-operation and Development.

Office of Government Commerce. (2009). *Managing Successful Projects with PRINCE2*. Edition Manual.

Project Management Institute. (2008). *A Guide to the Project Management Body of Knowledge (PMBOK Guide).* Upper Darby: Project Management Institute Inc.

Rai, S. (2012). Engaging young employees (Gen Y) in a social media dominated world – Review and Retrospection. *Procedia: Social and Behavioral Sciences, 37*, 257–266. doi:10.1016/j.sbspro.2012.03.292

Standish Group International. (1999). *Chaos: A recipe for success*. The Standish Group International, Inc.

van Aken, T. (1995). *De weg naar projectsucces*. Elsevier/De Tijdstroom.

Zandhuis, A., Legerman, A., & Stellingwerf, R. (2012). *ISO 21500 in practice: A Management Guide: The International Guideline for Project Management.* Van: Haren Publishing.

Chapter 3
Managing Project Communication:
Using Social Media for Communication in Projects

Esther van Dokkum
HU University of Applied Sciences Utrecht, The Netherlands

Pascal Ravesteijn
HU University of Applied Sciences Utrecht, The Netherlands

ABSTRACT

While social media use has rapidly grown all over the world the use in business context is growing at a steadier pace. Mostly social media is used by businesses as a communication channel aimed at customers either to promote products and services or as part of their web care activities. The use of social media as a means for internal communication is limited; this is especially true for projects. However social media can improve organizational communications and where communication within organizations is important in general, in the context of project management it is a critical success factor. Therefore research was conducted on how social media can be used to enhance communication within projects. In this chapter a framework that can be used to apply social media in project communication is described. The framework shows how social media tools are used by different roles and for different events during a project.

INTRODUCTION

Nowadays social media and Internet have become integrated in our lives. Before social media became 'the next best thing' it started with the introduction of WIT (WWW Interactive talk) where people could connect with other friends (Vlietstra, 2001). Years later in 2002 Friendster and in 2003 Myspace gained popularity (Hayden & Tomal, 2012). Friendster enabled users to create profiles and connect virtually with friends and Myspace, which was also a social network, gained popularity among teenagers and young adults. These were the first social platforms that were popular with a great majority. In 2004 Facebook

DOI: 10.4018/978-1-4666-9867-3.ch003

started as a site for college students from Harvard. Nowadays, Facebook has grown to become one of the biggest players in social media platforms. So far social networks were text based, a platform for the sharing of videos was missing. This changed when in 2005 YouTube offered this possibility through a platform that allowed users to freely upload and share videos on the Internet. In 2006 Twitter made an entrance in the social media world and allowed people to communicate through short, 140 character posts, called tweets. It wasn't until 2011 that Google introduced their own social networking platform: Google+. In this short overview of social media networks Pinterest should not be excluded. Pinterest started in 2012 as a social scrapbooking site and has rapidly grown to over 10 million users in its first year (Hayden & Tomal, 2012).

According to Kaplan and Haenlein (2010) social media has become a bigger part of our lives during the past several years. During this time there has been a shift in how social media is used. First social media applications were mostly used for communication between people while today social media is also used by businesses to reach consumers (Augar & Zeleznikow, 2013). Social media has become serious business not only for communication between Business and Consumers but also for Business-to-Business communication (Augar & Zeleznikow, 2013). Different social media platforms each have their own advantages and disadvantages and it is important for a business to choose the right social media platform to reach the desired target group. Social media has also found its way into the workplace. This opens up possibilities for new ways of communication within organizations. It helps to improve organizational communications, which results in a lower frequency of emailing, phone calls as well as meetings (Gunter, Riehle, Krasnova & Schondienst, 2009). Social media provides (knowledge) workers an efficient alternative for internal communication (Bohringer & Richter, 2009).

As described above social media can help in communicating efficiently. Communication within organizations is important in general but in the context of project management it is a critical success factor (Martin, 1976; Locke, 1984; Pinto & Slevin, 1989; Belassi & Tukel, 1996; Bohm, 1999; Isaacs, 1999; Schwalbe, 1999; Kerzner, 1998). Therefore we conducted research on how social media can be used to enhance communication within projects. This is done via the development of a framework that can be implemented to prescribe how social media tools can be used for different events during a project. In this study we build on prior research in which we determined the possibility of developing templates to help organizations in their social media communication strategy (Martina et al., 2014). Templates have been developed for different scenarios. These have subsequently been tested in a pilot study for an organization, which used the templates in the organization of a conference. While the templates that are developed were not specifically developed with projects in mind it did trigger this research as we think that templates could be well suited for use for communication in projects. However before templates can be developed and put to effective use a framework for the use of social media should be developed. For this we will also discuss several norms that are related to the use of social media within a project, by project members, the project manager and other stakeholders.

Thus, the goal of this chapter is to develop a framework that project managers can use in order to apply in social media to projects. This chapter is structured as follows: In the second part a literature review is provided. The third part discusses the research approach. Subsequently the fourth part presents the findings of the research, while the fifth part describes future research possibilities. The chapter ends with the conclusion in last part.

LITERATURE REVIEW

In this paragraph we will first describe the phenomenon of Social Media, its influence on how we communicate and how it can be used in an organizational context. This is followed by a discussion on project management and why communication is such an important factor in the relation to the success rates of projects. Finally the two topics are brought together in an effort to create a framework for the use of social media in project management, which is then described in the paragraph 'Constructing a Framework for the use of Social Media in Projects'.

Social Media

Social media has created a new environment, which has increased the volume, and speed of daily communication. It has become an easy, alternative channel for communication and connecting people. This has given people a voice and it has stimulated discussions on shared interest regardless of the distance (Badea, 2014; Moise & Cruceru, 2014; Guliciuc, 2014). The use of social media has increased over the last years. Web 2.0 allows the creation and exchange of user-generated content. For example the social network Facebook had on average 1.35 billion active users each month in 2014 while in the same year Twitter had 288 million active users (Statista, 2015).

Dumbrell and Steel (2014) state that social media are: "technologies providing an open platform in which peers can share information (of varying topics) with other peers. Where social media differs from previous communication methods (e.g. phone calls, email) is the capability for individuals to publicly connect with, and thus share information with, greater numbers." Social media is therefore a complex system composed of a very large number of elements with non-linear interactions within an online application that has similar characteristics with Internet applications (Weisbuch, 2007; Kaplan, 2010). Social media has changed the way we communicate, Hearning and Ussery (2012) claim that due to these changes in the environment the way employees and employers view the workplace must change too.

There are many examples of social media and virtual networks, common examples are Twitter, Facebook, LinkedIn, Instagram, Pinterest, personal and professional web blogs, video web, forums, testimonials, case studies, infograpics, how-to's, making-off, reviews and podcasts (Azhar & Abeln, 2014; Moise & Cruseru, 2014; Muller, Ehrlich, Matthews, Perer, Ronen & Guy, 2014; Martina, Oppier, Fafie, Hoogland, Krouwel & Kroef, 2014). The members of social media can be categorised in four types: casual readers, reactive authors, active authors and proactive authors (Karaduman, 2013). This is a categorization that also holds when social media is used in an organizational context.

This new way of communicating through social media provides companies with new opportunities and abilities for strengthening existing relations but also creating new relationships with their internal and external stakeholders like: business partners, competitors, customers and prospects (Karaduman, 2013; Moise & Cruceru, 2014). Social media has shifted the organizational and geographical boundaries. New resources have come within reach and this creates a corporate social network were employees can easily connect and help each other do their jobs more productively (Banes, 2009).

Social media can be used by companies for different purposes: announcing job openings, networking, branding, showcasing, disseminating project news, training and industry information, advertising events such as workshop, exhibitions etc. (Azhar & Abeln, 2014; Moise & Cruceru, 2014). Within an organization, social media can be used as a medium were users and group members share, interact, co-create, delegate tasks, facilitate information flows, discuss and modify content, promote value consolidation of organizational culture, build awareness, increase sales, stimulate creativity and manufacture loyalty (Guliciuc, 2014; Riemer & Richter, 2010; Banes, 2009). This provides a organization with an improved communication process that consists of valuable information and opportunities for business-critical skills (Krüger, Brockmann & Stieglitz, 2013).

Social Media Models and Frameworks

There are several models that describe the use of different social media in the environment of a business (see Table 1). Karaduman (2013) developed a model of "re-classification of social media presence / media richness and self-presentation / self-disclosure". This model provides insight in the influences of the different types of social media in self-presentation and self-disclosure. It provides top-level executives with guidance in the use of the right social media communication channels to engage with their customers and investors. Social networking (for example Facebook) and micro-blogging (for example Twitter) have a high self-presentation / self-disclosure and a medium social presence / media richness.

Dumbrell and Steele (2014) investigated the use of social media technologies amongst older adults in organizations. They created a framework with the requirements of the capabilities for older adults within a social media-used knowledge management. They claim that the key factors in the use of social media are: affordability, trust and ease-of-use. If these factors have been met than social media technologies can provide a self-organisation information network were workers can have: peer-to-peer sharing, content evaluation and push nature.

Kruger et al. (2013) presented a framework with guidelines for social media for enterprises. They claimed that social media could be placed in an internal- and external context, which each have their own perspective in communication and are embedded with norms. Also they found that it is important to recognize different roles in the use of social media for management and employees.

In comparison Muller and Stocker (2011) divide social media in perceived usefulness-, individual and organizational benefits. For perceived usefulness they recommend that shared information is visible to all users, social media should be used to announce interesting events, it can improve writings skills and can be used to follow internal experts. Furthermore it is possible to identify trends and create

Table 1. A summary of social media models and frameworks.

Name	Model/Framework
Karaduman (2013)	Model: re-classification of social media presence / media richness and self-presentation / self-disclosure.
Dumbrell and Steele (2014)	Framework: the requirements of the capabilities for older adults within a social media-used knowledge management.
Kruger et al. (2013)	Framework: guidelines for social media for enterprises.
Muller and Stocker (2011)	Model: divide social media in perceived usefulness-, individual and organizational benefits.
Gunter et al. (2009)	Model: a modified and extended version of Unified Theory of Acceptance and Use of Technology (UTAUT) to improve organizational communication with micro-blogging.
Riemer and Richter (2010).	An overview of micro blogging interaction types in enterprises

transparency in relation to interesting internal events. Searching relevant contacts or finding relevant information, easy access to expert knowledge, expanding an user's own social media network, learning from followers and gaining an informational edge are topics that provide perceived individual benefits. Finally the perceived organisational benefits are: improved flow of information, support for worldwide social networking, advanced knowledge management practice and useful discussions about experiences, leading to innovative thinking and better products.

Gunter et al. (2009) created a modified and extended version of Unified Theory of Acceptance and Use of Technology (UTAUT) to improve organizational communication with micro-blogging. The objects reputation, communicational benefits, signal-to noise ratio and codification effort and expected relationships lead to performance expectancy. This leads to, along with privacy concerns and facilitating conditions, behavioural intentions, which is followed by behaviour. Riemer and Richter (2010) provide an overview of micro blogging interaction types in enterprises. The categories are: ask question, share information, discuss and clarify, coordinate others, provide update and record information.

The main advantage of using social media is the lower cost but it also is an effective way of working (Moise & Cruceru 2009; Bohringer & Richter, 2009). Using social media reduces costs because employees can find relevant information without having to avoid restrictions on activities and this creates awareness which makes them less passive and therefore it reduces the frequency of communication by email, phone cells and meetings (Dourish & Bellotti, 1992). This creates an environment with fewer interruptions and more task performance time (Gunter, Riehle, Krasnova and Schondienst, 2009; Martina, Oppier, Fafie, Hoogland, Krouwel & Kroef, 2014). On the other hand there are costs associated with understanding, creating and maintaining social media (Azhar & Abeln, 2014; Moise & Cruceru, 2014; Dahnil, Marzuki, Langgat & Fabeil, 2014; Hearing & Ussery, 2012a; Hearing & Ussery, 2012b; Muller & Stocker, 2011). Furthermore, social media creates security risks; privacy issues and workers can become overloaded with information. Social media also requires a great effort of the employee to keep up to date.

Due to the great influence of social media on how information is obtained and exchanged, companies need to prepare a policy with netiquette's for the integration of social media in organizational communication. Therefore, there needs to be a strategy with a set of qualitative- and quantitative performance indicators and goals for interaction and conversion rates with the suitable channels, tools etc. (Badea, 2014; Krüger, Brockmann & Stieglitz, 2013; Banes, 2009). These must be communicated with the employees, so they understand the corporate policy (Moise & Cruceru, 2014).

Projects have different members and this creates different roles and task within social media. Research has shown that 80.6% of stakeholder's thinks that social media is an important channel for CEO's to utilize (Karaduman, 2013). As a matter of fact, by using social media top-level executives become accessible, visible and connected. It provides the stakeholder's with insight in the vision of an organization. The gap between the employees and management will become smaller and employees feel that they belong to a group (Badea, 2014). This influence provides mangers with the possibilities to ensure recourse and create an environment for innovation and experimentation. The same can be stated for the roles in the context of projects.

Before describing the role of Social Media in the context of project management we will first discuss what project management is, how it evolves and what influences its success.

Project Management

Within organizations many innovations such as new products and/or services and changes like IT implementations are organized as projects (Silvius et al., 2012). To manage these projects there are different methods available. One of the most famous is the PRojects IN Controlled Environments (PRINCE) 2 methodology. PRINCE 2 was originally developed in 1989 for the UK Government (Office of the Government Commerce, 2009) specifically for managing IT projects, however today it is widely used in all types of project contexts. In an IT context PRINCE2 was often used in conjunction with the waterfall method for developing software. The waterfall method consists of distinct stages that are executed sequential. Standard phases are defining requirements, design, development, testing, and implementation. Even though PRINCE2 and the waterfall method have been used a lot in practice both have been criticized for being too rigid leading to unfulfilled expectations and failure of IT projects (Hollaway, 2005; Laplante, & Neill, 2004). Research on the success rates of IT projects show a range between 16% and 44% (Basten et al., 2013). To increase the success rates organizations have more recently started to use Agile methods in IT development and project management. According to Chasalow (2008) "Agile methods rely on delivering working code in short cycles, having the working code reviewed by customers, and then following up with another iteration either improving on the capabilities just delivered, or adding additional features." While Agile started in 2001 (Highsmith, 2001) with the formulation of the Agile Manifesto many of the underlying concepts (e.g. prototyping) have been around for a lot longer (Chasalow, 2008; Naumann & Jenkins, 1982). It is still to early to conclude whether Agile will increase the success rates of IT projects or that on average one-third of the projects will still fail.

The key to successful projects might not depend on the methodology as such. Research on the critical success factors of managing projects shows that, amongst others, setting up 'information and communication channels' is crucial (Cleland & King, 1983). Communication within the project management domain and in general as part of problem solving is found to be important by many researchers (e.g. Martin, 1976; Locke, 1984; Pinto & Slevin, 1989; Belassi & Tukel, 1996; Bohm, 1999; Isaacs, 1999; Schwalbe, 1999; Kerzner, 1998). The emphasis on communication is also found in agile methods as they explicitly focus on 'Individuals and interactions over processes and tools' and 'Customer collaboration over contract negotiation' (Highsmith, 2001). Communication does not only influence the successful completion of a project but according to Räkers (2009) it also has a large impact on the costs of a project. Räkers states "communication costs are one of the most relevant drivers for project efficiency". Furthermore he concludes that the more complicated a project is the more expensive the communication will become and therefore it is advised that stakeholders in a project, and specifically team members, should communicate face-to-face regularly. In this chapter we show that Social Media can also be used to enable communication in projects. As mentioned above Social Media can reduce costs of communication within an organization. This can also be true for communication as part of project management. For instance Social Media can be used for communication during the different phases in a project as described by PRINCE2 or in an Agile approach such as SCRUM (Schwaber & Beedle, 2002) for daily 'Scrum' meetings or during sprint reviews.

The Use of Social Media in Project Management

To be able to develop an approach to using Social Media in Projects it is important to know which actors are involved in a project. In this research we focus on the two methods that are described above: PRINCE2 and the Agile SCRUM approach.

PRINCE2 is a structured project management method with four different perspectives of: seven principles, seven themes, seven processes and tailoring (Hedeman & Seegers, 2009). PRINCE2 recognize three levels of organization: directing (Project Board), managing (Project Manager) and delivering (Team Manager). "The project board is the highest management level of a project and recognizes an executive, senior user, senior supplier and project assurance. The executive is the key decision maker and accountable for the success of a project. The senior user represents the interest of the users on the Project Board. The senior supplier represents the interest of the suppliers on the Project Board (Hedeman & Seegers, 2009) The project manager is responsible for the daily management of the project on behalf of the Project Board. The team manager ensures the project activities, for this he or she can use the team members. (Hedeman & Seegers, 2009)

If a project is managed according to an Agile Scrum approach it is possible to distinct three SCRUM roles: the Product Owner, the Team, and the Scrum Master (Schwaber, 2004). The Product Owner is responsible for representing everybody that is involved in the project. He or she represents all stakeholders and can therefore be seen as the champion of the project. On the other hand the Scrum Master is the Scrum project manager besides managing the project, he or she, if necessary, teaches others how to use the Scrum process. The Team is responsible for performing the appropriate activities to reach the project goals, for example developing software functionality.

Although there are important differences there is some similarity between the roles in Scrum when compared with the roles in PRINCE2. The Project Owner can be compared with the Project Board (more specifically with the role of senior user), the Scrum Master – while not a manager – does have some similarities with the Project Manager and the Scrum Team with the Team Manager and his team members in PRINCE2. As PRINCE2 is still more commonly known and also has more regulated communication activities we will use the roles of PRINCE2 in this research (Project board, Project Manager /Team Manager (which are both managing roles) and Team Members).

RESEARCH APPROACH

To determine how social media can be used to enhance communication in managing projects a three-step approach was taken. First the research findings by Martina et al. (2014) were studied. Martina et al. developed templates to help organizations in their social media communication strategy. These templates provide guidelines to organizations on when to use social media (type of event), how to use it (type of message, number of messages) and where to use it (type of social media channel). The templates have been tested in a pilot study in which an organization used the templates in the communication strategy for a conference that was organized. While the templates were not developed with projects in mind we determined that the idea could be used for communication during project management. However projects have different characteristics and therefore the conditions for using social media might be different. To determine whether this is true a literature review was done (step 2). For this we used the PRISMA Statement approach (Moher et al. 2009). PRISMA Statement focuses on the activities that ensure a transparent and complete reporting of the literature review by the researchers (Moher et al. 2009). For this the "definitions of systematic review and meta-analysis used by the Cochrane Collaboration" is adopted (Green & Higgins, 2005). According to Moher at al. (2009) a systematic review consists of a clearly formulated question, which in turn is used to identify, select and evaluate relevant research in a systematic manner. This includes an analysis of the data from the studies that are included in the review. During the analysis it is possible to use statistical methods (meta-analysis) as a means to analyse and summarize the results of the included studies. In our literature study a statistical analysis is not included.

The third and final step in our research approach is to construct a framework that can be used to enhance communication within projects. For this the design science research approach by Hevner et al. (2004) is taken. While this approach is developed for researching information systems (IS) we deem this approach valid since its goal is to build and validate an (IS-) artefact, just as we have the goal to create an artefact (framework) for the use of social media in project management.

In design science research the environment justifies the research and its relevance by the needs from the business (Hevner et al., 2004), in this context the need for better project communication and management. As part of the development of the framework a knowledge base provides existing knowledge (from the literature study) such as methods, frameworks and theories to build the new theories and/or artifacts. Also methods for the justification/evaluation of the developed framework is provided by the knowledge base. In the research process, the business needs and applicable knowledge are combined to create the framework (Hevner et al., 2004). In this chapter an explorative descriptive research that ends with the proposed framework is described. While this is not part of the research described here the framework should be evaluated with formal methods to validate research. Based on findings during the evaluation, the developed framework can then be refined (Hevner et al., 2004). However this is subsequently the next research project.

CONSTRUCTING A FRAMEWORK FOR THE USE OF SOCIAL MEDIA IN PROJECTS

To develop a framework that project managers can use, in order to apply social media in project communication, we combined different social media models that are described in the literature review.

The framework (see Figure 1) is based upon the management levels of PRINCE2: Project Board, Project Manager/Team Manager and Project Team Members. As described above the Project Board contains several roles but in this model we only use the role of executive. The executive is accountable and key decision maker. Therefore he has the most communication with the members of the project in comparison to the other members of the Project Board.

The framework consists of an external and internal context. In the external context there is the Project Board and in the internal context are the Project Manager and Team Members. For all management levels there are sets of norms (see Figure 2 based on the research by Kruger et al. (2013)), which are the foundation of the communication with social media within projects. These norms can be divided in three categories: legislation, learning ability and output. Legislation consists of violation of data protections principles, violation of copyright, violation of privacy, violation of reputation and trust. These norms must be adhered to in all forms of communication whatever channel is used. Norms related to learning abilities are: that the information shared must be visible to all participants, it should expand the participant's own social network, create abilities to learn from followers and improve the flow of information.

Figure 1. A framework for the use of social media in project communication

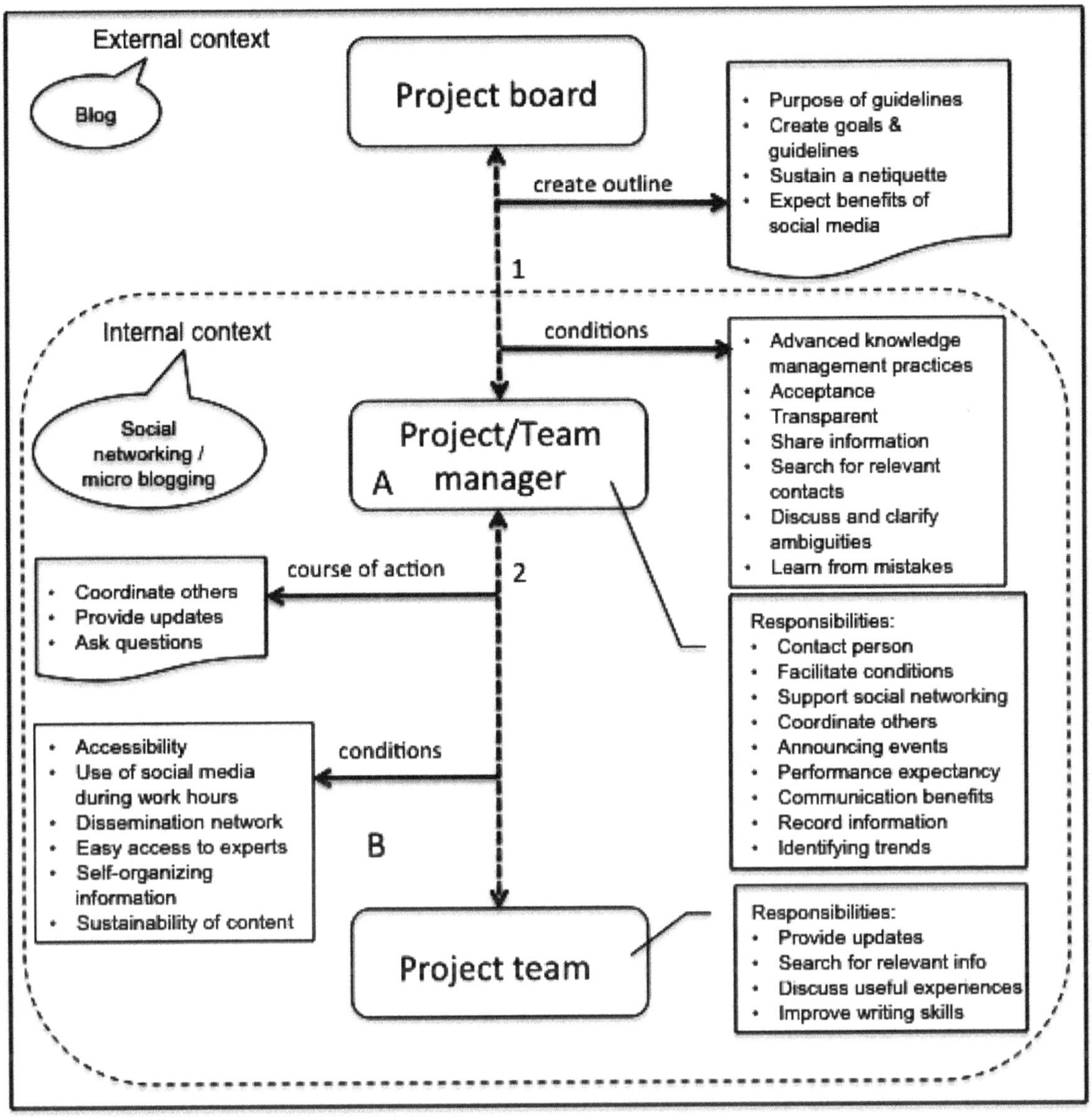

While these norms are not founded in legislation, and therefore not mandatory, they provide guidance in relation to the social media policies to be used in project communication. If these norms are not met than there is little value in using social media as a communication channel. Finally the output norms consist of affordability (cost effective), the fact that the social media channel must be easy to use and should be peer-to-peer. Failing to meet these norms means that the use of social media will be inefficient.

The framework can be used by different roles related to projects. How depends on the role and its relation to other roles. At first we will describe the relations between the roles in this model (the numbered lines) and subsequently we will explain the task(s) that each role contains. Hereby we focus on A) the Project Manager / Team Manager and B) the project team (member).

Figure 2. Norms when using social media in project communication

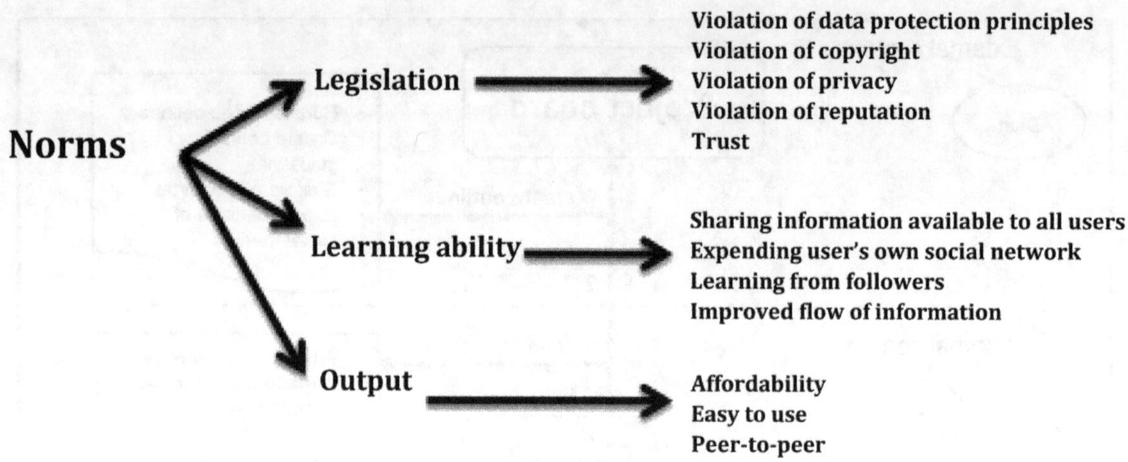

1. Project Board vs. Project Manager

The Project Board is located in the external context. In this context it is important to use a social media platform with high presentation/self-disclosure, in the literature we found that a blog provides the best solution. It allows the Project Board to communicate with the Project Manager. The Project Board can use social media in different ways to communicate with the Project Manager. Together they should create a common understanding of the purpose of using social media in project communication. Furthermore guidelines should be created that also describe the goals of social media use. These guidelines should be used to sustain a certain netiquette's and keep a clear eye on the expected benefits of social media. The conditions that should be met to be able to create such an outline are: advanced knowledge of management practice, acceptance of the social media platform, transparency, sharing information, search for relevant contact(s) that can be part of the social media platforms, take place in discussions, clarify ambiguities and stand up to mistakes. To be able to connect with the other members of the project it is essential that the Project Board has insight in the way a project is managed and is able to communicate this. Whether direct communication with the project members will take place is something the Project Board and Project Manager should discuss. However by sharing information with the members across the project, an environment can be created were every member can learn and feel more involved in the project. By being transparent, the members can experience the process and interact (sharing their knowledge) which creates a learning environment. The Project Board can follow the process. So if agreed upon the Project Board does not only connect with the Project Manager but also with project team members. Furthermore from their role the are able to invite other members to discuss issues and if necessary communicate in relation to possible mistakes. To create such an environment the Project Board must accept the social media platform and use it to share information in a transparent manner.

2. Project Manager / Team Manager vs. Project Team

The Project Manager/Team manager (the name of roles and how tasks are divided might differ depending on the context at hand, from here on we only mention the role Project Manager) and Project Team members are in the internal context therefore they can use micro-blogging channels to communicate with each other. While these are medium level in the means of presentation and self-disclosure it can still be used for communication, as these roles will also regularly interact in a face-to-face setting. Social media can then be used for short messages, for instance to quickly communicate a question, event or answer.

There are several ways of communication via social media between the Project Manager and the Project Team. Social media can be used by the Project Manager to coordinate others. Also team members can coordinate each other. Both parties can provide each other with updates or ask questions. To create an active environment and attain the benefits of the use of social media, the social media platform has to be publicly accessible. The project managers must allow project members to use social media applications during work hours. Advocate social networks as a means of easy access to expert knowledge and also let the users self-organize the information. The content needs to be updated constantly and experts should be actively involved so that team members can connect to them.

A. Role of Project Manager

The Project manager has a set of conditions to adhere to when communicating via social media. He is responsible for, and also the contact person to, the team members and also the linking pin to the project board. Therefore he needs to facilitate and support social networking. The Project Manager needs to coordinate others in the use of the platform, announce interesting events, provide the team and project board with performance expectancy and also explain the communication benefits of the use of social media. Furthermore, as all the information published on social media is recorded, the Project Manager can use this for trend analysis.

B. Role of Project Team Members

The project team is the target group and can use social media to discuss their project experience. Team members should constantly provide updates and start discussions about their tasks and experience. Only then team members in their search for relevant information will regard a social media platform as a useful resource. Regular posts of information on the social platform can lead to innovative thinking and thereby to better project results. Another advantage is that this will improve the writing / communication skills of team members, which can also lead to other benefits to the organization outside of the projects context.

Above the constructed framework for the use of social media in project management communication is described. In the remainder of this chapter further research activities and some final recommendations are stated.

FUTURE RESEARCH DIRECTIONS

As is shown in this chapter, the use of social media in support of internal communication is still limited. The suggested framework is based on earlier research in which templates for communication in different situations were developed. As the earlier templates have proven to be useful, the expectation is that the framework described in this chapter also is of practical value. However as the framework has not yet been used it should be evaluated on its applicability. For this we suggest the following formal methods to validate this research. First a Delphi study can be conducted in which experts are interviewed in several rounds to gather their remarks on both the theoretical foundations, their application in the framework and the overall usability. Second several case studies should be performed in which projects apply the framework. After each case study further refinements to framework can be made such as for instance extra instructions on its use, creation of more information related to different roles, development of best-practices. Finally more research is necessary into security and privacy issues that are related to the use of social media in project management communication. As social media platforms essentially tend to be open it is important to determine if the norms that are developed to be used in relation to the framework, and should be seen as a integral part of it, are sufficient to tackle any issues related to security and privacy.

CONCLUSION

In this chapter it is stated that social media can improve organizational communications, especially so in the context of project management where communication is one of the major critical success factors. Communication does not only influence the successful completion of a project but it also has a large impact on the costs of a project. Communication costs are one of the most important drivers for project efficiency. Furthermore the more complicated a project is the more expensive the communication will become. It is for this reason that it is advised that stakeholders in a project, and specifically team members, should communicate regularly. We believe that social media can play an essential role in improving communication.

Therefore, to help organizations that are wondering how to use social media a framework is developed that can be used to implement guidelines on how social media (tools) can be used for different events during a project. The developed framework consists of an internal- and external context, which each have their own perspective in communication and are embedded with norms. Furthermore different roles are defined who each use social media in a distinct way.

Important success factors in the use of social media are: affordability, trust and ease-of-use. If these factors have been met than social media technologies can provide a self-organisation information network were workers can have: peer-to-peer sharing, content evaluation and push nature.

REFERENCES

Augar, N., & Zeleznikow, J. (2013). 'I just saw this on Facebook, I need it now': Exploring Small Business use of Facebook. *Proceedings of 24th Australasian Conference on Information Systems.*

Azhar, S., & Abeln, J. (2014). Investigating social media applications for the construction industry. *Procedia - social and behavioral sciences*, 85, 42-51.

Badea, M. (2014). Social media and organizational communication. *Procedia - social and behavioral sciences*, 149, 70-75.

Banes, S. (2009). Social Media: lessons or the enterprise. *Orange Business.com*. Retrieved from http://www.orange-business.com/en/blogs/connecting-technology/social-media/social-media-lessons-for-the-enterprise

Basten, D., Pankratz, O., & Joosten, D., (2013). Assessing the assessors - an overview and evaluation of IT project success reports. ECIS 2013 Completed Research.

Belassi, W., & Tukel, O. I. (1996). A new framework for determining critical success/failure factors in projects. *International Journal of Project Management*, *14*(3), 141–151. doi:10.1016/0263-7863(95)00064-X

Bohm, D. (1999). *On Dialogue NY.* NY: Lee Nichol.

Bohringer, M., & Richter, A. (2009). Adopting social software to the intranet: A case study on enterprise microblogging. *Proceedings Mensch und Computer*, *2009*, 1–10.

Carlson, N. (2014). Pinterest CEO: Here's How We Became The Web's Next Big Thing. *Business Insider.com.* Retrieved from http://www.businessinsider.com/pinterest-founding-story-2012-4?op=1#ixzz3SPFYLzP6

Chasalow, L. (2008). What makes agile development different?: A case study of agile in practice. *Proceedings of SAIS 2008.*

Cleland, D. I., & King, W. R. (1983). *Systems Analysis and Project Management.* New York: McGraw Hill.

Dahnil, M., Marzuki, K., Langgat, J., & Fabeil, N. (2014). Factors influencing SMEs adoption of social media marketing. *Procedia - social and behavioral sciences*, 148, 119-126.

Dourish, P., & Bellotti, V. (1992). Awareness and coordination in shared workspaces. *CSCW*, *92*, 107–114.

Green, S., & Higgins, J. (2005). Glossary. Cochrane handbook for systematic reviews of interventions 4.2.5. The Cochrane Collaboration. Retrieved from http://www.cochrane.org/resources/glossary.htm

Guliciuc, V. (2014). Complexity and social media. *Procedia - social and behavioral sciences*, 149, 371-371.

Gunter, O., Riehle, D., Krasnova, H., & Schondienst, V. (2009). Modelings microblogging adoption in the enterprise. *Proceedings of the fifteenth Americas conference in information systems* (pp. 1-10).

Hayden, B., & Tomal, R. (2012). A History of Social Media. *CopyBlogger.com.* Retrieved from http://www.copyblogger.com/history-of-social-media/

Hearing, G., & Ussery, B. (2012a). The times they are changin' the impact of technology and social media on the public workspace, part I. *The Florida Bar Journal*, 86(3), 35–39.

Hearing, G., & Ussery, B. (2012b). The times they are a changin': The impact of technology and social media on the public workplace, part II. *The Florida Bar Journal*, 86(4), 20–24.

Hevner, A. R., March, S. T., Park, J., & Ram, S. (2004). Design science in information systems research. *Management Information Systems Quarterly*, *28*(1), 75–105.

Highsmith, J. (2001). History: The Agile Manifesto. Retrieved from http://www.agilemanifesto.org/history.html

Hollaway, A. (2005). *IT Project Failures, Accountancy Age.* KPMG Highlights.

Isaacs, W. (1999). *Dialogue and the art of thinking together.* NY, NY: Doubleday.

Kaplan, A. M., & Haenlein, M. (2010). Users of the world, unite! The challenges and opportunities of Social Media. *Business Horizons*, *1*(53), 59–68. doi:10.1016/j.bushor.2009.09.003

Karaduman, I. (2013). The effect of social media on personal branding efforts of top level executives. *Procedia - social and behavioral sciences*, 99, 465-473.

Kerzner, H. (1998). *Project Management: a systems approach to planning, scheduling, and controlling*. New York: Van Nostrand Reinhold.

Krüger, N., Brockmann, T., & Stieglitz, S. (2013). A framework for enterprise social media guidelines. *Proceedings of the Nineteenth Americas Conference on Information Systems*.

Laplante, P. A., & Neill, C. J. (2004). The demise of the waterfall model is imminent and other urban myths. *Queue*, *1*(10), 10–15. doi:10.1145/971564.971573

Locke, D. (1984). *Project Management*. New York: St Martin's Press.

Martin, C. C. (1976). *Project Management*. New York: Amaco New York.

Martina, E., Oppier, D., Fafie, D., Hoogland, D., Krouwel, L., & Kroef, v.d. (2014). Minor social media & virtual networks. Utrecht: BuDeCo.

Moher, D., Liberati, A., Tetzlaff, J., & Altman, D. G. (2009). Preferred reporting Items for systematic reviews and meta-analyses. The PRISMA Statement. *PLoS Medicine*, *6*(6). PMID:19621072

Moise, D., & Cruceru, A. (2014). An empirical study of promoting different kinds of events trough various social media networks websites. *Procedia: Social and Behavioral Sciences*, *109*, 98–102. doi:10.1016/j.sbspro.2013.12.426

Muller, J., & Stocker, A. (2011). Enterprise microblogging for advanced knowledge sharing: The references@BT case study. *Journal of Universal Computer Science*, *17*(4), 532–547.

Muller, M., Ehrlich, K., Matthews, T., Perer, A., Ronen, I., & Guy, I. (2012). Diversity among enterprise online communities collaborating, teaming, and innovating though social media. *CHI*, *12*, 1–10.

Naumann, J. D., & Jenkins, A. M. (1982). Prototyping: The new paradigm for systems development. *Management Information Systems Quarterly*, *6*(3), 29–44. doi:10.2307/248654

Office of the Government Commerce. (2009). *Managing successful projects with PRINCE2*. Norwich.

Pinto, J. K. & Slevin, D. P. (1989). Critical success factors in R&D projects. *Research Technology Management*, 32(1), 31-35

Räkers, M. (2009). A communication efficiency model for ETL projects in financial data warehousing. *Proceedings of ECIS 2009*.

Riemer, K., & Richter, A. (2010). Tweet inside: microblogging in a corporate context. BLED Proceedings 1-17.

Schwaber, K. (2004). *Agile Project Management with Scrum (Developer Best Practices)*. Washington: Microsoft Press.

Schwaber, K., & Beedle, M. (2002). *Agile Software Development with Scrum*. Upper Saddle River, NJ: Prentice Hall.

Schwalbe, K. (1999). *Information technology project management* (2nd ed.). Course Technology, Thomson Learning.

Silvius, A. J. G., van der Brink, J., & Köhler, A. (2012). *The impact of sustainability on project management, in the project as a social system, Henry Linger and Jill Owen* (pp. 183–200). Victoria: Monash University Publishing.

Statista. (2015). Number of monthly active Facebook users worldwide. *Statista.com*. Retrieved from http://www.statista.com/statistics/264810/number-of-monthly-active-facebook-users-worldwide/\

Statista. (2015). Number of monthly active Twitter users worldwide from 1st quarter 2010 to 4th quarter 2014. *Statista.com*. Retrieved from http://www.statista.com/statistics/282087/number-of-monthly-active-twitter-users/

Vlietsra, J. (2001). *Dictionary of Acronyms and Technical Abbreviations*. London: Springer London. doi:10.1007/978-1-4471-0263-2

Weisbuch, G. (2007). Tackling Complexity in Science: General Integration of the Application of Complexity in Science. Retrieved from http://www.soms.ethz.ch/research/complexityscience/EU_complexity_report.pdf

KEY TERMS AND DEFINITIONS

Agile: Agile methods rely on delivering working products/prototypes (as it is based in IT this is originally software code) in short cycles, having the working product/prototype reviewed by customers, and then following up with another iteration either improving on the capabilities just delivered, or adding additional features.

PRINCE2: PRojects IN Controlled Environments (PRINCE) 2 methodology. PRINCE 2 was originally developed in 1989 specifically for managing IT projects, however today it is widely used in all types of project contexts.

Project: Is a temporary endeavor undertaken to create a unique product, service or result. It's temporary in that it has a defined beginning and end in time, and therefore defined scope and resources. And it is unique in that it is not a routine operation, but a specific set of operations designed to accomplish a singular goal.

Project Management: Is the application of knowledge, skills, tools, and techniques to project activities to meet the project requirements.

SCRUM: Is a management and control process that cuts through complexity to focus on building products/services (originally software) that meets business needs. Management and teams are able to get their hands around the requirements and technologies, never let go, and deliver working products (software), incrementally and empirically.

Social Media: Are technologies providing an open platform in which peers can share information (of varying topics) with other peers. It differs from previous communication methods in that it enables individuals to publicly connect with, and thus share information with, greater numbers.Social media is therefore a complex system composed of a very large number of elements with non-linear interactions within an online application that has similar characteristics with Internet applications.

Chapter 4
Social Media for Project Management

Amir Manzoor
Bahria University, Pakistan

ABSTRACT

In the past, project managers could assume that most team members were in a single office location. Project management software was installed on a desktop workstation and status reports were delivered at weekly meetings. Social media use can provide real time information to project stakeholders and meet the demand of the "24 hour workday". Social media use can reduce traveling expenses and help document best practices & project learning. This chapter explore how project managers can use social media tools and how social media tools fit effectively into each project.

INTRODUCTION

In the past, project managers could assume that most team members were in a single office location. Project management software was installed on a desktop workstation and status reports were delivered at weekly meetings. The projects had monthly executive review. Today, the scenario has totally changed. In modern project management, it is very likely that at least one team member would likely be physically separated at least part of the time. The project executives look to view multiple projects as a portfolio while project sponsors expect real time access to project data. On top of it, we have global project management teams that have a 24-hour workday (Bredillet, 2006a; Symonds, 2013).

Social media provides many benefits. It influences how people communicate and support real time communication among all team members at the same time (Kaewkitipong, Chen, & Ractham, 2012). It helps develop relationships and build trust. Use of social media increases transparency and provides a cultural context for communication. In project management, use of social media can provide multiple benefits (Li, Chen, Zhang, & Fu, 2012). It can be used for knowledge sharing & project visibility as well as to identify, organize, and deploy project teams. It can support collaboration across departments and collaborate with remote resources. Social media use can provide real time information to project stakeholders and meet the demand of the round-the-clock workday. Social media use can reduce travel-

DOI: 10.4018/978-1-4666-9867-3.ch004

ing expenses and help document best practices & project learning (Leitch, 2014; Lousberg, Wamelink, Atkin, & Borgbrant, 2009; Microsoft, n.d.). The 2011 Social Media in a Project Environment Survey results showed that 20% more people used blogs for business use than in 2010. Over 90% of respondents used social media tools to stay in touch with colleagues while a quarter of respondents used social media tools for managing project teams. Over 75% of respondents felt that social media tools could improve the way they managed projects. Online Project Management Communities have also given boost to use of social media. Currently there existed around millions of project management professionals on LinkedIn with an estimated 1 million YouTube videos on project management (Girlsguidetopm, 2012).

In today's world, where project leaders are faced with strict deadlines and scare resources, social media is a fascinating idea. Use of social media in project management offers opportunities to achieve results through instant collaboration and information exchange (Ollus, Jansson, Karvonen, Uoti, & Riikonen, 2009). Social media is not new to project managers. What is new is the use of new social media tools to enable the process of collaboration and working with different groups of people (Ollus, Jansson, Karvonen, Uoti, & Riikonen, 2011). Social media is here to stay. Its use in project management offers great potential benefits that businesses and project managers shouldn't ignore. The objective of this chapter is to explore how project managers can use social media tools. The other important questions to be explored are how social media tool fit effectively into each project, what some guidelines for their use are, and how project managers should leverage the functionality of social media tools.

USE OF SOCIAL MEDIA FOR PROJECT MANAGEMENT

A project is a temporary social system where people come together to work towards a common goal – whether it's launching a satellite into space, getting your political party re-elected or launching a groundbreaking new product before the competition does. The key to making projects run smoothly is understanding how you make a temporary social system perform better – the key question for any project manager. Social media has been somewhat hijacked in terms of publicity by brands like Twitter and Facebook with a common misperception being that social media is mainly about private gossip and wasting time (Enterprise Apps Today, 2012). This is missing the point completely. Social media is a revolution in media and communication. The world was once Mad Men-like, where communication was a one-way street. You listened to the radio, watched TV, read the newspaper, obeyed the CEO and so on. Social media has now transformed this landscape into a two-way street with many lanes, where any one individual can communicate with whomever they want. Quickly, efficiently and for free. This is why social media promises to be a liberator of projects. As project managers around the world can attest, the main reason projects fail is misinformation and miscommunication (Reusch, Khushnood, Khan, & Aslam, 2010). As Gossart (2013) states "the single biggest problem with communication is the illusion that it has taken place."

Project management today is more challenging than ever. There exist many unique challenges. The project teams are becoming more and more ad hoc in nature (Huemann, 2006). Project requirements constantly shift during project life cycle and many times delivery requirements follow very tight deadlines. Increased use of virtual project teams has made it more difficult to disseminate knowledge across the team. To respond to this new and complex job of project manager, new project management methodologies, collaboration technologies, and communication techniques have been developed to foster team work and help project manager meet delivery requirements of the project. These technologies, while useful, also poses a dilemma for project managers. They now need to ensure their project teams are not overburdened with administrative work so much that the project tasks are delayed and at the same time maintain engagement of team members.

To deal with these challenges, project managers are increasingly seeking technology assistance to streamline collaboration. Project Management 2.0 (PM 2.0) or Social Project Management is the latest technology-enabled collaboration movement. PM 2.0 is defined as the use of web 2.0 technologies to enable project teams to better share information, increase collaboration and to empower teams to get things done (Kerzner, 2014). One of the most common PM 2.0 technology is Project Wiki. Using Project Wiki, all team members can update the tasks and their status, and add project documentation. Some other notable PM 2.0 technologies include blog, Voice over IP (VoIP), Internet search engines, and Wi-Fi. Web 2.0 technologies are general purpose technologies and as such it is unclear whether their use is specific to project management or just provide general collaboration. While Web 2.0 technologies help project management, their use comes with a price. Users need to maintain accounts with different service providers and use of multiple technologies may be required for the same type of interaction in different projects. The organizational use of free Web 2.0 technologies is limited due to many privacy, regulatory, or security reasons. Another issue is that few of Web 2.0 technologies are integrated with the organizational information technology (IT) infrastructure. Web 2.0 technologies definitely enhance project collaboration and make it easy to manage and track project tasks. However, due to the distributed nature of these technologies, these technologies can create challenges for project managers in aggregation of information about the project. The ultimate objective of PM 2.0 is to engage the whole social network of the project community in achieving project goals. This focus ensure that organizational goals, rather than project team goals, are fulfilled by having expert people in the project teams. This is accomplished by engaging the largest number of appropriate social network ties in accomplishing the goals of all the projects of an organization. It is recognized that to be successful, project teams need to have experts in delivering the project goal and these teams also need to be able to apply that expertise in the right place, at the right time (Schettini & Weiss, 2011).

The defined hierarchical communications and collaboration channels created by traditional project management practices can reduce information and communication overload but they are slow and can filter out important information (Klynstra, 2012). Social project management removes this deficiency by leveraging the collective knowledge of the wider social network of project community. Let's take an example. In traditional project management, a team member submits an issue to the project manager. Project manager than organize a series of meetings and use different communication and project management tools to discuss the issue. Project manager adds a task to the project plan, estimate it, and add it to execution plan. In social project management, a team member would add an issue to a PM 2.0 tool and propose a task to resolve this issue. After estimation, the project manager has the authority to accept the task and assign the task to a member for its execution. The member can also self-select him to execute the task. It is also possible that the submitted issue could be broadcasted to the project community to eventually reach a subject expert through social connections of project community. This subject expert can post a solution that everyone can see. By the time project manager see the issue, the issue most probably would be resolved. This way social project management enables fastest resolution of issue and best possible outcome (Leitch, 2014).

SOCIAL PROJECT MANAGEMENT PLATFORMS AND TOOLS

There exist many available social project management platforms and tools.

Podio

Podio is a freemium cloud-based collaboration service that supplies a web-based platform for organizing team communication, business processes, data and content in project management workspaces. Users can also select business apps from an online app store or build their own according to project needs. Podio can be used for a variety of collaboration purposes. The Podio Activity Stream is a great way to get started using the platform as a social intranet. You can share files on the Podio activity stream, like messages on the Podio activity stream, or ask a question on the activity stream. Then, use an app pack like Podio's pre-built Social Intranet that comes with apps like Bulletins, Staff Meetings and Departments, to get started. Podio tasks can help you keep track of projects and remind yourself or other users of an assignment's due date. Create a task with a keyboard shortcut, or create a task from an email by sending a message to an email address that Podio provides for each workspace and app. Podio is tightly integrated with Google Docs, Box.net and most recently, Dropbox. By connecting your Podio account to these services, you can quickly share files you've saved on those networks with coworkers in Podio. Podio can also be used for anything from CRM software for tracking leads and opportunities to social intranet for internal office communication. Podio can make recruiting new hires with web forms and managing the web app development process as easy as adding an app pack.

MangoApps

MangoApps is next generation of Intranet, Messaging and Team Collaboration tools that makes teamwork, file sharing, and collaboration easy. MangoApps is based on a modular software architecture. Users can use each module as stand-alone application or combine it with other modules. MangoApps offers multiple functionalities such as company-wide collaboration, a fully customizable company Intranet, user profiles and social networking, facility to store and share documents, wikis, collaboration with groups and projects, ideas management through brainstorming, event calendar, task management, and online forms and trackers. Administrators can personalize MangoApps with their company logo and other information and can customize MangoApps for easy navigation. MagoApps can integrate with more than 50 enterprise systems including email, Active Directory, SharePoint and LinkedIn. MangoApps can be deployed as Software-as-a-Service or on premise solution. From a functionality perspective, both deployment solutions are identical. However, on premise deployment provides you more control over hardware and software. You can control and manage all aspects of the service. You can create a secure MangoApp network that can be accessed via a VPN. You can set up LDAP directory based authentication and setup an IMAP server to fetch emails and convert them into feeds. MangoApp can be accessed using a mobile app, desktop, or web. All communication is encrypted. To collect new information for your company, you can create and customize online web forms. These forms can be automatically integrated with online trackers so that you can immediately track, take action, and manage collected data. You can create an event calendar with unlimited number of events. On your idea pages, you can share your ideas with colleagues so that you can get their comments expand on them. You can provide photos, files, and documents to strengthen the idea presented. You can use Groups & Projects feature to create a place for team collaboration. You can all project files at one place. Automatic version history allows you to access documents at various stages and you can use MangoApps internal search engine to find your documents. MangoApps allow people to create their profile from scratch or important their existing profile form LinkedIn.

MOOVIA

Moovia is designed to provide a collaborative environment for teams to work on projects. It creates a network with social media features and Google Docs integration to effectively share and work together on projects of any size. It is completely free of charge to use Moovia. Users are not restricted by space or number of projects. Some of the notable features of Moovia include free team collaboration and project management, social network environment, Google Docs integration, cloud-based storage, and multiple project management tools. This application is clearly targeted to those familiar with agile tools. This would not be recommended for teams working on projects or other non-professionals unfamiliar with Burndown or Gantt charts. Business may find that once familiar with the interface, it will make project management easier. Moovia is free for any number of projects and members and very quick to start (specially if connecting with your social accounts). It's light and safe, meaning good performance and data protection and provides a great tool for team communication. It has a "cockpit" view of the project (important things and issues will come to users eyes) and users can connect with people (like a social network), and invite them to a project. Users can manage their projects in a graphical way, with the Burndown and Gantt charts and create sprints and tasks easily with inline editing (no extra screen to edit information).

CONVO

Email chains among multiple teammates makes it difficult to track what's important and actionable. With Convo, however, you can send short, powerful messages instead of email chains. These collaborative tools enable you to disseminate information quickly and appropriately. Convo's Annotation feature enables you to point out particularly relevant pieces of information and to mark up exactly what you need to say. For remote teams, Convo enables other offices, contractors, or those traveling to stay connected in the most focused way. This is a prerequisite for ensuring that your project is complete with maximum efficiency. Keeping everyone informed in real-time about the status of tasks is crucial to ensuring that everyone is on track with the project and is using their time in the best possible way. Internal email is cumbersome when needing to keep everyone informed about the status of tasks or projects. Convo is built to produce while keeping coordinated with your team. It's efficient to keep all your files and conversations together. With Convo, the Groups feature keeps your company organized for different parts of work. For example, Groups can be team-based such as a Marketing Group so everyone on that team can keep updated or a Group that is project-based like a "new website project" so conversations and feedback stay in one place. When you have improved structure around teammates, posts, files, and links, everything is easy to find when you need it. If a new teammate joins the team, a simple @mention will give him access to previous discussion and knowledge. Convo fosters a highly collaborative, effective, and time saving workflow.

Huddle

Huddle is a team collaboration software that provides secure storage, sharing of documents and collaboration with people inside and outside the organization. Huddle provided cloud-based file storage and can automatically synchronize them across all devices. All team members always have access to the latest version of documents. You can also set permission, manage versions, and create audit trails to manage access to your documents. Project management using Huddle is a breeze. You can assign tasks and track complex projects across distributed teams and devices. The tasks can be tracked real time and an intelligent dashboard always keeps you updated with latest project-related information. Huddle provides many security features to protect data. Huddle provides data encryption, network security, user authentication and full administrative control. Huddle is used by both enterprises and government organizations to bring together the entire business network of partners, colleagues, clients and contractors into one central online environment. Currently, more than 100,000 organizations worldwide use Huddle. Approximately 80% of departments of UK central government use Huddle. Some notable enterprise that use Huddle include Kia Motors, National Grid, and Panasonic Europe. Some notable UK government organizations using Huddle include ministry of Justice, Department of Environment, and Department for Business Innovation and Skills.

Genius Live!

Genius Live! is a social collaboration platform for project & portfolio management. Genius Live! allows you capture threaded discussions across the entire lifecycle of the project. Project team members can submit comments and respond to feedback from other team members. These discussions can also be documented. For every document in a project, users can create a distribution list. These lists can greatly improve communication and information sharing among team members by providing automatic updates to members if there is any change in document or a new document is created. Genius Live! allows organizations to define their own workflows. These workflows can include flow cycles, phase reviews, and approvals. Automatic email notifications is a great feature to enhance team communication and collaboration. Users get automatic email notifications when they are assigned to new tasks or if there are any changes in their assigned tasks.

Socialcast

Socialcast is an enterprise social networking and collaboration platform that enables real-time communication and collaboration at work. It also provides integrated project management, secure real-time messaging and enhanced community management. Socialcast provides traditional productivity tools such as email, calendars, and schedules. Socialcast also provides knowledge management tools. Socialcast allows team members to exchange ideas, review document drafts or share updates. Organizations can use Socialcast to provide real-time information and document sharing among employees using a news feed (much similar to feeds provided by Facebook or LinkedIn). Socialcast can integrate with Microsoft SharePoint, corporate intranets, and popular email clients (such as Gmail and Microsoft Outlook). This integration can supplement existing organizational workflows. Socialcast Messenger is a free mobile app that allows to have ad-hoc conversations with individuals or teams, and share files while keeping the communication secure. An improved interface allows community administrators configure and customize communities. This interface can also be used to provide central management of security and employee access as well as integration with other business systems (e.g. Reporting).

Bitrix24

Bitrix24 provides tools for task management, document sharing, and time tracking all available on company's Intranet. The Activity Stream feature provide a unified view of all feeds that show every new addition to Intranet. This way all employees can be keep updated about ongoing activities. They can also contribute to the ongoing discussions and can customize the activity stream to choose which updates they want to receive. Using Activity Stream, you can schedule events, provide files, and receive immediate feedback from other users. The Like Button in Activity Stream provide users ability to show their opinions by liking the content. Such liking of content helps refine search results because liked content is given priority in search results. Therefore, useful and popular content can be easily found. You can user conversations to easily collaborate with others on a task or document. When starting a new conversation, user can add a document or image. Private conversations can also be started with one or more users. There is also an instant messenger that can be used to send private messages. A great motivational tool provided by Bitrix24 is Badges. Users can use badges to show their appreciation towards colleagues and supervisors can use these badges to give organization-wide visible awards to employees. These badges are shown both in the Activity Stream and user profile. You can aso make important announcements using Announcement Message feature in the Activity Stream. These announcements are made company-wide and they are remain visible until the user mark them as read. You can create unlimited photo albums in the Photo Gallery. All photo galleries are tightly integrated with Activity Stream. Thumbnails of photos can be liked and commented on. Standard workflows (Leave Requests, Business Trips, Expenses, Purchases, and General Requests) can be used via Activity Stream. You can integrate Bitrix24 with popular social media sites. For example, you can use #b24 hashtag to place Twitter tweets into your intranet's Activity Stream, and post clock-in information and number of completed tasks onto Facebook or Twitter. Bitrix24 is available as a cloud-hosted or self-hosted service. It comes with a desktop app for video calls, messaging and file sync. Bitrix24 is also available as a mobile app.

GUIDELINES FOR USE OF SOCIAL MEDIA IN PROJECT MANAGEMENT

Social media is being increasingly used in organizations and projects. Social media does provide opportunities of interaction and exchange of ideas that can be very beneficial for project management. However, project managers and project teams need some clear, concise, and non-ambiguous guidelines for social media use in projects. These guidelines are necessary because use of social media in project management should be limited to the extent necessary and its use should be aligned with organizational goals and objectives. Excessive and unnecessary use of social media in projects can bring undesirable consequences for organizations (such as privacy, data security etc.). Leveraging use of social media while minimizing risks of its use is a great challenge for organizations planning to use social media in projects. Following are some guidelines that organizations can use to achieve this critical objective.

Limit Social Media Interactions and Develop Policies of Social Media Use

Organizations embracing social media for project management should identify the project stakeholders and then limit the social media interactions for projects to only those stakeholders. Project managers should also be tasked with developing policies of social media use in projects. A project is unique for any organization despite the fact that it is a small part of overall organizational activities. This is because every project has some unique characteristics. A project aims to deliver a certain output in a defined period of time using a set of scare resources. In this context, a project manager may be tempted to use some risky tactics, such as social media, in project. These tactics may not be align well with on-going operations of the company. An organization may be very conservative and may not like the idea of free and dynamic interactions provided by social media. As such, suitable policies should be established first before start using social media in the projects in order avoid any negative impacts on project's dynamics.

Make Social Media Part of Project Communication Planning Process

A project manager is responsible for assessing the project communication requirements. If a project manager is looking to incorporate social media in project communication than it should first be assessed by the project manager. It is a good idea that such assessment is made part of the project communication planning process. Doing so, project managers would be in a better position to analyze current project requirements and decide which social media strategy to pursue.

Align Social Media Use with Project and Corporate Goals

There are many types of social media and each has its own pros and cons. While the social media itself is not limited but its use in project communication has to be limited in order align its use with project and overall corporate goals. Therefore, project managers should carefully choose the type of social media to be used in a project that would serve the interests of the project and the organization.

Monitor Social Media Use

Use of social media can bring increased collaboration, team synergy, effective processes, innovative thinking etc. However, use of social media also entails many risks such as risk of loss of intellectual property, increased distractions, risks of privacy etc. Therefore, it is important that the use of social media in projects should be monitored. Balancing the costs and benefits of social media use is a challenging task. A project manager should perform a careful risk-return analysis to ensure benefits of social media use outweigh the risks. It is a good idea if this monitoring is part of the project monitoring and controlling process. Such monitoring would help monitor and tailor the project strategy during project life cycle in way that fits project objectives.

Start Small and Build it Up

When project managers start using social media, they should first start its use at a small scale. Once they achieve some initial level of acceptance of social media by project community, then they should incrementally increase its use. This incremental increase in use of social media use would provide team members time and opportunity to digest this new idea and also results in development of feedback loops that catch up and adjust the system. For example, a project manager may first start using a project wiki and build up from there.

Build a Community around Social Media Use

Project managers should understand that social media is based around the concept of community. Therefore, the use of social media in project management should be focused on building a community of project stakeholders. This community building should be the first and fundamental objective of social media use in the projects. Once this objective is achieved, project managers can think of achieving some other goals through social media.

Find a Social Media Champion

Every change management effort needs a champion. Use of social media can be source of big change for organizations. It is natural that a resistance to such change would exist in almost every organization. Therefore, organization should first find a champion to lead their campaign of social media use in projects. This champion would be tasked with attracting people to use social media as a new environment of interaction and idea exchange. Organizations should understand that building social media maturity in project teams or organizations is a prerequisite for widespread use of social media in projects.

PRACTICAL IMPLICATIONS AND RECOMMENDATIONS

According to social project management, all barriers to communication in a project should be removed and people should be empowered to receive the information they need as and when they need it. This argument is based on the premise that every project is considered a social enterprise. Social project management further advocated free communication across project boundaries to increase information and idea sharing with a wider social fabric within an organization. Social project management argues that project community member should have continued access to key project information (such as project goals) that could affect the project team or project deliverables.

While access to key project information is fundamental goal of every project team, many a times this goal is not achieved. This is because project teams are often confined to find this information within project community while the information and expertise often exist outside project team and project community. Many a times, the project team can leverage this information by simply identifying it. Social project management opposes this traditional black box thinking of project teams and project communities. Social project management promotes communication beyond formal project communities to engage wider social fabric of the organization to gain access to the required information. This way the entire social network in an organization can become a project team.

Communication, Communication, Communication

Many project managers spend significant amounts of time planning around resources while ignoring the social dynamics of their teams. According to Pink (2011), there are three sources of work motivation: autonomy, mastery and meaning. People need space to bring creative solutions to problems. They need to be trusted so that they could grow their tasks. And there must be some meaning in whatever we do. Use of social media tools alone cannot provide these three factors. However, social media tools can provide project team members the freedom to open up conversation and dialogue and collectively highlight issues that were not brought up before when people were confined in their organizational silos.

Social Innovation

So far innovation and creativity have been considered a solo endeavor where a lone player comes up with an idea and then single headedly leads the innovation effort. The current research show that an innovation flourishes as a result of social encounters (Greenhow, Peppler, & Solomou, 2011). Idea sharing promoted through these social encounters provide new insights and involves more stakeholders that help developing an idea into a reality. To support this idea, let's take example of GPS invention (Johnson, 2011; Moulaert, MacCallum, & Hillier, 2013). The GPS technology was invented by US scientists to listen to the signals transmitted by Russian satellites. When the inventors shared this technology with their fellow scientist they suggested they could use Doppler-Effect to improve the technology to locate exact position of the satellite. As the word about GPS technology spread, the GPS inventors were suggested that this technology could also be used to locate the position of an object on earth using a satellite orbiting outside the earth's surface. This suggested use of GPS was actually opposite to what the GPS was actually developed for. We can see that the current form of GPS is the result of suggestions made by many people, a social network. When ideas are exposed to social networks, they are enriched. Someone else can nudge an aha moment, which happens when we talk a problem through or bounce ideas off each other. Then suddenly problems and ideas we've been working on for days, weeks or years, come into sharp focus. Rather than the prepared mind, maybe chance favors collaboration more (Johnson, 2010).

Real Knowledge is Beyond Organizational Silos

Traditionally, project managers and team members try to find the required information within the company boundaries and seldom make any effort to connect to outside world. This could also happen because organizational policies do not promote such practices. Approximately half the online population is member of some brand community or community of practice. Many of them are experts in their fields. There exist huge knowledge to benefit from if the geographical barriers are removed while team members seek knowledge (Nielsen, 2014). One should not forget that each such member of online communities has his/her own social network. Acquaintance with one member of online community means potential acquaintance with this social network. Utilizing outside knowledge can make your project transparent and open to so many interested people. Of course, an organization will need a carefully devised strategy to enable this process.

Track and Follow the Conversations

Innovative companies create an environment where sharing ideas and information is a key success factor. These companies hire talented individuals as project team members. These team members are imaginative and bold enough to challenge authority and develop new meanings of things. The success and failure of a project is dependent on how effectively these individuals are able to share their thoughts and insights. Social media tools can provide tracking and monitoring of conversations among project team members so that no team member miss out on any conversation. This way of working is the way of working for the next-generation of working.

Social Media is More Engaging

We can consider social media as a magazine developed executively for an individual. This magazine has everything an individual care about the most. No wonder social media could be a time-thief as many individuals may be tempted to use it frequently because it is more engaging. Social project management aims to leverage this characteristic of social media to better manage the project. Social project management use social media tools to provide an easy-to-use and recognized user interface that people can use to share ideas and have conversations. Team collaboration in social media based project environments is more engaging and inspiring.

Social Project Management Software is Not Social Media

Social project management software advocates adopting the model of social networking software to the project management process. This is because use of social media outside the organizations has provided opportunities of sharing ideas, information, and social interaction without any time and geographical barriers. However, it doesn't mean that the social project management software is same as social networking site (such as Facebook). A social networking sites (such as Facebook) is developed around the goals of an individual user. In contrast, a social project management software is developed around the goals of a project community and the organization.

Essence of Project Management is Unchanged

Social project management is meant to facilitate the traditional project management process by using social media tools. These social media tools enable the team collaboration process and enhance communication among team members. The way social media tools are applied produce no change in the tasks to be performed. Social project management changes the way tasks are executed and provide different outcomes of various tasks.

Team Empowerment

Social project management should empower each member of project team. Each team member must be clear about what he/she is expected to work on and the outcomes. Project manager should be able to perform real-time monitoring of the project. Project stakeholders should be able monitor the project and the project team. Team members, project managers, and project stakeholders would need information that is most relevant to them. This required information must be in a format conducive to goals of each member of project community. Social project management software should be able to provide such information enable team empowerment.

Integration is Essential

The objective of social project management is to integrate the project into the organizational social network. Social project management software should provide seamless integration with the core collaboration platforms of the organization in order integrate project teams to the collaborative and social fabric of the enterprise. Social project management software should be such a part of social technology fabric of the organization that provide a unified location for project management and collaboration. Without such integration, a social project management software will have little value for a project manager looking to broadcast needs and to find available expertise to complete tasks.

FUTURE RESEARCH DIRECTIONS

In a world that is always-on, constantly online and where the mobile phone has become the most common device for accessing the net, project managers need to update their operations to a real-time world (Bredillet, 2006b). There are many ways in which to do this but one of the first steps is to adapt the tools offered online. This is a technological shift but it can also act as a corporate culture shaper. Instead of seeing the organization as a set of boxes, it becomes an ongoing conversation between human beings. Instead of a static project plan- a melting pot of insights, ideas and perspectives. This promises to change not only project management but the way entire companies and organizations functions in the 21st century. The question is; can you afford not to take part in this conversation? The answer to this question is critical for the future of social project management and this is an area that needs further investigation.

CONCLUSION

Depending on how it is used, social media can either be a powerful tool for team collaboration or digital distractors that can take the project off track. Since social media is still in its nascent stages, little information is available about its practical use. However, this lack of information does not warrant exclusion of this powerful tool from the project manager's toolkit. Project managers should carefully research social media tools to determine their fit into the project and the organization itself. Project managers should set guidelines, develop policies, leverage the functionality of social media. Social media is here to stay. More and more project managers are expected to embrace social media use in their projects. Project managers are using social media in day-to-day project activities bringing instant collaboration and information exchange. One key area to utilize this technology is the much needed project status update. While social media is not cutting edge. New social media tools are just a way to enable the process of collaboration. Those project managers unfamiliar with social media and open environment may find it difficult to adjust this free movement of information. These managers need serious thinking about social media as a new tool of interaction and communication and consider it as another medium for delivering the direction and communication that good project managers have always done.

REFERENCES

Bredillet, C. (2006a). Investigating the future of project management: a co-word analysis approach. *International Research Network for Organizing by Projects-IRNOP 7.*

Bredillet, C. (2006b). The future of project management: mapping the dynamics of project management field in action. In D.I. Cleland & R. Gareis (Eds.), *Global Project Management Handbook: Planning, Organizing and Controlling International Projects* (2nd ed.). Planning, Organizing, and Controlling International Projects.

Enterprise Apps Today. (2012, August 21). Social Media Meets Project Management. Retrieved from http://www.enterpriseappstoday.com/social-media/social-media-meets-project-management.html

Girlsguidetopm. (2012). Social Media in a Project Environment: 2011 Survey Results. Retrieved from http://www.girlsguidetopm.com/social-media-in-a-project-environment-2011-survey-results/

Gossart, H. (2013, September 16). Communication- The single biggest problem with communication is the illusion that it has taken place (George Bernard Shaw). Retrieved from http://www.ncea.org/department-news/communication-single-biggest-problem-communication-illusion-it-has-taken-place

Greenhow, C., Peppler, K. A., & Solomou, M. (2011). Building creativity: Collaborative learning and creativity in social media environments. *On the Horizon*, *19*(1), 13–23. doi:10.1108/10748121111107672

Huemann, M. (2006). *Project management personnel in the project-oriented company.* Global Project Management Handbook.

Johnson, S. (2010). Where good ideas come from. *TED.* Retrieved from http://www.ted.com/talks/steven_johnson_where_good_ideas_come_from?language=en

Kaewkitipong, L., Chen, C., & Ractham, P. (2012). Lessons learned from the use of social media in combating a crisis: A case study of 2011 Thailand flooding disaster. *Proceedings of the 33rd international conference on information systems*, Orlando, FL, USA.

Klynstra, M. (2012, August 21). Social Media Meets Project Management. Retrieved from http://www.geneca.com/social-media-meets-project-management/

Leitch, R. (2014, March 13). Why Project Managers Should Embrace Social Media. Retrieved from http://www.business2community.com/social-media/project-managers-embrace-social-media-0802531

Li, M., Chen, G., Zhang, Z., & Fu, Y. (2012). A social collaboration platform for enterprise social networking. *Proceedings of the 2012 IEEE 16th International Conference on Computer Supported Cooperative Work in Design (CSCWD)* (pp. 671–677). IEEE. doi:10.1109/CSCWD.2012.6221890

Lousberg, L., Wamelink, H., Atkin, B., & Borgbrant, J. (2009). *Foundation of a practical theory of project management.* New York: SPON Press Taylor & Francis.

Microsoft. (n. d.). Use Twitter, Facebook and other social media to help manage projects and teams. Retrieved from https://support.office.com/en-us/article/Use-Twitter-Facebook-and-other-social-media-to-help-manage-projects-and-teams-1c9b9c86-e417-4763-91ed-35a5f6e86208?CorrelationId=b805fa25-81d5-4793-b446-c4495661dd22&ui=en-US&rs=en-US&ad=US#

Moulaert, F., MacCallum, D., & Hillier, J. (2013). Social innovation: intuition, precept, concept. *The International Handbook on Social Innovation: Collective Action, Social Learning and Transdisciplinary Research* (p. 13).

Nielsen. (2014, June 17). Global Consumers are Willing to Put Their Money Where Their Heart is When it Comes to Goods and Services from Companies Committed to Social Responsibility. Retrieved from http://www.nielsen.com/us/en/press-room/2014/global-consumers-are-willing-to-put-their-money-where-their-heart-is.html

Ollus, M., Jansson, K., Karvonen, I., Uoti, M., & Riikonen, H. (2009). On services for collaborative project management. In *Leveraging Knowledge for Innovation in Collaborative Networks* (pp. 451–462). Springer. doi:10.1007/978-3-642-04568-4_47

Ollus, M., Jansson, K., Karvonen, I., Uoti, M., & Riikonen, H. (2011). Supporting collaborative project management. *Production Planning and Control*, *22*(5-6), 538–553. doi:10.1080/09537287.2010.536624

Pink, D. H. (2011). *Drive: The surprising truth about what motivates us*. Penguin.

Projectplace. (n. d.). Social Project Management - Our Philosophy. Retrieved from https://www.projectplace.com/about-us/social-project-management/

Reusch, P. J., Khushnood, M., Khan, R. A., & Aslam, S. (2010). After the Crisis we need Social Project Management. Proceedings of the International Business Research Conference, University of Northern Florida UNF, Jacksonville.

Schettini, F., & Weiss, B. (2011, October 3). Social Media: A Growing Factor in Project Success. *CIO Insight*. Retrieved from http://www.cioinsight.com/c/a/Expert-Voices/Social-Media-a-Growing-Factor-in-Project-Success-806642

Symonds, M. (2013, July 15). Where does social media fit into project management? *Parallel Project Training*. Retrieved from http://blog.parallelprojecttraining.com/project-management-articles/where-does-social-media-fit-into-project-management/

ADDITIONAL READING

University Alliance. (n. d.). These Social Media Tools are Excellent for Project Management. Retrieved from http://www.usanfranonline.com/resources/social-media/social-media-an-excellent-project-management-tool/

Wrike. (2014, June 3). 11 Ways To Use Social Media To Find Project Management Resources (or just about anything!). Retrieved rom https://www.wrike.com/blog/11-ways-to-use-social-media-to-find-project-management-resources-or-just-about-anything/

Yongkui, L., & Yujie, L. (2009). Social network model of complex projects organization. *Proceedings of the International Conference on Management and Service Science MASS'09* (pp. 1–6). IEEE.

KEY TERMS AND DEFINITIONS

Collaboration: It refers to a working practice whereby individuals work together to a common purpose to achieve business benefit.

Collaborative Project: A collaborative project allow groups of people to work together to create online content.

Distributed Project: A distributed project is a project that is done across multiple business worksites or locations.

Networking: It refers to creating an active group of acquaintances and associates through regular communication for mutual benefit.

Project Champion: A project champion is a person with an overall responsibility for delivery of the project.

Social Media: Social media is the collective of online communications channels that allow people to create, share or exchange information, ideas, and pictures/videos in virtual communities and networks.

Social Networking: It refers to the practice of using a platform to build social networks or social relations among people who share similar interests.

Section 2
The Human Factor and Social Media

Chapter 5
The Influence of Social Media on Teamwork Aspects:
Introduction of a Conceptual Model to Measure the Influence Social Media has on Teamwork

Frank Molendijk
HU University of Applied Sciences Utrecht, The Netherlands

ABSTRACT

Social media has become an integral part of society compared to only ten years ago and has changed the way we communicate. On the other hand organizations are increasingly working in teams. Key in teamwork is communication, according to Salas et al. communication is invaluable in teamwork. However what is the influence of social media on teamwork with this major adjustment in the way we communicate? This chapter introduces a conceptual model to measure the influence of social media on teamwork aspects.

INTRODUCTION

The research field of social media is relatively new and is receiving increasing more attention over the last years. Social media has influence on all levels in our way of living and more importantly the way we work and communicate with each other. Some even say that social media is a revolution happening (Qualman, E. 2013) and one of the most powerful online networking tools which has been integrated into our social and economic life in the real world (Gerritsen et al. 2014).

Most of the work that people do requires some degree of corporation and communication with others, some kind of teamwork. This is not limited to any specific industry or business model. Over the last decade the way we communicate has changed drastically due to social media, however the influence of this has yet to receive sufficient attention. This is underlined by the research done by Treem et al (2012) which concluded that the study of social media use within organizations is in its infancy.

DOI: 10.4018/978-1-4666-9867-3.ch005

Whereas most of the current research field has studied the influence that social media (dubbed as social networks) has for consumers and organization in all different fields, primarily marketing and e-commerce (outward). There is little to no research done on the influence that social media has on teamwork or the internal organization (inward). In the end social media all comes down to communication, and communication is essential within a team and organization. This research project focuses on how social media influences teamwork within teams. Knowing how social media influences teamwork and having a model in measuring the influence per social media function offers organizations a method in creating guidelines. This brings us to the research question of this research project:

Which functions that are used in social media influence (certain aspects) of teamwork?

In addition the following sub questions are defined:

- What functions are offered by social media to support teamwork?
- Which social media's are used by individuals (business / private?
- What etiquettes are agreed upon (before or reactive)?
- Which aspects of teamwork, based on the TWQ framework of Hoegl and Gemuenden, are influenced by social media?.

This article starts with the literature study, results and provides the definition of both social media and teamwork aspects. Afterwards the research method used is outlined, why this was chosen. To finalize the findings, conclusions and closing comments on this research project and possibilities for future research are described.

LITERATURE REVIEW

Social Media

The first known use of the term social media in print is believed to have occurred in 1997, when then AOL executive Ted Leonsis commented that organizations needed to provide consumers with "social media, places where they can be entertained, communicate, and participate in a social environment" (Treem, J.W. & Leonardi, P.M. 2012). In addition the first popular social networking site, SixDegrees.com (1997 to 2001) was introduced in that same year. It was named after the six degrees of separation concept and allowed users to list friends, family members and acquaintances both on the site and externally; external contacts were invited to join the site (Wikipedia, 2014). This was the start of a period in which a large number of nowadays highly popular social media platforms came to see the light of day. Some examples includes the wiki-based encyclopedia Wikipedia (2001), LinkedIn (2002), MySpace (2003), Facebook (2004), Twitter (2004), Hyves (2004), Youtube (2005), Yammer (2008), WhatsApp (2009) and Instagram (2010).

Since the rapid growth of social it is apparent that social media is not something to be dismissed as a youthful or consumer oriented hobby. There are many definitions and interpretations of social media.

Andreas Kaplan and Michael Haenlein (2010) define social media as "A group of Internet-based applications that build on the ideological and technological foundations of Web 2.0, and that allow the creation and exchange of User Generated Content". *Boyd et all (2008) define social network sites as* "Web-based services that allow individuals to (1) construct a public or semi-public profile within a bounded system, (2) articulate a list of other users with whom they share a connection, and (3) view and traverse their list of connections and those made by others within the system. The nature and nomenclature of these connections may vary from site to site."

Treem et al (2012) state the default approach in many academic writings has been to define the term social media by pointing toward the types of technologies that people recognize, implicitly, as social media (such as blogs, wikis, social tagging, etc.). And Kietzmann et al. (2011) define social media as "*Mobile and web-based technologies to create highly interactive platforms via which individuals and communities share, co-create, discuss and modify user-generated content*". Due to the comprehensive definition of Kietzmann et al. and their overarching honeycomb framework, this definition served as the reference of social media in this research project. Kietzmann et al. (2011) also defined seven functional building blocks which can be offered via social media platforms (Figure 1). These functional building blocks are: identity, conversations, sharing, presence, relationships, reputation and groups.

Teamwork

Teamwork has received extensive academic and literature focus over the past decades. Back in 1997 Cohen and Bailey emphasized the importance of teams for organizational success in modern economy. Researchers of the ALL (Adult Literacy and Life skills survey) framework go even further and state that teams are becoming the primary building block of most organizations and due to its prevalence in society, teamwork has been identified as an important life skill. According to Salas et al teams have the potential to offer greater adaptability, productivity, and creativity than any one individual can offer and provide more complex, innovative, and comprehensive solutions to organizational problems.

Cohen and Bailey define four type of teams (work teams, parallel teams, project teams and management teams) and define a team as "*an collection of individuals who are interdependent in their tasks, who share responsibility for outcomes, who see themselves and who are seen by others as an intact social entity embedded in one or more larger social systems (for example, business units or the organization), and who manage their relationships across organizational boundaries*". In the comprehensive research done by Salas et al they asked the question: What ensures the success of a team? They answered "Teamwork".

Figure 1. The honeycomb framework of social media functions (Kietzmann et al. 2011)

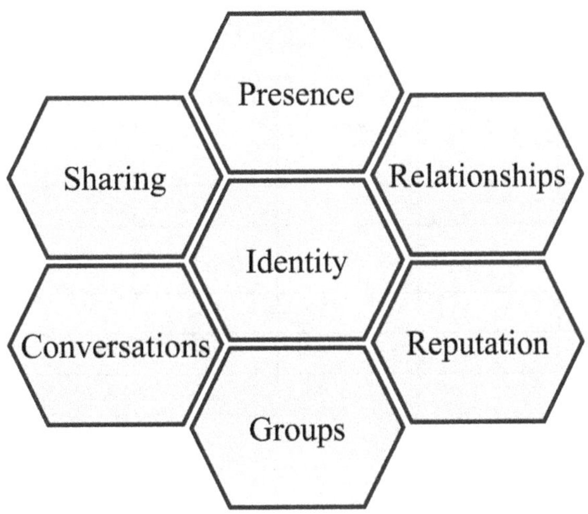

Oser et al. state that teamwork can be defined as a team's ability to exhibit team behaviors relevant to task performance in changing environments. Kozlowski et al define teamwork as the knowledge and skills that enhance the quality of team member interactions, i.e., coordination, cooperation, communication. Salas et al. describe teamwork as a set of interrelated thoughts, actions, and feelings of each team member that are needed to function as a team and that combined to facilitate coordinated, adaptive performance and task objectives resulting in value-added outcomes.

According to Rousseau et al. there was lack of a consensus concerning the conceptual structure of teamwork behaviors. Therefore they reviewed the frameworks of teamwork behaviors in the literature on work teams (teamwork). Rousseau et al did an extensive research and comparison of existing frameworks, during the literature review of this research project every framework of teamwork behaviors that was included in the Rousseau et al research (Table 1, 544 – 545, Rousseau et al) was checked for applicability. One of the frameworks that stood out was the framework of Hoegl and Gemuenden which focused solely on the quality of interactions within teams rather than team members and provided a comprehensive framework (TWQ). Hoegl and Gemuenden state the most elementary component of their framework is communication within a team. However what is the influence of social media on communication? Hoegl and Gemuenden are not alone with their statement that communication is one of the essential components within teamwork. Brannick et al describe communication as a major component of the teamwork process. Kozlowski et al define communication as a primary means to enable more proximal factors like coordination and cooperation. And according to Salas et al. communication is invaluable in teamwork.

The goal of this research project is not to define how a team must be developed or measure how it performs. It is purely focused on the influence that social media has on existing teamwork aspects and provide a comprehensive model of how this can be measured within an organization or team.

With existing teamwork aspects we refer to the facets as defined by Hoegl and Gemuenden proposed in their teamwork quality (TWQ) framework which is shown below in Figure 2.

They stated that teamwork quality is positively related to the performance of teams with innovative projects and to the personal success of team members. As defined by the research question the focus of this research are certain aspects of teamwork, being the quality of teamwork. Therefore the "Team Performance" and "Personal Success" of the TWQ framework are not be discussed further in this research paper.

Table 1. Conceptual model based on Hoegl and Gemuenden TWQ and Kietzmann et al social media frameworks

	Identity	**Presence**	**Relationship**	**Reputation**	**Groups**	**Conversations**	**Sharing**
Communication							
Coordination							
Balance of member contribution							
Mutual support							
Effort							
Cohesion							

Figure 2. Hoegl and Gemuenden teamwork quality (TWQ) framework

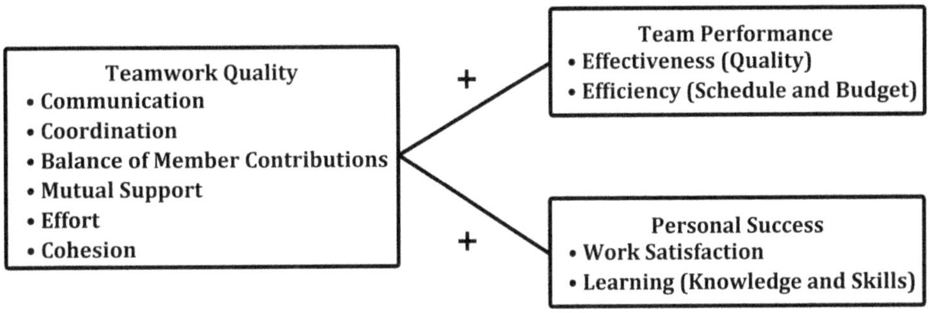

Social Media and Teamwork

Social media is a relative new phenomenon which has received more academic attention over the last decade. However most of the research done on social media is focused on the outward usage in for example advertising or customer support. Teamwork on the other hand has received widespread academic attention over the last several decades, these results have been shared with you in the above paragraphs. However what academic research has been done on the influence that social media has on teamwork?

Although there are valid resources for social media and even more for teamwork, there is very little to no research done on the influence that social media has on teamwork aspects. It is surprising that this is the case since teamwork is all about communication and corporation, exactly these two aspects (especially the first) have changes the most with the rise of social media. Therefore this research has combined the literature findings of the different sources to combine these into a conditional model which is introduced later in this paper.

The Study

Conceptual Framework

Following the literature review the conceptual model was developed using both frameworks of Hoegl and Gemuenden and Kietzmann et al. The conceptual model, shown in Table 1, makes use of these two existing frameworks.

The combined conceptual model, shown in Table 1, can be used to measure and visualize the influence that different social media functions have on teamwork aspects. In order to determine the influence of social media a quantitative research method has been chosen. To determine the influence of social media on teamwork aspects an extensive questionnaire was developed based on the seven functional aspects of social media and each of the six teamwork facets. The questionnaire was build up in several segments which logically relate to each other. With the exception of the generic questions, each question is build up from two dimensions and created as questions which can be answered in certain scales based on the Likert methode. One part of the question relates to the dimension "Teamwork Quality" based on the TWQ Framework of Hoegl and Gemuenden. The second part of the question relates to one of the seven social media functions based on the honey comb model of Kietzmann et al. Each of the research focused questions can be answered with negatively, slightly negatively, neutral, slightly positive, positive or I do not know.

Respondents

As this is an quantitative research with the use of an online questionnaire a suitable target group was selected. The questionnaire was sent via a personal invite, with three reminders, to 242 employees of a large global operating IT service provider. For this research project a margin of error percentage of 10% and 90% trustworthiness was used. The selected target group consist of the below population and in which of the three classifications they belong (Table 2).

Engagement managers are mainly project managers and team managers in general. These people are actively managing a large team, share information, maintain relationships and above all coordinate between different stakeholders. Subject matter experts consists mostly of infrastructure professionals and architects who are used to working with new technology and platforms. These individuals almost always work in teams and are IT savvy people who tend to use new techniques or online platforms faster than other individuals. The group of "Others" is quite small compared to the other classification groups. Respondents in this group vary from Project Management assistances, secretaries and sales professionals.

The questionnaire was shared with 242 respondents. These respondents have been selected explicitly based on their role in the organization and high level of teamwork. In total there were 25 generic questions in the questionnaire to determine some common baseline such as age, gender, role in organization and whether they use social media. The other 42 questions where focused in answering the core research question of this project. What is the influence of social media, on certain aspects, of teamwork? The questions in the questionnaire where divided in 7 open, 2 ranking, 16 open and 42 Likert scale questions.

Over a period of four weeks the respondents were given the opportunity to complete the survey, Table 3 shows the percentage of respondents that complete the survey.

According to Hamilton (2009) it is more important to have a high percentage rate if the goal of the research is to establish generalization in a large population. Response rate is of less importance if you are trying to create insight into a certain subject. Based on the meta-data used by Hamilton a total response rate of 13.35% was the average.

Of all the respondents who completed the survey 8% was female, 49% was between the age of 25 and 44, 97% work in teams and 97% of them uses social media. In total all respondents had 3,1 devices in average on which they used social media. In addition to the devices all the respondents were asked to select which social media platforms they used privately and for business matters. Figure 3 shows the outcome and which platform are used for private and or business matters.

Table 3. Overview of response rate / percentage

Classifications	Response	Response %
Engagement Managers	27	34.60%
Subject Matter Experts	30	22.10%
Others	8	28.60%
Total	*65*	*28.4%*

Table 2. Target group research project

Classifications	Population	Needed Response
Engagement Managers	78	37
Subject Matter Experts	136	46
Others	28	21
Total	*242*	*104*

Figure 3. Data analysis social media platforms

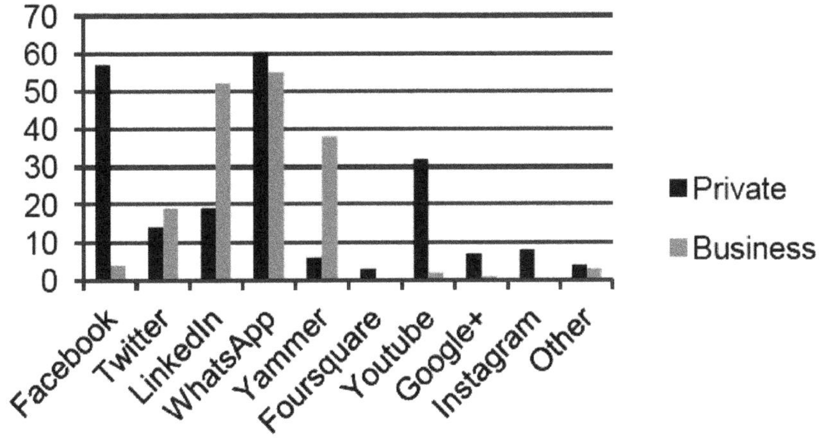

Interesting facts is that for personal matters each respondent made use of 3.2 social media platforms where for business matters each respondent made use of 2.7 social media platforms. Another interesting fact is that in both private and business matters WhatsApp ranks #1.

One of the sub questions of this research project was "What etiquette are agreed upon (before or reactive)?" The findings in Figure 4 conclusively show that 57% of the respondents find that their organizations understand the impact of social media. However only 20% of the respondents state that there are agreed etiquettes in place on an organizational level and only 8% of the respondents stated that there are etiquettes in place within their team.

FINDINGS

Overall

Table 4 shows the results of all respondents in the conceptual. It clearly shows what the influence is of the different social media functions on the six facets of teamwork as defined by Hoegl and Gemuenden.

Figure 4. Data analysis understanding and etiquettes in organization

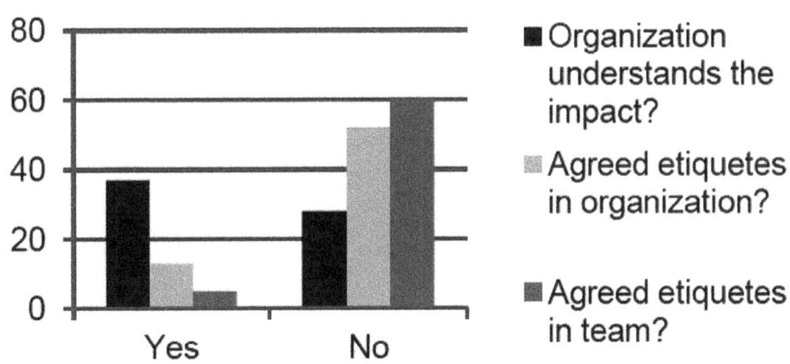

Table 4. Summary of results for all respondents

	Identity	Conversations	Sharing	Presence	Relationships	Reputation	Groups
Communication	Slightly positive (3,6)	Slightly positive (4,3)	Slightly positive (4,3)	Slightly positive (4,1)	Slightly positive (3,8)	Slightly positive (3,5)	Slightly positive (3,8)
Coordination	Neutral (3,2)	Slightly positive (4,1)	Slightly positive (3,9)	Slightly positive (3,9)	Neutral (3,4)	Neutral (3,2)	Slightly positive (3,7)
Balance of Member contribution	Neutral (3,2)	Neutral (3,2)	Slightly positive (3,6)	Neutral (3,2)	Neutral (3,1)	Neutral (2,9)	Neutral (3.1)
Mutual support	Neutral (3,3)	Slightly positive (3,9)	Neutral (3,3)	Slightly positive (4,0)	Neutral (3,4)	Slightly positive (3,5)	Slightly positive (3,5)
Effort	Neutral (3,0)	Slightly positive (3,9)	Slightly positive (3,8)	Neutral (3.1)	Slightly positive (3,8)	Neutral (3,0)	Neutral (3,3)
Cohesion	Slightly positive (3,6)	Slightly positive (3,8)	Neutral (3,4)	Neutral (3,2)	Slightly positive (3,6)	Slightly positive (3,5)	Slightly positive (3,8)

An interesting observation is that, according to the respondents, none of the social media functions have a negative of slightly negative influence on teamwork aspects. The standard deviation had an average of 1,14 on all cells.

Ranking

In addition to the questions which could be answered based on the Likert scales, all the respondents where asked to rank the social media functions and teamwork facets from highest to lowest influence. Tables 5 and 6 show the results of these rankings.

Results of the Three Respondent Groups Compared

Table 7 shows the results based on the three respondent groups. Each of these groups have been analyzed to determine if there is a large difference with the overall results or if there are certain correlations to be seen. Engagement managers are mainly project managers and team managers in general.

Table 5. Social media ranking results including average ranking position

#	Social Media Function	Average Ranking
1	Conversations	2,02
2	Presence	2,68
3	Sharing	3,54
4	Relationships	4,17
5	Reputation	5,09
6	Groups	5,23
7	Identity	5,26

Table 6. Teamwork facets ranking results including average ranking position

#	Teamwork Quality Aspect	Average Ranking
1	Communication	1,22
2	Coordination	2,58
3	Mutual support	3,78
4	Balance of mem contribution	3,78
5	Effort	4,71
6	Cohesion	4,92

Compared to the overall results of the engagement managers answered all the questions the most neutral of all groups. This might be related to the fact that this group of professionals is not actively using these new platforms or that the functions offered by social media have yet to prove themselves compared to more "traditional" instruments such as e-mail, telephone and personal sessions. The subject matter expert group consists mostly of infrastructure professionals and architects who are used to working with new technology and platforms.

These individuals almost always work in teams and are IT savvy people who tend to use new techniques or online platforms faster than other individuals. In addition the organization in which this research was conducted is a large IT service provider which can boost the effect of these experts. Compared to the other classification groups the subject matter expert group has the highest amount of "Positive" influences on various social media functions. The group "Other" respondents is quite small compared to the other classification groups. Compared to the other classification groups it stands out that these group of respondents score relatively high, compared to the engagement managers, on social media functions "Identity", "Sharing", "Reputation" and "Groups". However due to the small population (12%) there cannot be drawn any conclusions based on these results. Off all the respondents only 0.70% of the questions were answered with "Negative" influence and 3.74% of the questions were answered with "Slightly negative". Keep in mind that the 65 respondents answered 2.730 Likert questions in total. Only 5.57% of the answers provided by the respondents where answered with "I do not know".

Discussion

In this research project the research question "Which functions that are used in social media influence (certain aspects) of teamwork?" was at the center. In addition some sub questions provided extra guideline for the questionnaire. The method to determine the influence of social media on certain aspects of teamwork was done with the help of existing frameworks to create a new conceptual model. This model proved to be very helpful and easy to use once it was developed and the needed questions where defined.

Identity

Out of all the social media functions Identity scored the lowest of them all and has the least influence on teamwork. However it is the belief of the researcher that this is due to the fact that the research took place with respondents who all worked on projects and mostly already know one another from previous projects or are part of the same team. In addition the organization in which this took place is service oriented in which most of the persons are working in teams. This function of social media is primarily valuable if you want to know more of this person, if you already know him or her there is no need to use this function.

Groups

Just as with the function of Identity, Groups is a function of social media has a relative neutral influence on teamwork. As already stated the organization in which this research took place is already focused on groups and teams based on the type of service or project one is working on. Therefore the creation of

Table 7. Summary of results per respondent group Engagement Managers (EM), Subject Matter Experts (SME) and Others (OTH)

	Identity			Conversations			Sharing			Presence			Relationships			Reputation			Groups		
	EM	SME	OTH	EM	SME	OTH	EM	SME	OTH	EM	SME	OTH	EM	SME	OTH	EM	SME	OTH	EM	SME	OTH
Communication	3,1	4,2	3,9	4,0	4,6	4,4	4,0	4,7	3,8	3,6	4,6	4,3	3,9	3,9	3,9	3,1	3,9	4,1	3,3	4,5	3,9
Coordination	3,1	3,3	3,6	3,8	4,5	3,9	3,4	4,3	4,0	3,4	4,4	3,8	3,2	3,5	3,6	3,0	3,4	3,5	3,4	4,2	3,6
Bal. of contr.	3,1	3,2	3,6	3,2	3,2	3,4	3,3	3,7	3,9	3,0	3,3	3,3	3,1	3,2	3,1	2,6	3,2	2,9	3,0	3,2	3,0
Mutual support	3,2	3,2	4,0	3,7	4,1	4,1	3,3	3,2	3,6	3,6	4,4	4,2	3,0	3,7	3,2	2,9	4,0	3,8	3,3	3,8	3,4
Effort	2,9	3,1	2,9	3,4	4,5	3,4	3,4	4,3	3,5	2,7	3,3	3,4	3,3	4,4	3,3	2,7	3,2	2,9	2,9	3,6	3,5
Cohesion	3,4	3,6	4,1	3,6	4,0	3,9	3,4	3,3	3,3	3,2	3,1	3,3	3,6	3,6	3,4	3,2	3,8	3,5	3,3	4,2	4,0

Legenda:

- (white) = Neutral
- (grey) = Slightly positive
- (black) = Positive

groups within Yammer or other platforms does not seem to be used. One could ask themselves if WhatsApp does not count as a group function provided via social media. It seems that most of the respondents does not make this link and relate WhatsApp toe conversations, this again shows the close integration of social media which spans over several function areas of the honeycomb framework.

Reputation

This functional area of social media has a low influence on teamwork aspects. Again this seems to be related to the type of respondents. If one would do a similar research within an organization which is focused on recruitment or an HR department this functional area of social media it could result in a higher rating on the scale. Again this shows the diversity of social media since each function has an added value depending on the type of department or organization.

Relationships

This function is closely related to identity and groups, as stated the respondents all knew most of their colleagues and thus this social media does not add any value within the current teamwork. Social media only enabled the way to maintain and create the already existing relationships via other platforms such as LinkedIn, Yammer, Facebook and WhatsApp.

Sharing

The top three starts with the functional block sharing. Most of the respondents stated that social media enabled more direct communication and enabled easy exchange of information via these platforms. Some comments from the respondents include "I am able to work better and faster with my team members" "A powerful medium which can be used informing others very quickly" and "...can be easily used to quickly gather shared information.". Team leads, project managers and infrastructure professionals seem to embrace this function, mostly in the form of WhatsApp. However the fact that there are no agreed etiquettes in advance do create a serious risk, what type of information is allowed on this public platform? What are the security restrictions with customer confidential data?

Presence

Second place is reserved for the social media function Presence. Although this function was already available for some time via personal computers the rise of social media created extra outlets which can be used. An interesting fact is that again the female respondents showed a big difference compared to the male and other respondents.

Conversations

As already stated multiple times in this research project the academic community universally agreed on the fact that communication is the key aspect within teamwork. Communication consists primarily of conversations, verbally of digitally. Exactly this aspect of teamwork is influenced the most, in a positive way, by social media. All the respondents agreed on this aspect.

CONCLUSION

Answering the Research Question and Sub Questions

The research done within the selected organization showed that all functions, as outlined by Kietzmann et al, offered by social media had either a neutral, slightly positive or positive influence (depending which classification grouped referred to) on all aspects, as defined by Hoegl and Gemuenden, of teamwork. The earlier ranking shows which aspects of teamwork are influenced most by social media according to the respondents. The below reactions of some respondents underline the key outcomes of this research project best.

Improves the interaction, improves speed of solution of (smaller) matters
Always quick access to all needed information. quick info sharing
WhatsApp can be used easily to quickly access groups of team members.
Social media is crucial within teams for communication purposes.
Can be very good and efficient and non-intrusive
Quick and easy contact with other team members

The above quotes shows the power of social media and the impact that this have on teams within organizations. In addition it is apparent that organizations and team leaders need to catch up with this new of communication and align this accordingly with the team. Results of the questionnaire clearly shows which functions of social media can be used on certain aspects of teamwork. Table 4 shows the results of all respondents and shows which social media platforms have the most influence on certain aspects of teamwork. It clearly shows that conversations, presence and sharing need to be given extra attention due to their influence. In addition it shows that communication, coordination and mutual support are teamwork aspects that have the most to gain via social media platforms. The fact that social media has the biggest influence on communication within teams is not surprising since communication is exactly what has changed drastically by social media. Thus it is somewhat concerning that the research uncovered the fact that there are little to no (known) agreed etiquettes in place for social media usage within this organization.

Sub question "*What functions are offered by social media to support teamwork?*" is answered with the framework of Kietzmann et al being conversations, presence, sharing, relationships, reputation, groups and identity. Each function has, depending on the team, functions to offer which can support teamwork in one way or another.

Sub question "*Which social media's are used by individuals (business / private?*" is answered with Figure 3 which clearly shows the high degree of integration and penetration that social media has on a personal and business level. WhatsApp proved to be the most used social media platform in all.

Sub question "*What etiquettes are agreed upon (before or reactive)*?" was answered with Figure 4 which showed that 57% of the respondents find that their organizations understand the impact of social media. However only 20% of the respondents state that there are agreed etiquettes in place on an organizational level and only 8% of the respondents stated that there are etiquettes in place within their team. All the employees that did answer with "Yes" where inconclusive, not in line with one another and some of them referred to guidelines which could be found somewhere on the intranet. This is a major gap and needs to be addressed quickly, especially with project teams and or delivery teams which are client facing.

Sub question "*Which aspects of teamwork, based on the TWQ framework of Hoegl and Gemuenden, are influenced by social media?*" is basically answered with the previous sub questions. All aspects of teamwork defined in the TWQ framework are influenced by social media. However how much influence varies slightly between the different defined categories groups and per social media function offered.

External Validation

In addition to the purely quantitative research the results have been discussed with several individuals who are working for different organizations in different sectors. In total the results have been validated with four individuals. During the validation it was confirmed that the conceptual model used provided valuable insight to the four individuals. In addition all the results were discussed in detail, specifically the ranking results and conceptual model with the combined results (table 7). All four individuals agreed with the top three ranking results and proved to have valuable insights such as the guidelines which were in place on an organizational level and the WhatsApp groups used within the team to gain better and faster communication.

FUTURE RESEARCH DIRECTIONS

This paragraph contains suggestion for future research that would contribute to both the scientific community and the practical applications on the area of social media and the influence it has on teamwork aspects.

An obvious future step would be to do the same research project within another organisation in a less IT savvy environment to determine if there are differences in the results. This could provide valuable information to determine if less IT savvy people have a completely different view of what the influence is of social media. In this organisation one should try to involve a larger group of female respondents to verify the positive difference in male and female respondents.

This research project used a quantitative research approach with a low percentage of qualitative input from the respondents. Future research can focus on a small group of respondents to get a better insight in their mindset and detailed personal experiences. This could include with a research approach to identify a certain department of team that makes no use of social media, determine the quality and effectiveness of this team, "implement" social media via the earlier given guidelines and let them work for a couple of months via this new way of working. Afterwards the exact same quality and effectiveness test needs to be done to determine the before and after, this would give us valuable insights into the exact influence of social media.

Finally, one could focus a new research project specifically to create detailed guidelines and etiquettes of social media usage based on qualitative research in different organizations.

REFERENCES

Baker, D.P., Horvath, L., Campion, M., Offermann, L., Salas, E. (n. d.). *Measuring Adult Literacy and Life skills*. The ALL Teamwork Framework. Statistics Canada – Catalogue no. 89-552-MIE, no. 13.

Berthon, P., Pitt, L., & Campbell, C. (2008). Ad lib: When customers create the ad. *California Management Review*, *50*(4), 6–30. doi:10.2307/41166454

Boyd, M. D., & Ellison, N. B. (2008). Social Network Sites: Definition, History, and Scholarship. *Journal of Computer-Mediated Communication*.

Brannick, M. T., Salas, E., & Prince, C. (1997). *Team Performance: Assessment and Measurement: Theory, Methods and Applications*. Lawrence Erlbaum Associates Inc.

Bryman, A., & Bell, E. (2007). *Business research methods*. Oxford university press.

Castka, P., Bamber, C.J., Sharp, J.M. (2003) Measuring teamwork culture: The use of a modified EFQM model. The Journal of Management Development, 22(1/2), 149.

Cohen, S. G., & Bailey, D. E. (1997). What Makes Teams Work: Group Effectiveness Research from the shop floor to the Executive Suite. *Journal of Management*, *23*(3), 239–290. doi:10.1177/014920639702300303

Cross, M (2014). The Social Media Security: Leveraging Social Networking While Mitigating Risk. Syngress – Elsevier.

Daft, R. L., & Lengel, R. H. (1986). Organizational information requirements, media richness, and structural design. *Management Science*, *32*(5), 554–571. doi:10.1287/mnsc.32.5.554

Deloitte Consulting. (2011). *Social Computing. Tech Trends 2011 – The natural convergence of business and IT*.

Dunbar, R. I. M. (1992). Neocortex size as a constraint on group size in primates. *Journal of Human Evolution*, *22*(6), 469–493. doi:10.1016/0047-2484(92)90081-J

Engeström, Y. (2001). Expansive learning at work: Toward an activity-theoretical reconceptualization. *Journal of Education and Work*, *14*(1), 133–156. doi:10.1080/13639080020028747

Galegher, J., Kraut, R. E., & Egido, C. (2014). *Intellectual Teamwork: Social and Technological Foundations of Cooperative Work*. Psychology Press.

Goffman, E. (1959). *The presentation of self in everyday life*. New York: Doubleday Anchor Books.

Gross, N., & Martin, W. E. (1952). On group cohesiveness. *American Journal of Sociology*, *57*(6), 546–554. doi:10.1086/221041

Hamilton, M. B. (2009). Online survey response rates and times: background and guidance for an industry SuperSurvey.

Heivadi, T., Khajeheian, D. (2013). Construction of Social Identity in Social Media: An investigation of Iranian Users' Appearance in Facebook. *Interdisciplinary Journal of Contemporary Research in Business,* 4(12).

Hoegl, M., & Gemuenden, H. G. (2001). Teamwork Quality and the Success of Innovative Projects: A Theoretical Concept and Empirical Evidence. *Organization Science*, *12*(4), 435–449. doi:10.1287/orsc.12.4.435.10635

Internetworldstats.com. (2012). Internet Usage in the European Union - EU27 Retrieved from http://www.internetworldstats.com/stats9.htm#eu

Jordan, P. W., Thomas, B., Weerdmeester, B. A., & McClelland, I.L. (Eds), (1996). Usability Evaluation in Industry. London: Taylor & Francis Ltd.

Kaplan, A., & Haenlein, M. (2010). Users of the world, unite! The challenges and opportunities of Social Media. *Business Horizons*, *53*(1), 59–68. doi:10.1016/j.bushor.2009.09.003

Kietzmann, J., Hermkens, K., McCarthy, I., & Silvestre, B. S. (2011). Social media? Get serious! Understanding the functional building blocks of social media. *Business Horizons*, *54*(3), 241–251. doi:10.1016/j.bushor.2011.01.005

Kozlowski, S. W. J., & Bell, B. S. (2001). Handbook of psychology: Vol. 12. *Work Groups and Teams in Organizations* (pp. 333–375). Industrial and Organizational Psychology.

Likert, R. (1932). A Technique for the Measurement of Attitudes. *Archives de Psychologie*, *140*, 1–55.

Mangold, W. G., & Faulds, D. J. (2009). Social media: The new hybrid element of the promotion mix. *Elsevier Business Horizons*, *52*(4), 357–365. doi:10.1016/j.bushor.2009.03.002

Mullen, B., & Copper, C. (1994). The relation between group cohesiveness and performance: An integration. *Psychological Bulletin*, *115*(2), 210–227. doi:10.1037/0033-2909.115.2.210

Oser, R., McCallum, G.A., Salas, E., & Morgan, B.B., Jr. (1989, March). Toward a definition of teamwork: an analysis of critical team behaviours. Human Factors Division Naval Training Systems Center, Orlando, FL.

Pinto, M. B., & Pinto, J. K. (1990). Project team communication and crossfunctional cooperation in new program development. *Journal of Product Innovation Management*, *7*(3), 200–212. doi:10.1016/0737-6782(90)90004-X

Qualman, E. (2013). *Socialnomics: How Social Media Transforms the Way We Live and Do Business*. John Wiley & Sons.

Rousseau, V., Aubé, C., Savoie, A., (2006) Teamwork Behaviors A Review and an Integration of Frameworks. *Small Group Research*, 37(5), 540-570.

Salas, E., Sims, D. E., & Burke, C. S. (2005). Is there a "Big Five" in teamwork? *Small Group Research*, *36*(5), 555–599. doi:10.1177/1046496405277134

Schau, H. J., & Gilly, M. C. (2003). We are what we post? Selfpresentation in personal web space. *The Journal of Consumer Research*, *30*(3), 385–404. doi:10.1086/378616

Short, J., Williams, E., & Christie, B. (1976). *The social psychology of telecommunications*. Hoboken, NJ: John Wiley & Sons, Ltd.

Silvestre, B.S., Kietzmann, J.H., McCarthy, I.P., Pitt, L. (2012) Unpacking the social media phenomenon: towards a research agenda. *Journal of Public Affairs (Special Issue)*, 12(2), 109-119. DOI:10.1002/pa.1412

Sponselee, M.G.M., (2014). Social Media & Project Management. The effects of Social Media on Project Management.

Treem, J.W. & Leonardi, P.M. (2012). Social Media Use in Organisations: Exploring the Affordances of Visibility, Editability, Persistence and Association. *Communication Yearbook,* 36.

UNData. (2014). Mobile-cellular telephone subscriptions. Retrieved from http://data.un.org/

White, D.S. (2010). Social Media growth from 2006 to 2010. Retrieved from http://dstevenwhite.com/2010/08/08/social-media-growth-from-2006-to-2010/

Wikipedia. (2011). SixDegrees.com. Retrieved from http://en.wikipedia.org/wiki/SixDegrees.com

Wikipedia. (2012). Catfish: The TV Show. Retrieved from http://en.wikipedia.org/wiki/Catfish:_The_TV_Show

Wikipedia. (2014). United Breaks Guitars Retrieved from http://en.wikipedia.org/wiki/United_Breaks_Guitars

Zeng, B. & Gerritsen, R. (2014). What do we know about social media in tourism? A review. *Tourism Management Perspectives.*

KEY TERMS AND DEFINITIONS

Facebook: An online social networking service headquartered in Menlo Park, California.

Foursquare: A local search and discovery service mobile app which provides a personalised local search experience for its users.

LinkedIn: A business-oriented social networking service.

Social Media: Mobile and web-based technologies to create highly interactive platforms via which individuals and communities share, co-create, discuss and modify user-generated content.

Teamwork: A set of interrelated thoughts, actions, and feelings of each team member that are needed to function as a team and that combined to facilitate coordinated, adaptive performance and task objectives resulting in value-added outcomes.

Twitter: An online social networking service that enables users to send and read short 140-character messages called "tweets".

WhatsApp: An instant messaging app for smartphones that operates under a subscription business model and since recently part of Facebook.

Yammer: A freemium enterprise social networking service that was launched in 2008 and sold to Microsoft in 2012.

Chapter 6
Investigating the Intention to Use Social Media Tools Within Virtual Project Teams

Jerry Giltenane
Aspiracon, Ireland

ABSTRACT

Enterprise social media tools are becoming more prevalent in project management, particularly where project teams have to operate on a global and virtual basis. It is becoming more critical that organisations understand the key attributes of such technology to encourage their teams to use them in order to achieve the perceived benefits. In this chapter we search for answers to the factors that influence the adoption of such tools in a virtual project setting by testing the applicability of the much cited technology adoption model known as the Unified Theory of Acceptance and Use of Technology (UTAUT). The model is modified to suit the sphere of virtual teams and focuses on the behavioural intention to adopt social media technology. The purpose of examining such a model is to see if it can explain some of the key factors that may influence the adoption of social media within virtual project teams.

INTRODUCTION

Virtual teams have become a common entity in today's business world and the growth of virtual teams is increasing due to improving technology, globalization (Beyerlein, Johnson, & Beyerlein, 2001), the growth of the knowledge economy and the search for talent regardless of location (Lepsinger & DeRosa, 2010) as well as increasing rates of outsourcing (Harrin, 2010a). Virtual teams also contribute to the tightening requirements of cost efficiency (IFIP, 2004) and external global pressures continue to demand that organizations be fast and more responsive. Given these trends, it is no surprise that virtual teams are now commonplace in project management.

Social media or collaboration technologies are also becoming much more common place within the corporate organization due to the perceived benefits of adoption. In a 2007 study of 2100 corporate organizations, Melcrum (2008) noted that the two biggest benefits perceived to arise from internal use

DOI: 10.4018/978-1-4666-9867-3.ch006

of social media were improved employee engagement and improved internal collaboration. Taking these benefits into account, it is clear that within project management that the use of social networking tools will become much more prevalent amongst project managers over the next 10 years. Project management may be particularly suitable for the adoption of social media given for instance that Camarinha (2009) considers project management to be a social effort in the first place and due to the importance of project collaboration quality in project management (Dietrich, Eskerod, & Sandhawalia, 2010). Celik, cited in (Dinsmore & Cabanis-Brewin, 2010) notes that social media can also help speed up the internal communication process, referring to social media as "being parallel processing for people rather than computers. Given the huge role people play in project management, the potential for social media to improve communication structures in project management is strong and as a result improve the outcomes of projects in terms of success and contribution to organisation progress and growth.

Although the use of social media tools is becoming more popular in project management, it is still a relatively new trend and hence there is little in the literature on factors influencing the adoption social media within project management. A reflection of the growing importance of the intersection of project management and social media is the formation within the PMI organization of a new media council whose main aim is to develop and gain an understanding of the role of tools such as social media have to offer project management. Given the growth of virtual teams in project management and the increased importance of collaboration and management across borders, social media tools may be seen as an effective solution to improve project communication and hence improve project effectiveness (Binder, 2007). The unique importance of collaboration and information sharing to project management means that many companies are beginning to deploy social media tools to help project teams as they can easily justify the benefit (Walkey, 2009). With the increased importance of communication in virtual teams it is clear that the internal adoption of social media is of particular importance to virtual project teams.

Aside from the perceived benefits of social media for use in project management, it is also a key fact that many young people joining the workforce today (members of the Y generation) will become project team members of the future and are very familiar with social media as a technology and a communications framework and as a result almost demand and expect the use of it internally in companies and in reality will see enterprise social media as an extension of a communication channel that they use every day outside work. It is important the organization understand this, as the youth of today are the project managers of the future and in today's fast moving and fluid world, it is important that organizations can plan and adapt such new communication channels to support the next generation.

With the increased emphasis on project management's trend towards virtualization as well as continuing need to deliver project success, the author believes that the adoption of social media can help project communication and hence improve project success rates. Taking into account the potential benefits, this chapter will focus specifically on the actual factors that affect behavioral intent to use social media in general amongst virtual teams as knowledge of the key adoption factors will be critical to understanding the attributes that must be in place for successful adoption. In particular the chapter will focus on the search for answers to the factors that influence the adoption of such tools in a virtual project setting by testing the applicability of the much cited technology adoption model known as the Unified Theory of Acceptance and Use of Technology (UTAUT). The model is modified to suit the sphere of virtual teams and focuses on the behavioral intention to adopt social media technology. The purpose of examining such a model is to see if it can explain some of the key factors that may influence the adoption of social media tools.

LITERATURE REVIEW

There are many models and much research into the area of technology adoption in the literature. An understanding of why individuals or organisations adopt various technologies is of critical importance, not only to the manufacturers and producers of information technology systems, but also to implementation managers, team leaders and to society in general. Many information systems technology adoption models are based on psychology theory and this section will review some of the key models and their history. Particular focus has been put on user acceptance of technology since the seventies due to the expansion of technology and increasing failures for system adoption (Chuttur, 2009). This section will review and explore some of these models and the progression of this particular field of study.

Diffusion of Innovations

One early popular model is that of Diffusion of Innovations, first proposed as far back as the nineteen century but more familiar as the model as described by Everett (1962) which was based on earlier work by Ryan and Gross (Darrow, 2007). The model concentrates on reasons how and why and at what rate adoption of new technical and concepts take place in markets, organizations and cultures in general. Many would be familiar with the model in terms of the classification (innovators, early adopters, early majority, late majority and laggards) that it puts on people, depending on how quickly they adopt something new compared to others and is a concept often seen in marketing studies.

Although the main focus of the diffusion model was to understand the rate of adoption over time (Kautz, 1995), the model is still of particular interest to technology adoption factors in that part of the theory (probably less well known part) attempts to describe the stages in an individual decision making process to adopt a new idea. Figure 1 Illustrates Everett's five step decision section of the diffusions model. The first three stages in particular (Knowledge, Persuasion and Decision) describe the process where an individual goes from knowing little or nothing about the concept, to becoming interested and finally working out the advantages and disadvantages and subsequently making a decision.

Figure 1. Five stages in the decision innovation process

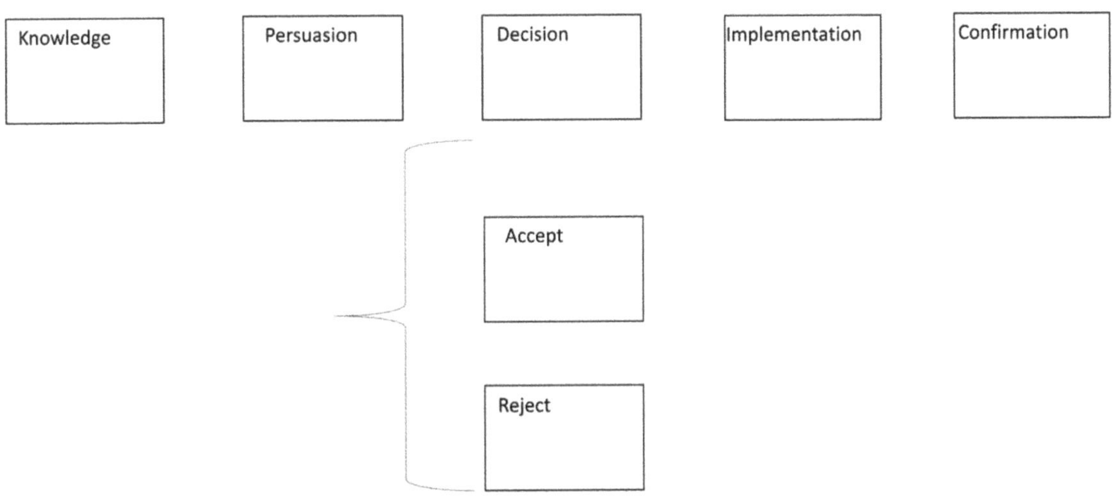

The model has a long and enduring history of conceptual and empirical study (Dearing, 2009), but has some limitations in that it can be more descriptive as against being more explanatory and is not so useful in predicting outcomes (Clarke, 1999) as well as drawbacks in cases where people struggle to understand the innovation in the first place (Shawaludin, 2010).

Theory of Reasoned Action Model (TRA)

The theory of Reasoned Action was developed by Fishbein and Ajzen as an update to a previous theory known as Information Integration theory. The central premise of the theory is the ability to predict behavioral intention based on attitude and behavior.

The theory can be summarized as follows in figure 2, where

AB = one's attitude toward performing the behavior.

SN = one's subjective norm related to performing the behavior (influence of other people etc).

The main development over previous models was the introduction of the notion of predicting behavioral intent as against predicting actual behavior. Intent can be seen as good indicator of future use. The model does however note that actual behavior can be limited by various factors outside of one's own attitudes. An example would be lack of funds to purchase an item, despite positive attitude to purchase an item. It has been applied to a wide range of situations from reporting alien adductions to using condoms, so it therefore is a general use theory as opposed to just a theory for technology acceptance (Dillard & Pfau, 2002).

Although the model had been used to serve as a theoretical foundation for many of the specific technology models, (Kautz, 1995), Dillard and Pfau also criticize the model in that they point out that the model is limited to volitional behavior and they note that habitual behaviors can be considered non-volitional in that past behaviors can create a habit and almost take the decision outside of one's control and hence such behavioral intentions would not be covered by this model. Sheppard et al. (1998) also note the volitional weakness and also adds that the model does not cover choices very well and also suggests that when subjects intentions are assessed, that they may not have all the required information to make a decision.

In 1985, Aizen developed this model further and proposed a new version entitled the Theory of Planned Behavior (TPB). Figure 3 breakdowns the revised model into it various constructs.

Figure 2. TRA model

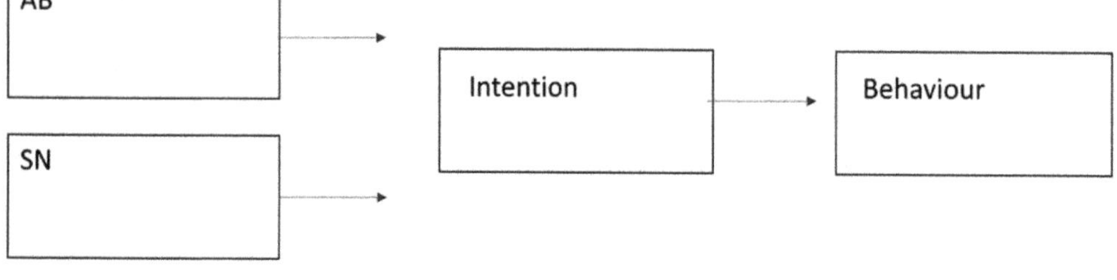

Figure 3. TPB constructs

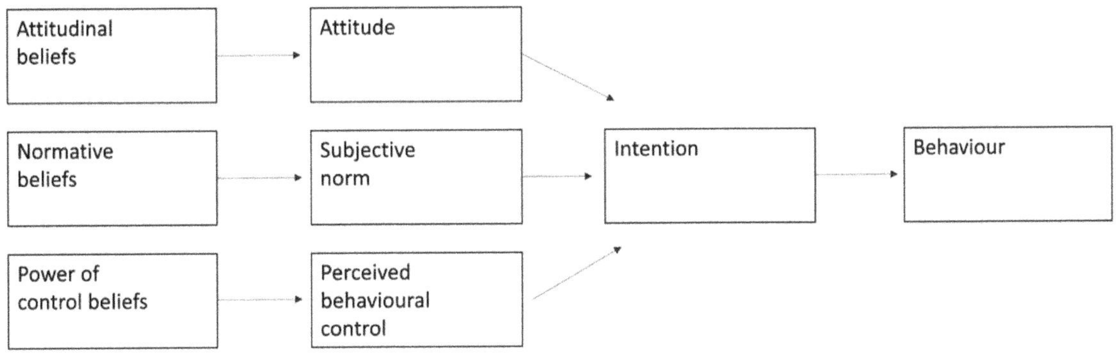

The revised model is much more complicated than the original TRA model, but the key fundamental difference is that TPB takes into account the fact that not all behaviour is completely under one's self control and the construct of control beliefs was added to account for this (Twente, 2010). Control beliefs are:

The perceived presence of factors that may facilitate or impede performance of a behavior. It is assumed that these control beliefs -- in combination with the perceived power of each control factor -- determine the prevailing perceived behavioral control. (Aizen, 2010).

The model has been since used in many cases to predict adoption behaviour in various IT information technologies ranging from internet banking in Taiwan (Shih & Fang, 2004), e-commerce adoption for consumers (Pavlou & Fygenson, 2006) to more recent studies on internet sales systems (Angel & Ignacio, 2010). Despite a strong record in research, the model still has a number of issues as summarized below (Baum, 1997):

- Although intentions may be seen to have a casual effect on behaviour, self-behaviour prediction may not influence behaviour directly.
- Ignores the action phase. Does not consider factors that translate intention into actual action.
- Complexity. The survey questionnaire for the model is generally considered long and over complex for the behaviour being studied.

Technology Acceptance Model (TAM)

The Technology Acceptance Model (TAM) is a further adaptation of the TRA and TPB models and is specifically applied to the field of Information systems and was created by Davis in 1995. The TAM model is based on the theory that perceived usefulness and perceived ease of use determines an individual's intention to use a system with intention to use serving as a mediator of actual system use. (Furneaux, 2006). The critical difference between TAM and the previous models is the inclusion of perceived usefulness and perceived ease of use into the model, replacing the attitudal constructs in the previous models discussed. Figure 4 illustrates the basic TAM model.

There have been various iterations of the model over the years and involved the inclusion of subjective norms plus other constructs related to Information Technology such as quality of output, computer

Figure 4. Basic TAM constructs

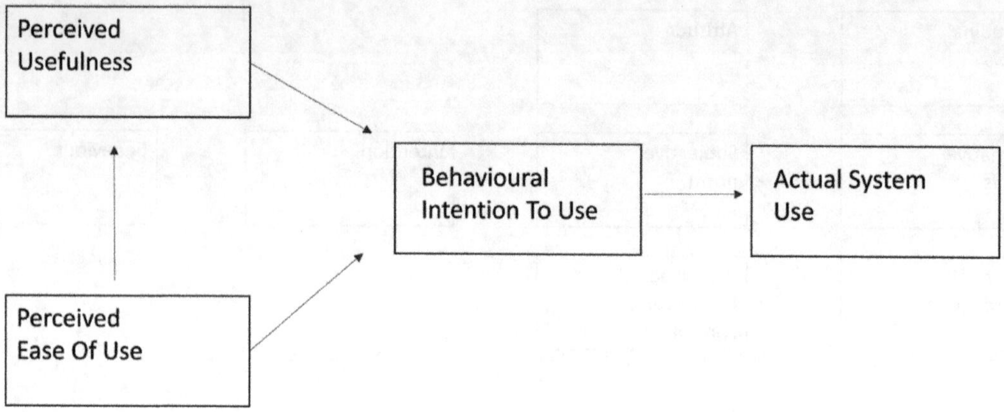

self-efficacy, computer anxiety and playfulness. TAM, like the TRB model contains strong behavioral elements which assume that when someone forms an intention to act, that they will be free to act without limitation. In reality constraints do exist such as limited ability, time, environmental or organizational limits and these will limit the freedom to act (York University, 2010)

TAM is a highly cited model and became one of the most popular models in IT adoption research (Merchant, 2007). One of the key advantages of the model has been the ability to customize it with additional constructs such as trust, quality expectations and satisfaction and some researchers have for instance added Hofstede's cultural dimensions to the model (Merchant, 2007). In a comparative study Taylor & Todd, (2001) demonstrated that TAM is better than PTB at predicting behavior. However there are mixed opinions regarding the model's theoretical assumptions and practical effectiveness. According to Chutter (2009), research in TAM lacks sufficient rigor and relevance that would make it a well-established theory for the IS community. Both (Chutter, 2009) and (Salovaara & Tamminen, 2010) also note that in many cases, self-reported data is used to measure system use instead of actual data and notes that self-reported data is subjective and therefore unreliable. Salovarra & Tamminen (2010) also note that many studies based on TAM lack longitudinal studies and often deal with just short exposures to technology.

The Unified Theory of Acceptance and Use of Technology Model

Venkatesh et al. (2003) conducted a review of the key models available and resulted in the creation of a new model to combine and replace these key models. The model was called the Unified Theory of Acceptance and Use of Technology Model (UTAUT). Figure 5 illustrates the various constructs of the model.

In summary, the theory indicates that four key constructs (performance expectancy, effort expectancy, social influence, and facilitating conditions) are direct determinants of usage intention and behavior. Gender, age, experience, and voluntariness of use are claimed to have a moderating influence on the impact of the four key constructs on usage intention and behavior (Furneaux b, 2005).Table 1 defines the various constructs in more detail.

The UTAUT model has been empirically tested with 70% of dependent variable variance accounted for (adjusted R^2), which is much higher than either TAM or TPB models (Qingfei, Shaobo, & Gang,

Figure 5. UTAUT model constructs

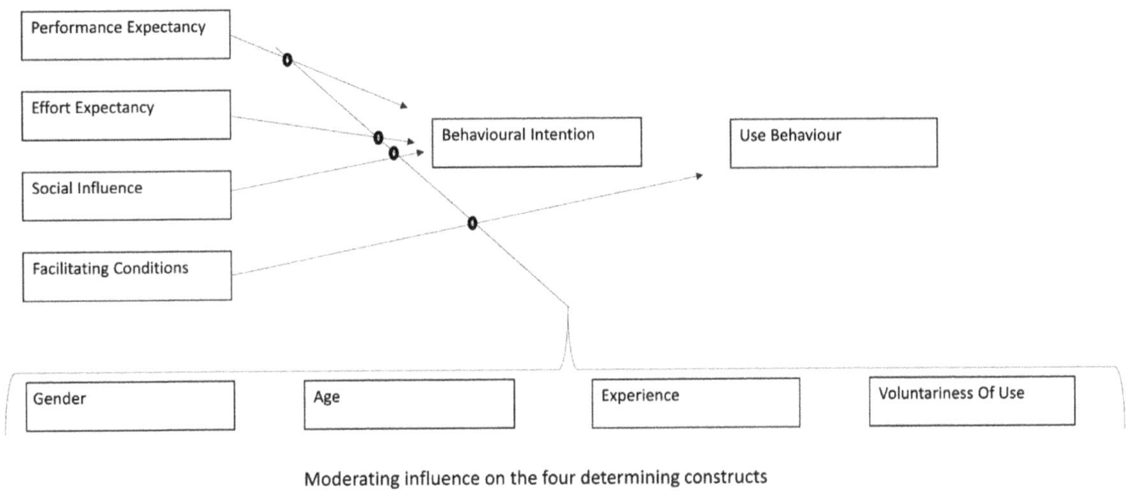

Table 1. UTAUT constructs

Performance expectancy	The extent to which an individual perceives that using a system will enhance his or her productivity, and thus lead to performance gains.
Effort expectancy	The extent to which using a system is free from effort—effort expectancy is conceptually and empirically identical to perceived ease of use from TAM.
Social influence	The extent to which an individual perceives that important others think that he or she should use the target system.
Facilitating conditions	Is the perception regarding the availability of organizational and technical resources to support use of the target system
Gender, Age, Experience and Voluntariness	These factors influence the above constructs

2008). As with any model, it is not without its flaws. For instance Dishaw et al. (2004) argue that the model fails to include task constructs, which they feel are critical in information technology. Bilandzic & Weckermann (2008) also argue that since 2003, not much work has been done to the model to improve it aside from tweaking it to adopt to various types of IS situations and reflects a lack of progression in this specific field of research. Venkatesh himself acknowledges these issues and notes that the model does require adaptations in order to cater for specific technology areas (Venkatesh V., 2010b). Overall, however he argues that UTAUT model provides a "*Useful tool for managers needing to assess the likelihood of success for new technology introductions and helps them understand the drivers of acceptance in order to proactively design interventions targeted at populations of users that may be less inclined to adopt and use new systems*".

The model is consistently used in a wide range of settings and in most cases, the basic model provides the theoretical underpinnings with many studies adapting the model to suit the environment of technology in question. A search of the literature did not find use of the model in the study of technology adoption in virtual teams and in fact there is very little literature on technology adoption in general for virtual teams and this therefore is a significant gap in the literature.

Modifying the UTAUT Model

With social media becoming a key issue in project management and with the increasing use of virtual teams, understanding what impacts adoption of such new tools will be very useful information. Social media tools in general help improve communication, a key element of project management. For virtual teams, there is a need for organisations to put in place appropriate information technology communications systems to address some of the key issues associated with virtual teams such as trust and communication. There has been a lack of empirical research in terms of project management and social media and virtual teams. In particular, little research has been executed on the factors influencing individual's intent to use social media within a virtual setting. Given that enterprise social media is a newly emerging technology and with a strong history of using technology adoption models to predict intention to use, the UTAUT model is clearly a good model to use to explore such adoption factors.

In line with the current thinking, the research will adapt the model for use in a survey with an additional construct for team trust. A theme that emerges frequently in the literature is that trust is generally considered one of the major issues when it comes to virtual teams as opposed to traditional co-located teams due to lack of face to face interaction, cultural and communication difficulties. Such a view is supported by many authors such as (Mancini, 2010), (Harell & Daim, 2009) and (Kimble, 2011). Time zone constraints also contribute to communication disadvantages due to a reliance on asynchronous communication methods (Lee-Kelley, 2006), (Cleland & Gareis, 2006). Such trust and communication issues can be compounded by team members' reluctance to participate in shared knowledge works due to members varied backgrounds, degree of demographic diversity and lack of prior joint work experience (Hong & Vai, 2009). It should be noted that the UTUAT model is designed to test whether its constructs are a good predictor of intention to use as against actual usage levels and therefore the research conducted is focused on the adoption factors that impact intention versus actual usage.

RESEARCH DESIGN AND METHODOLOGY

Having identified the UTAUT model as a suitable model for this purpose. The UTAUT model as presented by Venkatesh has shown strong exploratory predictive power for intention of 70% and hence can provide a set of suitable hypothesis to test. A survey was conducted based on the UTUAT model to allow us to:

- Indicate whether the use of existing technology adoption models help predict the use of social media in virtual project teams?
- Explore the key factors that influence the adoption of social media within virtual teams?

For the purpose of this specific research, the UTUAT model was used and was adapted as illustrated in Figure 6 in order to generate relevant hypothesizes.

The following adaptations were made from the original model:

- The inclusion of a new construct labelled team trust as an independent variable due to premise that trust would seem to be an important consideration when working in virtual teams.

Figure 6. Revised UTAUT model for this study

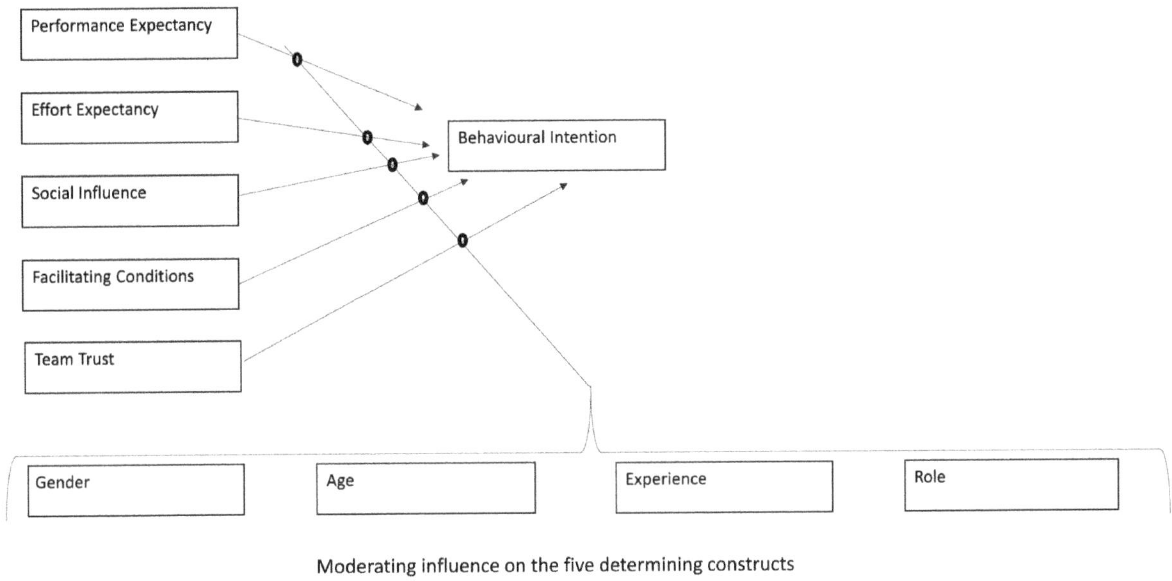

- Change in the independent variable 'facilitating conditions' to have a direct effect on intention (the dependent variable) as against actual usage as noted in the original model in the belief that facilitating conditions are important in terms of intent to use. This study is interested in adoption factors effecting intent as against actual usage.
- The use of gender, age, and virtual team experience will be considered as modifying factors. Voluntariness will not be included for this study. Role will be included as a modifying factor.

The revised UTAUT model allows the research questions to be rephrased as the following hypothesis:

- H_{01} The Unified Theory of Acceptance and Use of Technology (UTAUT) can successfully predict behavioural intention to use social media technology in a virtual team environment.
- H_{02} The various independent variables in the revised model positively impact behavioural intent to use social media technology in a virtual team environment.
- H_{03} Moderating factors such as age, virtual team experience, gender and role will have some influence of the overall model.

The research instrument deployed was an analytical survey eliciting quantitative data based on the original UTAUT model survey. The original survey questions were modified to cater for virtual teams and social media tools and extra questions added to cater for team trust. The design therefore chosen was of a fixed and mono nature. The survey instrument is suited to a deductive approach to allow the generation and statistical analysis of primary data to test the validity of the various constructs of the model adapted for this study. The survey is based on Venkatesh's original UTUAT survey instrument with the survey updated to take into account the context of enterprise social media and virtual teams as well as an extra set of questions on team trust. The study targeted those people who worked within organisations and are members of virtual project teams globally. The respondents targeted were mainly project managers but also catered for non-project manager team members. The definition of a virtual team used on the survey introduction to clarify the eligibility definition to partake in the survey for potential respondents in terms of virtual team membership was as follows: 'People who work over time, distance and organizational boundaries and primarily use technology to facilitate their primary communication needs'

Due to the potentially large population chosen and the difficulty associated with getting a good probability sample from such a large base, a non-probability sample was chosen. Non-probability sampling is often of use when one cannot determine the probability that every unit or respondent can be included in a sample. (Fricker, 2006) The sample chosen was based on a judgement sampling technique. Judgemental sampling is a type of convenience sampling. This type of sampling helps to reduce cost and times issues when administrating a survey and despite potential issues related to selection bias, this author is of the opinion that the distribution channels chosen will reflect accurately the population targeted. The following rule of thumb was taken from (Paillant, 2010, p. 150) that for a multiple regression analysis (this technique was the assumed method for analysis prior to the results) that there should be at least 15 respondents per independent construct. With 5 independent constructs, this would require a sample size of at least 75 respondents.

The survey was administered online via a select chosen number of distribution channels that reflected the population at large as best as possible. Surveys are the most implemented online research methodology used in social research (Poade, 2011). Online surveys have advantages of cost, time and ability to access a large number of potential respondents. Another key advantage is the fact that the researcher also has no involvement in the survey, eliminating possible bias (Ilieva et al., 2002). In his original study, Vankatesh noted that the survey could be administered three times, before implementation of the technology, one month after and three months after. The scope of this study does not allow for such a longitudinal time-span and hence the survey was administered once over a three week period between February 21 2011 and March 11 2011 and should be noted that the survey does not illicit usage data and is focused on behavioural intention.

The survey was designed and executed via the Survey Monkey tool. The link to the survey was placed on the following web sites and distribution channels:

- LinkedIn – Various Project management groups.
- LinkedIn – Henley alumina group.
- PMI Irish Site.
- Henley Newsletter.
- Twitter via project management hast-tag.

RESEARCH RESULTS

Cronbach's alpha was used to measure the reliability of the scales. Table 2 indicates that all items apart from facilitating conditions had good scores, indicating strong reliability. A score above .7 is considered a reliable scale (Paillant, 2010, p. 97).

Further analysis was undertaken for the facilitating conditions construct to see if the removal of any item would improve the score. Table 3 notes that there was no scope for improving the score through the removal of any one item and given the low initial score of .544, this construct will be removed from the

Table 2. Cronbach's alpha

Construct	Cronbach's Alpha Score
Performance Expectancy	.752
Behavioural Intent	.920
Effort Expectancy	.786
Facilitating Conditions	.544
Social Influence	.794

Table 3. Facilitating conditions analysis

	Scale Mean if Item Deleted	Scale Variance if Item Deleted	Corrected Item-Total Correlation	Squared Multiple Correlation	Cronbach's Alpha if Item Deleted
FC1	15.73	7.599	.231	.077	.547
FC2	16.61	5.808	.343	.124	.468
FC3	15.76	7.388	.293	.148	.502
FC4	15.87	5.947	.472	.237	.345

model due to the unreliable nature of the scale. This is disappointing, however the UTAUT model used in this paper has included this construct as an independent construct effecting behavioral Intent, where as in the original model, it was considered a factor that effected actual usage as against intent, hence the remaining model is still a valid model and suitable for analysis.

Inferential Analysis: Partial Least Squares

The survey results indicated that various constructs being measured were not of a normal distribution. This rules out the multiple regression statistical technique as a method for examining this adapted UTAUT model. In order for multiple regression analysis to be a viable analytic technique, the assumption that the distributions are normal is a critical pre-requisite (Paillant, 2010, p. 158). Therefore in order to validate and understand the strength of the proposed model, partial least squares analysis (PLS) has been used to determine the predictive effects of the various independent constructs on the dependent variable, behavior intent.

It is relatively common in the social sciences that distributions are not distributed normally (Lewis-Beck, Bryman, & Futing Liao, 2004, p. 113) and therefore the distributions seen in the survey were not unexpected. A review of past UTAUT papers have indicated that PLS is a common method for statically analysing the results of UTAUT based surveys (Kijsanayotin, Pannarunothai, & Speedie, 2009), (Chen & Tsou, 2007) and (Marimuthu & Dean, 2007).

The analysis presented will be without statistical significance and this must be noted a potential weakness. However Garson indicates that PLS is favoured as a predictive technique as against an interpretive technique model. Hinseler, Ringle, and Sinkovics cited in (Garson, 2011) note that "PLS path modelling is recommended in an early stage of theoretical development in order to test and validate exploratory models." Therefore the use of PLS is can be considered a valid and correct tool to examine the validity

Table 4. Proportion of variance explained

Latent Factors	Statistics				
	X Variance	Cumulative X Variance	Y Variance	Cumulative Y Variance (R-square)	Adjusted R-square
1	.603	.603	.492	.492	.486
2	.221	.824	.055	.547	.536
3	.074	.898	.003	.550	.533
4	.102	1.000	.000	**.550**	**.527**

of this model. The sample size of 84 achieved for this survey is also a valid sample size for this analysis as Chin cited in (Garson, 2011) recommends that at least 10 cases per measured variable are used. In this case, 84 respondents more than suffice with six constructs being measured in the model. Given that multicollinearity is not a significant factor with this technique, no tests on construct multicollinearity were carried out for this analysis.

Core Model Results

$H_{01:}$ *The Unified Theory of Acceptance and Use of Technology (UTAUT) can successfully predict behavioural intention to use social media technology in a virtual team environment. Result: True*

Table 4. indicates that the model has an R Square of.550 and an adjusted R-square of .527. Given the model is not overly complex, this paper will use the .55 R-square figure. This figure indicted that the independent constructs account for 55% of the behavioral intent. The figure may not be as high as the original models 70%, but given the modifications to the original model, the result indicates that the model does help to predict a relatively large portion of the dependent variable and hence this hypothesis is considered to be true.

H_{02}: *The various independent variables in the revised model positively impact behavioural intent to use social media technology in a virtual team environment. Result: True*

Table 5. notes that performance expectancy contributed .566 (56%) to the predictably of the model and was the strongest independent factor of all four. Hence this hypothesis is considered true. Table 5

Table 5. Dependent variables analysis

Independent Variables	Dependent Variables
	Behavioral Intent
Performance Expectancy	.566
Team Trust	-.257
Social Influence	.285
Effort Expectancy	.318

also notes that team trust contributed -.257 (-26%) to the predictably of the model and was a significant independent factor. Interestingly the negative figure indicates a negative correlation between trust levels and intent to adopt social media technologies. This is somewhat surprising and may in fact be an indication that with lower trust levels, team members may be more inclined to use social media in order to perhaps address the trust issues.

Modifying Factors Analysis

$H_{03:}$ Moderating factors such as age, virtual team experience, gender and role will have some influence of the overall model. *Result: True for virtual team experience, gender, age but false for role*

Table 6 indicates that the moderating factors do have a strong influence on the overall model predictability. SPSS was used to split the respondents into groups by the select cases method and then PLS ran for each group. It should be noted that due to small sample sizes in some cases such as the number of females (35) and operational staff (20), some care needs to be used in interpretation. For the females, those with more than 5 years virtual team experience and those over forty years, the model had a very high prediction rate of over 80%, which is a very strong score. The model did not vary so much based on role and hence role is not considered to have any strong modifying effect (although care should be given to the fact that the survey only had 20 operational staff).

DISCUSSION

Intention Rates

The survey question on actual intention did indicate a strong intent to use social media technology over the six months within a virtual project team setting. This is indicative of the perceived benefits that social media collaboration tools purport to bring and indicates potentially that people working in virtual environments certainly envisage that such tools can be of great use in their day to day project work. Given the relatively high usage intention rates, it is important that organizations put in place the

Table 6. Moderating factors effect on behavioral intent predictability

	Group	R Square
Gender	Males	55%
	Females	82%
Role	Project Manager / Program Manager	55%
	Operational Member	62%
Virtual Team Experience	More than 5 years' experience	80%
	Less than 5 years' experience	43%
Age	More than 40 years old	80%
	Less than 40 years old	46%

required foundations both at a technical and support level to ensure that such intention does not turn to frustration, in cases where organizations are not yet ready or aware of the potential of such tools and potential benefits. If the benefits of social media tools turn out to be realistic, the strong intention rates are a positive development for the future of project management. Given the expected rise in the use of outsourcing in the future (Brady, 2009) and the development of relatively cheap technology such as cloud computing, it can be expected that many more people will find themselves working in a virtual environment and combined with high usage intention rates, the use of social media type technology will have a big part to play in project organizations communication and information systems over the medium term.

Model Validity

The analysis has indicated a predictive rate of 55% in terms of behavioural intent for social media tool adoption. Although this is below the 70% achieved by Vankatesh, the study shows that revised model used in this study still exhibits strong predictive ability. Therefore for project organisations who are considering rolling out social media technology, the results of the study are of great interest. The model helps to paint a comprehensive picture of the key factors that should be in place in organisations in order to encourage the use of social media tools. This is of use given that many organizations today are expecting to start or to improve their internal collaboration toolset and any information that helps deliver a more efficient and successful roll out is of huge benefit, particularly in the current economic environment, where cost of IT infrastructure and ownership has become a key factor (Rosenberg, 2009).

Performance Expectancy

Performance expectancy was defined as the extent to which an individual perceives that using a system will enhance his or her productivity, and thus lead to performance gains .This construct had a strong positive correlation to behavioural intent and was the strongest factor of the four constructs. Organisations need to be cognitive of the importance of ensuring that social media tools deployed or pending to be deployed, need to be designed such that they clearly aid staff productivity and that such tools are not just rolled out for the sake of it. It would be of importance to ensure that not too many tools are deployed, as this may lead to clutter and may in fact negate any potential performance benefit that arise. To help ensure that the tools deliver on performance expectancy, this author recommends that end users are polled and involved in the process of both tool selection or design, such that user requirements are correctly captured and built into the final iteration of the tool. Another key is to potentially retire any legacy applications that may still be in use as a proliferation of tools will potentially diminish any expected benefit. The fact that this was the strongest factor is not a surprise and is potentially related to the Vroom's expectancy theory of motivation where outcomes and not needs are what motivate people to do certain acts. A study in 2000 by (Chen & Lou, 2000) into the behavioural factors effecting intent to use groupware (the social media of it time) noted that the one key factor was the potential to improve one's job competence and this fact still applies today to the adoption of social media technology as reinforced by this study's findings. The authors also make the sensible recommendation that it is important to advertise and make very public what the key benefits of any new technology are and this is a lesson that certainly will also apply to social media technology roll out plans

Effort Expectancy

Effort was defined as the extent to which using a system is free from effort. The research reinforced that effort expectancy is an important element in introducing new technologies such as social media. (Basagila, Caporarello, & Pennarola, 2007) note that when it comes to designing these tools, it is important to take into account simultaneously both the instrumental and effortless side of technology. This may be easier for the design of internal social media tools primarily due to the popularity of the huge range of external social media platforms available such as Twitter and this author believes that the public external tools should be used as a blueprint to base any internal applications on. One key reason for this is that many people joining organizations already use social media in their personal lives and having corporate technology based on a similar experience to what people are already used to, will make it easier for staff to adopt to whatever internal social media tools are offered. In many ways this will also reduce training costs as well as the learning curve will be shorter if aspects of the public external tools are used and copied where possible.

Social Influence

Social influence was defined as to the extent to which an individual perceives that important others think that he or she should use the target system. The results reveal that social influence is also an important contributing factor in the adoption of social media internally. Given the nature of social media and its ability to reach out to people, this was to be expected and not a new phenomenon. (Munkvold, 2003) notes that it is often important to obtain a critical mass of users in order to make a technical adoption in an organization successful and that social influence is a critical part in this early stage of adoption and that peer pressure can often be as important in the early stages of adoption as the actual characteristics of the technology itself. This author believes that one potential solution that organizations can use to help manage the direction of social influence is the possibility of creating a post of social media manager in the organization who could help be an advocate for the technology within organizations. Many organisations now for instance have created a social media department who main aims of responsibility are to promote and work with staff in the use, distribution and training of social media tools. It is also important for leaders to become involved in the building of online communities within organizations (Dasgupta, 2006) and perhaps if organisations wish to improve adoption rates of any technology in virtual environments, particular emphasis should be placed on the role corporate leaders have in the rollout process.

Team Trust

Team trust was defined as the degree of trust between each project team member in each other's ability to get the job done well and efficiently. Perhaps the main surprise of the research was the relatively significant negative correlation between team trust levels and intention to adopt social media. This may be in part due to the fact the trust levels in teams are relatively low compared to co-located teams and perhaps in such an environment, social media technology may be seen as a way to bridge trust gaps and build relationships. This implies that teams where trust levels are high, there may not be as much of a demand or intention to use the new social media technologies as perhaps the existing communication channels that are already in place are adequate given higher levels of trust. Regardless trust levels are certainly a significant contributing factor and must be studied as part of any plan to roll out new social media tools across a virtual team environment. This author strongly believes that social media tools can help bridge trust issues and bring people closer together and perhaps this is even more critical in teams where trust levels are low or at the beginning of team formation in order to help promote the strong growth of swift trust early in a team's life cycle.

Modifying Factors

The key conclusion that one can make from the analysis on the modifying factors is that the composition of the team will have some effect on acceptance and willingness to use social media. The stark contrast in the trust construct between female and males is a good example. (Furumo & Pearson, 2007) found in a study on gender based communication in virtual teams that females have more trust in short term project teams then males, but notes that trust does not seem to vary between same sex team versus mixed teams. The key for those tasked with implementing social media as a communication channels in virtual teams is to take into account the composition of the team and understand that a one size fits all approach may not work due to the diversity of team members. A recommendation may be to have as part of the project start up process, a step to review with all the team members what may be considered the most appropriate social media tools to use, from those available within the organisation.

Limitations of the Study

As noted, a measurement of significance is not possible with partial squares analysis within SPSS. However it is possible to use what is called the bootstrap method which requires a level of coding and complexity and tool availability for SPSS in order to derive a level of significance. This was beyond the current scope of this current research and capabilities. The research still gives good indication of the predictive effects and this disadvantage is a noted side effect of the core partial square analysis. A future, more prolonged study may find it more practical to attempt to use the bootstrap method to attempt to get some significance level for the partial least squares test.

As referenced in the analysis, the reliability of the facilitating conditions construct was poor and hence this construct was not used. The construct items were based on the original UTAUT survey instrument and were therefore from a valid source. Further testing would be required to test and develop scales that may be more applicable and reliable in a virtual project environment setting.

Team trust was added as a new construct to the original model due to the importance of trust noted in the review of current thinking. The overall model created accounted for 55% of the behavioural intention variance and there is no doubt that potentially more constructs such as collaboration levels etc. could be used to see if the predictive nature of the model could be improved, but the author was wary of having too many questions on the survey and potential for respondents not completing the survey as a result.

FUTURE RESEARCH DIRECTIONS

This study concentrated on investigating intention factors as against actual usage. In the future, it would be beneficial to do a cross sectional study with a repetitive sample to measure both intention and actual usage over a period of time. This would help to further the knowledge base and also help derive how strong the correlation is between intention to use and actual usage in a virtual project environment. Given the papers findings on the negative correlation on trust and behavioural intention, it would be also of interest to explore this further in the virtual project setting. Given the importance of trust in teams and rapid move to more collaborative communication technology such as social media, further research in this area is much warranted. As noted in the previous section, the further refinement of the model with the additional of other constructs would also be welcome in an effort to improve the model's predictive ability.

CONCLUSION

The primary focus of this study was to examine the factors that influence intention to use social media technology in a virtual project environment. The review of current thinking indicated a lack of any great research or insight into this specific area and this is perhaps not a surprise given the relatively newness of social media as a technology, particularly the use of such technology within a virtual project organization. The current thinking review did however re-enforce the author's initial views that the growth of virtual teams and the increased awareness of the potential of new social media technology that can be used within an organizational team are becoming important issues, particularly in light of the continued lack of progress in making project management better at delivering project success. Of particular interest was the wide range of models that the review of current thinking exposed as viable models in the technology acceptance area that were suitable for the research question for this dissertation. The UTAUT model in particular was determined to be a powerful model that could certainly help explain and predict behavioural intention for the scope of this paper. Given the lack of use of this model in the virtual project team space, the use of and customization of the model, the research design chosen and the analysis and findings, This research certainly can contribute to both the body of knowledge on technology adoption in general and in particular to the sphere of social media and virtual teams, given the dearth of research in this area.

The findings validate to a strong degree the findings of previous studies using the model and although the predictive percentage of 55% is not as good as Venkatesh's 70% result, it is still a respectable result and indicates the models suitability for further refinement in the virtual project team area and indeed virtual teams in general. In some respects, one could argue that this was just another implementation of a well cited model, however, given its lack of use in this chapters subject area, I consider it a relatively important piece of research that may encourage other perhaps in future to add and develop further. The model of course does not explain 45% of the behavioural intention and perhaps with larger samples and more time span and resources, more of this unknown 45% can be discovered. For this study, team trust was added as an independent variable and therefore ensured that the model was not an exact copy of the original, and as a result was an attempt to add value and bring the model further along the road, which in itself is also an important contribution to the use of the UTAUT model.

REFERENCES

Aizen, I. (2010). *TPB*. Retrieved Jan 13, 2011, from http://www.people.umass.edu/aizen/: http://www.people.umass.edu/aizen/tpb.diag.html#null-link

Angel, H. C., & Ignacio, R. (2010). The influence of the commercial features of the Internet on the adoption of e-commerce by consumers.Find More Like This. *Electronic Commerce Research and Applications*, *9*(6), 562–657. doi:10.1016/j.elerap.2010.04.006

Basagila, S., Caporarello, M., & Pennarola, F. (2007). Individual Adoption of Convergent Mobile Technologies in Italy. In A. D'Atri, & M. De Marco (Ed.), *Interdisciplinary Aspects of Information Systems Studies: The Italian Association for Information systems: Italian Association for Information Systems (ItAIS) Annual Conference* (pp. 63 - 68). San Servolo: Springer.

Baum, A. (1997). *Cambridge handbook of psychology, health, and medicine*. Cambridge: Cambridge University Press.

Beyerlein, M. M., Johnson, D. A., & Beyerlein, S. T. (2001). *Virtual Teams*. Emerald Group.

Bilandzic, M., & Weckermann, D. (2008). Technology Acceptance Research – current development and concerns. *Proceedings of the 2nd Workshop on Information Systems and Services Sciences 2008 (2nd WISSS 08)* (pp. 57-65). Technische Universität München: Garching. Retrieved from www.winfobase.de

Binder, J. C. (2007). *Global project management: communication, collaboration and management across borders*. Gower Publishing.

Brady, R. (2009). *Growth in Outsourcing, Like it or Not.* Retrieved from www.businessweek.com

Camarinha, M., Paraskakis, L., & Afsarmanesh, I. (2009). Leveraging Knowledge for Innovation in Collaborative Networks. *Proceedings of the 10th IFIP WG 5.5 Working Conference on Virtual Enterprises, PRO-VE,* Thessaloniki (p. 457). Springer.

Chen, J., & Tsou, H. (2007). *Information technology adoption for service innovation practices and competitive advantage: the case of financial firms.* Retrieved from http://informationr.net/ir/12-3/paper314.html

Chen, Y., & Lou, H. (2000). Toward an Understanding of Behavioural Intention to Use a Groupware Application. *Challenges of information technology management in the 21st century: 2000 Information Resources Management Association International Conference* (pp. 419 - 421). Alaska: Idea Group (IGI).

Chutter, M. Y. (2009). Overview of the Technology Acceptance Model: Origins, Developments and Future Directions. *Sprouts: Working Papers on Information Systems, 9*, pp. 9-37.

Chuttur, m. (2009). *Overview of the Technology Acceptance Model: Origins, Developments and Future Directions.* Retrieved from http://sprouts.aisnet.org

Clarke, R. (1999, September 26). *A Primer in Diffusion of Innovations Theory.* Retrieved from http://www.rogerclarke.com

Cleland, D. I., & Gareis, R. (2006). *Global project management handbook: planning, organizing, and controlling international projects*. McGraw-Hill Professional.

Darrow, R. (2007, October 30). *Diffusion of Innovations research.* Retrieved from http://docjourney.wordpress.com

Dasgupta, S. (2006). Virtual Reality User Acceptance. In Encyclopedia of virtual communities and technologies (p. 567). Idea Group (IGI).

Dearing, J. W. (2009, September). *Applying Diffusion of Innovation Theory to Intervention Development*. Retrieved from http://rsw.sagepub.com/content/19/5/503.short

Dietrich, P., Eskerod, P., & Sandhawalia, B. (2010, September). The Dynamics of Collaboration in Multipartner Projects. *Project Management Journal*, *41*(4), 59–78. doi:10.1002/pmj.20194

Dillard, J. P., & Pfau, M. (2002). The Persuasion Handbook. *Sage (Atlanta, Ga.)*.

Dinsmore, P. C., & Cabanis-Brewin, J. (2010). *The AMA Handbook of Project Management*. AMACOM Div American Mgmt Assn.

Dishaw, M. T., Strong, D. M., & Brandy, B. D. (2004). The Impact of Task-Technology Fit in Technology Acceptance and Utilization Models. *Proceedings of the Tenth Americas Conference on Information Systems* (p. Paper 416). New York: AMCIS.

Everett, R. M. (1962). *Diffusion of Innovations*. Glencoe: Free Press.

Fricker, R. D. (2006). *Sampling Methods for Web and E-mail Surveys*. Retrieved from http://www.nps.navy.mil

Furneaux, B. (2006). *Theories Used in IS Research*. Retrieved from www.istheory.yorku.ca

Furneaux b, B. (2005, September 30). *Theories Used in IS Research: Unified Theory of Acceptance and Use of Technology*. Retrieved from www.istheory.yorku.ca

Furumo, K., & Pearson, M. J. (2007). Gender-Based Communication Styles, Trust, and. *Journal of Information, Information Technology, and Organizations*, *2*, 1–14. Retrieved from www.jiito.org

Garson, D. G. (2011). *Partial Least Squares Regression*. Retrieved from http://faculty.chass.ncsu.edu

Harell, G., & Daim, T. U. (2009). Virtual Teams and the Importance of Building Trust. *IT Professional Magazine*, *11*(6), 46–49. doi:10.1109/MITP.2009.135

Harrin, E. (2010a). *Social Media for Project Managers*. PMI.

Hong, J. F., & Vai, S. (2009). Knowledge-sharing in cross-functional virtual teams. *Journal of General Management*, *34*(2), 21–37.

IFIP. (2004). Virtual enterprises and collaborative networks. *Proceedings of the IFIP 18th World Computer Congress: TC5/WG5.5 - 5th Working Conference on Virtual Enterprises*, Toulouse, France (p. 255a).

Ilieva, J., Baron, S., & Healy, N. M. (2002). *Online surveys: Pros and cons*. Retrieved from www.ser-professoruniversitario.pro.br/

Kautz, K. (1995). Diffusion and adoption of information technology. *First IFIP WG 8.6 Working Conference on the Diffusion and Adoption of Information Technology* (p. 133). Aslo: Springer.

Kijsanayotin, B., Pannarunothai, S., & Speedie, S. M. (2009). Factors influencing health information technology adoption in Thailand's community health centers: Applying the UTAUT model. *International Journal of Medical Informatics*, *78*(6), 404–416. doi:10.1016/j.ijmedinf.2008.12.005 PMID:19196548

Kimble, C. (2011, January/February). Building effective virtual teams: How to overcome the problems of trust and identity in virtual teams. *Global Business & Organizational Excellence*, *30*(2), 6–15. doi:10.1002/joe.20364

Lee-Kelley, L. (2006, April). Locus of control and attitudes to working in virtual teams. *International Journal of Project Management*, *24*(3), 234–243. doi:10.1016/j.ijproman.2006.01.003

Lepsinger, R., & DeRosa, D. (2010). *Team Success: A Practical Guide for Working and Leading from a Distance*. John Wiley and Sons.

Lewis-Beck, M. S., Bryman, A., & Futing Liao, T. (2004). *The Sage encyclopedia of social science research methods* (Vol. 1). Sage. doi:10.4135/9781412950589

Mancini, D. J. (2010). Building organizational trust in virtual teams. *Journal of Behavioral Studies in Business*, *2*, 1–5.

Marimuthu, M., & Dean, A. M. (2007). *The Influence of Perceived Service Value on Information System*. Retrieved from http://conferences.anzmac.org/ANZMAC2007/papers/M%20Marimuthu_1a.pdf

Melcrum. (2008). *How to use social media to engage employees*. Retrieved from http://www.melcrum.com

Merchant, S. (2007). Exploring the Influence of Cultural Values on the Acceptance of Information Technology: An Application of the Technology Acceptance Model. Journal of Issues in Informing Science and Information, 4, 431.

Munkvold, B. E. (2003). *Implementing collaboration technologies in industry*. Springer. doi:10.1007/978-1-4471-0073-7

Paillant, J. (2010). *SPSS Survival Manual* (4th ed.). McGraw-Hill.

Pavlou, P. A., & Fygenson, M. (2006). Understanding and predicting electronic commerce adoption: an extension ofthe theory of planned behavior. *MIS Quaterly*, *30*(1), 115–143.

Poade, D. (2011). *Sampling and Response: The experience of conducting an online student survey*. Retrieved from www.research.plymouth.ac.uk

Qingfei, M., Shaobo, J., & Gang, Q. (2008). Mobile Commerce User Acceptance Study in China: A Revised UTAUT Model. *Tsinghua Science and Technology*, *13*(3), 257–264. doi:10.1016/S1007-0214(08)70042-7

Rosenberg, D. (2009). *Reducing IT infrastructure costs via outsourcing*. Retrieved from http://news.cnet.com

Salovaara, A., & Tamminen, S. (2010). *Accept or appropriate? A design-oriented critique on technology*. Retrieved from www.hiit.fi

Shawaludin, A. (2010). *Diffusion of Innovations: Theoretical Perspectives and Future Prospects of Diffusion Studies*. Retrieved from http://www.nmconf.uob.edu.bh: http://www.nmconf.uob.edu.bh/download/english_article/010.pdf

Sheppard, B. H., Hartwick, J., & Warshaw, P. R. (1998, December). The Theory of Reasoned Action: A Meta-Analysis of Past Research with Recommendations for Modifications and Future Research. *The Journal of Consumer Research*, *15*(3), 325–343. doi:10.1086/209170

Shih, Y.-Y., & Fang, K. (2004). The use of a decomposed theory of planned behavior to study Internet banking in Taiwan. *Internet Research*, *14*(3), 213–223. doi:10.1108/10662240410542643

Taylor, S., & Todd, P. A. (2001). Understanding Information Technology Usage: A test of Competing Models. *Information Systems Research*, *6*(2), 144–176. doi:10.1287/isre.6.2.144

Twente, U. o. (2010). *Theory of Planned Behavior/ Reasoned Action*. Retrieved from http://www.utwente.nl

Venkatesh, V. (2010b). *User Acceptance of Information Technology: Toward a Unified View*. Retrieved from www.vvenkatesh.com

Venkatesh, V., Morris, M., Davis, G., & Davis, F. D. (2003). User Acceptance of Information Technology: Toward a Unified View. *MIS Qquarterly*, *27*(3), 425–478.

Walkey, G. (2009, Sep 16). *Guest Blogger – What do Project Managers need to know about Social Media?* Retrieved from www.arraspeople.co.uk

York University. (2010, Nov 18). *Technology acceptance model*. Retrieved from http://www.fsc.yorku.ca

ADDITIONAL READING

Adams, B. D., Bruyn, L. E., & Chung-Yan, G. (2004). *Creating a measure of trust in small military teams*. Retrieved from www.dtic.mil

Adams, S. L., & Anantatmula, V. (2010). Social and Behavioural influences on team process. *Project Management Journal*, *41*(4), 89–99. doi:10.1002/pmj.20192

Adenfelt, M. (2010). Exploring the performance of transnational projects: Shared knowledge, coordination and communication. *International Journal of Project Management*, *28*(6), 529–538. doi:10.1016/j.ijproman.2009.10.004

Barnes, N. D., & Barnes, F. R. (2009). EQUIPPING YOUR ORGANIZATION FOR THE SOCIAL NETWORKING GAME. *Information Management Journal*, *43*(6), 28.

Beyerlein, M. M., Johnson, D. A., & Beyerlein, S. T. (2001). *Virtual Teams*. Emerald Group.

Brown, S. A., Dennis, A. R., & Venkatesh, V. (2010). Predicting Collaboration Technology Use: Integrating Technology Adoption and Collaboration Research. *Journal of Management Information Systems*, *27*(2), 9–53. doi:10.2753/MIS0742-1222270201

Chiocchio, F. (2007, March). Project team performance: a study of electronic task and coordination communication. *Project Management journal*.

Crossley, K., Clark, L. A., & Clark, R. W. (2010). Developing Multidimensional Trust Without Touch in Virtual Teams. *Marketing Management Journal*, *20*(1), 177–193.

Gholami, R., Ogun, A., Koh, E., & Lim, J. (2010). Factors Affecting e-Payment Adoption in Nigeria. *Journal of Electronic Commerce in Organizations*, *8*(4), 51–67. doi:10.4018/jeco.2010100104

Gibson, C. B., & Cohen, S. G. (2003). *Virtual teams that work: creating conditions for virtual team effectiveness*. San Francisco: John Wiley and Sons.

Hollingsworth, C. (2010, March). PMPs ON FB? OMG!: Project managers are all over social media, but is it really helping them get the job done? *PM Network*, *24*(3), 40–46.

Kaplan, A., & Haenlein, M. (2010). Users of the world, unite! The challenges and opportunities of Social Media. *Business Horizons*, *53*(1), 59–68. doi:10.1016/j.bushor.2009.09.003

Kerzner, H. (2010). *Project Management: Best Practices: Achieving Global Excellence*. John Wiley and Sons.

Kijsanayotin, B., Pannarunothai, S., & Speedie, S. M. (2009). Factors influencing health information technology adoption in Thailand's community health centers: Applying the UTAUT model. *International Journal of Medical Informatics*, *78*(6), 404–416. doi:10.1016/j.ijmedinf.2008.12.005 PMID:19196548

Kuruppuarachchi, P. R. (2009). Virtual team concepts in projects: A case study. *Project Management Journal*, *40*(2), 19–33. doi:10.1002/pmj.20110

Lindley, C., Edwards, C., Fraser, K., Gudelsky, S., Holmquist, J., Thornton, K., & Sweetser, K. (2010). Adoption of social media for public relations by nonprofit organizations. *Public Relations Review*, *36*(1), 90–92. doi:10.1016/j.pubrev.2009.10.003

Lipnack, J., & Stamps, J. (2008). *Virtual Teams: People Working Across Boundaries with Technology*. NetAge.

Manchester, A. (2009). Three common problems solved with internal social media. *Strategic Communication Management*, *4*(9), 9.

McAfee, A. P. (2006). Enterprise 2.0: The Dawn of Emergent Collaboration. *MIT Sloan Management Review*, *47*(3), 21–28.

Newhouse, P. C. (2001, Fall). Applying the Concerns-Based Adoption Model to Research on Computers in Classrooms. *Journal of Research on Computing in Education*, *33*(5), 1–21.

Newson, A., Houghton, D., & Patten, J. (2008). *Blogging and other social media: exploiting the technology and protecting the enterprise*. Gower Publishing Ltd.

Pells, D. L. (2008, June). Seven Good Reasons for the Rapid Growth of Project Management in IT and why that Trend will Continue. *PM World Today*, *10*(6), 1–14.

Qualman, E. (2011). *Socialnomics: How Social Media Transforms the Way We Live and Do Business*. John Wiley and Sons.

Ratcheva, V. (2008). The knowledge advantage of virtual teams -- processes supporting knowledge synergy. *Journal of General Management*, *33*(3), 53–67.

Robert, L. P., Denis, A. R., & Yu-Ting, C. H. (2009, Fall). Individual Swift Trust and Knowledge-Based Trust in Face-to-Face and Virtual Team Members. *Journal of Management Information Systems*, *26*(2), 241–279. doi:10.2753/MIS0742-1222260210

Schwalbe, K. (2009). *Information Technology Project Management*. Cengage Learning.

Turner, R. (2007). A Handbook for Project Management Practitioner. In R. Turner (Ed.), Gower Handbook of Project Management (pp. 1-20). Gower Publishing.

Chapter 7
Barriers to Social Media Adoption on Projects

Elizabeth Harrin
Otobos Consultants Ltd, UK

ABSTRACT

This chapter considers the reasons behind the lack of adoption of social media tools in a project environment. It discusses how project practitioners can overcome concerns about the lack of overall strategy, lack of senior management sponsorship, lack of a proven business case, security issues, information overload and the blurring of lines between professional and personal data online in order to realize the benefits of social and collaboration tools. It concludes that social tools are a fundamental part of the current and future project management landscape and that 'social' should be intelligently incorporated into working practices in order to meet a need instead of being a response to outside trends.

INTRODUCTION

More and more of our life is run online and the growth in internet tools has impacted how we communicate and connect with friends and colleagues. Whether it's organizing a party or sharing photos of our children, there's an app for everything, including productivity and project management tools to assist with work. Smartphones and tablets combined with online, cloud-hosted project management software and apps make it possible to check project status and collaborate with colleagues at any time, from wherever you can get an internet connection.

While it's clear that the ability to be 'always on' offers benefits to the project manager who travels extensively or for other reasons cannot be tethered to a desktop computer, it does mean that it's possible to check in with project team members and monitor status even at times when you aren't supposed to be working. The delineation between the work/life balance is no longer as clear cut as it used to be. This is compounded by the convergence of the personal and the professional in relation to data especially when it comes to virtual working. Project managers only want to carry one device, and expect to be able to manage their personal and professional networks from it.

DOI: 10.4018/978-1-4666-9867-3.ch007

Social media is a valuable asset to project teams as the tools allow for improved and enhanced collaboration especially within virtual teams. As more project work is being carried out by virtual teams, social communication techniques offer the project manager another tool to lead and manage the team. CIOs even state that the major use of social tools at work is to manage projects (Kiron et al, 2013). Social technologies used within the enterprise have the potential to raise the productivity of a knowledge worker by 20-25 per cent (Chiu, 2012).

Projects are all about people working together to deliver shared objectives, and the 'sharing' and 'collaboration' features of social media couldn't be more perfect to fit with that goal. Research into the value of project management like the (albeit small scale) study by Pollack and Adler (2014) show that project management practices improve productivity. Layering social media tools onto a project environment should therefore offer businesses a step-change in output.

One would expect, therefore, take up of social communication tools to be rife within the project management community. However, social media usage in the workplace is actually declining. In 2012, participation in professional discussion groups and social media networks decreased from the 2011 totals. Corporate social media usage is lower now than it was in 2009 (Hagel et al, 2013).

In the context of this chapter, the term 'social media tools' is used to include social collaboration and communication tools of all kinds including those used in the enterprise behind a secure firewall.

The objectives of this chapter are to look at the reasons behind the lack of take up of social communication tools on projects and consider how project practitioners can overcome these in order to realize the benefits that social media products have to offer project teams.

The chapter first looks at the background surrounding the impact of digital business on workplaces and how this enables organizations to operate differently. The chapter then discusses the barriers facing companies who wish to adopt digital and social tools in the project management environment. Finally, it discusses how project teams and senior managers can address and overcome the barriers to change in order to realize the benefits of new ways of working, before concluding with further research directions.

BACKGROUND

It wasn't that long ago that faxes were commonplace in offices. Offices may still have one, tucked away in case of need or to send urgent contracts. However, it's more common today for modern offices to operate with the minimum of paper moving between teams and buildings.

Interested readers can find more information about the growth of social media both for consumers and businesses elsewhere[1]. Businesses that use social technologies and social media are more likely to lead their market sector, have greater market share than their competitors and use management practices that result in higher margins (Bughin & Chui, 2010). The top business benefits for companies using social tools internally according to a McKinsey study (Bughin & Chui, 2010) are:

- Increased speed of access to knowledge (77 per cent).
- Reduced communication costs (60 per cent).
- Increased speed of access to internal experts (52 per cent).
- Reduced travel costs (44 per cent).

In turn, these business benefits drive further innovation in the areas of collaboration and productivity. The impact that digital business is having on the workplace has resulted from the convergence of four technological trends: social, mobile, cloud and information. Gartner calls this the Nexus of Forces (Howard, 2014).

Social supports an ongoing shift to collaboration as a way to achieve corporate goals; in the project management environment it has long been recognized that the command and control style of management was ineffective when compared to a collaborative, servant-leadership style.

There are now as many wireless subscriptions in the US as there are people (Hagel et al, 2013) and phones now serve many more functions than simply taking calls. *Mobile* services that support location-based data and other social tools now offer contextual information. Project managers are often highly mobile workers and this trend reflects their need to access data while out of the office.

The growth of *cloud* solutions lowers infrastructure costs for businesses and enables rapid deployment. Project managers using cloud-based software solutions enjoy fast fix times and increased feature releases, as well as the confidence that their project data is backed up routinely. Cloud also partners with mobile: as project teams are no longer tethered to a desktop environment, their data needs to be accessible from everywhere and cloud solutions offer flexible ways to deliver that. The resulting changes to the traditional application architecture models are changing to reflect that.

Finally, *information* and the 'big data' trend open up opportunities for businesses to analyze and improve processes like never before. Business intelligence becomes a differentiator as it enables organizations to tailor their customer interactions and provide better service by utilizing information they already have.

This increase in mobility and collaboration goes beyond online shopping and offering customers e-commerce options. Consumer-facing and employee-facing technologies are improving the user experience in the online environment.

These four trends are enabling businesses to:

- Improve interactions with customers.
- Launch new products.
- Differentiate from competitors.
- Reach new customer segments.
- Improve operational efficiency.

However, no major transformation in the status quo comes without its challenges. Despite these obvious advantages, take up has been slow. The tools that deliver these benefits to project managers within the organization have actually seen a decrease in adoption in several areas. For example, social media usage in the workplace is currently on the decline. Research shows that participation in professional discussion groups and social media networks dropped to below 2011 levels. Overall, corporate social media usage is lower today than was seen in 2009 (Hagel et al, 2013). Let's look at why that could be.

BARRIERS TO ADOPTION

Social media use on projects is not about boosting morale in the project team by sharing funny videos of cats. The use of social media tools in the workplace is designed to foster communication and collaboration with purpose: the purpose of getting projects done. With that as the stated aim, organizations that wish to benefit from these new ways of working need to overcome the challenges of putting these tools in place and increase adoption.

Research by MIT Sloan Management Review (Kiron et al, 2013) highlights several common barriers to adopting social business models. The four main barriers identified are:

- Lack of overall strategy.
- Lack of senior management sponsorship.
- Lack of proven business case.
- Security concerns.

While this research study relates to businesses in general, for the purposes of this chapter the assumption is made that these challenges are also relevant for the project environment within a business. It seems fair to conclude that a project environment is a sub-set of a larger business and therefore the barriers to adopting social tools at the macro level will be similar or identical to the ones faced by project leaders.

My own informal research with project practitioners[2] also identified a further barrier to adoption: that of the perception of such a wave of data that project managers feel unable to cope. When asked what they feel the largest hurdle is for adopting social media tools in a project environment, 49 per cent of respondents to my survey said that information overload was their greatest concern. The full results from this survey can be found in Table 1.

In this section I will expand on the four barriers to social tool adoption identified by the MIT Sloan research and also the concerns around information overload. Furthermore, I'll address an additional point: that of the increasing blend of personal and private data in a cloud-based architecture model. These six points offer the framework for identifying issues that prevent project-based organizations adopting the tools that could raise their productivity by 25 per cent.

Barrier #1: Lack of Overall Strategy

Executives can find it hard to get any social media tool adoption in the project environment approved for lack of an overall corporate strategy. With only 61 per cent of businesses having policies in place governing commenting about company confidential information, financial data and business insider

Table 1. What do you feel is the biggest hurdle to using social media tools on projects?

Barrier	Percent
Information overload	49.3
Lack of buy-in from project team	14.0
Too much time/resources required	10.9
Lack of competence with the technology	7.9
Not of sufficient value to stakeholders	7.9
Employees will waste time	6.1
Inability to measure success	3.6

N=164

information on social networking sites (Flynn, 2009), it seems fair to assume that formal corporate-wide strategies are unlikely to be in widespread use. Where social media strategies are present, they are often focused on externally-facing sites such as on official corporate Twitter feeds or blogs.

A lack of understanding around the business value of internally-facing tools can also hamper their inclusion in wider business strategy. A major difficulty for businesses here is in finding data and case studies that prove the benefits over a long enough periods for senior business leaders to make appropriate decisions. As the tools have not been around that long, it is difficult to find reference sites and data that will feed into and support a fully-fledged digital strategy.

Furthermore, PMI research shows that only 64 per cent of organizations effectively manage strategic initiatives. This implies that even if there is a strategy in place that covers digital working and the use of social tools for collaboration purposes, it is possible that it is not implemented as effectively as it could be (PMI, 2014a).

Barrier #2: Lack of Senior Management Sponsorship

Over 85 per cent of CEOs believe it is important that they champion the adoption of new technology (Snowden, 2015). Senior management sponsorship is frequently identified as one of the top causes of project success (see for example, Berman et al, 2008; James et al, 2013) and a factor in reducing resistance to change (see for example, Lundy & Morin, 2013). Yet over a third of executive project sponsors are frequently or always overstretched (PMI, 2014b).

Even in businesses where sponsorship is not a significant problem, there is some evidence that senior managers do not champion social media use. Research by Stanford shows that only 7.7 per cent of directors receive reports summarizing social media metrics for their businesses (Larcker, undated). The researchers conclude that the data is either not collected, not considered valuable or too low level for senior managers to give it much time. A further conclusion from that report is that executives and board members may view social media as 'beneath them'. They assert that there is the possibility that senior business leaders view these tools as only for marketing or public relations purposes.

This lack of willingness to invest time in understanding social tools and the value they add, plus the general busyness of senior managers who would be available to take on the sponsorship role compounds the problem of lack of leadership for internal social media initiatives.

Businesses that are unable to provide a committed, active sponsor for a social media initiative are unlikely to get their project off the ground. Without someone championing the cause and highlighting the productivity and collaboration benefits that users could see from the tools, projects are unlikely to start well – if at all – or deliver the promised benefits.

Barrier #3: Lack of Proven Business Case

Eighty-eight per cent of CEO's feel that value has been created from their digital investments in the area of operational efficiency (Snowden, 2015), but how is that actually measured? Often business cases are predicated on informal staff surveys or 'gut feel'.

Given that the benefits of social media tools are often the intangible elements shown in Table 2, proving the value of adopting these tools can be difficult. How do you measure increased collaboration? The fragmented use of social tools across a business also makes it hard to produce a cohesive business case and to track ongoing benefits at portfolio level.

Table 2. The benefits of social media functionality are often hard to quantify

Functionality	Benefit
Wiki	Faster access to organizational knowledge and project lessons learned
Discussion forum	Rapid access to subject matter experts; open asynchronous collaboration channel
File sharing	Collaborative access to documents for co-creation of content; faster document review; reduces number of revisions of document and ensures project team have instant access to the latest version of the file
Social networking	Intra-company collaboration; ability to identify experts and connect with the project team to build trusting relationships
Blogs	Publish and discuss articles; share information with a wider audience and reduce need for project newsletters or printed project marketing materials
Shared workspaces	One-stop shop for project teams to access all project-related media, manage and track task progress

For companies without robust approaches for preparing business cases for technology projects, securing any investment for new software can be difficult. The inability to quantify predicted return on investment or to produce any hard metrics that can be easily translated into measurable project success criteria can stop projects before they start.

It is not often possible for businesses to look outside and draw on case studies or research, as there is a paucity of practical research in this area. On top of this, companies could be (rightly) reluctant to share proprietary information about their business imperatives and return on investment as this could be seen as company confidential information and a core driver of differentiation in the marketplace. The immaturity of many of the products available for consideration provides further complexity. New tools do not have longevity and credibility in the marketplace which (again, rightly) makes it difficult to justify an investment in what is effectively a start-up company.

Barrier #4: Concerns about Security

Over 40 per cent of project practitioners using social media tools do so without the knowledge of their organization's IT department (Harrin, 2011). This is a major security concern as it puts corporate assets and project information at risk.

This 'under the radar' adoption shows grassroots enthusiasm for new ways of working but is also a major risk at PMO and organizational level, as well as for individual projects that may risk data deletion or the leakage of commercially sensitive project plans. Leakage may not be malicious. An accidental click or inadvertently changing the settings on a file could make it available to external users such as contractors. It's a lot easier to control project communications of a sensitive nature when you are having face-to-face conversations with the meeting room door closed, although even then you cannot always rely on the discretion of your employees.

IT departments and PMOs should be concerned with how to keep project data safe and auditable. Cloud-hosted solutions have many benefits but what happens if the supplier decides to leave the market? Where is data stored and how can it be retrieved should it be accidentally deleted? These are valid concerns for the organization that wishes to adequately secure and control its assets.

There is also the issue of dealing with system abuse. With abuse ranging from high profile cyber attacks like that on Sony Pictures in 2014, to a disgruntled employee deleting files before leaving the business, organizations need robust approaches to tackle potential business security threats.

Barrier #5: Concerns about Information Overload

My own discussions with project practitioners show information overload and dealing with the perceived deluge of information from additional communication channels to be a major concern and barrier to adoption (webinar held with PMI Learning, Education & Development Community of Practice, 2013).

Traditional project management communication channels including conference calls, emails and meetings often have the project manager in attendance. There is therefore the perception that the project manager has some degree of control over the communication and is aware of the important information pertaining to moving the project forward.

Project practitioners assume that social media tools will create a stream of data that will be impossible to manage. This results in concerns over the loss of control of the data flows and worries about being deluged with unwanted communications through subscriptions to social media alerts. There is a concern that data they do actually want to see will be lost in the vast output of updates and chatter through the social media tool.

Barrier #6: Concerns about Personal and Private Boundaries

The 'personal cloud' is a result of a shift in consumer behavior. It's now common for an individual to access multiple apps and services from one or more devices. All personal data can be synchronized and made available on all a user's devices, resulting in a personal cloud unique to that individual made up of the data stored in services that the user accesses regularly (Cearley, 2014). For a project manager this may include:

- A project management app for managing scheduling and resources.
- Corporate email services.
- Personal email services.
- Corporate social network services e.g. Yammer.
- Personal social network services e.g. Facebook.
- Online document storage with both personal and corporate accounts.
- Browser access with both personal and corporate bookmarks/favorites.
- Music, radio or video streaming for corporate or personal use.

While there are obvious advantages to having your personal data accessible from anywhere, the disadvantage is the blurring of lines between the personal and professional. Project managers may want to access personal data on the corporate network, or avoid carrying two phones: one for personal use and one for professional use. Flexible and remote working models have increased the preference for a single interface into all data sources. Knowledge workers are rarely nine-to-five employees who switch off as soon as they leave the office – if they were even in the office to start with.

With the blending of professional and personal lives, and the merging of the associated data sources, the boundaries between personal and professional become less distinct. More and more companies are opting for Bring Your Own Device policies, which offer the employee the ability to choose which gadget they will use for work purposes. However, hardware that is out of the control of a corporate IT department may not be patched or protected against viruses in the same way that company-issued technology would be.

The difficulties in navigating the technical challenges of the personal cloud must be addressed, and this can be a barrier to adopting social media tools in the workplace.

The concern centers on ensuring employees do not store sensitive corporate information such as project timescales for a market-sensitive initiative, in a public space. Companies face the possibility of data leakage: sensitive corporate information being migrated to publicly accessible platforms or the personal cloud without the project manager necessarily realizing the impact of this, or that it has even happened. When personal and professional resources are so entwined on a device it isn't hard to save a file to the wrong place without malicious intent but with potentially disastrous consequences for the business and the individual.

This has a major implication for the secure storage of project information and the requirement to share with third party suppliers or contractors.

SOLUTIONS AND RECOMMENDATIONS: OVERCOMING THESE BARRIERS

As discussed above, there are benefits to adopting social media tools in a project environment. Businesses have operated successfully for many years with traditional team tools and collaboration approaches, so there is no 'burning platform' imperative for many companies to make the leap to new technology.

However, when the barriers to adopting tools are not addressed, and technology is not used to its full advantage, businesses miss out on the benefits of increased productivity, greater collaboration, and speed of access to information and experts discussed above. Therefore it is worth spending time assessing the barriers to adopting these tools in an organization and preparing targeted responses as required.

This section considers each of the six barriers already discussed and offers solutions and recommendations for overcoming these.

1. Addressing Lack of Strategy

Social media and collaboration tools should only be used as a response to a particular project problem or the desire to improve project management practice. It is never a good idea to implement a tool because it's what everyone else says they are doing. Social media use in the project environment does have benefits but the tangible results you will see depend on your choice of tool, your implementation strategy, successful adoption, the user group and other factors relating to your particular situation. Therefore it's important to have a strategy prior to adopting any new way of working.

What do you want to achieve? This is the question executives should ask themselves prior to starting any tool selection activities. For example:

- Increase collaboration amongst virtual team members.
- Facilitate the sharing of lessons learned.
- Streamline document management and make it easy to search for project files.
- Make it easier to find resources with the right skills from across a vast global business for secondment to a project team.
- Standardized, cross-project reporting or portfolio dashboards.

These are all very different needs which would be addressed by a different tool and different local adoption strategy. An online, cloud-based full project management suite with collaboration features would be a good choice for increasing teamwork amongst virtual employees. A wiki is a good tool for sharing and searching for lessons learned across multiple projects. A document management system with advanced search features would make it easy to search for project files, but an in-house professional social network would make it easy to search for project resources. Dashboards pull data in real-time from project management systems so an 'always on' online system would give you the most flexibility for that.

All of these require both a technical strategy for the selection and implementation of the tool and a business strategy to change the way work gets done on projects.

Developing a strategy starts with appointing someone at a senior level to be responsible for social tools, most likely a senior figure in the Project Management Office. The PMO should feel empowered to be able to lead this change and to give themselves permission to make changes to the working practices of project teams in the same way as they would do by introducing a training program to upskill staff or publishing a new template. In a business culture where this is not the case, then the PMO should seek management guidance and authority to implement a new strategic approach to delivering projects using social tools.

An additional strategic role is that of senior sponsor: someone who can lead the cultural change and create an environment where a social project management culture can thrive. Both these executives will help to make social 'the way projects are done around here'.

For any strategy to be successful, the appropriate resources need to be allocated to the implementation and delivery of it. Part of defining a project social media strategy should be identifying the subject matter experts, extended team members and budget and time requirements necessary to deliver any strategy effectively. Without this, strategy is just a documented wish list.

Finally, ensure that the strategy addresses project issues and dovetails into any larger social media strategy for the organization. A project social media strategy should be aligned to the policies and practices already embedded in the wider business and should reference them where necessary.

Creating a Social Media Strategy in a Project Environment

A strategy is a codified version of a vision for how projects are done. It sets out how that vision will be made reality and ensures that the supporting infrastructure required for delivery is present in the organization. The strategy pyramid, depicted in Figure 1, is a good starting point for managers who have not had to think in this way before. Work down the strategy pyramid from the top.

Figure 1. The strategy pyramid

1. Define your vision, bounded by the benefits you wish to see from your social media tool use.
2. Write a specific, measurable, achievable, realistic and time-bound statement about what you plan to do in order to achieve that vision. This is your strategy statement.
3. Ensure your existing portfolio management structure will support your strategy. Will you be able to use existing governance and project process models to manage the work or do you need to revise your methodologies?
4. Define the individual projects required to achieve your vision: this will encompass one or more tool deployments.

It is worth reviewing what existing projects are in the current portfolio. There may be some that will assist you on the way to delivering your social media strategy such as upgrading base infrastructure (browser versions etc), implementing a Bring Your Own Device policy or other IT initiatives that will support your goals.

2. Addressing Lack of Senior Management Sponsorship

The only practical way to address the lack of senior management sponsorship is to put a senior management sponsor in post. This should be someone who can champion and support the initiative and will ideally be responsible for the implementation.

Some companies like L'Oréal and Burberry have embedded digital leadership in their senior management structures, either through the role of a Chief Digital Officer or a governing council tasked with ensuring business leaders support digital working practices (Catlin, Scanlan & Willmot, 2015).

However, it's important to note that the project sponsor that gets this social project initiative started is not necessarily the right person to be managing deployment of additional functionality in a year's time. It's a myth that sponsors cannot change part-way through a project: it is far more important to select the right person for the job in hand at any given part of the project life cycle. The tasks and focus required from the project sponsor change depending on the project stage:

- **Initiation:** Project sponsor requires organizational expertise and influencing skills to ensure that the project starts in the best possible way.
- **Planning:** Project sponsor requires a strategic view.
- **Execution:** Project sponsor's role focuses on removing roadblocks and creating an environment for the project team to carry out their tasks.
- **Closing:** Project sponsor focuses on reviewing and measuring project benefits and value delivered.

Consider whether the person chosen to sponsor your social media deployment is skilled in all of those areas. If not, a shift of senior leadership at strategic moments in the project may well help see the project through to successful completion. It can also make the burden of sponsorship less as it effectively splits the sponsor role between several key players, requiring each of them to be involved for a shorter period of time.

While there are of course benefits to having the same sponsor for the duration, there are also benefits is deconstructing the role which could help address the unwillingness of executives to actively engage as project sponsor. Equally, the leadership of the broader digital strategy will also evolve over time. When social working becomes the norm, the requirement for a Chief Digital Officer or equivalent role can drop away as the principles become embedded in normal business practice.

If no sponsor can be found, it is recommended that any social initiative is put on hold until someone with the right senior levels of influence can commit to leading the project.

3. Addressing Lack of Business Case

For many senior managers, a business case with a return on investment is a requirement before a project is approved. When so many of the metrics related to social media tools are difficult to quantify, the business case looks weak.

However, the majority of businesses seem to be addressing this by not requiring the social media deployment projects to track their benefits. Only 40 per cent of businesses with mature and effective social media practices within the workplace measure their results (Towers Watson, 2013), so if you choose not to measure anything at all you will be in the majority.

There is some logic to this. Conference calls, email and face-to-face meetings are also tools that foster collaboration and effective working within teams. No one puts together a business case for them and then regularly tracks the benefits of these communication methods, assessing their impact on project success or the productivity of project teams. A social media tool designed to enhance knowledge work should be considered in the same 'category' of technology: a fundamental channel for connecting project teams to the data and resources they need to be effective.

If you do decide that there is a requirement for gathering metrics, the advantage is that online and social tools capture vast amounts of data in the form of logs and audit trails. This makes it possible to see the number of users, 'shares' of data, documents stored and accessed, and assess usage across the project management teams.

However, usage does not always equal a return. Gathering statistics about how many people are using the lessons learned wiki will not tell you what they are using it for. It doesn't matter if 5000 people are using it if they are not the people who will then apply the lessons to future projects. Far better to have a much lower usage number: say, the 50 project managers leading critical business projects who have a real need to tap this source of organizational knowledge. In other words, it's important to measure the metrics that matter and that have a clear link to improved project management performance. When project sponsors and decision makers can see the link between adopting social project management tools and project success (even if this is an unproven or anecdotal benefit), it follows that achieving business case approval will be easier.

Finally, it is worth saying that the lack of a business case for social media adoption in the project environment might not be that great a concern after all. Social media tools are often seen as a 'right to play' rather than something that will provide a tangible return on investment.

4. Addressing Security Concerns

Communication through social tools relies on a devolved communication model – the project manager cannot (and should not) moderate all discussions. They may not even see all the discussions, and the lack of control that is inherent in this model may give rise to feelings of information overload which will be addressed below. Devolving the responsibility for communications to the team can present the security concerns as was shown above.

There are five pillars to a successful, secure social media tool deployment as can be seen in Figure 2.

Access controls may seem inconsistent with the transparent and open principles of social media tools. However, in a workplace environment they are critical for ensuring the right people have access to the right data. Choose tools that allow granularity of access to prevent, for example, financial project data being shared with external contractors working on the team.

Users should have individual usernames and passwords and the tools should not be available on an open access basis. In other words, logging in should be compulsory. Single sign-on technology and enabling cookies will ease the burden of remembering another password and prevent users from having to reset their password too often.

Back ups enable businesses to recover data in case of a disaster event. This could be anything from a project team member leaving their laptop on a train to flooding in the server room rendering the computer hardware useless. Cloud technologies make backing up project data easier as this is managed by, and is the responsibility of, the service provider. However, consider what would happen if the business chose to move to another tool provider or the provider went out of business. Make sure project data can be retrieved.

Collaboration tools that are hosted in-house also require backing up. Extend existing back up processes and business continuity plans to cover the social and collaboration tools in use across the project teams. This will provide everyone with confidence that essential project information can be retrieved if necessary.

Audit trails enable system administrators to see who logged in to the system and what tasks they performed. They go hand in hand with access controls, and users should be made aware that their use of the system can be tracked. Not all social tools have the facility to log and store an audit trail of system actions, so if a feature is of particular interest to project stakeholders it would be prudent to check that the applications under consideration have this feature.

Project teams should always use *authorized software*: products that have been vetted and approved by a corporate IT department or equivalent. This addresses the issue of individuals using apps that are not

Figure 2. Elements of a secure social media system (adapted from Harrin, 2010)

secure, are not backed up and do not enable project data to be shared in a confidential way. Unauthorized tools can create problems for project teams later on: who will support the product or upgrade it if there is an issue with it in the future? Downloading unapproved software can introduce vulnerabilities into the software estate such as viruses.

Unfortunately it is easy to download tools from the internet, especially as many of the products that are under discussion here are available for free.

System policies enable managers to track access and manage the behavior of users. They should include a formal process for requesting access to the collaboration tool for new starters and an equivalent process for removing users when their need to access the system has ended. There may also be a requirement for template non-disclosure or confidentiality agreements for use by third-party contractors or other partners requiring access to the application.

A clear policy around what constitutes acceptable behavior online can help moderate and inform users' interactions with each other via the tool. While existing HR policies can be invoked to deal with inappropriate workplace behavior online such as bullying or harassment, it's better to avoid these situations in the first place by clearly stating the code of conduct you expect project team members to adhere to online.

Existing IT policies and protocols may already cover these areas and may simply need to be amended or extended to include the use of collaboration tools.

To conclude this section, security concerns can be actively addressed by a social media tool adoption project. The PMO lead (or individual project manager in the absence of any structured initiative) should involve IT professionals and work with them on defining the best solutions for the project/project environment.

5. Addressing Information Overload

The issue of information overload for project managers is really an issue of control. Where communication channels are devolved and the project manager is not in attendance during the discussion, there is a concern that they will no longer be able to stay on top of progress and monitor the project work.

What's needed here is a mindset shift: devolved communication actually demonstrates greater levels of trust and accountability than a micro-management approach, and assuming that the project team members are trustworthy and competent, can create an empowered team environment.

In order to bring about this change in mindset it is worth considering whether there really is an issue with too much information or whether that is a convenient label for a different, underlying issue. Allcott (2014) identifies four root causes of feeling overloaded with information that are not actually to do with having too much information to process. They are:

- **Lack of Control:** What project managers often mean when reporting the feeling of being overloaded with information is that they can't control it. This isn't information overload: it's a personal time management problem and an internal struggle with feelings of being unable to control the environment.
- **Looking Foolish:** There is a learning curve with any new tool or process. Project team members at all levels sometimes choose not to admit that they don't understand the technology. It may not be an information overload problem but simply an issue of user training.

- **Risk of Ambiguity:** Data in this social environment is potentially unstructured, vague or ambiguous. There is also ambiguity in the way with which it should be handled. It may be unclear who is picking up the task (or even if there is a task to be done at all). This isn't a problem with the information itself but an issue with how to manage uncertainty and clarify communications.
- **Conflict:** There are often change requests that get processed through one of many social channels at short notice on fast-paced projects. Alongside conflicting priorities, your stakeholders and team now have more channels than ever to discuss and challenge decisions. It can certainly feel as if you are being overloaded with competing opinions, but it's actually an issue around dealing with conflict.

Implementing good project management practices across all areas of the project will help address these and in turn alleviate erroneous feelings of information overload. Efficient change and task management, conflict management techniques and systemizing as much as possible will enable project teams to deal with the information in unstructured formats provided by social collaboration tools.

When project teams, and project managers in particular, really do face information overload, there are a number of solutions to address this. Harrin (2010) offers six strategies to deal with an overwhelming amount of data that requires processing, namely:

1. **Starting Small:** This helps clarify the scale of the problem (if any). Implement tools and functionality in an iterative way, measuring the impact of, for example a project wiki, before adding deeper collaboration functionality.
2. **Filter Incoming Information:** Set up rules so that alerts for tasks that need to be done urgently are flagged to your inbox. Anything that is 'for information' can be diverted to a mailbox folder or other location for review at a convenient time.
3. **Segment the Conversations:** Encourage separate discussion threads for separate topics and only involve the individuals who can actively contribute.
4. **Turn off the Information:** Unless essential, opt out of real-time alerts. Unsubscribe from alerts about discussions you no longer need to monitor. Over time project managers will develop greater trust and an internal 'filter' to sift through the incoming data and establish what is of value.
5. **Arbitrate:** Social collaboration tools offer a voice to the many. Project managers should not be afraid to step into the discussion, take executive decisions and move the debate forward. Social media does not equal an environment where everyone has to agree on a solution before the project can move on.
6. **Use Mobile:** Make use of time that may not have been previously accessible for work with mobile apps, but be aware of the 'always on' culture and take time to switch off as well.

These approaches, combined with an appreciation of the mindset change required to lead in a different business paradigm, will enable project managers to foster a collaborative and trusting workplace with high levels of efficiency.

6. Addressing Personal and Private Boundaries

The business and personal risks presented by the blurred lines between corporate and individual information managed in a single cloud environment is probably the hardest concern for project managers to address. In many respects, this issue goes further than the sharing of project-related data on personal devices and stretches into corporate IT strategy.

Clear social media policies about what is acceptable for the use of project social media tools will help, along with a constant reiteration of what is acceptable. Again, involving the IT professionals from the organization will be essential as will incorporating any project management or collaboration apps into the business' Bring Your Own Device policy.

Project leaders should model acceptable behavior and not engage in any online data sharing that is potentially a risk. Project managers should lead by example and not be afraid to call out others when their behavior doesn't seem appropriate: they may not know what the workplace standards are, especially if they have only just joined the workforce.

At the time of writing, the only guaranteed way to fully address this concern is to keep professional data on a separate network without the requirement to share or collaborate in the cloud. However, this approach could fail to deliver many of the productivity benefits project leaders expect because of resistance from employees.

The boundaries between the personal and professional are only likely to get closer as employees demand a more seamless experience and a better work/life balance facilitated by technology. This is an area where thought leadership and cultural change will make a difference. Further research and the sharing of best practice on projects and in wider business contexts is needed.

FUTURE RESEARCH DIRECTIONS

It's always difficult to predict the future with any certainty, not least in an area such as social media which is changing rapidly in response to consumer and corporate demands. However, there are some trends that will support ongoing growth of social media adoption in the workplace for communication and collaboration in the project environment.

Mobile Device Management

Mobile device management is already a requirement for many businesses, but there will continue to be challenges. Project managers, like other employees, are demonstrating a willingness to invest in their own devices installed with the personal apps they use to manage their work/life balance (Cearley, 2014). This involves a high degree of personalization: the apps of choice for one individual will not be the same as another's.

Policies and Management

Current approaches to managing the personal cloud and the delineation of company confidential project information and personal information will need to be constantly revised as employees adapt flexible working practices. Without this, project teams will find their efforts to deliver effectively and in a collaborative environment hampered by lack of access to the right tools. In turn, they will find ways around IT policies in order to ensure they can work effectively.

Beyond Software

The current focus of this chapter has been on social media tool adoption for project teams. Tools are software. However, the rise of technologies like smart machines and 3D printing will mean that project managers need to be aware of interfaces with physical devices. The Internet of Things will increase the requirement for project teams to have access to online and social tools. They will be able to send the specifications of the prototype direct to the 3D printer over a wireless network from within the project management scheduling tool. As more routine jobs are managed by smart devices, digital businesses will require 50 per cent fewer process workers and 500 per cent more key digital business jobs (Plummer, 2014). Businesses who wish to remain competitive will have to find ways to overcome the barriers to social media tool adoption for their project teams.

The impact of these trends will be to continue the workplace disruption we have seen over the past few years. Project leaders face the need to re-engineer project processes in order to incorporate new technologies and ways of working. Project managers who can adapt to the new economy, incorporate big data findings and display excellent social skills will be in demand.

Themes for Future Research

This chapter has only focused on environments where knowledge sharing and collaborative working would happily form part of the project management culture with the tools, management and leadership to support them. The role of culture in the perception of the value of trust during knowledge sharing has been the subject of research (Wiewiora, 2014) and further investigation into the impact of culture in social media tool adoption would be an interesting avenue for future research.

CONCLUSION

Social media tools are here to stay. The brands, functionality and interoperability will certainly evolve over time but online collaboration software is fundamental to the ways in which the digital natives in project teams live their lives. This will spill over into the workplace whether project leaders are ready for it or not. Millennials and subsequent generations will be the project stakeholders and sponsors on future projects: they will expect the use of social media tools and full integration with their personal cloud.

There are also operational and delivery benefits of working in a collaborative, social way, as has been shown. Social communication should be integrated into the way project teams work and not just an 'add-on'. Project-based organizations must have a strategy for social tool adoption backed up by policies on social media. Initiatives must be led by credible senior managers to prevent issues and to overcome some of the barriers to adoption driven by lack of understanding or direction.

By embracing new technologies and dealing with the difficult questions of strategy, business case and security, project teams will be able to lead the field in knowledge work and remain competitive.

REFERENCES

Allcott, G. (2014). *How To Be A Productivity Ninja*. London: Icon Books.

Berman, S., et al. (2008). *Making Change Work*. IBM Global Business Services. Retrieved from http://www-935.ibm.com/services/us/gbs/bus/pdf/gbe03100-usen-03-making-change-work.pdf

Bughin, J., & Chui, M. (2010). *The rise of the networked enterprise: Web 2.0 finds its payday*. Retrieved from http://www.mckinsey.com/insights/high_tech_telecoms_internet/the_rise_of_the_networked_enterprise_web_20_finds_its_payday

Catlin, T., Scanlan, J., & Willmott, P. (2015). *Raising Your Digital Quotient*. Retrieved from http://www.mckinsey.com/insights/strategy/raising_your_digital_quotient

Cearley, D. W. (2014). *The Top 10 Strategic Technology Trends for 2014*. Gartner. Retrieved from https://www.gartner.com/doc/2667526?ref=clientFriendlyURL

Chiu, M., Manyika, J., Bughin, J., Dobbs, R., Roxburgh, C., ..., Westergren, M. (2012). *The social economy: Unlocking value and productivity through social technologies*. McKinsey Global Institute. Retrieved from http://www.mckinsey.com/~/media/McKinsey/dotcom/Insights%20and%20pubs/MGI/Research/Technology%20and%20Innovation/The%20social%20economy/MGI_The_social_economy_Full_report.ashx

Flynn, N. (2009). *2009 Electronic Business Communication Policies and Procedures Survey*. Retrieved from http://www.epolicyinstitute.com/2009-electronic-business-communication-policies-procedures-survey-results

Hagel, J., Seely-Brown, J., Samoylova, T., & Frost, M. (2013). *2013 Shift Index metrics: The burdens of the past*. Deloitte Center for the Edge, Deloitte University Press. Retrieved from http://dupress.com/articles/the-burdens-of-the-past

Harrin, E. (2010). *Social Media for Project Managers*. Newtown Square: PMI.

Harrin, E. (2011). *Social Media in A Project Environment: Survey Results*. Retrieved from http://www.pm4girls.elizabeth-harrin.com/social-media-in-a-project-environment-2011-survey-results/

Howard, C., Natis, Y. F., Harris-Ferrante, K., Proctor, P. E., Cain, M. W., ..., Anderson, E. (2014). *Transform your business with the Nexus of Forces*. Retrieved from https://www.gartner.com/doc/267381528

James, V., Rosenhead, R., & Taylor, P. (2013). *Strategies for Project Sponsorship*. Tysons Corner: Management Concepts Press.

Kiron, D., & Palmer, D. Nguyen Phillips, A., & Berkman, R. (2013). *Social Business: Shifting Out of First Gear*. MIT Sloan Management Review/Deloitte University Press. Retrieved from http://cdn.dupress.com/wp-content/uploads/2013/07/DUP446_SB_Report_Final.pdf

Larcker, D. F. (n. d.). *Social Media Use Among Directors and Senior Managers*. Stanford Graduate School of Business, Center for Leadership Development and Research. Retrieved from https://www.gsb.stanford.edu/sites/default/files/13SocialMedia.pdf

Lundy, V., & Morin, P.-P. (2013). Project leadership influences resistance to change: The case of the Canadian public service. *Project Management Journal*, *44*(4), 45–64. doi:10.1002/pmj.21355

Plummer, D. C., Fiering, L., Dulaney, K., McGuire, M., Da Rold, C. ..., Marian, K. (2014). *Top 10 strategic predictions for 2015 and beyond: Digital business is driving 'big change'*. Retrieved from https://www.gartner.com/doc/2864817?srcId=1-4782295242

PMI. (2014a). *Enabling Organizational Change through Strategic Initiatives*. PMI. Retrieved from http://www.pmi.org/learning/pulse.aspx#

PMI. (2014b). *Executive Sponsor Engagement: Top driver of project and program success*. PMI/Boston Consulting Group. Retrieved from http://www.pmi.org/~/media/PDF/learning/tranlations/2015/executive-sponsor-engagement-uk.ashx

Pollack, J., & Adler, D. (2015). Does project management affect business productivity? Evidence from Australian small to medium enterprises. *Project Management Journal*, *45*(6), 17–24. doi:10.1002/pmj.21459

Snowden, S., & Cheah, P-K. (2015). *A Marketplace Without Boundaries? Responding to Disruption*. PwC 18th Annual CEO Survey. Retrieved from http://www.pwc.com/gx/en/ceo-survey/2015/assets/pwc-18th-annual-global-ceo-survey-jan-2015.pdf

Towers Watson. (2013). *How the fundamentals have evolved and the best adapt: Change and communication ROI study report*. Retrieved from http://www.towerswatson.com/DownloadMedia.aspx?media=9AD1B8E9-813C-4FE8-AED2-0E753B1E098F

Wiewiora, A., Murphy, G., Trigunarsyah, B., & Brown, K. (2014). Interactions between organizational culture, trustworthiness, and mechanisms for inter-project knowledge sharing. *Project Management Journal*, *45*(2), 48–65. doi:10.1002/pmj.21407

KEY TERMS AND DEFINITIONS

Blog: Web-based publishing tool for sharing article-style content in chronological order. Can have a single or multiple authors such as the project sponsor.

Bring Your Own Device: A policy whereby staff members can connect their personal mobile devices such as smartphones and tablets to the corporate network.

Digital Native: An individual brought up in the digitally-enabled world, who has never 'lived' analogue or off-line working practices.

Information Overload: The feeling of having too much data to process. Being unable to manage incoming work effectively due to volumes.

Wiki: A collection of web pages acting as a hyperlinked knowledge repository and data set.

ENDNOTES

1 I recommend *Friends With Benefits: A Social Media Marketing Handbook* by Darren Barefoot and Julie Szabo (No Starch Press, 2009). While this book is now quite old, its explanation of the rise of 'social' is clear and still relevant today.

2 This was done as part of a webinar I delivered to the PMI Learning, Education and Development Community of Practice during December 2013.

Section 3

Tools and Technologies of Social Media

Chapter 8
Analyzing the Landscape of Social Media

Gilbert Silvius
LOI University of Applied Sciences, The Netherlands & University of Johannesburg, South Africa

ABSTRACT

The rapid spread of social media provides a new reality for organizational communication and team collaboration. This also applies to projects and project management, where logical application areas are stakeholder engagement and team collaboration. This last application area will be most beneficial to international projects with geographically dispersed teams. However, the landscape of social media is not unified. There are remarkable differences between regions, countries and generations. This chapter explores these differences, by discussing different perspectives on the social media landscape.

INTRODUCTION

The emergence of the online social networks has been the most interesting web development in recent years (Wellman 2005). Social media are changing the way people communicate, share information and find information (Mayfield, 2008). The rapid spread of blogs, social networking sites, and media-sharing technology (such as YouTube), aided by the proliferation of mobile technology, provides a new reality for organizational communication and team collaboration. Social media therefore also provide opportunities for managers of projects and programs to communicate effectively with their team members or (external) stakeholders. However, in order for this communication via social media to be effective, it is important to use the media and channels that reaches the intended audience. And in the rapidly developing landscape of social media, these media and channels are rapidly changing and not unified. For managers of projects and programs it is therefore essential to understand the regional and generational differences in the social media landscape.

It is not easy to exactly describe what social media is/are. An often cited definition from Kaplan and Haenlein (2010) who define social media as "a group of Internet-based applications that build on the ideological and technological foundations of Web 2.0, and that allow the creation and exchange of User

DOI: 10.4018/978-1-4666-9867-3.ch008

Generated Content" (p.61). Elaborating on this definition, Werder et al. (2014), define social media as "a web-based service or platform based on web 2.0 technology that enables the sharing, co-creation, discussion and modification of user-generated content.". This definition refers to social media as a specific application, whereas Kaplan and Haenlein refer to social media as "a group of … applications". We experience that the term social media is most often used in the plural form, referring to a group of services or applications. However, which applications are considered to be included in this group is not always clear.

But also without an exact definition or boundary, the applications that may be considered as social media, together make up the 'landscape' of social media. This paper aims to provide project management professionals insight in this landscape. And more specifically, in the differences of this landscape when organized into certain perspectives. The reason for this being that the social media landscape is not unified as many assume. For example China is known for banning popular foreign social media sites, such as Facebook, Twitter, Google+, YouTube, Dropbox, Picasa and Instagram. Rather than eliminating social media, these banns resulted in a flourishing state-approved set of Chinese-owned equivalents, such as Renren, Sina Weibo and Youku. And the Chinese social media are thriving. With a home market of over 640 million internet users, some Chinese social media are approaching the number of users of their Western equivalents. Also in Europe there are remarkable differences in the social media landscape. For example the well-known professional networking site LinkedIn has not succeeded to build a leading position in the German-speaking market (D-A-CH: Germany, Austria and Switzerland). German based Xing leads the DACH market of professional networking sites, with more members than LinkedIn.

For managers of international teams and projects, understanding these geographical differences in the social media landscape is crucial when selecting a social media strategy. But there are more aspects to take into account, for example age. The social media landscape is very dynamic and younger generations tend to be early adopters of new social media, sometimes with the motivation to have an alternative next to the mainstream social media that also older generations use.

As stated earlier, this chapter aims to give an overview of the social media landscape and to illustrate also differences in the landscape when organized into certain perspectives. In order to do this, the next paragraph first suggests some meaningful perspectives on the social media landscape. The subsequent sections than discuss the landscape of social media by these different perspectives.

The contribution this chapter makes to the topic of social media in project management, is that it makes project professionals aware of the fact that there is not one unified social media landscape. A project manager that wants to effectively apply social media in his or her project, either in the communication within the project team or in the communication with stakeholders, should tune his/her social media strategy to the needs and practices of the intended communication partner. Recognizing the differences in social media use amongst geographical regions, generations and other variables is a condition for an effective social media strategy. In general, and also in projects.

PERSPECTIVES ON THE SOCIAL MEDIA LANDSCAPE

As presented in the introduction of this chapter, it makes sense to consider the social media landscape through different perspectives. What perspectives are meaningful may provide an endless discussion. In the next sections, we discuss the social media landscape amongst the following perspectives.

- Functionality.
- Global size and growth.
- Geographical market position.
- Generational differences.
- Gender differences.

With this choice of perspectives, we do not claim, or aim, to be complete. Other perspectives can be added. However, we aimed to tackle the most relevant perspectives for the intended readership, being project management professionals, of this book.

In our study of the perspectives, we used secondary data of academic and professional studies and statistics to create meaningful insights. Also here, we adopted the perspective of the project management that plans to use social media in his or her project.

SOCIAL MEDIA LANDSCAPE: A FUNCTIONAL PERSPECTIVE

Different social media provide different functionality to their users, such as microblogging, sharing pictures or video's, connecting to people, collaboration, networking, etc. In order to structure these functionalities, several professional websites and blogs present colorful illustrations that order the social media landscape in some kind of functional classification. Functionalities mentioned functionalities in these classifications are for example: Publish, Share, Discuss, Promote, Influence, Network and Find. And although these terms refer to identifiable functionality, they do not provide a clear and recognized classification framework of the functionality of social media. Also in more academic publications some functional classification frameworks can be found. Richter and Koch (2008), propose a framework of six basic functionalities of social networking services:

- Identity management
- Expert finding
- Context awareness
- Contact management
- Network awareness
- Exchange

However, the most referenced model of social media functionality is the 'honeycomb' model (see Figure 1) of seven functional building blocks: identity, conversations, sharing, presence, relationships, reputation and groups, as developed by (Kietzmann et al, 2011).

Table 1 provides a short description of the seven functionality building blocks of this framework. The table adds also some examples of social media that provide the functionality of the respective building block. These examples do not aim to provide a complete listing of all relevant social media providing this functionality, but to provide illustrations of relevant social media.

An observation from this table should be that different social media provide different functionalities and that no single social media site provides all functionality. This implies that project managers that plan to apply social media in their projects, should develop a social media strategy, in which a mix of particular social media is selected that together provide the required functionalities.

Figure 1. The honeycomb of social media functionality (Kietzmann et al, 2011)

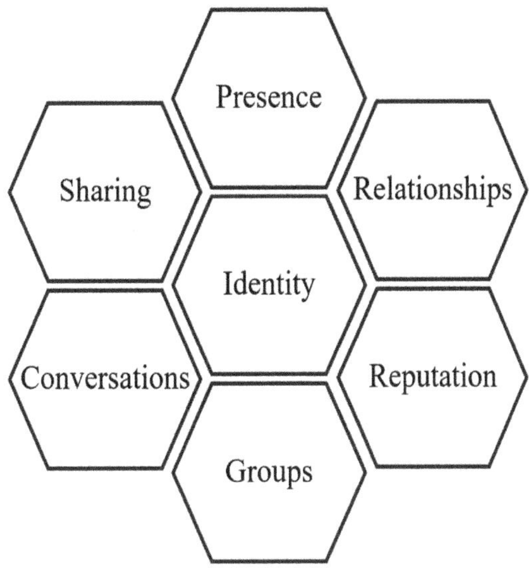

Table 1. Functionality building blocks of the honeycomb model

Functionality building block	Description	Examples of social media providing this functionality
Identity	The functionality for individuals and organizations to show themselves, including their experiences, interests, hobbies, thoughts, feelings, likes and dislikes.	Facebook, Linkedin, Xing
Presence	The functionality to show that users are available.	Skype, Microsoft Lync
Relationships	The functionality with which users can relate or associate themselves to/with other users.	Facebook, Linkedin, Xing
Reputation	The functionality that allows users to build a standing for themselves, in comparison to other users.	Linkedin, Xing, Twitter, Sina Weibo
Groups	The functionality to which users can form communities and sub communities.	LinkedIn, Facebook, Yammer
Conversations	The functionality to communicate to or with other users.	WhatsApp, WeChat, Facebook Messenger, Yammer
Sharing	The functionality to exchange, distribute, and receive content.	YouTube, Dropbox, Yammer, Instagram, Picasa

Werder et al. (2014), suggest a framework for the development of a social media strategy (Figure 2), that consists of three key components: Scope, Capabilities and Governance.

In this framework of social media strategy, Scope refers to the actors, their interaction and the social media platforms, that are addresses in the strategy. Capabilities refer to the objectives and activities of the use of social media, as supporting objectives of the (project's) objectives. Governance refers to the measuring, evaluating and directing of the social media activities, as well as managing the risks associated with it (Noy & Ellis, 2003).

Figure 2. The social media strategy framework (Werder et al., 2014)

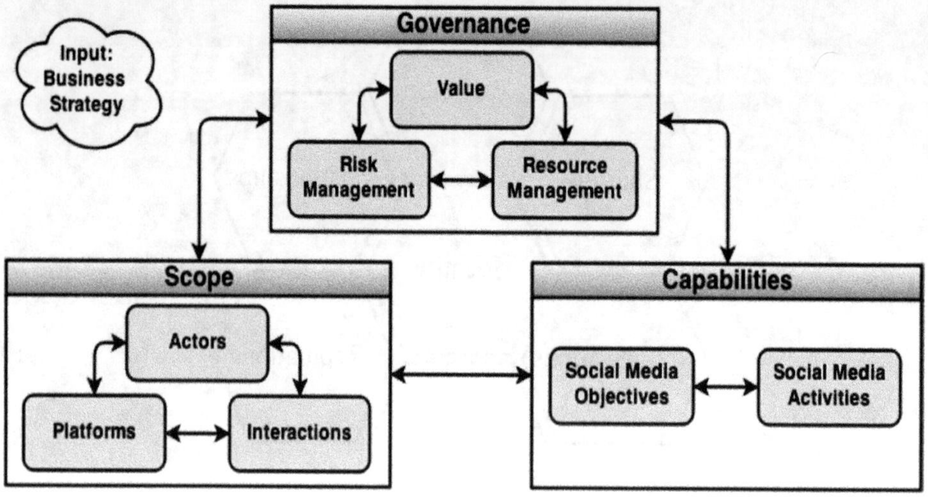

SOCIAL MEDIA LANDSCAPE: GLOBAL SIZE AND GROWTH

The number of active social media accounts is estimated to have passed 2 billion, equaling about 30% of earth's population and about two-thirds of all internet users (Parcells, 2015). Research conducted by GlobalWebIndex suggests that the average social media user spends 2 hours and 25 minutes per day using social networks and microblogs.

According to the statistics portal www.statista.com, Facebook continues to be the largest global social network, measured by number of active accounts or users. Table 2 shows the 18 largest online social media networks and their countries of origin.

From this table it shows that the many of the largest social media originate from the United States, but that their Chinese equivalents are on the rise. And while Facebook remains to be the largest social media site, the growth in number of user has significantly slowed down. In 2014, the fastest growing social media were Tumble, Pinterest, WhatsApp and Instagram, all with spectacular growth rates, measured in active users.

Where the growth of Facebook in number of users has almost come to a halt, the engagement of its users is still growing. In 2014 70% of Facebook engage with the site daily, a significant increase from the 63% who did so in 2013 (Duggan at all, 2015).

A trend in the use of social media is that of the use multiple platforms. 52% of online adults now use two or more social media sites, a significant increase from 2013, when it stood at 42% of internet users. Table 3 shows this usage of multiple social media platforms, based on the 2014 Social Media update (Duggan et al., 2015).

From this table, again the leading position of Facebook shows. Users of the other platforms, typically also have a Facebook account, with percentages from 86 to 94%, where in the reversed situation these scores are much lower, between 29 and 34%. It should be mentioned that the study referred to in this table, focused on social media usage in the United States.

Table 2. Social media networks by size (active users)

Position	Social media	Country of origin	Number of active users (end 2014) [* 1 million]	Growth of active users in 2014
1	Facebook	United States	1415	2%
2	Tencent QQ	China	829	
3	WhatsApp	United States	700	75%
4	QZone	China	629	
5	Facebook Messenger	United States	500	52%
6	WeChat	China	468	42%
7	LinkedIn	United States	347	54%
8	Skype	United States	300	
9	Google+	United States	300	16%
10	Instagram	United States	300	64%
11	Baidu Tieba	China	300	
12	Twitter	United States	288	26%
13	Viber	Israel	236	32%
14	Tumblr	United States	230	120%
15	Snapchat	United States	200	55%
16	LINE	Japan	181	45%
17	Sina Weibo	China	167	
18	VK	Russia	100	

Table 3. Percentage of particular social media sites that also use another particular site

	Use Facebook	Use LinkedIn	Use Twitter	Use Instagram	Use Pinterest
% of Facebook users who …	-	33%	29%	34%	34%
% of LinkedIn users who …	86%	-	39%	35%	40%
% of Twitter users who …	91%	47%	-	58%	42%
% of Instagram users who …	94%	38%	52%	-	47%
% of Pinterest users who …	88%	40%	34%	43%	-

SOCIAL MEDIA LANDSCAPE: A GEOGRAPHICAL PERSPECTIVE

As already mentioned in the introduction of this chapter, the social media landscape is not globally unified. Potential reasons for local differences may be governmental imposed restrictions, different levels of penetration and/or strong local players.

Imposed Restrictions

The well-known Chinese ban on popular social media sites Facebook, Twitter, Google+ and YouTube, opened the opportunity for local equivalents. Thriving on their rapidly developing home markets, these Chinese-owned social media are now amongst the largest social media sites, as Table 2 showed. And they are expanding to the rest of the world. So is WeChat, the internationally branded Chinese equivalent of WhatsApp, now challenging its Western example, both in size as in functionality.

For international projects that include a team in China, the social media strategy should consider the quite specific social media landscape in this country. However, also other countries and regimes sometimes impose restrictions on social media sites. Some examples:

- Turkey has had temporary bans on Twitter and YouTube and is today still restricting blog sites.
- India has restricted the use of Blogger as a platform for political statements.
- Egypt temporarily banned Twitter in 2011 during the protests against then president Hosni Mubarak.
- Morocco, Indonesia, Russia, Malaysia, Pakistan and several other countries all blocked specific videos from YouTube for political of religious reasons.
- In May 2015, Russia's communications oversight agency threatened to fine or even block Facebook, Google and Twitter under a controversial law on alleged illegal blogging.

In none of these markets, other than China, did the ban or restricted use lead to the development of strong local social media, such as in China.

Penetration

Social media penetration differs substantially per country. Based on research by eMarketer, Table 4 presents the penetration, as percentage of population, of social network use in selected countries.

From Table 3 shows that there are significant differences in penetration of social media between countries. Reasons for this may be technical (internet penetration, or broadband penetration, in general), economical (related to the affordability of internet devices and access) or social (related to social values or traditions). The study of these factors are beyond the aim of this chapter. We merely intended to illustrate that geographical differences in social media use do exist and that this is something to take into account when using social media in (international) projects.

Local Players

It may be hard to imagine today, but social media did not start as a global market. It started as a local-by-local market. Many of the now global social media sites, such as Facebook, started locally in a home market and expanded from there. In their expansion, these global social media often conquered markets from local players. For example, in the Dutch market, Hyves, the local market leading social network until 2010, completely vanished as a result of the rise of Facebook in the Netherlands. And in France, LinkedIn needed until the end of 2013 to conquer market leadership in its segment on local player Viadeo.

Table 4. Penetration of social network use by country

	Social network user penetration by country [% of population]				
	2013	2014 (expected)	2015 (projected)	2016 (projected)	2017 (projected)
Norway	63%	67%	69%	71%	73%
Netherlands	64%	66%	68%	80%	71%
Sweden	57%	60%	62%	64%	66%
South Korea	54%	57%	59%	61%	62%
Denmark	53%	57%	60%	63%	64%
Finland	51%	55%	58%	60%	63%
United States	52%	53%	54%	55%	56%
Canada	51%	53%	54%	55%	56%
United Kingdom	50%	53%	54%	55%	56%
Australia	49%	52%	56%	59%	61%
Russia	42%	46%	49%	51%	53%
Argentina	41%	45%	48%	49%	51%
Germany	41%	44%	46%	48%	50%
France	39%	41%	43%	44%	45%
Japan	38%	40%	42%	43%	44%
Spain	37%	40%	42%	44%	45%
Brazil	35%	38%	40%	43%	44%
Italy	34%	37%	38%	40%	40%
Mexico	31%	35%	39%	43%	47%
Indonesia	27%	31%	35%	39%	42%
China	26%	28%	30%	32%	35%
India	8%	11%	13%	15%	17%

And although the trend of LinkedIn gaining market share and Viadeo losing seems irreversible, Viadeo remains an important social network for professional contacts in France, next to LinkedIn.

In the German speaking DACH countries, Germany, Austria and Switzerland, the market position of LinkedIn is still challenged by local player Xing. In fact, Germany based Xing is the leading professional social network in the three countries together, with over 7 million users versus almost 6 million for LinkedIn, and has given up its international ambitions to protect its home market position. Whether this strategy will keep Xing on top is to be seen. Its leading position in the DACH countries is now only based on the German market, as LinkedIn took over the number one spot in Austria in the summer of 2014 and is already leading in Switzerland for many years. Home market Germany will therefore be the last 'fortress' for Xing. However, with a far larger number of paid subscriptions, sounds revenues and more advanced privacy settings, Xing may be in a good position to defend their position for some more years.

In the earlier sections, it was already discussed that local social media dominate the Chinese market. Another market where local social networks should not be neglected is Russia. VK, originally VKontakte, is the largest Russian social network in Europe. At the end of 2014, VK had some 280 million user accounts, and an estimated number of active users of 100 million. In Table 2 it is ranked as the 18th largest social network in the world. VK is especially popular among Russian-speaking users, particularly in Russia, Ukraine, Belarus, Kazakhstan and Uzbekistan. The functionality and use of VK is much like the use of Facebook. VK allows users to message each other publicly or privately, to create groups, public pages and events, share and tag images, audio and video, and to play browser-based games.

As conclusion of this paragraph, we observe that the social media landscape is globalizing, but that local differences should not be ignored. The reasons for these local differences may be resulting from government imposed restrictions, differing penetration levels or the presences of strong local players. Either way, the message resulting from these local differences should be that managers of international projects also in their use of social media in their projects, have to consider local circumstances and situations.

SOCIAL MEDIA LANDSCAPE: A GENERATIONAL PERSPECTIVE

Different age groups are differently represented on the individual social media. In general, older generations, aged 55 and up, are less active on social media than youth and professionally active generations. However, differences also show per specific social media site. The 2014 Social Media update of the Pew Research Centre (Duggan et al., 2015), illustrated this for the social networks Facebook, LinkedIn, Twitter, Instagram and Pinterest. Table 5 summarizes the usage figures, as percentage of internet users, they found.

Table 5 confirms the general conclusion that the younger generations are most active on social media. However, the data also show that the 65+ generation is the fastest growing age group in terms of social media usage.

On the most popular network, Facebook, all generations have developed a significant presence. On this site, the age profile of active users on sites such as Facebook is shifting upwards as the youngest networkers embrace newer sites the most enthusiastically. It is reported that younger generations shift their activities from Facebook to newer social media, such as Instagram, Snapchat and Pinterest, in order to not be exposed to their parents and grandparents, that are also active on Facebook. Table 4 shows this effect most clearly for Instagram, with Snapchat not being included in the study.

Not surprisingly, on the professional network LinkedIn, the professionally active generations have the highest user penetration. However, on this platform, the younger generation, together with the 65+ generation, the fastest growing user group.

Table 5. Use of selected media by age group

	Facebook		LinkedIn		Twitter		Instagram		Pinterest	
Age group	**2013**	**2014**	**2013**	**2014**	**2013**	**2014**	**2013**	**2014**	**2013**	**2014**
18-29	84%	87%	15%	23%	31%	37%	37%	53%	27%	34%
30-49	79%	73%	27%	31%	19%	25%	18%	25%	24%	28%
50-64	60%	63%	24%	30%	9%	12%	6%	11%	14%	27%
65+	45%	56%	13%	21%	5%	10%	1%	6%	9%	17%

SOCIAL MEDIA LANDSCAPE: A GENDER PERSPECTIVE

From the same study (Duggan et al., 2015), we extracted the use of the different social media by gender. This is summarized in Table 6.

From this overview it appears that women are more active on the more personal social media, such as Facebook, Instagram and Pinterest. The difference is exceptionally large on Pinterest: 42% of online women now use this platform, compared with 13% of online men.

Men have a slightly higher usage of the professional network LinkedIn and on Twitter.

LIMITATIONS

Writing a publication on 'the social media landscape' is both challenging and limited. The challenge is provided by the fact that clear and undisputed data on usage of the different social media are not always available. Especially in the quickly developing market of social media platforms, usage data and statistics are constantly changing and it is practically impossible to stay completely up-to-date. This dynamic context also provides the main limitation of this chapter. The social media landscape is constantly developing and project management professionals that plan to use social media in their projects should inform themselves about the actual situation in the markets they aim for.

CONCLUSION

The rapid spread of social media provides a new reality for organizational communication and team collaboration. This also applies to projects and project management, where logical application areas are stakeholder engagement and team collaboration. This last application area will be most beneficial to international projects with geographically dispersed teams. However, the landscape of social media is not unified.

This chapter provided a discussion of the social media landscape amongst the following perspectives.

- Functionality.
- Global size and growth.
- Geographical market position.
- Generational differences.
- Gender differences.

Table 6. Use of selected media by age gender

	Facebook		**LinkedIn**		**Twitter**		**Instagram**		**Pinterest**	
Gender	**2013**	**2014**	**2013**	**2014**	**2013**	**2014**	**2013**	**2014**	**2013**	**2014**
Men	66%	66%	24%	28%	17%	24%	15%	22%	8%	13%
Women	76%	77%	19%	27%	18%	21%	20%	29%	33%	42%

Based on an analysis of secondary data from academic publications, professional studies and statistics, we showed on each of the perspectives, that an effective use of social media in or by projects, requires a thorough analysis of the specifics of the region or target group at hand.

We would like to encourage project professionals to utilize the potential of social media in stakeholder communication and team collaboration. However, we recommend that these professionals inform themselves about the actual use of social media by the stakeholders they plan to engage with. Especially in the rapidly developing world of social media, the effectiveness of particular sites may change 'overnight'.

FUTURE RESEARCH DIRECTIONS

The emergence and rapid development of social media and online social networks did not go unnoticed. Many companies today are applying social media for branding, online marketing, sales, customer service and support, and product development (Culnan et al., 2010). And also in research, the use of social media in customer engagement is frequently studied. For the context of projects, this field of application has some analogy to project marketing and or project stakeholder engagement. With the differences in the social media landscape, discussed in this chapter, one direction of further research should be the effectiveness and limitations of social media in stakeholder engagement towards different groups of stakeholders.

Another logical application area of social media in projects is that of communication and collaboration within the team. Also in this field of application, the differences in the social media landscape discussed in this chapter, may affect the applicability and effectiveness of specific social media, especially within international (project) teams. This therefore also provides an interesting direction for further research: how to develop the most effective social media strategy for team communication and collaboration within international project teams.

International teams often imply also intercultural teams. The cultural aspect of social media use was not discussed in this chapter, however, also this perspective provides a relevant direction for further research. What are the cultural aspects of using social media in project teams?

We encourage that scholars and practitioners cooperate to develop more knowledge about the effective use of social media in projects, both in stakeholder engagement and in team communication and collaboration.

REFERENCES

Culnan, M. J., Mchugh, P. J., & Zubillaga, J. I. (2010). How large U.S. companies can use twitter and other social media to gain business value. *MIS Quarterly Executive*, *9*(4), 243–260.

Duggan, M., Ellison, N. B., Lampe, C., Lenhart, A., & Madden, M. (2015). Social Media Update 2014. *PewResearchCentre*, Retrieved from http://www.pewinternet.org/2015/01/09/social-media-update-2014/

Kaplan, A. M., & Haenlein, M. (2010). Users of the world, unite! The challenges and opportunities of Social Media. *Business Horizons*, *53*(1), 59–68.

Mayfield, A. (2008). What is social media? Retrieved from http://www.icrossing.co.uk/fileadmin/uploads/eBooks/What_is_Social_Media_iCrossing_ebook.pdf

Noy, E., & Ellis, S. (2003). Risk: A neglected component of strategy formulation. *Journal of Managerial Psychology*, *18*(7), 691–707. doi:10.1108/02683940310502395

Parcells, F. E. (2015). Social Media trends 2015. Retrieved from http://www.slideshare.net/feparcells/social-media-trends-2015-44900830

Richter, A., & Koch, M. (2008). Functions of Social Networking Services. *Proceedings of COOP '08: the 8th International Conference on the Design of Cooperative Systems.*

Wellman, B. (2005). Community: From neighborhood to network. *Communications of the ACM*, *48*(10), 53–55. doi:10.1145/1089107.1089137

Werder, K., Helms, R. W., & Jansen, S. (2014). Social media for success: A strategic framework. *Proceedings of the Pacific Asia Conference on Information Systems.*

KEY TERMS AND DEFINITIONS

Baidu Tieba: The largest Chinese communication platform provided by the Chinese search engine company, Baidu. It is an online community bound tightly with internet search services, one of the main business of Baidu.

Facebook: An online social networking service headquartered in Menlo Park, California. Users can create a user profile, add other users as "friends", exchange messages, post status updates and photos, share videos and receive notifications when others update their profiles. Additionally, users may join common-interest user groups.

Google+: A social network, owned by Google, that allows users to post photos and status updates to the stream or interest based communities, group different types of relationships (rather than simply "friends") into Circles, a multi-person instant messaging, text and video chat called Hangouts, events, location tagging, and the ability to edit and upload photos to private cloud-based albums.

Instagram: An online mobile photo-sharing, video-sharing and social networking service that enables its users to take pictures and videos, and share them on a variety of social networking platforms, such as Facebook, Twitter, Tumblr and Flickr.

Line: A proprietary application for instant communications on electronic devices such as smartphones, tablet computers and personal computers. Line users exchange texts, images, video and audio, and conduct free VoIP conversations and video conferences.

LinkedIn: A business-oriented social networking service, launched in 2003. It is mainly used for professional networking.

QZone: A social networking website, which was created by Tencent in 2005. It allows users to write blogs, keep diaries, send photos, listen to music, and watch videos.

Sina Weibo: A Chinese microblogging (weibo) website. Akin to a hybrid of Twitter and Facebook, it is one of the most popular sites in China, in use by well over 30% of Internet users, with a market penetration similar to the United States' Twitter.

Skype: A telecommunications application software product that specializes in providing video chat and voice calls from computers, tablets and mobile devices via the Internet to other devices or telephones/ smartphones. Users can also send instant messages, exchange files and images, send video messages and create conference calls.

Snapchat: A photo messaging application. Using the application, users can take photos, record videos, add text and drawings, and send them to a controlled list of recipients. Users set a time limit for how long recipients can view their 'Snaps', the range is from 1 to 10 seconds, after which they will be hidden from the recipient's device and deleted from Snapchat's servers.

Social Media: A group of Internet-based services and/or applications, based on web 2.0 technology, that enable the sharing, co-creation, discussion and modification of user-generated content.

Tencent QQ: An instant messaging software service developed by Chinese company Tencent Holdings Limited. QQ also offers a variety of services, including online social games, music, shopping, microblogging, and group and voice chat.

Tumblr: A microblogging platform and social networking website founded by David Karp and owned by Yahoo! Inc. The service allows users to post multimedia and other content to a short-form blog.

Twitter: An online social networking service that enables users to send and read short 140-character messages called "tweets".

Viber: An instant messaging and Voice over IP (VoIP) app for smartphones developed by Viber Media. In addition to instant messaging, users can exchange images, video and audio media messages.

VK: The largest Russian social network in Europe. It is especially popular among Russian-speaking users, particularly in Russia, Ukraine, Belarus, Kazakhstan and Uzbekistan. Like other social networks, VK allows users to message each other publicly or privately, to create groups, public pages and events, share and tag images, audio and video, and to play browser-based games.

WeChat: A mobile text and voice messaging communication service developed by Tencent in China, first released in January 2011.[8] It is the largest standalone messaging app by monthly active users.

WhatsApp: An instant messaging app for smartphones that operates under a subscription business model and since recently part of Facebook.

Chapter 9
Social Media Use within Project Teams:
Practical Application of Social Media on Projects

Linky Van der Merwe
Virtual Project Consulting, South Africa

ABSTRACT

This chapter gives practical recommendations about the social media tools and applications for use on projects. It will introduce the reader to the most popular and widely used social media tools and will provide considerations for the selection of the best tools to integrate with projects. Platforms being described from a project management point of view are LinkedIn, Facebook, Twitter, Yammer, Google+, Blogs, Wikis, Instant Messaging, YouTube, Webinars, SlideShare, Podcasts and Vodcasts. Best practice recommendations are given for each tool from a project manager as well as a team member perspective. Advice is given about dealing with various challenges such as security concerns and managing the culture change. The current trends that will dictate and influence the use of social media on projects are also discussed.

INTRODUCTION

Social media is reshaping the way we manage projects, by changing the way we connect and communicate with our teams and stakeholders. Social media provides instant access to a broader audience than was previously possible through conventional communication means.

Picture this scenario. As the project manager of a large multi-national, cross country project, you need to manage your virtual project team. In response to stakeholder requirements, teams are mobilized quickly and cheaply. The project manager makes use of cloud-based project management software with built-in collaboration capabilities. Meetings are held weekly or more regularly using video- and teleconference facilities such as Microsoft Lync. A social media policy is in place and all team members have been briefed as to how it will be used, when and for which information.

DOI: 10.4018/978-1-4666-9867-3.ch009

The project manager uses a few selected social media tools as communication channels to engage with the team, to empower them to make decisions, to share information and collaborate, to streamline processes and engage the team with stakeholders, partners and vendors. A project Wiki is in place to collaborate on documents, intranet sites to engage the client and share the team's work, discussion boards to check the pulse across the team, as well as shared task lists to track the team's progress in real time. Formal progress feedback is provided through Dashboard reporting based on real-time project progress.

This is not a theoretical project, but a real-life scenario of how social media savvy project managers lead their projects and teams today, using social media as a communications and collaboration technology, in conjunction with more traditional methods.

The above scenario illustrates that one of the most rewarding aspects of social media is the ability to create virtual communities, allowing teams to share ideas and monitor all aspects of the project in real time. Communicating in this way builds community, trust and morale among team members.

This chapter will serve to educate project management practitioners about using social media within the project team. The objective is to provide best practice recommendations for using various popular social media tools from a project manager as well as a team member perspective.

The chapter starts with broad definitions of available social media tools for use on projects. It explains how to address social media concerns like enabling a new way of working and security. It then continues to provide practical advice on how to overcome challenges and how to establish rules of engagement. Recommendations are made for how to integrate social media onto projects. The most useful aspect of the chapter is the practical application of the popular social media platforms. It provides input to create a roadmap that is easy to apply on your own projects.

SOCIAL MEDIA AS COMMUNICATION CHANNELS

Since social media lends itself to be participatory, community based and interactive, it is ideal for engagement among project team members. Various social media tools can be used effectively as communication channels on projects. Team members use it on projects to share information and status, to collaborate and to connect with stakeholders and fellow team members.

With the common adoption of mobile devices in the work place, it is not surprising to hear from Joseph Guarino, owner of Evolutionary IT, in his presentation: "Social media for project managers" (Guarino, 2012) that social networking apps are the 3rd most used smart phone apps. He also stated that social networks and blogs account for almost half of all time online.

When organizations consider adopting social media as a communication tool on projects, one of the first decisions required, is to select appropriate enterprise collaboration software that has social media incorporated into the project management information system. For this type of software, there is normally a choice between Software as a Service (SaaS) which is easy to deploy with a potentially lower total cost of ownership, versus locally installed traditional enterprise software which is more complex and costly to manage. The advantage being that you have more control and you own the project management solution.

In addition to using a project management software solution or even without having an enterprise project management solution, as is the case with smaller organizations, there are popular social networks to select as communication tools on projects. You can differentiate between social media tools for use by project team members versus tools to use as a project manager for thought leadership and to deepen networks.

What follows are some high level descriptions of popular, available social media tools for use on projects.

LinkedIn

LinkedIn is the leading social media networking site for professionals with about 364 million (Statista.com 2015) users. It's emerging as a top source for business-related content, fueled by its Influencers program. The Influencer network consists of high-profile CEOs, entrepreneurs and thought leaders from every major industry. By following a few influencers, it will enrich your thinking and keep you up-to-speed with broader trends and developments affecting business (Smart Company, 2013). LinkedIn allows for information sharing across professions – across the global workplace. As a social networking site for professionals, LinkedIn will help you find experts in project management. It has fused resume, cover letter and references all into one. A study, conducted by Louise Worsley for an Open University module, shares finding on how project managers use LinkedIn. Over 50% of respondents use more than one social network weekly. And 85% use LinkedIn every week mainly for creating, maintaining and growing professional relationships. The other reasons for using LinkedIn are seeking information on practices and seeking answers to specific questions. (Worsley, 2015)

Facebook

Although Facebook, with about 1.9 billion (Statista.com 2015) users worldwide, is normally associated with being a social platform to find old friends or to share personal details with your friends, it has risen as a business tool in the past 5 years. Most organizations will have a dedicated Facebook page, (see Project Management Institute) acting as a type of social media Wiki, accessible by all. Project managers can use Facebook to engage with other project managers, join relevant groups to find experts and ask them questions.

Yammer

Yammer with more than 8 million (2013) users, is like Facebook's equivalent, but in the corporate world, focused on the company. Yammer is an enterprise social software that's integrated with Microsoft Office 365 and SharePoint 2013. Yammer helps you discover relevant conversations, groups, files, and people across the company and for teams it gives greater context around the work they're doing. (Microsoft Office.com 2015)

Google+

Most people have a Google profile and it's very easy to join Google+. There are about 300 million (Digitalinformationworld.com 2015) active users on Google+. It offers Circles, Pages and Hangouts and there's tight integration between all Google's services. A good consideration is for project managers to join communities and network with other project managers across the world. Google+ could even be a contender for free project management tools. (Messieh, 2011)

Twitter

Twitter is the most popular micro-blogging tool today and boasts with about 302 million (Statista.com 2015) monthly active users worldwide. It allows you to send short messages to the internet, but limits the update to 140 characters and permits your "tweets" to be protected. The tweets appear on your homepage in a chronological stream, with the most recent comments at the top. Twitter has risen as a useful tool for project teams with many different purposes.

Blogs

Blogs are made up of posts, which are short articles that appear in reverse chronological order on the blog. Blogs have an archive facility which will display historical posts by day, week, or month. It can be a very handy platform to share project information and for team collaboration. "A secure blog can be used to share project information, air concerns and encourage discussion and resolution of problems by everyone involved on the project in an interactive way that cannot be achieved if a team is spread across the globe. A secure blog can be set up on an internal domain with controlled access to provide all the advantages of a blog without the security issues" as per Michelle Symonds. (Symonds, 2012)

Wiki

The Wiki is likely the oldest platform and it's a space in which users can add, modify and delete pages and content using a simple mark-up language. A compelling feature of a wiki is that its structure and content is created and maintained by the users themselves as it is grows and is being used. You can host a wiki on your own server (SharePoint) or use a service company (Socialtext) that offers hosted solutions that allow you to sign up and get started immediately. A wiki is useful to pull all project information together in one place.

Youtube

YouTube with more than 1 billion users (Statista.com 2015) offers hundreds of videos on project management methodology. It is also the 2nd most popular search engine after Google.

WhatsApp

WhatsApp Messenger is a cross-platform mobile messaging app which allows you to exchange messages without having to pay for SMS. With this free messaging service a project manager can facilitate a quick and easy group discussion.

Slideshare

SlideShare is a social network site with an average of 60 million visitors per month and is now owned by LinkedIn. It is used to share professional content like presentations, info-graphics, documents, videos, PDFs and webinars. A great SlideShare can help showcase your expertise and build thought leadership.

Webinar

A webinar is simply a seminar hosted on the web. It is also used to describe other types of meetings where the participants go to a website to see the presentation material. Participants use their web browser to access a website for that meeting. Several platforms exist to use for Webinars like GoToWebinar, Cisco WebEx, SharePoint and Lync. This is a great cost saving tool for geographically distributed project teams.

Podcasts

Podcasts are audio files that can be delivered on-demand and regularly through a mechanism that allows people to subscribe to the latest episodes, like RSS. This has become a very popular medium to share project management topics and to record interviews with experts that are then distributed as podcasts that can be downloaded. It is also widely used in academic settings and project management organizations like the Project Management Institute (PMI), provides podcasts as free education to their members. (PMI. org, 2015) Another form of podcasting is Vodcasts. It's a video stored in a digital form that broadcasts on a specific topic and can be distributed and accessed on demand. It can be downloaded from the internet and played on a computer or a mobile device. On projects a Vodcast can be used for pre-recording a training session for future access, like training of end-users on a new system.

ISSUES AND CHALLENGES

The nature of the modern workplace involving distributed and dynamic teams across time-zones with different cultures, languages and work etiquette calls for the use of enterprise collaborative software.

Virtual Teams

The typical circumstances, under which project teams will make use of the various social media tools, are when members are distributed geographically whilst working on projects.

This increase in virtual teams makes the communication process more challenging; therefore it becomes more difficult to establish strong relationships and bonds that lead to high levels of trust. Communications delivered through social media are potentially a valuable resource for developing trust between project team members. That said, social media tools alone will not drastically improve your projects. The use of social media tools will enable better, more timely communication and more effective knowledge sharing in a dispersed team.

Tension in the Workplace

Despite the wide-spread adoption of social media on projects, some IT departments and leaders remain wary. The fear is often that social tools will drain productivity. Yet, it is the same tools that many team members are already using to make themselves more productive.

The other concern is around information security which requires careful consideration regarding who should have access to social media tools at every level - project, program, portfolio and stakeholder. Be mindful of the security problems, like encryption, that can be encountered when using social media on projects. "Major social media sites such as Google+ and Twitter have enabled encrypted browsing by default, other social networks have left the option for manual adjustments", as highlighted by Jaclyn Bickerton from Raven5. (Bickerton, 2013)

Culture Change

The challenge of bringing in social tools is not because of the technical nature of using the tools themselves, but the cultural change that is necessary to be successful. That's because social isn't just another technology but something that enables entirely new ways of working. People think, act, and communicate in different ways. With social media it's about human beings doing what they do best, that is to socialize and to share.

More often project managers are expected to provide real-time information to stakeholders from any location at any time and social collaboration tools will help to meet the demands of the 24-hour workday. This in itself can present new challenges as stakeholders will have higher expectations to be engaged and to see earlier benefits from projects.

According to Adam Pisoni, co-founder of Yammer: "For enterprise social tools to be effective, they can't just be a destination. Social technology has to be woven into the apps people use every day to unite people, information, and application data in a way that drives greater effectiveness, performance, and agility". (Fast Company, 2015)

The nature of how we work is changing. With the increase in virtual teams and workers using mobile devices, new tools are needed that make it easier to connect, share, and organize across locations, teams, and devices. The technology options are abundant and cost effective.

As work becomes less routine, employees need easier access to the right knowledge and information, to make fast, informed decisions. Knowledge sharing and project visibility are critical as organizations look to project management as a strategic competency that drives new ideas and achieves business results.

Information Overload

With all the social media technology available as communication tools, they can result in more interruptions and therefore more distractions. The various streams of information that social media tools open up to the team, needs to be managed in order to avoid information overload.

In a field like project management which depends heavily on lessons learned and best practices to deliver repeatable results, the available pool of resources you can tap into via social media is very powerful.

Benefits of Using Social Media

Social media tools not only foster communication and availability; they allow for financial savings. The cost of traveling expenses and monthly telephone bills can be reduced by using a tele- and video-conference program to host a meeting.

When implemented and used effectively, social media will serve as a cornerstone of best practices and organizational knowledge. At the end of a lengthy project, it can be handed over to the operational team.

Within project teams it allows for real-time quick, and ad-hoc sharing of information. It provides project managers with the ability to provide real-time information to stakeholders from any location at any time. It is important to agree upfront what the criteria for stakeholder engagement and communication will be and to make that part of the project measures for success.

Project managers will benefit from a professional viewpoint by being able to discuss challenges with other project managers and hear from project managers in different sectors, providing an on-going roundtable that fosters continuous improvement.

Although social media has revolutionized the way we communicate on projects and can be a productivity booster for Project Management Organizations, it cannot replace the human factor. As technology has enabled organizations to automate certain processes, it still remains important to have human, face-to-face, interactions with project teams to follow up. Even when using social media as communication tools, the personal contact among team members remains critical for strong trust relationships and for resolving issues and concerns faster.

SOLUTIONS AND RECOMMENDATIONS

Integration on Projects

Steve Nicholls recommended that a winning strategy is to have an adaptable, step-by-step, ongoing formula to bring social media onto projects. Adopt a unique blend of social media according to the nature and size of the project, different members involved and the environment in which members are operating. (Nicholls, 2012)

According to a Microsoft Office support article, it is best to document how the team should use the tools, when to use the tools, what type of content should be contained, and not contained, in posts. There is a stronger chance of the tools being used when everyone understand some fundamentals about them. (Microsoft Office support, 2015)

Once the decision has been made to integrate social media onto a project, and it is documented, make sure that the project team is in agreement with which social media tools are to be used and how.

Communication among Virtual Teams

With the increase of virtual teams who are distributed geographically whilst working on projects, social tools are driving a faster flow of knowledge and information within and across organizations. Enterprise social tools apply social media principles to the workplace, making it easier for people to share files and information with colleagues, as well as to collaborate as teams across departments and locations.

Social media provides companies with the ability to quickly identify, organize and deploy teams, to collaborate across borders and between departments, and see a measurable organizational benefit.

Culture Change of Using Social Media On Projects

The most salient feature of social media is the focusing on building relationships among team members and with the key stakeholders (figure 1).

Figure 1. Creating a social network

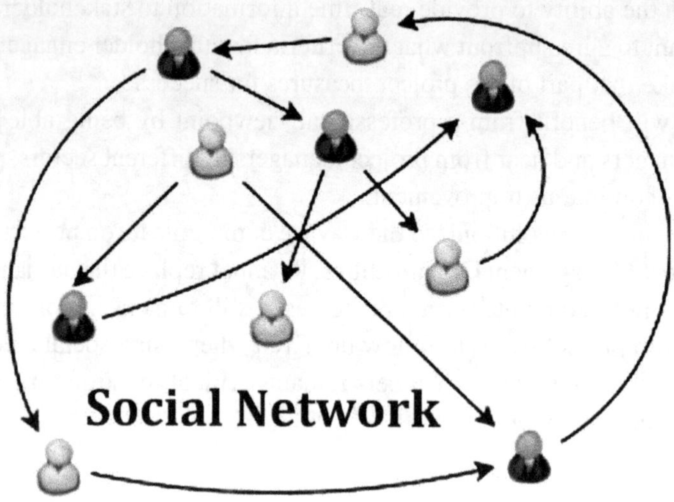

It creates a new culture on the team that is supported and enabled by various technologies and applications on desktops and mobile devices like laptops, tablets and smart phones. "People think, act, and communicate in a completely different way", Colleen Garton states in her book, "The use of social media in project management" (Garton, 2012). People belong to bigger networks within and external to their companies, they share stories, ask questions and research information, because they now operate in a world that's always connected.

How to Address Security Concerns

According to Colleen Garton, we hear much about the dangers of social media, but when we follow standard rules, guidelines and procedures, that helps to minimize risk. (Garton, 2012)

Evaluate the business and communication needs within your organization to determine who should have access to social media tools at every level - project, program, portfolio and stakeholder. Grant and restrict access as per the security guidelines. Ensure senior management develop and enforce (through training and Key Performance Indicators) organizational policies managing the use of mobile devices (an added security threat) and social media in general.

The project needs to align itself with the processes and guidelines adopted by your company to ensure responsible usage of social media and the sharing of information inside and outside of your team to protect company intellectual property. Find out if a social media policy exists. The policy gives guidelines for dealing with confidential and proprietary information and security issues.

Respect the firewall. Implement appropriate social media tools behind your firewall to increase security. This may be a challenge for virtual teams, so establish access rules and policies for remote users.

Present and discuss the policy with project team members. Protect your intellectual property by ensuring that your team knows and understands what can and cannot be shared via social media channels.

Productivity and Rules of Engagement

Establish rules of engagement. Define how social media is to be used by project managers within the organization. Will it be used for training, to manage projects, as a means for research, to network or all of the above? By defining the focus and purpose, it will enable selection of the right social media tools for your project team.

Once the social tools to be used as communication tools on your project, is documented, agreed and part of the Communications Plan, it would ensure the use of the tools in the most productive way. Limit distractions and information overload by sticking to the agreed tools to improve team collaboration.

Assign a social media monitor for each project. It could be a team member or the project manager to monitor social media use for each individual project. This will govern usage and help teams to adhere to social media policies.

RECOMMENDATIONS FOR EACH SOCIAL MEDIA TOOL

Depending on the agreed social media tools selected as communication channels, herewith some practical recommendations for popular platforms. The recommendations are given from two perspectives, one is from a project manager's point of view and the other is from a project team's point of view.

LinkedIn

For Project Managers

As a project manager, consider joining some project management related interest groups that exist on LinkedIn. Within the group, community is built with people who share common interests with the project manager. Connections are made with other project professionals and experts who can answer questions and provide advice. Specialized Forums (e.g. "Energies Project Management") allow for relevant information sharing and best practice discussions for the applicable industry in which the project exists.

Use LinkedIn to research existing or potential team members, partners or service providers to the project. A search for "project management group" delivers thousands or results (7000 results at the time of writing). In the search results, groups with the most members are displayed at the top and the number of active discussions is also shown. A search for "project manager" delivered more than 4.5 million results (Figure 2).

By posting relevant updates about your industry or levels of expertise, become a thought leader in your industry or connect with other thought leaders who you can build relationships with.

Give recommendations to your team members and ask a team member whose opinion is respected, to give you a recommendation at the end of each project. Of course when a project manager is ready to move on to the next project, LinkedIn is great for finding project management positions or to catch the attention of recruiters who are looking for job candidates!

Figure 2. LinkedIn search results for project manager

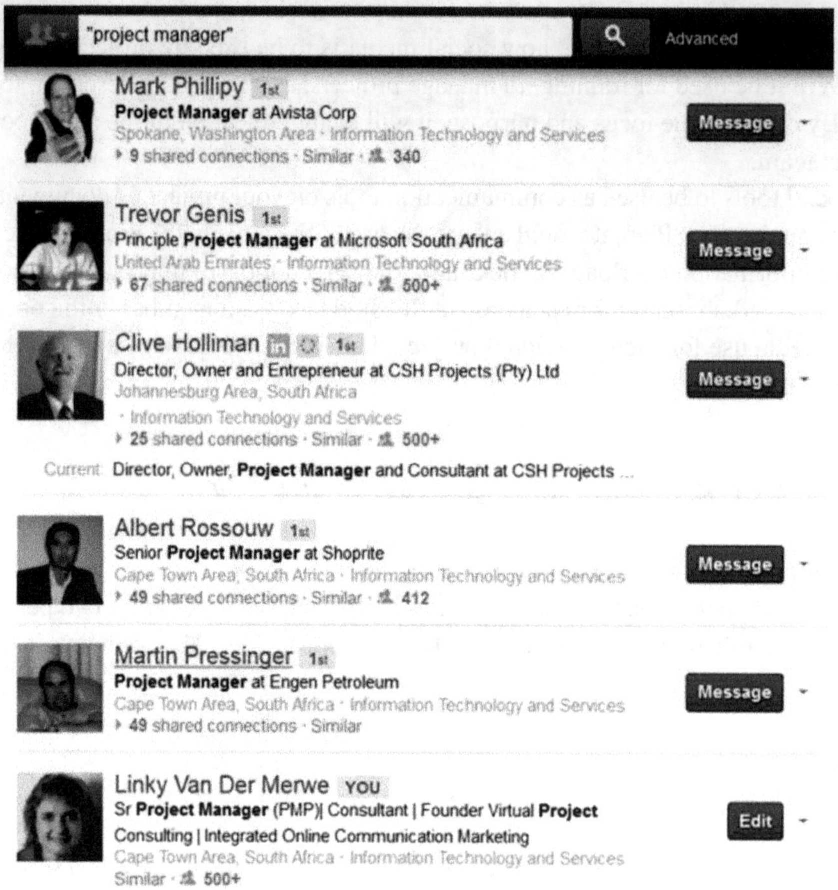

For Team Members

LinkedIn is great for networking with other professionals and people in the same industry. Team members can also research companies having similar projects, who they would want to work for once the project is complete. Research people in your industry who have worked on similar projects than you are, and ask them questions about lessons they've learned on those projects.

Facebook

For Project Managers and Team Members

Research Facebook pages of project management companies or institutions to find out what topics are being discussed, what training or software is offered and what events are hosted.

Like you do socially, project managers can become friends with project management experts, ask them questions or exchange other relevant professional information. Post links to project management articles and news and share with your project management friends. Also join relevant project groups, post updates and participate in discussions.

Instant messaging and video calling can also be used with team members if an enterprise collaboration tool is not available.

Yammer

For Project Managers and Team Members

Use Yammer to share announcements, create a team calendar of milestones, to create pages for different interests and to upload documents. Also consider posting your team norms, latest screenshots of the app for team members to comment on, and sharing video updates or team photos.

Yammer allows for more in-depth updates and comments can also be grouped into a "thread" beneath each post, allowing for a more conversational tone.

Consider this case study of using Yammer on a nation-wide project. Yammer was rolled out at a restaurant chain to 2500 managers and staff in its corporate office. When the company introduced a new burger to its menu, managers used the enterprise social network to deliver customer feedback straight from its restaurants. That helped them refine the recipe in a month which was a fraction of the time it would have taken in the past.

Another project that the same restaurant chain used Yammer - with great success, was to introduce the platform as part of a new interactive training program for their young workforce of hourly wage earners. To encourage engagement, they were reached through their mobile phones using Yammer. They could use it to ask questions and give feedback during training, as well as to upload videos of new practices. These practices could then be incorporated into future training. (Pisoni, 2015)

Google+

For Project Managers and Team Members

Use Google+ for social networking, to collaborate in real-time and to share ideas. On this platform you can join Pages and communities.

Invite all project team members to join Google+. Add the team members to a circle that's created for the project. Share specific project feedback and information only with this circle consisting of the project team members. Also use for chat (instant messaging).

With Google Hangouts, a live video chat that will create meaningful two-way communication can be used to connect with your team members, stakeholders and customers via a video chat. The conversation can also be recorded so that it can be viewed at a later time. During a Hangout you can share your screen and demonstrate new software or systems and receive immediate feedback. It is perfect to share data in real time, for a team to brainstorm or to teach. Team members can also join by telephone.

Find multiple interest groups to join discussions, watch webinars or to join other Google hang-outs. With built-in authorship verification, Google+ will serve up your relevant posts in search results.

Consider this case study. In Twitter when you do a search for #PMHangouts you will discover a Hangout for project managers who are members of the Sensible Project Manager Community on Google+

which was started by Mark Phillipy. Members of the community share ideas via Google+ Hangout about various project management topics. Those not making it to the hangout can view the conversation via Hangouts "On-Air" or view the archives of each hangout afterwards on the SensiblePM YouTube Channel.

Twitter

For Project Managers

Twitter can be most useful for project managers in general. Use the search function to find good articles about specific project management topics and best practices (figure 3).

Hashtags (keywords preceded by the #) are used to help index and filter topics. For example, the hashtag '#pmot' is used for tweets about "project management on Twitter". When you click on the hashtag, you will collect tweets that use the same tag and then be able to track conversations. This is a simple way that users can quickly filter for only tweets about specific subjects.

Also search for tweets by typing the hashtag in the Twitter search box. Other useful hashtags for PM's are: #projectmanager, #pmp, #project, #msproject, #project2010, and #pm.

Tools like TweetDeck help users manage multiple conversations at once. Twitter is a good option for fast, short (140 characters) interactions with easy indexing of topics. Every Friday there's #PMChat for Tweetups. This is an innovative way for project managers to get answers to project management questions and obtain different perspectives.

On the Home page of Twitter, your Twitter timeline can get cluttered very quickly. Twitter lists become useful as it allows you to group Twitter users. Make a list of other users who are also in Project Management, for example Project Managers. Every time you follow a person on Twitter who is also a project manager, you add them to your list.

By following this process a project manager will soon connect with project managers from all over the world to follow and collaborate with. Also follow other people's PM lists.

As project managers we can also contribute as part of the PM community. This can be achieved by sharing your knowledge and experiences on Twitter by posting a useful link or a lesson learnt. This way you can connect with people who have common interests and goals.

Figure 3. Twitter search results for #pmot

For Project Teams

Project team members need to use their own Twitter handles when using Twitter as a project communications tool. The social media monitor of the project can create a list consisting of the project team members relating to the project they are working on. The URL of the list is sent to the team members so that they can see who were added.

Create a Team hashtag # – a project team can decide on its own hashtags for the projects they're working on. For example if your team is working on a business application project, you could decide on a hashtag to use across Twitter, such as #busapp. Then use this hashtag to keep team members updated on daily progress. This is useful for a virtual and widely distributed team. It will work for projects where security is less of a concern. It's easy to use and allows for quick and near immediate communication.

Blogs

For Project Managers and Team Members

In the case of a long-term project, running over several months or even years, use a Project Blog to publish all project documentation. Decide whether you want to use external blogging sites or internal blogs. Many products are available internally for example Microsoft SharePoint or SharePoint Online (Office 365) contains a blogging feature that an organization can use to create a blog that is private to a project team. External sites include WordPress or Blogger.

A blog can be used to publish progress reports as well as for major milestone announcements. A blog is a great way to keep the team informed of the major phases that are coming up, as well as to recognize the good work the team has accomplished as milestones are passed.

Keep the blog interesting by posting pictures of a product in various stages, or of people who are making a product that aren't usually in the company newsletter. The social media Monitor would come in handy to keep the blog up to date on a weekly basis.

Use blog features such as comments fields, as well as tags and ratings features. Collect feedback as part of bi-directional communication.

Wiki

For Project Teams

A wiki is a good option if you want to create a space for a project team, but don't want to dictate how it's organized or actively manage it as an administrator. Use a Wiki as an online documentation platform that allows the creation and editing of interlinked websites. It is recommended to capture this data in a structured way as the project progresses.

Pull all the project information together in one place and stay connected with the project team. A Wiki can include a project blog, a place for to-do items, team profile pages, a file storage area, and more! Wikis are flexible and can serve as the backbone for a small team's shared notebook or an entire corporate intranet.

For Project Managers

Wikis can also be used at a PMO level for gathering lessons learned throughout the course of various projects. It's good as a knowledge base.

Since Wikis are easy to search (archive), project managers have fast access to information relevant to their work and can update that information with knowledge that could lead to future improvements.

Youtube

For Project Managers and Team Members

Many people prefer video to text with certain types of information. For distributed teams, set each group up with the means to create video updates. Not only will the status reports be more engaging, but putting faces to names creates a closer, more respectful team.

Let your stakeholders know your videos are intended to give them better and more compelling information.

An example of how a project management company makes good use of videos, is projectmanager.com – who distribute free videos as a marketing tool to educate people about project management and to promote their software (Figure 4).

Instant Messaging

For Project Managers and Team Members

Real time communication is provided by instant messaging or chat as well as other features beyond sending text. Teams can send links, attach files and even do video conferencing.

Figure 4. Jennifer Whitt, Director of ProjectManager.com uses White Board sessions that are very educational and easy to watch.

This is an enterprise wide tool where the technology client exists on all desktops and devices. It has the ability to show presence which will indicate if a person is available, busy, in a meeting or away from the network.

It's very effective to obtain quick answers to a question, that can't wait for an email reply, similar to a phone call, but quicker. This tool is generally well understood and often the fastest method to communicate between distributed team members.

The output from chats can be stored. The instant messaging tool may have settings that sends the chat to you as an email after the session ends, so check if this is turned on and use it if it is available. These can then become project documents and can be stored and archived in the same way as meeting minutes.

Examples of tools available are Microsoft Lync, also available in Office 365, as well as OpenFire and Spark. With WhatsApp the mobile messaging app, users can, in addition to basic messaging, create groups, send each other unlimited images, video and audio media messages.

SlideShare

For Project Managers

SlideShare is a great tool for a project manager to build visibility and thought leadership by sharing non-confidential presentations or documents about project management.

A search on "project management" will render thousands of presentations about project management and related topics.

Webinar

For Project Managers

There are companies who often host webinars covering useful project management topics, allowing attendees to be present through an internet connection. The technology allows attendees to ask questions and to have them answered live by the presenter.

An example of such a webinar event, is the annual International Project Management day in November hosted by the International Institute for Learning (IIL). Some project management training providers will host webinars weekly on relevant project management topics and allow contributions from people in the profession. Examples of such a webinars are Roeder Consulting and PM Centers USA who host free monthly webinars.

For Project Teams

A Webinar is a very useful platform for subject matter experts to present a topic to a virtual team attending from different parts of the country or even the world.

Podcasts

For Project Managers

Numerous project management topics are discussed on podcasts. Nowadays you can subscribe to podcast feeds using iTunes, Stitcher Radio or SoundCloud. It is convenient to download podcasts and listen to them at your own time.

Existing Project Management Professionals (PMP), can listen to podcasts that will count towards professional development units (PDU's). An example of a well-known Podcast service is "The Project Management Podcast" from Cornelius Fichtner.

Social Media Tool Selection

When developing a social media action plan for the project team use these five questions from Michael Klynstra to gather information from your team: (Klynstra, 2012)

1. How sensitive is content that would be shared? Twitter does offer capabilities to secure tweets and send direct messages away from the public. Yammer and a self-hosted wiki are examples of private spaces.
2. Is your communication unidirectional or bidirectional? If you are looking for a new way to communicate status, Vimeo allows for password-protected videos or setting access. To get your entire team talking together, look for a platform with a forum-style area such as a LinkedIn group or wiki for your team to post updates, and to comment and converse in a free-form way.
3. Do you have a social platform budget? While most platforms offer free or low-cost versions with basic functionality, tiered pricing can get you more. Based on your platform selection and tiered pricing structures, get a sense of what it will cost.
4. What social platforms do team members use today? Take a poll on what people use, to gauge levels of interest in trying something out. Introducing social tools always introduces the challenge of adoption, so to think about how to get people engaged.
5. Keep it Personal or make it Professional? Work with your team to determine what info will be shared; whether team members should use their personal accounts or create professional accounts.

FUTURE RESEARCH DIRECTIONS

Social Software

The forecast from Forrester is that Enterprise social software is to become a $6.4 billion market worldwide by 2016 and that organizations will continue to increase their spending on enterprise collaboration software. Technology options have become abundant and cost effective.

The implication of this is that social media will become more widely available as part of enterprise tools and will be vital to facilitate communication among project team members.

A sure sign of this being a trend that will continue, is that several companies have incorporated social media into project management information systems, for example:

- AtTask
- CentralDesk
- Liquid Planner
- MangoProjects
- ProjectPlace
- Teambox
- Zoho Projects

Project Collaboration

According to Wrike, a project management software company, project collaboration remains essential for the growth of business today. There are three main trends shaping project collaboration and driving the adoption of new tools.

1. Remote work is becoming more common as more people in multiple industries start working remotely.
2. The number of "accidental project managers" is rising as people need to take on the project management role without certification or experience in project management methodologies and practices.
3. Collaboration via Cloud Services is on the rise. In order for distributed teams to keep working together and to have visibility into one another's work, they are using cloud service for example storage services such as Dropbox, Sky Drive or Google Drive. Communication tools like Skype and Google Hangouts are used more to facilitate meetings and work management tools like Wrike enterprise collaboration software.

Another collaboration solution is "Crowd-sourcing" which will allow teams to tap into a much broader range of expertise and experience of possible solutions, at all times of the day and night, globally.

Virtual Work Teams

The trend of geographically dispersed project teams will continue with the increase of company mergers and acquisitions bringing teams together from various locations. There are also more Generation Y and Millennials demanding a level of work-life balance that involves less travel and more time at home with family.

Both of these trends mean that increasingly, project teams may be spread among various locations and even time zones. The successful project manager will need to know how to use project collaboration tools and effectively manage virtual teams.

Communities of Best Practice

Social media provides an excellent vehicle for fostering communities of best practice while exposing project managers to a framework of experience, collaboration, and knowledge. This is learning that requires informal contact and a willingness to share information which is a perfect use of social media. The availability of industry thought-leaders willing to collaborate and mentor, can play a vital role in building up project management knowledge in organizations.

More research into case studies of projects where social media was successfully integrated, is required. With more project managers realizing the value of using social media tools on projects and with more enterprise project management software incorporating social media into systems, the adoption is expected to grow and more case studies will become readily available.

CONCLUSION

Project management practitioners should not ignore the growing trend of social media tools adoption, as well as the incorporation of social media into project management information systems. Just as knowledge and understanding of project management methodologies, processes and a project life cycle is vital to perform successfully as a project manager, an appreciation of social media as a communication and collaboration tool is now essential.

To aid project managers to understand social media better, the chapter focused on giving best practice recommendations for popular and well-known tools, both from a project manager and from a team member perspective. Advice is given on how to address concerns, overcome challenges and how to make the best social media selection for the project team by having an agreed social media action plan.

By starting at the right place, namely having a social media policy in place, adhering to the guidelines for privacy and security, analyzing which tools would best fit your organization and then agreeing on selected tools for use on projects, a project manager would be on track to integrate social media successfully onto projects.

Be practical and specific around the use of the tools, agree on the success metrics and what the expected benefits are, and regularly monitor these metrics. This will improve your ability to measure the performance afterwards.

Try using the selected social media tools on projects from beginning to end, so that you can learn from your mistakes and your achievements and share your story as a case study for future project managers.

REFERENCES

Harrin, E. (2011). *Get started using social media on your projects* (3rd ed.). Newtown Square, PA: Project Management Institute Press.

Pritchard, C. (2013). *The Project Management Communications Toolkit* (2nd ed.). USA: Artech House.

Nicholls, S. (2011). Social media in business (Ch. 2, p. 84). UK: Bookinars.

Garton, C., & McCulloch, E. (2012). Fundamentals of Technology Project Management (2nd ed.). The Use of Social Media in Project Management. Canada: MC Press.

Remidez, R., & Jones, N.B. (2012) Developing a Model for Social Media in Project Management Communications. *International Journal of Business and Social Science*, 3(3), 33-36. Retrieved from http://www.ijbssnet.com/journals/Vol_3_No_3_February_2012/3.pdf

Microsoft Office Support. (2015). Use Twitter, Facebook and other social media to help manage projects and teams. Retrieved from https://support.office.microsoft.com/en-za/article/Use-Twitter-Facebook-and-other-social-media-to-help-manage-projects-and-teams

First Round Review. (2015). Adam Pisoni explains how a culture shift toward transparency, experimentation and empowerment can make companies more successful. Retrieved from http://www.fastcompany.com/3042221/hit-the-ground-running/how-yammers-cofounder-impressed-bill-gates-with-a-story-about-a-burger

Digital Information World. (2015). Fascinating Social Media Stats 2015. Retrieved from http://www.digitalinformationworld.com/2015/02/fascinating-social-networking-stats-2015.html

The Statistics Portal for Statistics and Studies. (2015). Retrieved from http://www.statista.com

Project Management Institute. a professional membership association (2015). Retrieved from http://www.pmi.org/Learning/podcasts.aspx

Worsley, L. (2015). The LinkedIn effect: a new way of learning – Focus on project management communities. Retrieved from http://www.slideshare.net/PiCubed/the-linkedin-effect-a-new-way-of-learning

Young, T. (2013). Four million reasons why you should be on LinkedIn. Retrieved from http://www.smartcompany.com.au/leadership/professional-development/40412-how-linkedin-has-grown-to-be-an-influential-business-network.html#

Klynstra, M. (2012). Social media applied to project teams. Retrieved from http://www.geneca.com/social-media-meets-project-management/

Guarino, J. (2012). Social media for project managers. Evolutionary IT. Retrieved from http://www.evolutionaryit.com/presentations/social_media_for_project_managers.pdf

Jensen, J. 2012. Social media for project management. Retrieved from http://www.slideshare.net/jonniejensen/social-media-for-project-management

Symonds, M. 2012. Social Media in the project management arena. Retrieved from Parallel Project Training: http://blog.parallelprojecttraining.com/project-management-articles/social-media-in-the-project-management-arena/

Messieh, N. 2011. How Google+ could become an essential business tool. Retrieved from http://thenextweb.com/google/2011/07/13/how-google-could-become-an-essential-business-tool/

ADDITIONAL READING

Salesforce. (n. d.). Retrieved from http://www.salesforce.com/chatter/

Yammer. (n. d.). Retrieved from http://www.yammer.com

Jive software. (n. d.). Retrieved from http://www.jivesoftware.com

Socialtext. (n. d.). Retrieved from http://www.socialtext.com

Wrike. (n. d.). Retrieved from https://www.wrike.com/enterprise-project-management/

Telligent. (n. d.). Retrieved from http://www.telligent.com

Office 365. (n. d.). Retrieved from http://www.microsoft.com/en-us/office365/

Google business apps. (n. d.). Retrieved from http://www.google.com/enterprise/apps/business/

Pells, D. (2015). PM World Today: Current trends and future predictions. Retrieved from http://www.projectmanagement.ie/images/assets/pdf/currenttrends.pdf

Bonnie, E. (2015). Trends in IT Project Management for 2015. Retrieved from https://www.wrike.com/blog/trends-project-management-2015/

Valdellon, L. (2014). Where Collaboration is heading in 2015: Top 4 trends to watch. Retrieved from https://www.wrike.com/blog/collaboration-heading-2015-top-4-trends-watch/

Van Der Merwe, L. (2014). Project Manager – How to Integrate Social Media with your Projects. Retrieved from http://www.virtualprojectconsulting.com/project-manager-how-to-integrate-social-media-with-your-projects-2/

Van Der Merwe, L. (2014). Can Social Media drive project success? Retrieved from http://www.virtualprojectconsulting.com/can-social-media-drive-project-success/

Van Der Merwe, L. (2012). Project managers are you Twitter smart? Retrieved from http://www.virtualprojectconsulting.com/project-managers-are-you-twitter-smart/

Van Der Merwe, L. (2013). Practical use for social media in project management series. Retrieved from http://www.virtualprojectconsulting.com/practical-use-for-social-media-in-project-management/

Mullaly, M. (2012). The Social Storm. Retrieved from http://www.projectmanagement.com/articles/271280/The-Social-Storm

Wood, M. (2014). Social Media: A key to project success? Retrieved from http://www.projectmanagement.com/articles/287660/Social-Media--A-Key-to-Project-Success-

Donoghue, M. (2014). Social media policy: Protecting yourself and your project team. Retrieved from http://www.projectmanagement.com/articles/283197/Social-Media-Policy--Protecting-Yourself-and-Your-Project-Team-

Bickerton, J. (2013). Top 10: Social Media security issues with Infographic. Retrieved from http://www.raven5.agency/blog/top-10-social-media-security-issues-2013

KEY TERMS AND DEFINITIONS

Enterprise Social Software: Enterprise social software describes social networking and collaboration tools used in large organizations. It's a category of software systems that primarily functions to allow user collaboration and communication, for example instant messaging, wikis and blogs.

Google Hangout: A live video chat similar to a Skype video call.

Hashtag: A Hashtag, #, is put in front of a word and then used to help index and filter the subject matter of your tweet.

Info Graphics: Graphic with pictures and words to explain difficult or often boring concepts in an interesting and visually appealing way.

LinkedIn Influencer Program: The Influencer network consists of high-profile CEOs, entrepreneurs and thought leaders from every major industry.

PMO: Project Management Office, a department within an organization that maintains the governance and standards for project management within the organization.

RSS: Really Simple Syndication: RSS is the acronym used to describe the de facto standard for the syndication of Web content.

Software as a Service (SaaS): A software distribution model where the software is hosted by a vendor or service provider and made available through over the network. It is licenses on a subscription basis and it is centrally hosted. The main benefits to customers are that you don't have to invest in additional hardware and you only pay for what you use.

SoundCloud: An audio platform enabling users to upload, record and promote their sounds.

Stitcher Radio: An on-demand internet radio service providing radio shows and podcasts.

Vimeo: A video-sharing website in which users can upload, share and view videos.

Chapter 10
An Integrated Approach to Collaborative Learning in Projects

Giuliana Teixeira Veronese
Stefanini IT Solutions, Brazil

Marcirio Chaves
Nove de Julho University, Brazil

ABSTRACT

Information Technologies 2.0 (IT 2.0) is transforming the project management by improving communication and collaboration. It provides better experience than the traditional software package allowing document sharing, integrated task tracking, enforcing team processes and agile planning. Despite the benefits brought by IT 2.0, their use to promote lessons learned (LL) remains unexplored. For many project managers to obtain and integrate information from different tools of previous similar projects remains a challenge. This chapter emphasizes the need of combining traditional LL processes and methods with IT 2.0. It describes the IT 2.0 uses and how these technologies can support LL processes and methods in project settings. It delivers a proposal focusing on both IT 2.0-centered LL processes and an updating of traditional LL methods with IT 2.0. This proposal aims to help project managers to improve the management of LL and, as a result, the project learning.

INTRODUCTION

Projects are executed in the organization to produce and develop goods and services and present challenges during their lifecycle including contractual problems, inaccurate estimation, low team performance, lack of knowledge of providers and turnover of professionals. Identify each challenge and act proactively looking for solutions to each specific situation that occurs is crucial to achieve the projects objectives. The use of processes, methods and techniques that allow to document and distribute the knowledge obtained in each experience during the projects lifecycle is a valuable tool for organizations ensuring to reduce costs and risks and to increment productivity and competitive edge.

DOI: 10.4018/978-1-4666-9867-3.ch010

Lessons learned (LL) is a well-known project management tool and can be defined as the learning gained during the process of performing a project. This learning should be usefully applied on future projects to promote the recurrence of desirable outcomes and to avoid or mitigate possible problems. Project managers used to have difficulties to manage LL during the project. Schindler and Eppler (2003) found that the main causes of the lack of documentation of LL on projects are time, motivation, discipline and skills. On the other hand, nine percent of the respondents were willing to contribute to the documentation due to the time and level of effort required. In this same vein, Petter and Vaishnavi (2008) found that 64% of participants in an experiment reported having learned from the documents filed by his peers. These data are encouraging to raise awareness about the management of LL in the project team.

To minimize the time and effort, web 2.0 tools (IT 2.0, henceforward, e.g. microblogs, blogs and wikis) can be an alternative to be explored. Emerging IT 2.0 and applications start to gain visibility and use by project managers to better support daily tasks and processes (Grace, 2009; Shang, Li, Wu, & Hou, 2011). Despite the use of IT 2.0 be broad in Project Management (PM) (e.g. creation of deliverables, status reports, 'great ideas' saved for later, standards and practices), this chapter focuses on their use to cope with LL. IT 2.0 need to be better grasped to store, capture, share and disseminate LL in a project. Although some projects successfully deal with LL, this subject remains being an appellant challenge to project managers, since as Polanyi (1966) stated 'we can know more than we can tell.' One of the issues approached in this chapter is to provide facilities to capture LL from the project team. The aim of this chapter is to present theoretical background about LL processes and methods and discuss how to use IT 2.0 to support LL in PM. Instead of using commercial and legacy LL systems such those listed by Weber et al. (2001), free IT 2.0 can provide a simple, easy and more efficient way to deal with LL.

USING INFORMATION TECHNOLOGY 2.0 IN PROJECTS

The uses of IT 2.0 include supporting knowledge management, collaboration and communication, training, and innovation (Andriole, 2010). IT 2.0 have also the potential to complement, enhance, and add new collaborative dimensions to the processes of storing, capturing, sharing, disseminating and applying LL. Further, these technologies afford the advantage of reducing the technical skill required to use their features, allowing users to focus on the exchange of LL and collaborative tasks themselves without the distraction of a complex technological environment. The main IT 2.0 to be applied to PM and LL include wikis, blogs and microblogs, which are described in the following.

A *wiki* is a web application which allows people to edit content in collaboration with others. Wikis has been used to support creation and sharing of knowledge within communities in projects and organizations since at least ten years ago (Bean & Hott, 2005, Majchrzak, Wagner, & Yates, 2006, Wiewiora & Murphy, 2015). Wikis have unique features such as collaborative authorship, instant publication, versioning and simplicity of authorship. Grace (2009) highlights other advantages in the usage of wikis, including ease of use, central repository for information, tracking and revision feature, collaboration among organizations and solve information overload by e-mail. Parker and Chao (2007) emphasize their use to enhance the learning process. Wikis have been also used to support the following organizational processes: knowledge codification, communities of practice, interaction with third parties, information systems development and maintenance, management activities and organizational response in crisis situation (Lykourentzou, Dagka, Papadaki, Lepouras, & Vassilakis, 2012). One type of wiki widely used internally in a corporate context is Corporate Wiki (Grace, 2009). Majchrzak, Wagner and Yates

(2006) conducted a survey with 168 corporate wiki users in which emerged three main types of benefits from corporate wikis: enhanced reputation, work made easier, and helping the organization to improve its processes. Wikis allow implementing the process or task of socially constructed knowledge creation. In a PM perspective, corporate wikis can be implemented to support collaboration among coworkers. Choosing a wiki platform can be also a challenging task of a project manager, who can take into account the wiki's selection and implementation framework proposed by Grace (2009). Wikis platforms usually contain a set of built-in or embedded IT 2.0 such as blogs, Rich Site Summary (RSS), and tagging. RSS is a set of web feed formats used to publish frequently updated works such as wiki and blog entries, audio and video in a standardized format. RSS allows project members to be automatically notified of updates in a wiki or a blog been used in a project, eliminating the need of periodic visits to search for updates in these sites.

A *blog* is a discussion or informational site published on the Web and consisting of entries typically displayed in reverse chronological order. Most blogs are interactive (i.e. open to comments by visitors) and have a set of characteristics that allow them to gain popularity. The technical and behavioral characteristics of project blogs are very lightweight, chronologically sequenced, easily skimmed, and entries easily accessed (Grudin, 2006). In a survey of 212 blog participants, Hsu & Lin (2008) found that ease of use and enjoyment, and knowledge sharing (altruism and reputation) was positively related to attitude toward blogging. Chai e Kim (2010) made a relationship between trust and the sharing of information in blogs environment and results indicated that trust has a positive impact on information sharing. Gholami and Murugesan (2011) add the main applications in which blogs are being used in projects and organizations: 1. for collaboration of team members in a distributed software team (collaboration tool from one to many); 2. Exchanging ideas and conduct brainstorming; 3. Sharing information about the employee profile (containing personal and professional information); and 4. Providing interaction among project team and stakeholders.

Microblogging 'allow[s] users to exchange small elements of content such as short sentences, individual images, or video links' (Kaplan & Haenlein, 2010). It is a broadcast medium in the form of blogging that allows users to write brief text updates (usually less than 200 characters) and publish them, either to be viewed by anyone or by a restricted group which can be chosen by the user. Notable active microblogging services are Twitter, Identi.ca, Tout and Yammer. The simplicity and ability to post frequently seem to be what attract most to the concept. The characteristics also make the use of microblogs successful include 1. Creation of ambient awareness; and 2. Push-push-pull communication (Kaplan & Haenlein, 2011). Creation of ambient awareness refers that in combination, different tweets sent out over time can paint a very accurate picture of a person's activities. This feature allows project managers follow the progress of a team as well as the individual members. Push-push-pull communication refers to the feature of one author's tweets are automatically pushed onto the Twitter main page of all followers. If the receiver of the message finds the news so interesting and intriguing that he decides to give it an additional push by re-tweeting it to their own followers. Once the message has been pushed and pushed again through the whole network, it may motivate some user to go out and 'pull' additional information on the subject from other sources. This feature makes it easy to augment the knowledge among the members of a project. Literature is rich in examples of use of microblogs by organizations (Günther, Krasnova, Riehle, & Schoendienst, 2009). Directly related to the main topic of this chapter, Günther et al. (2009) refer that microblogs improve internal organizational transparency and knowledge sharing, reduce e-mail overload and facilitate the need to find specialists in specific subjects. Considering that LL are often informally reported microblogging has the potential to support this communication among coworkers.

In addition to wikis, blogs and microblogs, other IT 2.0 tools and services can be used in projects. A social bookmarking service is a centralized online service which enables users to add, annotate, edit, and share bookmarks of web documents (Noll & Meinel, 2007). In the context of PM, the use of a platform of bookmarking (e.g. diggo.com) among members of a project is crucial to capture and share LL from external environment. Technical problems are often discussed in specialized forums and blogs which store and describe a set of recurring problems and solutions. Once a project member find a useful LL in a forum or blog, he/she can bookmark the web site or page and share it with co-workers. Moreover, the search process is facilitated by the use of tags. For instance, LL about the planning phase of a project can be bookmarked with the tag 'planning', which can help further searches about this topic.

Finally, as social networks (e.g. Facebook), VoIP (Voice over Internet Protocol - e.g. Skype) and Web-based Office Suite (e.g. googledrive.com) can be considered the most popular IT 2.0, this chapter will not describe them. Next section describes how to better leverage IT 2.0 and applications to support the management of LL along a project.

THE MANAGEMENT OF LESSONS LEARNED

Learning organizations are 'organizations where people continually expand their capacity to create the results they truly desire, where new and expansive patterns of thinking are nurtured, where collective aspiration is set free, and where people are continually learning how to learn together' (Senge, 1991, p.8). LL are an intrinsic part of learning organizations. Project Management Institute (2013) defines LL as the knowledge gained during a project which shows how project events were addressed or should be addressed in the future with the purpose of improving further performance.

Although the literature is rich in the definitions of LL, this paper adopts the one proposed by Secchi, Ciaschi, & Spence (1999). 'A lesson learned is a knowledge or understanding gained by experience. The experience may be positive, as in a successful test or mission, or negative, as in a mishap or failure. Successes are also considered sources of LL. A lesson must be significant in that it has a real or assumed impact on operations; valid in that is factually and technically correct; and applicable in that it identifies a specific design, process, or decision that reduces or eliminates the potential for failures and mishaps, or reinforces a positive result.' LL can be categorized as follows (Weber et al., 2001):

- **Informational** (e.g. how employee's duties could be changed during times of emergencies);
- **Successful** (e.g. capture effective responses to a crisis);
- **Problem** (i.e. describe examples of actions that failed and potential ways to resolve them).

However, Weber et al. (2001) suggest categorizing lessons by their contribution rather than, or at least in addition to, the type of experience from which they were derived (e.g. success or failure).

Lessons Learned Processes

The literature on learning organizations has described a set of LL processes named as follows: collect, capture, gather, verify, store, share, distribute, disseminate, reuse, and apply. Weber et al. (2001) propose four LL processes: collect, verify, store, and disseminate. They also highlight the sub-processes into each of process proposed by them.

Five sub-processes compose the collection process: passive collection, reactive collection, after action collection, proactive collection and active collection. Passive collection occurs when organizational members submit their own lessons using a form (e.g. online). In reactive collection, members are interviewed to collect lesson. After action collection is accomplished during or near the completion of a project. In proactive collection, lessons are captured while problems are solved. Active collection can be carried out through two ways: 1. Active scan attempts to find lessons in documents and in communications among organization's members; 2. Problems demanding lessons are identified and a collection event is planned to obtain relevant lessons.

The process of verification focuses on validating LL for correctness, consistency, redundancy, and relevance. The store process addresses issues related to the representation (e.g., level of abstraction) and indexing of lessons, formatting, and the repository's framework. Lesson representations can be structured, semi-structured, or in different media (e.g., text, video, audio) (Weber et al., 2001).

The process of dissemination is also decomposed into five sub-processes: Passive dissemination, which users search for lessons in a (usually) standalone retrieval tool. In active casting lessons are broadcast to potential users via a dedicated list server. Broadcasting uses bulletins are sent to everybody in the organization, as is made in some LL organizations. In the active dissemination sub-process, users are dynamically notified of relevant lessons in the context of their decision-making process. In the proactive dissemination sub-process the system builds a model of the user's interface events to predict when to prompt users with relevant lessons. Finally, the reactive dissemination occurs when users realize they need additional knowledge, they can invoke a help system to obtain relevant lessons and related information (Weber et al., 2001).

The essential processes to simplify the management of LL are described below:

- **Raise Awareness:** This process deals with the social aspects and people in the context of LL. Raise awareness means convince and motivates projects managers and team members about the relevance of the document LL. This process is supported by existing theories (Sense, 2004; Jugdev & Wishart, 2014) and by the Social Processes framework (Brookes et al., 2006);
- **Capture:** The process of bringing together information or knowledge from different sources has been indistinctly denominated gather and collect in the PM literature. In this paper the process of capture includes to gather and collect LL. To gather means to bring together information which are spread around within a short distance; to collect means to get examples of something from different people or places that are physically separated; and to capture is to represent or record in lasting form (Hornby & Turnbull, 2010). In a PM perspective, the capture of LL includes information spread around within a short distance and people physically separated. LL can be captured through text, audio, video or image;
- **Storage:** The storage process searches to define the environment where LL will be stored. It should consider a range of formats to allow the capture process to collect talks (audio and video), technical procedures (image and video), and formal and informal documentation (text);
- **Share and Verify:** Share LL means to make them available at the same time for a team of experts who focuses on validating them for correctness, consistency, redundancy, and relevance (Weber et al., 2001). Moreover, each lesson need to meet the criteria proposed by Secchi, Ciaschi, & Spence (1999): to be significant, valid and applicable;

- **Distribute or Disseminate:** To spread the knowledge contained in the LL by a team, department or organization;
- **Apply or Reuse:** To make useful the LL on current and further projects;
- **Withdraw:** To recognize when an LL is no longer useful on current and further projects.

IT 2.0-centered Lessons Learned Processes

IT 2.0 is transforming the PM in a thousand of organizations by improving communication and collaboration. The new generation of web-based collaborative tools (e.g. application lifecycle management tools) provides much better experience than the traditional software package allowing document sharing, integrated task tracking, enforcing team processes and agile planning. Despite of the benefits brought by IT 2.0, the use of these technologies to promote LL remains completely unexplored. For many project managers to obtain and integrate information from different tools of previous similar projects in global organizations remains a challenge.

As presented in the previous sections to promote LL reuse the literature defines processes to collect, validate, store, and disseminate. This section discusses the application of IT 2.0 in the LL context presenting interesting differences in the implementation of the core of LL processes. One of the objectives is to provide an integrated vision of a set of technologies that could be used by project members promoting the application and reuse of LL. This proposal suggests an innovation in the knowledge management letting the project team collaborate and share information easily. Figure 1 outlines such vision.

Figure 1. Using IT 2.0 in project management
Source: Chaves and Veronese (2014)

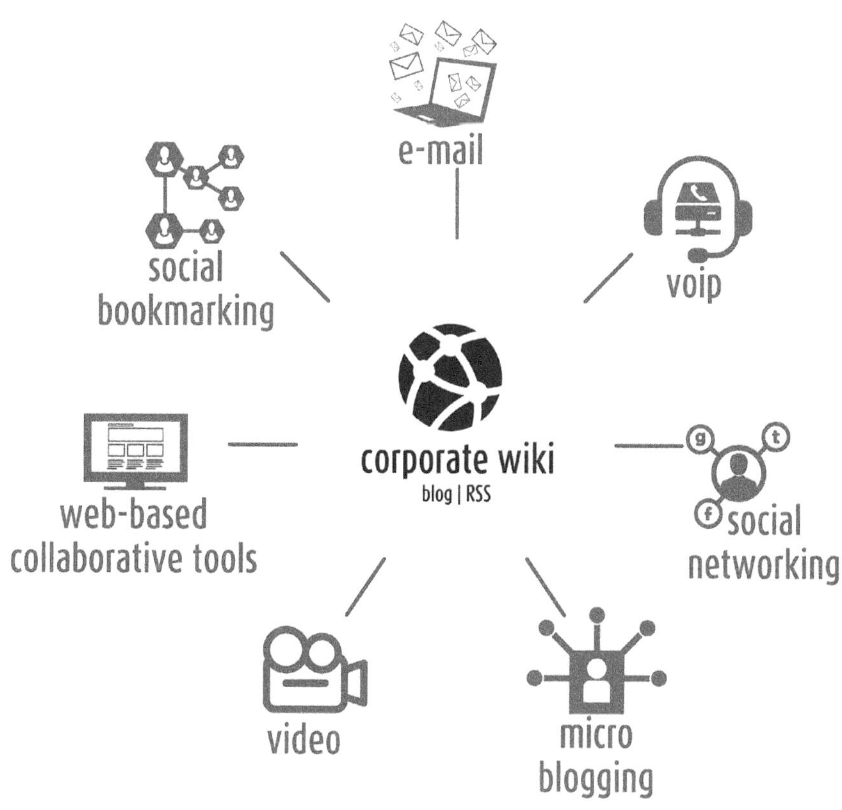

In this proposal a wiki platform is used as a centralized repository of LL collected during the entire project life cycle. The centralized repository facilitates the access of all information related to the projects. The blog and RSS technologies are built-in or embedded in order to facilitate LL capture and dissemination respectively. In spite of providing a flexible structure and taking into account the different preferences of project members (e.g. one prefers use voice, other texts), this proposal presents a broad use of IT 2.0. Orbiting around the wiki platform are the following technologies: microblogging, social bookmarking, social network, video, VoIP and web-based collaborative tools.

Due to the strong acceptance of internal and external social networks (Andriole, 2010; Moqbel, 2012), the organization or the knowledge management officer should define and adopt a social network model in order to promote communication and dissemination. LL can be also shared by the team members through posts in microblogs using hashtags in order to facilitate information retrieval. The wiki should present minimal structured information to identify the project and URLs of collaborators to allow that all members have access to the discussions posted in the social network. Videos recorded in meetings or in the execution of technical procedures, relevant conversations carried out through VoIP and URLs of the documents in web-based collaborative tools should be also stored in the wiki. The flexibility provided by IT 2.0 allows integrating project information managed for different applications and media.

Figure 1 indicates that corporate wikis are the most complete tool to support LL. In this sense, instead of introduce all technologies at the same time in a project, the proposal is a phased adoption in order to verify which technologies can better fit with the project features and how they can be explored to promote LL. It can start with the implementation of a wiki and gradually accommodate other technologies considered relevant to the project. Technologies such as blog and RSS can be easily integrated in the project because they come built-in or embedded in the platform.

Storing Lessons

Weber et al. (2001) propose to deal explicitly with storing after the verification process. The project managers must to define which technologies will be used and how they will be integrated with each other in order to combine the technologies that better fit with the project´s features (e.g. projects related to user experience can disseminate more useful LL using videos). Furthermore, define how the information will be stored is also a point of attention. Structured data requires the use of forms and metadata which makes the process slow and bureaucratic inhibiting the capture of LL. In our proposal LL can be stored in text format or in different media. Therefore, the semi-structured approach better fits to store LL using IT 2.0. In order to facilitate the information retrieval some templates can be defined to present basic information about the project (e.g. name, project manager and scope) or LL in textual data (e.g. in question/answer or problem/solution format). According to Figure 1, several tools are used to store LL and a wiki centralizes their contents through links to external sources such as documents in web-based collaborative tools, videos in video-sharing websites or web pages in social bookmarking web services.

Capturing Lessons

The process of capturing LL involves sub process, methods and technologies. The passive sub-process usually is performed through a set of forms in a legacy system. In our proposal, the passive sub-process is carried out exploring the best features of the IT 2.0 such as collaborative authorship (wiki), speedy communication (microblog) and easy integration (web-based collaborative tools, video, calls on VoIP). The most appropriated methods to perform passive collection are project review, retrospective meetings, learning history, micro article and journaling.

Interviews with project team are used in order to cope with the reactive sub-process. To innovate, the results of this collection could be shared through videos becoming this LL capturing process more dynamic and attractive for the participants.

The after action sub-process is performed during the entire project's lifecycle conducive to the project´s team members review important events allowing them analyzing what and why happened and how to improve the results to execute the same, or similar, tasks. Due to the features of this sub-process, the most appropriate technologies are Wiki and microblogs since they enable coworkers to capture lessons throughout the project.

The main goal of the proactive sub-process is share important events in the moment that they are happening (e.g. project member solving a problem). Microblog, Web-based Collaborative tools and videos can improve this LL capturing sub-process.

Although the storage and capture processes are described in sequence, they occur almost simultaneously, once a project member reports a lesson in this structure, the lesson is stored automatically. Finally, it is important to mention that the more available methods and technologies, higher probability of lessons be captured by the project team.

Sharing and Verifying Lessons

The main goal of sharing and verifying processes is to validate the accuracy and applicability of submitted lessons. LL are submitted by team members in order to be validated by domain or subject matter experts. Due to the collaborative aspects provided by the IT 2.0, the sharing and verification processes can be significantly improved. A team member that find a technical solution for a problem in a forum can easily share the URL of the web page using a social bookmarking tool. Once the other members have access to this information, they can contribute criticizing or providing more details and posting this information, for instance, in the project´s wiki. This approach provides a first level verification which team members collaborating to improve the LL description becoming it more accurate.

The second verification level can be conducted by a set of subject matter experts in order to determine whether or not a lesson is pertinent for a particular project, department or can be applied to the organization as a whole. Once decided the relevance of the published information, it can be highlighted in some specific communication channel(s) (e.g. intranet, internal social network and corporative wiki) in order to disseminate for a large number of people.

Disseminating Lessons

The dissemination process allows users to retrieve information from past experiences on specific topics and directly communicate last verified LL to various audiences. Passive dissemination can be performed using wiki platforms, blogs, microblogs and social networks. RSS is a useful tool to promote active casting dissemination. LL related to a specific topic are sent to an interested group of users (e.g. Project's members are only notified about the lessons relevant to their project´s tasks).

Broadcasting is carried out through bulletins which are sent to everybody in the organization using e-mail. Proactive dissemination can be partially performed using a bookmarking service through the automatic suggestion of tags when project members are tagging websites or web pages. Discussions group can be a useful tool to support reactive dissemination allowing the project team share project issues and obtain information from their partners. It is also interesting to observe that the traditional methods to capture LL do not refer (or explicitly mention) to the use of technologies as VoIP and videos. This tool should be considered while capturing LL. Finally, some processes to deal with LL which involve the application, reuse and withdraw them are not being considered in this proposal once they are post-implementation processes.

Some of IT 2.0 described in this chapter can be applied in other processes than those presented in the previous section. Microblogging could be used to share LL, but become more complex the first level of sharing and verification processes when project members need to augment its content. LL can also be captured through social networking; nevertheless, the verification process is remarkably complicated once the subject matters experts need to check post by post. Moreover, LL retrieval is more difficult in the social networks when compared with other tools such as wikis.

Figure 2 presents an IT 2.0-centered perspective of the LL processes. It summarizes the most appropriated technologies to be used with each process. Corporate Wikis appear as more comprehensive technologies to support the four main processes. Adjoining, wiki technology can easily integrate the huge amount of information provided by different web-based collaborative tools used during the project lifecycle.

Web-based collaborative tools and social bookmarking are also indicated to deal with storage, capture, share and verification processes. The dissemination process can be better performed using blogs, social networks, microblogging, RSS and e-mail than web-based collaborative tools or social bookmarking. VoIP and video are more suitable for the storage and capture processes. Blog is appropriated for capturing and disseminating LL, while social networking can be used to support the processes of sharing and disseminating.

Although Raise Awareness is part of the core processes in the LL implementation, it cannot be related with any technology in particular, but the IT 2.0 technologies presented in this section should be used as a motivator factor to the project team to capture and share their experience during the project lifecycle.

Figure 2. IT 2.0-centered lessons learned processes. St: Storage, C: Capturing, Sh: Sharing, V: Verification and D: Dissemination

Source: Extended from Chaves and Veronese (2014)

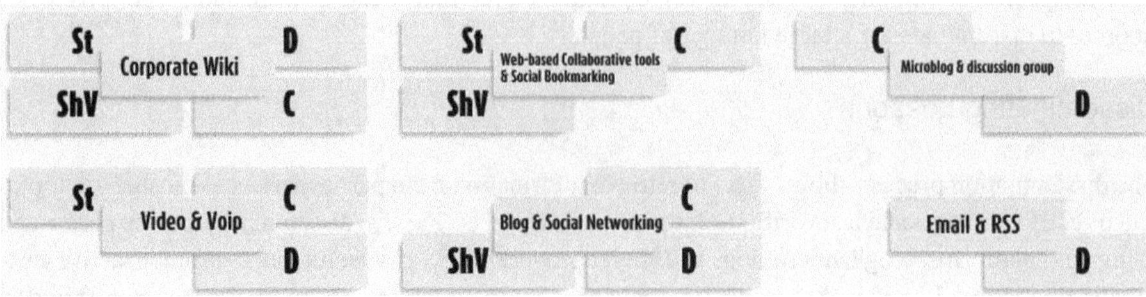

Lessons Learned Methods

Lessons learned are relevant ways of gathering and sharing (Secchi et al., 1999) formal and informal project knowledge (Jugdev, 2012). Project learning has been captured and shared through structured project lessons (project reviews) and less structured Community of Practice (CoP). Both project reviews and CoP are methods organized in the scope of a set of processes.

Schindler & Eppler (2003) classify methods to foster learning in two groups. Process-based methods stress the relevant steps and their sequence in course of a project's time line while documentation-based methods focus on aspects of the content wise representation of the experiences and the storage of contents within the organization (Schindler & Eppler, 2003). The four process-based methods are project review or project audit, after action review, post-control and post-project appraisal. Post-control is carried out exclusively at project's end and post-project appraisal is performed approximately two years after project completion. Considering that project processes are generally temporary and unique, with nonroutine features, hindering learning, the retention of the knowledge generated along the project should be done since the beginning. According to Bentley (2010) the LL Report is gradually built up (and acted on) during the project and handed over as one of the products at Project Closure. Project review or project audit can be characterized as follows: participants are project team and third parties that are involved into the project. Its purpose is status classification, early recognition of possible hazards, and it has also a team-internal focus. The interaction mode is face-to-face meetings and the main benefits include the improvement of team discipline, prevention of weak points and validation of strategies. After action review has as participant the project team and its purpose are learning from mistakes and knowledge transfer inside the team. The interaction mode is cooperative team meetings. and the main benefit is the immediate reflection of the own doings to improve future actions.

On the other hand, the documentation-based methods described by Schindler & Eppler (2003) are micro articles, learning histories and RECALL. A micro article is written in an informal style with a framework that consists of a topic, an introductory short description of its content and a keyword part for indexing the article (Schindler & Eppler, 2003). Learning history is a written story consisting of the main events of a project arranged in a chronological order. Contrary to micro article that has at most one page, a story can contain between twenty and one hundred pages following a story-telling approach. Once compiled, learning histories are validated in discussions with the people involved. RECALL was a prototype used by National Aviation and Space Agency (NASA) where users could submit their LL directly using a Web browser. After the insertion, users were asked to answer a set of questions to the system to add relevant context information. The most appropriated documentation-based methods described by Schindler & Eppler (2003) to use with IT 2.0 are micro articles and learning histories. RECALL was an example of prototype supported by a LL system and used internally at NASA, which makes difficulty to adapt to the reality of the most project-based organizations.

Finally, the journaling method consists of a journal, which is an articulated narrative that follows from the reflective, and critical thinking about one's learning experiences or specific learning events (Loo, 2002). The three-stage model of reflective learning is composed by (1) awareness, the present situation, (2) critical analysis, which connects present with the past and future, and (3) learning, the development of a new perspective based upon one's critical analysis and the application of new knowledge to the learning situation under reflection (Loo, 2002).

Updating Lessons Learned Methods with IT 2.0

LL methods are plentiful in literature, as summarized in Table 1. The applicability identifies in which phase of the project the method is more appropriated to be applied. Participants are all people involved in the project that should participate of the LL capturing and sharing processes. In some of then the facilitator role is required in order to establish an open environment motivating the participation of all members. The duration is a superficial estimation of the required time to implement the method documented in the papers that detail these methods. The organizations that have applied these methods are evidence that the learning in projects is a concern, independently of organizations´ size or industry sector. The IT 2.0 column presents the most appropriated technology to support each method. Von Zedtwitz (2002) describes research and development projects in which were applied the post-project reviews. Suresh (2006) used an empirical study with 26 small and medium organizations of construction industry in which the post-project reviews was applied. Carrillo and Anumba (2002) report that the community of practice is a method commonly used to manage knowledge in big constructions corporations. Probst and Borzillo (2008) present a study with more than 20 organizations of different business sectors that have applied communities of practice. On other hand, retrospective reviews are usually applied in the IT domain in different organizations size as part of agile frameworks.

Some LL methods propose the register and analysis of experiences lived by the team members after the project conclusion. Important details of these experiences can be lost if they are only registered and analyzed in the end of the project. Therefore, in order to maximize the use of the knowledge obtained in each relevant experience it is necessary to document all information just after its occurrence (Anbari, 1985). Furthermore, due to the dynamic nature of organizations, professionals usually can move to other areas making all knowledge about crucial took actions and decisions during the project lifecycle be lost. The continuous register of experiences as part of the methodology of the project management, promotes the discipline in project team allowing their performance review, reflection about the project progress and definition of the corrective actions.

The definition of how they should be registered remains as one of the biggest challenge to the LL capture processes. Large applications forms that considers to register the vision of each participant as suggested by the Post-project appraisal and the Learning histories can be very expensive and not fit with some organizations´ needs. The format of LL register should be strongly related to the tools used to share their knowledge in order to become the access easy, dynamic and that achieves all interested people.

Meetings are crucial to discuss LL and concretize the knowledge transferred. They can vary in the format, periodicity and duration but it is fundamental to assure a collaborative environment where each participant feels himself as a transformer agent. To promote this kind of environment the presence of a facilitator or a moderator is suggested in many methods. The moderator should guide the project team to execute an objective analysis and the definition of corrective actions.

The Retrospective Meetings (RR) and Appreciative Lessons Learned Methods (4ALL) define a framework to manage the meetings and their results. The moderator does a follow up in the corrective actions removing impediments and supporting the project team in the necessary changes. This follow up is important to the project team perceives the evolution assuring the compromise of everyone in each corrective action.

The main objective of this section was to present and discuss the aspects of the main LL methods found in the literature. Each method owns a set of specific characteristics that can be combined with a knowledge transfer methodology that better fits with the organizational environment and kind of the project.

Table 1. Updating Lessons Learned Methods with IT 2.0

Criteria / Learning methods	Applicability	Participants	Duration	Organizations that have used this method	First reference	IT 2.0 suggested
Project Review	During the project lifecycle	PM, Project team and stakeholders	variable	Kennedy Space Center	Faas (1977)	Wiki
Post-project review	At the end of the project	PM, Project team and stakeholders	variable	Hewlett-Packard, DaimlerChrysler, SAP and Unisys	Skeen (1977)	Wiki
Post-project appraisal	2 years after the end of the Project	PM, Project team and stakeholders	6 months	BP and Boing	Gulliver (1987)	Wiki
Community of Practice	During the project lifecycle	PM, facilitator, project team and stakeholders	variable	Siemens, Oracle, IBM, CERN e Pioneer	Lave and Wenger (1991)	Wiki
Post-project evaluation	During the project lifecycle	PM, facilitator, project team and stakeholders	Between 20 minutes and 2 hours	BP, Siemens and USA Army.	Center (1993)	Wiki
Retrospective meetings	At the end of the project or project phase	PM, facilitator, project team and stakeholders	3 hours	Google, Stefanini IT Solutions, CI&T	Sutherland and Schwaber (1995)	Web-based Collaborative Tool
Micro articles	During the project	PM and project team	Maximum one turn	Not found in the literature	Willke (1998)	Wiki and Blog
Learning Histories	During the project	PM and project team	Many days	Sloan School of Management at MIT	Roth e Kleiner (1998)	Wiki and Blog
Light-weight documentation (LID)	After a short activity(from 1 to 3 months)	PM and project team	Maximum 2 hours	DaimlerChrysler	Schneider (2000)	Wiki, Web-based Collaborative Tool
Ba: Shared context	During the Project lifecycle	PM, facilitator, and project team	Variable	Not found in the literature	Nonaka, et al. (2000)	Wiki, Web-based Collaborative Tool
Journaling	Twice per week	PM and project team	Maximum one turn	University of Lethbridge (experiment done by students of Administration)	Loo (2002)	Wiki, Web-based Collaborative Tool
4ALL	After Project conclusion	PM, moderator, project team	1 or 2 turns	Ericsson	Baaz et al. (2010)	Wiki

Source: Extended from Veronese (2014).

The implementation of learning methods only is successful when it becomes a part of the organization culture. Individual efforts usually are not efficient if the knowledge management is not a compromise of the higher senior management. When the knowledge capture and share is not part of the organizational culture daily activities takes priority on the LL processes become the results useless. Other key aspects that should be considered to implement the LL methods are presented below:

- **Organizational Environment:** Challenges of project-oriented environments are different of a matrix organization structure. In projectized organizations is easier integrate learning objectives with the project objectives. Matrix environments need to integrate learning objectives with the objectives of different areas.
- **Definition of Tangible Objectives:** The definition and follow up of the objectives during the implementation process of learning methods allow the evaluation of their benefits and consequently the awareness of stakeholders and senior management level about the importance of knowledge transfer processes.
- **Analysis of the Average Time of Project Execution:** In short projects (3 to 6 months) dynamics methods as microblogging and retrospective meetings should be applied. For large projects, which last more than 6 months Learning Histories and Post-project evaluation can be used with detailed formats.
- **Continuous Reviews:** It is a best practice that avoids loss of knowledge and promotes disciplined teams that analyze the team performance, the results of actions taken and the definition of new corrective actions.
- **Dynamic Capture:** The methods and formats of capture should be dynamics and easy access allowing that participants feeling motivated to share their experiences. IT 2.0 is complementing and transforming the PM through collaborative tools that allow disseminate the information in different social medias (i.e. video, voice, social network and discuss groups).
- **Facilitator:** With a suitable training, the facilitator can guide the project team becoming the process more agile and directing the participants and ensuring a collaborative environment.
- **Follow Up:** In order to motivate all participants, it is crucial that each involved person identify the results of defined actions in the retrospective meetings allowing each participant become a transformer agent.

Furthermore, a combination of different methods of capture and analysis should better support the management of LL. Some methods used during the project execution can be combined with methods used exclusively after the project conclusion. For instance, the use of LID method during the project execution and the adoption of workshops after the project conclusion as an alternative to retain and disseminate the knowledge.

FURTHER RESEARCH DIRECTIONS

The implementation of a new technology in an organization is a challenging process. Standing & Kiniti (2011) list a set of challenges related to the use of wiki in organizations, which includes: management support, absence of organized culture of collaboration and knowledge sharing, lack of clear guidelines and policies for wiki use, risk of vandalism and the uncertainty over quality control and evaluation, wiki usability and accessibility, and failure to integrate the wiki within established work practice. Organizations should consider all these challenges before to implement wikis and other IT 2.0.

Depending on the dimension of an organization, the maturity process of the technologies implemented can vary according to the number of users involved in the project. Moreover, it is relevant to motivate the users to share their knowledge. The dynamic environment provided by IT 2.0 can help in the identification of leaders and promote innovation. The most active users of wikis, blogs and microblogs can be considered potential leaders in a team helping in the raise awareness process.

As mentioned by Williams (2003) learning from projects needs a more sophisticated approach than simply register experiences. This approach changes the knowledge management increasing group communication making project managers identifies new skills in the team. Manage the amount of information generated along the project is another critical factor of success in the implementation of IT 2.0 in PM that should be addressed in future works.

Future works also include the empirical validation of the ideas outlined in this chapter in project-based organizations using the action-research and case study research methods. Along this validation process, it will be possible to find the main limitations of the proposal as well as its extension with regards the processes, methods and the introduction of other IT 2.0.

CONCLUSION

This chapter presented an overview of traditional LL processes, the main learning methods and IT 2.0. Although the literature is plentiful of works about LL methods, how to apply the new tools brought by IT 2.0 in the projects knowledge management remains almost unexplored. The main objective of this chapter was to provide an integrated vision of a set of technologies that could be used by project members promoting the application and reuse of LL. This proposal suggests an innovation in the knowledge management letting the project team collaborate and share information easily. Virtual team can work together much more efficiently by using this new-generation of tools that require a low cost investment to implement. This innovative way to manage projects by using these set of technologies is also being called PM 2.0 and represents an increase in the ability for project teams' collaboration.

REFERENCES

Anbari, F. T. (1985). A systems approach to project evaluation. *Project Management Journal*, *16*(3), 21–26.

Andriole, S. J. (2010). Business impact of Web 2.0 technologies. *Communications of the ACM*, *53*(12), 67–79. doi:10.1145/1859204.1859225

Baaz, A., Holmberg, L., Nilsson, A., Olsson, H. H., & Sandberg, A. B. (2010). Appreciating Lessons Learned. *Software, IEEE*, *27*(4), 72–79. doi:10.1109/MS.2009.198

Bean, L., & Hott, D. D. (2005). Wiki: A speedy new tool to manage projects. *Journal of Corporate Accounting & Finance*, *16*(5), 3–8. doi:10.1002/jcaf.20128

Bentley, C. (2010). *PRINCE2: a practical handbook*. Amsterdam: Elsevier/Butterworth-Heinemann.

Brookes, N. J., Morton, S. C., Dainty, A. R. J., & Burns, N. D. (2006). Social processes, patterns and practices and project knowledge management: A theoretical framework and an empirical investigation. *International Journal of Project Management*, *24*(6), 474–482. doi:10.1016/j.ijproman.2006.03.005

Busby, J. S. (1999). An assessment of post-project reviews. *Project Management Journal*, *30*(3), 23–29.

Carrillo, P. M., & Anumba, C. J. (2002). Knowledge management in the AEC sector: An exploration of the mergers and acquisition context. *Knowledge and Process Management*, *9*(3), 149–161. doi:10.1002/kpm.146

Center, U. A. C. A. (1993). *A leader's guide to after-action reviews (Training Circular 25-20)*. KS: Fort Leavenworth.

Chai, S., & Kim, M. (2010). What makes bloggers share knowledge? An investigation on the role of trust. *International Journal of Information Management*, *30*(5), 408–415. doi:10.1016/j.ijinfomgt.2010.02.005

Chaves, M. S., & Veronese, G. (2014). A Proposal to Manage Lessons Learned in Projects: Web 2.0 Technologies to Promote Innovation. *International Journal of Innovation*, *2*(1), 1–17.

Cheah, Y., Khoh, S. B., & Ooi, G. B. (2011). An ontological approach for Program Management Lessons Learned: Case study at Motorola Penang Design Centre. *Proceedings of the IEEE International* Conference on *Industrial Engineering and Engineering Management IEEM* (pp. 1612-1616).

Collier, B., DeMarco, T., Fearey, P., (1996). A defined process for project postmortem review. *IEEE Software Journal*, 65–71.

Faas, R. C. (1977). *Decision making in project review: processes, participation, and performance in Michigan multi county comprehensive health planning*. Agric Econ Rep Dep Agric Econ Mich State Univ.

Gassler, G., Hug, T., & Glahn, C. (2004). Integrated Micro Learning – An outline of the basic method and first results. *Interactive Computer Aided Learning, 4*.

Gholami, B., & Murugesan, S. (2011). Global IT Project Management Using Web 2.0. *International Journal of Information Technology Project Management*, *2*(3), 30–52. doi:10.4018/jitpm.2011070103

Grace, T. P. L. (2009). Wikis as a knowledge management tool. *Journal of Knowledge Management*, *13*(4), 64–74. doi:10.1108/13673270910971833

Grudin, J. (2006). Enterprise Knowledge Management and Emerging Technologies. *Proceedings of the 39th Hawaii International Conference on System Sciences* (p. 57a). IEEE.

Gulliver, F. R. (1987). Post-project appraisals pay. *Harvard Business Review*, *65*(2), 128.

Günther, O., Krasnova, H., Riehle, D., & Schoendienst, V. (2009). Modeling Microblogging Adoption in the Enterprise. Proceedings of AMCIS 2009.

Hornby, A. S., & Turnbull, J. (2010). *Oxford advanced learner's dictionary of current English*. Oxford: Oxford University Press.

Hsu, C.-L., & Lin, J. C.-C. (2008). Acceptance of blog usage: The roles of technology acceptance, social influence and knowledge sharing motivation. *Information & Management*, *45*(1), 65–74. doi:10.1016/j.im.2007.11.001

Jugdev, K. (2012). Learning from Lessons Learned: Project Management Research Program. *American Journal of Economics and Business Administration*, *4*(1), 13–22. doi:10.3844/ajebasp.2012.13.22

Jugdev, K., & Wishart, P. (2014). Mutual Caring—Resolving Habituation Through Awareness: Supporting Meaningful Learning From Projects. *Project Management Journal*, *45*(2), 66–82. doi:10.1002/pmj.21406

Kaplan, A., & Haenlein, M. (2011). The early bird catches the news: Nine things you should know about micro-blogging. *Business Horizons*, *54*(2), 105–113. doi:10.1016/j.bushor.2010.09.004

Kaplan, A. M., & Haenlein, M. (2010). Users of the world, unite! The challenges and opportunities of Social Media. *Business Horizons*, *53*(1), 59–68. doi:10.1016/j.bushor.2009.09.003

Kotnour, T., & Vergopia, C. (2005). Learning-Based Project Reviews: Observations and Lessons Learned from the Kennedy Space Center. *Engineering Management Journal*, *17*(4), 30–38. doi:10.1080/10429247.2005.11431670

Lave, J., & Wenger, E. (1991). *Situated Learning: Legitimate Peripheral Participation*. Cambridge: Cambridge University Press. doi:10.1017/CBO9780511815355

Levitt, R. E. (2011). Towards project management 2.0. *Engineering Project Organization Journal*, *1*(3), 197–210. doi:10.1080/21573727.2011.609558

Levy, M. (2009). Web 2.0 implications on knowledge management. *Journal of Knowledge Management*, *13*(1), 120–134. doi:10.1108/13673270910931215

Loo, R. (2002). Journaling: A learning tool for project management training and team-building. *Project Management Journal*, *33*(4), 61–66.

Lykourentzou, I., Dagka, F., Papadaki, K., Lepouras, G., & Vassilakis, C. (2012). Wikis in enterprise settings: A survey. *Enterprise Information Systems*, *6*(1), 1–53. doi:10.1080/17517575.2011.580008

Majchrzak, A., Wagner, C., & Yates, D. (2006). Corporate wiki users: results of a survey. *Proceedings of the International Symposium on Wikis* (pp. 99–104). Odense, Denmark: ACM Press. doi:10.1145/1149453.1149472

Moqbel, M. (2012, *February 29–March*). Explaining user acceptance of social networking: Employees' Perspective. *Proceedings of the Southwest Decision Science Institute Forty Third Annual Conference* (Vol. 3, pp. 110-118).

Noll, M. G., & Meinel, C. (2007). Web Search Personalization Via Social Bookmarking and Tagging. In K. Aberer, K.-S. Choi, N. Noy, D. Allemang, K.-I. Lee, L. Nixon, … P. Cudré-Mauroux (Eds.), The Semantic Web (Vol. 4825, pp. 367–380). Springer Berlin Heidelberg. doi:10.1007/978-3-540-76298-0_27

Nonaka, I., Toyama, R., & Konno, N. (2000). SECI, *Ba* and Leadership: A Unified Model of Dynamic Knowledge Creation. *Long Range Planning*, *33*(1), 5–34. doi:10.1016/S0024-6301(99)00115-6

Parker, K., & Chao, J. (2007). Wiki as a Teaching Tool. *Interdisciplinary Journal of E-Learning and Learning Objects*, *3*(1), 57–72.

Petter, S., & Vaishnavi, V. (2008). Facilitating experience reuse among software project managers. *Information Sciences, 178*(7), 1783–1802. doi:10.1016/j.ins.2007.11.020

Polanyi, M. (1966). *The Tacit Dimension.* Garden City, N.Y., USA: Doubleday & Co.

Probst, G., & Borzillo, S. (2008). Why communities of practice succeed and why they fail. *European Management Journal, 26*(5), 335–347. doi:10.1016/j.emj.2008.05.003

Project Management Institute. (2013). *A guide to the project management body of knowledge (PMBOK® guide)* (5th ed.). Project Management Institute.

Roth, G., & Kleiner, A. (1998). Developing organizational memory through learning histories. *Organizational Dynamics, 27*(2), 43–60. doi:10.1016/S0090-2616(98)90023-7

Scarborough, H., Swan, J., & Preston, J. (1999). *Knowledge management: a literature review*. London: Institute of Personnel and Development.

Schindler, M., & Eppler, M. J. (2003). Harvesting project knowledge: A review of project learning methods and success factors. *International Journal of Project Management, 21*(3), 219–228. doi:10.1016/S0263-7863(02)00096-0

Schneider, K. (2000). LIDs: a light-weight approach to experience elicitation and reuse. In *Product Focused Software Process Improvement* (pp. 407–424). Springer Berlin Heidelberg.

Schwaber, K., & Sutherland, J. (2013). *The Scrum Guide - The Definitive Guide to Scrum: The Rules of the Game*. Scrum Org.

Secchi, P., Ciaschi, R., & Spence, D. (1999). A Concept for an ESA Lessons Learned System. In P. Secchi (Ed.), *Proceedings of Alerts and LL: An Effective way to prevent failures and problems (Tech. Rep. WPP-167).* The Netherlands: ESTEC.

Senge, P. M. (1991). The fifth discipline, the art and practice of the learning organization. *Performance + Instruction, 30*(5), 37–37.

Sense, A. J. (2004). An architecture for learning in projects? *Journal of Workplace Learning, 16*(3), 123–145. doi:10.1108/13665620410528498

Shang, S. S. C., Li, E. Y., Wu, Y.-L., & Hou, O. C. L. (2011). Understanding Web 2.0 service models: A knowledge-creating perspective. *Information & Management, 48*(4-5), 178–184. doi:10.1016/j.im.2011.01.005

Skeen, D. R. (1977). User involvement with EDP systems development. In *Proceedings of the fifteenth annual SIGCPR conference* (pp. 62-71). ACM. doi:10.1145/800100.803233

Standing, C., & Kiniti, S. (2011). How can organizations use wikis for innovation? *Technovation, 31*(7), 287–295. doi:10.1016/j.technovation.2011.02.005

Suresh, S. (2006). *Knowledge management in small and medium enterprises in the United Kingdom construction industry* [PhD thesis]. Glasgow Caledonian University, Scotland, UK.

Sutherland, J. V., & Schwaber, K. (1995). Business object design and implementation: OOPSLA '95 workshop proceedings. The University of Michigan.

Swan, J., Scarbrough, H., & Newell, S. (2010). Why don't (or do) organizations learn from projects? *Management Learning*, *41*(3), 325–344. doi:10.1177/1350507609357003

Veronese, G. S. (2014). Métodos para Captura de Lições Aprendidas: Em Direção a Melhoria Contínua na Gestão de Projetos. *Revista Gestão e Projetos*, *5*(1), 71–83. doi:10.5585/gep.v5i1.250

Von Zedtwitz, M. (2002). Organizational learning through post–project reviews in R&D. *R & D Management*, *32*(3), 255–268. doi:10.1111/1467-9310.00258

Weber, R., Aha, D. W., & Becerra-Fernandez, I. (2001). Intelligent lessons learned systems. *Expert Systems with Applications*, *20*(1), 17–34. doi:10.1016/S0957-4174(00)00046-4

Wenger, E., McDermott, R., & Snyder, W. M. (2002). *Cultivating Communities of Practice: A Guide to Managing Knowledge*. Boston: Harvard Business School Press.

Westbrook, R. N. (2012). Online Management System: Wielding Web 2.0 Tools to Collaboratively Manage and Track Projects. *Journal of Library Innovation*, *3*(1), 86–100.

Wiewiora, A., & Murphy, G. (2015). Unpacking 'lessons learned': Investigating failures and considering alternative solutions. *Knowledge Management Research & Practice*, *13*(1), 17–30. doi:10.1057/kmrp.2013.26

Williams, T. (2003). Learning from projects. *The Journal of the Operational Research Society*, *54*(5), 443–451. doi:10.1057/palgrave.jors.2601549

Willke, H. (1998). *Systemisches Wissensmanagement*. Stuttgart: Lucius & Lucius Verlagsgesellschaft.

Zhang, J., Qu, Y., Cody, J., & Wu, Y. (2010). A case study of micro-blogging in the enterprise: Use, value and related issues. *Proceedings of the SIGCHI Conference on Human Factors in Computing Systems* (pp. 123–132). ACM Press. doi:10.1145/1753326.1753346

KEY TERMS AND DEFINITIONS

Knowledge Management: The process of capturing, developing, sharing, and effectively using organizational knowledge. It refers to a multi-disciplined approach to achieving organizational objectives by making the best use of knowledge.

Lessons Learned: The learning gained during the process of performing a project or a knowledge or understanding gained by experience.

Project: A project can be defined as a temporary endeavor undertaken to create a unique product or service.

Project Lifecycle: By definition, a project has a beginning and an end and passes through several phases of development known as life cycle phases. These phases are varied depending upon the industry involved but all follow the same basic steps. It is important to realize that the project life cycle for each project may differ, in both the number of phases it may have and the detail within each of these phases. The five main phases of the project life cycle are as follows:

Start-Up: This phase is where the project objectives are defined and the conceptual aspects of the project agreed. This may be the phase where a problem is identified and potential solutions suggested.

Planning: This phase is where the project is broken down into manageable areas of work and planned in terms of time, cost and resources. This is a continuous process and will extend throughout the execution phase of the project.

Execution: During this phase the work is implemented, controlled and monitored.

Close-Out: The final phase of the project life cycle is close-out and demobilization, where resources are reassigned, the project is handed over and the post-project review is carried out.

Project Management: The body of knowledge concerned with principles, techniques, and tools used in planning, control, monitoring, and review of projects.

Stakeholders: A person, group or organization that has interest or concern in a project. Stakeholders can affect or be affected by the organization's actions, objectives and policies. Some examples of key stakeholders are creditors, directors, employees, government (and its agencies), owners (shareholders), suppliers, unions, and the community from which the business draws its resources.

Web Based Collaborative Tools: In the project management context, web collaboration refers to web, social and software tools used to facilitate the project team communication allowing that multiples users updates documents, sharing information and follow up the state of the project activities. Some examples are Team Concert, Enterprise Project Management, Team Software Foundation, among others.

Chapter 11
'Smart' Project Management:
Smartphone 'Apps' for Project Management

Céline M. Silvius
De Montfort University, UK

Gilbert Silvius
LOI University of Applied Sciences, The Netherlands & University of Johannesburg, South Africa

ABSTRACT

Mobile devices and applications are changing the way individuals gather, process and share information. A development which also applies to project management. This chapter reports an explorative study on the functionality of 50 project management apps. The apps were analyzed on the variables: type of functionality, project management processes supported, methodology/standard supported, topics covered, website support, languages supported, project roles supported, number of team members supported and number of projects supported. Our analysis showed that the functionality of project management apps today is mainly focused on two application areas: (A) Supporting the role of the project manager individually in the planning/organizing processes of the project and (B) Supporting team communication and team collaboration. Lacking in functionality seems to be the communication/collaboration with project sponsor and other stakeholders. Based on our study we recommend project managers to be selective when starting to use project management apps.

INTRODUCTION

The process of how individuals gather, convert or share information is increasingly influenced by smartphone applications, better known as 'apps'. One needs only look at the sheer numbers of apps available in leading app stores, a number that reached approximately 1.6 million apps in 2015 (Wikipedia, 2015), to conclude that smartphones and tablets have earned their position as information processing devices. The shift to mobile apps when processing information has changed the landscape of information processing, even when most of the popular apps, such as games, entertainment or social media apps (Bushey,

DOI: 10.4018/978-1-4666-9867-3.ch011

2013), are not aimed at professional use. The mobile accessibility of apps is quickly making them also the 'user interface of choice' for business professionals, when disclosing or creating information in their professional context,. It may be concluded that the shift to mobile applications and the related improvement in communication has been the result of the ease with which mobile devices can be accessed (Godwin-Jones, 2011).

Through providing access to online information at the tips of one's fingers (Brown & Chalmers, 2003), mobile devices and related apps provide great potential for business professionals and as such also for project managers. While many providers for project management support tools, such as Trello and Asana, offer their services as apps, studies have not yet explored the possibilities of professional apps specifically aimed at project management. The study reported in this chapter, explored and analyzed available apps for project managers. Using a structured approach, the study classified a selective sample of 75 apps on a classification framework that comprised of nine variables.

The remainder of this chapter is structured as follows. The following paragraph reports the selection of apps for the study and describes the sample. Next, the third paragraph outlines the classification framework and its associated variables used for the assessment of app functionality. Paragraph four then presents the findings of the study. The chapter finalizes the study with conclusions and suggestions for further research in paragraph five.

The research advances existing research through the provision of insight in the app market specific to project management. This insight enables project managers and organizations to make more enlightened decisions regarding the use of apps in their work.

SELECTING PROJECT MANAGEMENT APPS

The operating system platforms for smartphones and tablets appear to be settling on IOS from Apple, Android from Google and, on some distance, Windows Phone from Microsoft. Figure 1 shows the number of apps available in the official app stores for these platforms.

The Google Play store has now over 1.6 million apps available, with an approximate number of downloads of over 70 billion (Wikipedia, 2015b). The number of apps available for the IOS platform is approximately 1.5 million, with over 75 billion downloads (Wikipedia, 2015). The Windows Phone store now has approximately 340.000 apps available (Statista, 2015) and in total some 3 billion downloads (Hachman, 2013). As the Windows Phone platform is clearly trailing the IOS and Android platforms, we focused solely on the latter two.

By entering the search term 'project management' in both the IOS app store and the Google play store, approximately 300 apps were identified in each store. However, several prominent apps do not include the word project management in their names, for example Basecamp. In order to also identify these apps, we searched for the term 'best project management app' in Google, from which we also selected apps which seemed relevant and were recommended to project managers. Based upon these searches, the number of downloads of the apps in the two stores and the evaluation of the apps in the stores, we selected 75 most prominent apps for our study. For practical reasons, we omitted apps that were not available in the English language. Table 1 presents the details of our sample, with the apps in alphabetical order.

Figure 1. The number of apps available in the leading app stores
(Source:Statista, 2015)

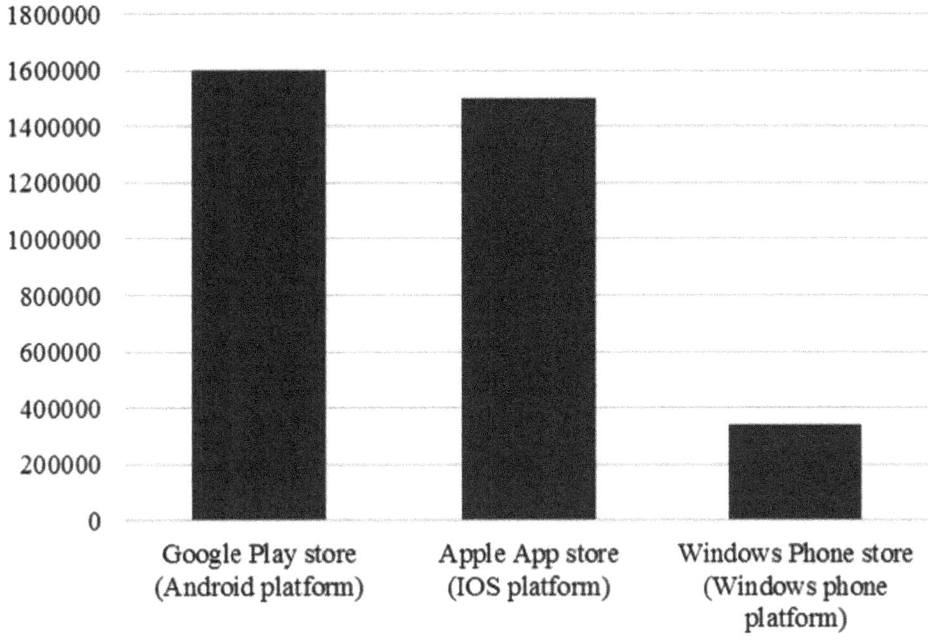

A first observation that can be made from Table 1 is that the availability of apps is still platform dependent. Of the 75 apps in our sample, only 46 apps (61%) are available on both the IOS and Android platforms. Moreover, of these 46 apps, only seven apps have the same version number on the two platforms, which could indicate that the other apps are available on both IOS and Android, may have version differences between the platforms. Of the 29 apps that are only available on one of the platforms, 14 apps are only available on Google play store, and 15 only in Apple's IOS app store.

CLASSIFICATION FRAMEWORK

As our study has an explorative nature, we were mostly interested in describing and analyzing the functionality of the apps. For this we developed the framework presented in Table 2.

The following section describes the variables and the answer values in more detail.

Type of Functionality

With this variable we intended to analyze whether the nature of the app was:

- **Educational / Instructional:** Learning / developing / testing project management competences;
- **Informative:** Providing information / data resources / knowledge on project management;

Table 1. The project management apps in the sample

	Name	Manufacturer	Platform		Version	
			IOS	Android	IOS	Android
1	Ace project	websystems inc	Yes	Yes	1.4	8
2	Agile and astute project management tips	The Anode Group Pty Ltd	Yes		1.3	
3	Apptivo	Apptivo	Yes	Yes	1.0.2	2.0.2
4	Asana	Asana	Yes	Yes	3.2.0.	1.125
5	AtTask	AtTask Inc.	Yes	Yes	1.4.0	1.7.2
6	Avaza	Spyk software pty ltd	Yes	Yes	1.1.16	1.1.14
7	Azendoo	Azendoo	Yes	Yes	1.18.0	1.18.0
8	Basecamp	Basecamp, LLC	Yes	Yes	1.1	1.1.7
9	Beesy	BeesApps	Yes		2.31	
10	Bitrix 24	Bitrix 24	Yes	Yes	2.7	2.6.0.2
11	Brax.Me	Roberto Cordero	Yes	Yes	1.0.6.6	1.0.6.177
12	Clarizen	Clarizen	Yes	Yes	5.4.0.4	5.4.0.4
13	Collaboration Tool - Teamwork	Digitalcurve Inc.		Yes		1.0.9
14	Comidor	B.open		Yes		0.0.3
15	Contractor: Project Management	Jobcrafts		Yes		2.5.5
16	Droptask	Think Productivity Ltd	Yes		1.4.2	
17	Easy Team Projects	Azendoo	Yes	Yes	1.9.5	1.9.5
18	Evernote	Evernote Corporation	Yes	Yes	7.6.5	0.9
19	eXo	eXo platform	Yes	Yes	2.4.1	2.4.1
20	EZ Share Pro	Antecea Inc.	Yes		3.0.1	
21	File Sharing	Infrascale Inc.		Yes		2.2.2
22	Flowdock	Flowdock	Yes	Yes		2015.08.03
23	Gantter VU	InQuest Technologies	Yes		1.1.0	
24	GanttMan	Martin Doudera		Yes		1.3.2
25	Google +	Google Inc.	Yes	Yes	4.8.3	5.1.1.88991728
26	gTasks	Appest Inc.	Yes	Yes	4.8.4	2.2.22
27	GQueues	GQueues	Yes	Yes	1.2.1	1.3.1
28	Hall	Hall.com	Yes	Yes	2.5.1	3.1.10
29	Huddle	huddle.net	Yes	Yes	2.5.3	1.1.0
30	Insightly	Insightly Inc	Yes	Yes	3.3.4	3.3.0
31	iBrainstorm	Universal mind	Yes		3.0	
32	iScope	Maihue Ltd.	Yes		1.5.2	
33	Learn Project Management	WAGmob		Yes		14.2
34	LiquidPlanner	LiquidPlanner Inc	Yes	Yes	4.53.0	4.53.0
35	Loopy Telegram pro messenger	Quo App Solutions Inc.	Yes	Yes	2.8	2.1.3
36	Microsoft OneNote	Microsoft	Yes	Yes	2.10.1	1.0
37	Mindjet Tasks	Mindjet LLC	Yes	Yes	2.3.1	1.1
38	Molasync	Molamola Inc.	Yes		2.0.2	

continued on following page

Table 1. Continued

	Name	Manufacturer	Platform		Version	
			IOS	Android	IOS	Android
39	Moxtra	Moxtra Inc.	Yes	Yes	2.9.16	2.9.4
40	Ontraport	Landon Ray		Yes		1.0.3
41	Paymo	Paymo S.L.R.	Yes	Yes	1.0.3	1.0
42	PM Connector	Ricardo Viana Vargas	Yes	Yes	2.1	2.0
43	Podio	Podio ApS	Yes	Yes	4.6.9	3.2.4
44	Producteev by Jive	Jove Software	Yes	Yes	6.4.1	1.1.1
45	Project Management	Apps Educations		Yes		1.2
46	Project Management Application	LnTInfotech	Yes		1.0	
47	Project Management Magazine	Project Management	Yes	Yes	1.17	2.1
48	Project Management System	Expert Village Media Technologies		Yes		2.4.4
49	Project Management Training	Projectmanager.com	Yes	Yes	1.0	3.0
50	Project Manager	Farid Kilani		Yes		1.1.1
51	Projectplace	Projectplace International	Yes	Yes	4.0.5	1.2.0
52	Project Planner HD	Peritum.Net	Yes		2.5.1	
53	Project Planning	J. de Montcheuil		Yes		4.1.3
54	Project Planning Pro	i2e Consulting LCC	Yes	Yes	1.7.7	1.4.4
55	Project Schedule (Free)	Thorsten Krämer		Yes		1.11.7
56	Pushbullet	Pushbullet	Yes	Yes	1.9	15.6.5
57	Redbooth	Redbooth Inc.	Yes	Yes	6.4.8	6.5.5
58	Smartsheet Project Management	Smartsheet.com	Yes	Yes	2.2.1	2.1.0.28
59	Sqwiggle	Sqwiggle Inc	Yes		0.1.9	
60	Task by TeamWork HD	Mobile Expert Co. Ltd.	Yes		2.0	
61	Teamfocus	Teamfocus pty ltd.	Yes	Yes	1.7	1.7
62	Teamwork	Teamwork.com	Yes	Yes	2.2	2.1.6
63	Teamwork	Tim Roadley	Yes		1.3	
64	Teamworks	Logistical Athletics Solutions		Yes		1.5.3
65	Teamwork by Scopevisio	Scopevision AG	Yes	Yes	1.18.0	3.1.12
66	Teamwork Stock Count	Teamwork Retail LLC	Yes		1.3.448	
67	Teamplace	Cortado AG	Yes	Yes	7.9.4	5.1.17.1
68	Todoist	Doist	Yes	Yes	10.1.5	8.0.5
69	Trello	Trello Inc.	Yes	Yes	2.7.1	3.1.0.566
70	Viadesk	Viadesk bv	Yes	Yes	1.12	1.12
71	Wrike - Project Management	Wrike Inc.	Yes	Yes	1.1.6	1.5.3.2
72	Workshare Mobile	Workshare	Yes	Yes	3.1.3	1.3.6
73	Wunderlist	6 Wunderkinder GmbH	Yes	Yes	3.2.0	3.3.1
74	xPlan	adnX SARL	Yes		3.7	
75	Zoho Projects	Zoho Corporation		Yes		1.6.14

Table 2. Classification framework for the project management apps

Variable	Answer values
Type of functionality	Educational / instructional
	Informative
	Executive
	Collaborative
	Administrative
Project management processes supported	Initiating processes
	Planning / organizing processes
	Implementing / execution processes
	Controlling / monitoring processes
	Closing processes
Methodology supported	No specific method
	PM BOK®
	PRINCE2®
	ISO 21500
	AGILE/SCRUM
	Other, …
Topics covered / supported	Requirements / scope
	Deliverables / Products
	Activities / WBS
	(Human) Resources
	Materials
	Suppliers
	Budget
	Time / Schedule
	Stakeholders
	Communication
	Risks
	Issues
	Reports

continued in following column

Table 2. Continued

Variable	Answer values
Also accessible through a website?	Yes/No
Languages available / supported	English
	German
	Spanish
	French
	Chinese
	Others, ….
Which project roles supported?	Project manager
	Project sponsor
	Project team member
	Other stakeholders
How many team members supported per project?	1
	2-5
	6-10
	>10
	N/A
How many projects supported simultaneously	1
	2-5
	6-10
	>10
	N/A

- **Executive:** Supporting the execution of project management processes;
- **Collaborative:** Supporting communication within the project team and/or other stakeholders;
- **Administrative:** Recording and/or archiving data about the project and/or project management processes.

An app could score in multiple functionality types.

Project Management Processes Supported

This variable scored the process group in which the app would most likely be used. For the identification of project management process groups, we used the five generic process groups that the PM BOK® and ISO 21500 recognize. As an app can support more than one process group, also on this question multiple answers were allowed.

Methodology/Standard Supported

This variable scored whether the app supported a specific methodology or standard. We identified the following methodologies/standards for this question: PM BOK®, PRINCE2®, ISO 21500 and AGILE/SCRUM. As an app can support more than one methodology, also on this question multiple answers were allowed, except when answering "No specific method".

Topics Covered / Supported

In this variable we scored which project management topics/themes/knowledge areas the app supported. For this we identified the following topics: Requirements / scope, Deliverables / Products, Activities / WBS, (Human) Resources, Materials, Suppliers, Budget, Time / Schedule, Stakeholders, Communication, Risks, Issues, Reports. Also on this question multiple answers were allowed.

Also Accessible through a Website?

This question refers to whether the app, or the database that the app accesses, is also accessible through a website ("Yes" or "No").

Languages Available / Supported

As we used English as one of the selection criteria for our sample, this question refers to whether the app supports any languages other than English.

Which Project Roles Supported?

This variable assessed the project roles that were supported by the apps. We distinguished the following roles in our analysis: Project manager, Project sponsor, Project team member and Other stakeholders. Multiple answers were allowed.

How Many Team Members Supported Per Project?

This variable scored the number of team members in a project that could use the app in their specific project.

How Many Projects Supported Simultaneously?

This variable scored the number of simultaneous projects that a user could use the app for.

Analysis of the apps was based on qualitative 'scoring' of functionality as presented in descriptions and on screenshots. Reviews of the apps were studied for additional information. The researchers scored the apps independently of each other and compared their analysis in order to enhance objectivity.

Next to the variables analyzing the functionality of the apps, the researchers recorded descriptive data of the apps: name, manufacturer, availability for IOS and Android mobile platforms, number of downloads from the Apple app store and the Google Play store, evaluation of the app in these stores and information on pricing.

FINDINGS

Annex A provides the specific data of the 75 apps we analyzed in this study. In this paragraph we will report the data for the analysis in a more condensed way. The findings are structured by variable.

Type of Functionality

Table 3 presents an overview of the functionality found in the apps in our sample.

From Table 3 it appears that the apps focus foremost on the collaborative and executive, with administrative functionalities following at some distance. The most frequently found functionality in our sample is collaboration (63%) in the form of supporting communication within the project team and/or with other stakeholders. Given the personal character of the mobile devices that apps are used on, these apps may be quite suitable for use in communication and collaboration. 48% of the apps support the execution of project management processes, and 35% provide administration functions. Informative and educational/instructional functionalities, for example checklists or description of methodologies, appear in only 5% resp. 7% of the apps.

Project Management Processes Supported

Table 4 shows that the most covered (91%) process group in the apps is planning/organizing. The second highest scoring process group is controlling/monitoring, that was covered by 72% of the apps. On some

Table 3. Overview of functionality of the project management apps

Variable	Answer Values	# apps	Percentage
Type of functionality	Educational / instructional	5	7%
	Informative	4	5%
	Executive	36	48%
	Collaborative	47	63%
	Administrative	26	35%

Table 4. Coverage of project management process groups

Variable	Answer Values	# apps	Percentage
Project management processes supported	Initiating processes	28	37%
	Planning / organizing processes	68	91%
	Implementing / execution processes	38	51%
	Controlling / monitoring processes	54	72%
	Closing processes	13	17%

distance, the process groups implementing / execution and initiating follow, with a coverage of respect. 51% and 37%.

The least covered process group is closing, with a coverage of only 17%. Apparently these processes are considered less suitable for the characteristics of the use of apps at this moment.

When we relate the results on this variable to the results on the previous variable, functionality, the impression arises that the main application areas of the apps are execution and administration during the planning of a project and communication and collaboration during project execution.

Methodology/Standard Supported

The apps in our sample all supported 'generic' project management. They did all not apply any specific project management method such as PRINCE2® or SCRUM. On a more detailed level of the support functionality, such as planning and scheduling of project activities, some apps supported specific methods such as Gantt chart, PERT and CPM.

Topics Covered / Supported

In this variable we scored which project management topics/themes/knowledge areas the app supported. As is presented in Table 5, the highest scoring topics were Time/schedule (87%) and Activities/WBS (85%). The high scores of these topics are likely to relate to the high scoring planning/organizing process group in the coverage of the project management process groups (Table 4). Also the topics (Human) Resources and Communication score high (resp. 77% and 72%), which appears to be consistent with the high scoring collaborative functionality we found earlier.

The topics Risk (5%), Materials (11%), Issues (13%), Requirements/scope (15%) and Suppliers (16%) all score relatively low. The 'middle' group, which we define as scoring between 20 and 50% is formed by the topics Stakeholders (21%), Budget (31%), Deliverables/Products (31%) and Reports (36%).

The considerable gap between the scores of Deliverable/Products (31%) and Activities/WBS (85%) can be considered remarkable, as both topics relate to the key 'structures' in project management. Also the relatively low score of the topic Stakeholders (21%) may be remarkable, as the communicative nature of the apps provides good opportunities for stakeholder engagement.

Table 5. Project management topics supported

Variable	Answer Values	# apps	Percentage
Topics covered / supported	Requirements / scope	11	15%
	Deliverables / Products	23	31%
	Activities / WBS	64	85%
	(Human) Resources	58	77%
	Materials	8	11%
	Suppliers	12	16%
	Budget	23	31%
	Time / Schedule	65	87%
	Stakeholders	16	21%
	Communication	64	72%
	Risks	4	5%
	Issues	10	13%
	Reports	27	36%

Also Accessible Through a Website?

65% of the apps were also accessible through a website, which enhances their use in group collaboration. The others only had the app as user interface. Most of the apps that were also accessible through a website were additions to already existing websites or collaboration platforms.

Languages Available / Supported

From the English download/viewing in the app-store in English it was often not made clear whether the apps also provide support of other languages. Only 13 apps (17%) explicitly provide support of other languages. For four of these, one other language is supported, where six apps provide support of a relatively large number of languages. Language support may be an important feature for international projects in which not all participants master the English language. Of course an app in the English language can still be used to support communication in another language which is put in by the user to communicate with other users.

Which Project Roles Supported?

Not surprisingly, the apps in the study all supported the role of the project manager (Table 6). Next to this role, 73% of the apps also supported the team member role.

Other roles in and around the project, sponsor (19%) and other stakeholders (9%), are supported by only a handful of apps. This appears to be in line with the relatively low score of the topic stakeholders, reported in Table 5 above.

Table 6. Project management roles supported

Variable	Answer Values	# apps	Percentage
Supporting which roles?	Project manager	75	100%
	Project sponsor	14	19%
	Project team member	55	73%
	Other stakeholders	7	9%

Table 7. Maximum number of team members supported per project

Variable	Answer Values	# apps	Percentage
How many team members supported per project?	1	29	39%
	2-5	7	9%
	6-10	0	0%
	>10	25	33%
	N/A	14	19%

How Many Team Members Supported Per Project?

Table 7 shows that 39% of the apps support only one team member using the app, indicating individual use. The paid versions of these apps, however, often support more users. 25 Apps support over 10 team members in a project. These apps may be considered in cases where the use of the app is aimed at team communication and collaboration.

How Many Projects Supported Simultaneously?

This variable scored the number of simultaneous projects that a user could support using the app. Table 8 shows that on this aspects of functionality, the sample included two groups of apps. One group that can support an individual project (24% of the apps) and one (46%) that can support multiple projects. This last group may be considered the more professionally positioned group of apps.

We should mention, however, that some apps provide a free-of-charge version that is limited in the number of projects supported, and a priced version with more functionality.

Table 8. Number of projects supported simultaneously

Variable	Answer Values	# apps	Percentage
How many projects supported simultaneously	1	18	24%
	2-5	4	5%
	6-10	0	0%
	>10	31	41%
	N/A	22	29%

CONCLUSION

Apps are changing the way individuals gather, process and share information. This development also applies to the project management profession. This paper analyzed a sample of 75 project management apps on the variables Type of functionality, Project management processes supported, Methodology/ standard supported, Topics covered / supported, Accessibility through a website, Languages available / supported, Project roles supported, Number of team members supported per project and Number of projects supported simultaneously. Our analysis showed some interesting findings:

- The availability of apps is still platform dependent. Of the 75 apps in our sample, only 61% are available on both the IOS and Android platforms, but version differences may appear.
- The professionalism, functional and technical support of project management apps differ hugely, with some being developed as experiment by entrepreneurial individuals and others being developed as professional products and extensions of other professional project management products.
- A substantial number of project management apps are additions to web based project management tools or collaboration platforms.
- Project management apps typically support the roles of the project manager and the team members, based on a generic approach to project management.
- Collaboration and communication within the project team appears to be the most frequently found functionality in the apps. Other frequently mentioned functionalities are the execution of project management processes and administration functions.
- The most covered process groups in the apps are planning/organizing and controlling/monitoring.

From the findings summarized above, it could be concluded that the functionality of project management apps today is mainly focused on two application areas:

1. Supporting the role of the project manager individually in the planning/organizing processes of the project, including specific planning methods such as WBS, Gantt chart, PERT and CPM.
2. Supporting team communication and team collaboration in the executing, monitoring and controlling processes of the project.

Lacking in functionality seems to be the communication/collaboration with project sponsor and other stakeholders. Given the potential role of mobile devices in communication, this may be a potential direction of further development. Mobile apps could also be used more extensively for educational purposes, which is now still relatively unexplored.

Based on our study we recommend project managers to be selective when starting to use project management apps. The number of stars or evaluations in the app-stores are quite often not very informative, making the case for a more serious selection process. The most professional apps that appeared in our study were developed as additions to web based project management tools or collaboration platforms, for example: Asana, Basecamp, Trello, Pushbullet, Podio, Projectplace and Wunderlist.

FUTURE RESEARCH DIRECTIONS

As the availability of apps for all sorts of applications is really booming, the use of apps in project management deserves serious academic attention. Some interesting questions would be:

- Does the use of apps change the way project managers plan, organize, monitor and/or control their projects? For example; Do apps intensify the communication the project manager has?
- Are apps also suitable for more structured project management tasks, such as for example creating Gantt charts? Or does the limited screen size of most mobile devices limit the effective use of apps to communication and messaging applications?
- What would be an effective framework of criteria to assess the quality of project management apps?

We encourage that scholars and practitioners cooperate to develop more knowledge about the effective use of apps in project management.

REFERENCES

Brown, B., & Chalmers, M. (2003). Tourism and Mobile Technology. *Proceedings of the European Conference of Computer Supported Cooperative Work (ECSCW)*, Helsinki (pp. 335-354).

Bushey, R. (2013). The 15 Most Pupola3 Free iPhone Apps of 2013. *Business Insider*. Retrieved from http://www.businessinsider.com/popular-free-iphone-apps-2013-12?op=1

Godwin-Jones, R. (2011). Emerging Technologies; Mobile Apps for Language Learning. *Language Learning & Technology*, *15*(2), 2–11.

Hachman, M. (2013). Windows Phone Store passes 200,000 apps, so let's make them better, Microsoft! *PC World*. Retrieved from: http://www.pcworld.com/article/2080804/windows-phone-store-passes-200-000-apps-so-lets-make-them-better-microsoft.html

Number of apps available in leading app stores as of July 2015. (2015). *Statista*. Retrieved from http://www.statista.com/statistics/276623/number-of-apps-available-in-leading-app-stores/

App Store (IOS) page. (2015, March 14). Wikipedia. Retrieved from http://en.wikipedia.org/wiki/App_Store_(iOS)

Google Play page. (2015b, March 14). Wikipedia. Retrieved from http://en.wikipedia.org/wiki/Google_Play_Store#Play_Store_.28Android_app.29

KEY TERMS AND DEFINITIONS

Android: An operating system for mobile devices developed by Google.

App: A computer program designed to run on smartphones, tablet computers and other mobile devices.

App Store: A digital distribution platform for mobile apps. The most developed app stores are Apple's app store for apps for IOS and Google's Google Play app store for apps for Android.

Google Play: The app store for apps for the Android operating system.

IOS: The operating system for Apple's mobile devices.

Mobile App: See "App".

Mobile Device: A small computing device, typically small enough to be handheld (and hence also commonly known as a handheld computer or simply handheld), having a display screen, often with touch input and/or a miniature keyboard and weighing less than 2 pounds (0.91 kg).

Smartphone: A mobile phone with an advanced operating system. A smartphone typically combine the features of a cell phone with those of other popular mobile devices, such as personal digital assistant (PDA), media player and GPS navigation unit. A smartphone typically also connects to the web.

Section 4

Cases and Applications

Chapter 12
Developing a Social Media Communication Plan

Ahdia Nazari
Omnia, Finland

ABSTRACT

Social media is accepted as an effective communications and promotion tool. Social media tools such as Facebook, LinkedIn, Twitter, blogging and podcasting are leveraged by different organizations for creating profiles, establishing communication, interaction and launching promotional activities. However, promoters might encounter certain challenges in targeting potential audiences and maintaining interest and the interaction of the audience in their social media profiles. The purpose of this chapter is to identify effective communication and content approaches, with a Finnish perspective, and to develop a social media communication plan.

INTRODUCTION

The emergence of social media websites facilitates communication and interaction with large numbers of people. The unique communication and promotional possibilities of social media are being leveraged by different organizations which enable conducting of direct conversations with the potential audience which is in contrast to the traditional communications of high degree presence of organization's direct control. The services of social media are democratizing communications and interaction, thus generating more interest and popularity in the use of social media websites for communication, dissemination of information and promotional purposes (Scott, 2010).

However, social media is a large media consisting of different promotional profiles in which unplanned targeting of the audience and non-strategic communication with them might be both time-consuming and distractive. Identifying and perceiving the sources of motivation and interest of the target audience are essential in developing connections with the audience and becoming interactive with them. Therefore, organizations need to focus more on developing attractive pages as well as interesting and valuable contents to gain and maintain interest and interaction of their audience on their profiles. The primary question of our study is to investigate effective social media communication, content and promotional

DOI: 10.4018/978-1-4666-9867-3.ch012

approaches under a social media communication plan for the Quicker Steps project to manage more efficient leverage of social media profiles and obtain differentiated social media profiles (Evans 2010, 16).

The Quicker Steps project is a project with the purpose of disseminating knowledge and best practices of the diverse cooperation and partnership solutions between higher education institutions and working life in Finland, Luxembourg, Austria and the United Kingdom in order to develop students' possibilities to quicker become employed from higher education, nevertheless the focus of the study is limited to the Quicker Steps project in Finland. Considering the substantial popularity of social media websites for communication and promotional purposes in Finland, the promoting team of the Quicker Steps project is also using the social media websites of Facebook and LinkedIn for communicating and promoting the purpose and current issues of the Quicker Steps project. The promoting team of the Quicker Steps project has managed to increase audience awareness of the project via Facebook and LinkedIn (The Quicker Steps project website). However, certain challenges in acquiring more audience awareness of the Quicker Steps project, increasing interest and conversation of the audience in Facebook and LinkedIn regarding the purpose of the Quicker Steps project are coped with. In order for the Quicker Steps project to become differentiated and interesting for the audience on social media, there is a need for developing more attractive, interactive and valuable communication and content approaches.

The objective of the study reported in this chapter is to investigate possible social media communication and content approaches to develop a social media communication plan for achieving audience awareness and promoting audience engagement in conversations regarding the purpose of the Quicker Steps project. However, the theoretical section of the chapter includes propositions regarding communication theory, social media websites and elements of a social media communication plan, that apply more generically. The empirical part of this chapter studies the methods and approaches of promoting audience awareness and interest of the Quicker Steps project on Facebook and LinkedIn and increasing their engagement in conversations.

The primary question of the study is formulated as *What types of communication and content approaches are efficient in attracting the potential audience and motivating them towards participation in conversations on the Facebook and LinkedIn profiles of the Quicker Steps project.* The author attempts to evaluate communication and content approaches under a social media communication plan for the Quicker Steps project to manage more interactive and interesting profiles in Facebook and LinkedIn.

THEORETICAL BACKGROUND

Communications Theory

According to Smith & Zook (2011, 120), communication is defined as the process of transmitting and exchanging of information through verbal, nonverbal and visual messages. Communication is not a unidirectional flow of information, meaning that communication is based on a reciproactive interaction between individuals in which information and intelligence are transmitted and shared. The process of delivering verbal, nonverbal and visual messages does not guarantee successful communication; the prerequisite for a functional and successful communication is receiving the message intended by the sender to be received. Messages that are rejected misinterpreted and misunderstood result in ineffective communication (Smith & Zook 2011, 120).

As people continue to reach their goals and acquire experience, communication skills become increasingly effective and valuable in achieving those goals. Good communication skills facilitate better understanding of other people and reduce the possibilities of being misunderstood. Therefore, communication is considered effective only in case the message is understood and the receiver is encouraged to act and contribute in different ways (Smith & Zook 2011, 120).

Communication Models

The communication model as shown in Figure 1 demonstrates the factors that affect a communication process which is indicative of the fact that communication is effective if the received message is the message that is sent. A message is sent in a proper way (encoding) through a media channel to the receiver and as the message is transmitted through the noise, it reaches (decoding) the receiver. The case illustrated is ideal; according to the model the sender is assumed to be active, the receiver passive and the message is comprehended well.

A correct/incorrect decoding of a verbal, nonverbal and visual message by the audience is not guaranteed; the message might be accepted, rejected, stored and distorted through the external factors e.g. noise, poor listening and fatigue. Thus the sender monitors the development of the feedback whether the receiver is changing thoughts, expressions, behaviors and attitudes in order to be able to modify the message or the media channel approached (Smith & Zook 2011, 123-124).

There are different types of communication models in which the primary factors are distinguished as sender, message and receiver e.g. there is the one-way communication model as shown in Figure 2 in which the sender is demonstrated as the sole communicator and the concern is assuring whether the message sent is received, thus not knowing whether the meaning conveyed through the message is shared between the sender and the receiver.

However, there is another communication process e.g. the two-way communication model as shown in Figure 3 in which the role of the receiver as a communicator is also recognized through the feedback. This is considered as a simple example of interactive communication in which the sender communicates with the receiver through feedback (Smith & Zook 2011, 123-124).

Different communication models are designed to meet the increasing needs and challenges of mass communication and promotion; the earlier described models are simplistic communication approaches and are not observed as alternatives for the current communication demands. In reality, communication is seen as a multi-step process in which opinion formers e.g. journalists, analysts and opinion leaders e.g. non-formal experts, advice providers who are in the position of influencing a target audience and

Figure 1. The communication process based on Schramm's 1955 model

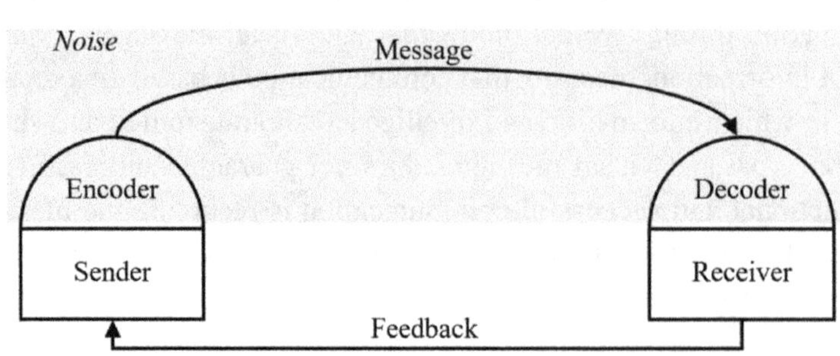

Figure 2. The one-way communication model

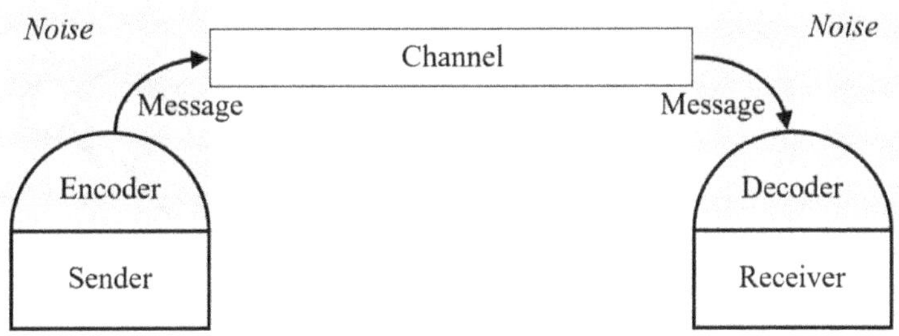

Figure 3. The two-way communication model

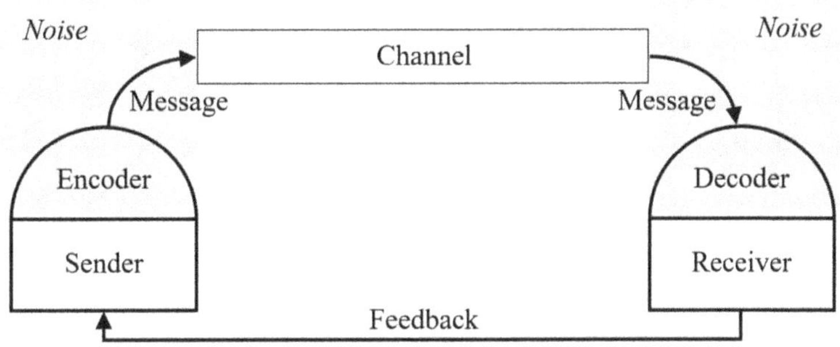

being trusted for promoting new products, services and solutions. In a multi-directional communication, opinion leaders talk to each other, they talk to their listeners and listeners become involved with discussion groups and internet groups, leading to group influence. These interventions suggest that perception, selection, motivation, learning, attitudes and group roles affect the communication process (Smith & Zook 2011, 125-126).

Furthermore, considering the current web communication models which are centered on branding, the primary and important method of communicating with the audience is being engaged in conversations. The existence of social networking websites and the facilitation of online communities are considered ideal channels of communication and spreading information through word of mouth. Through social web communities, an audience becomes interactive and reactive to different topics that are being discussed and thus the flow of communication transforms into a web of communications between the target audience and the opinion leaders as shown in Figure 4.

Organizations facilitate conversation topics for the target audience to monitor and listen to what is being discussed, thus generating reasons to develop strong relations with the target groups. This type of advanced web communication allows fast spread of information through word of mouth, as target groups become involved in conversations, creative ideas and interesting experiences are exchanged between target groups and from opinion leaders to the target audience and from opinion leaders to opinion leaders and from the organization as well. This information sharing includes both positive and negative discussions, which requires constant monitoring and observing of the organization (Smith & Zook 2011, 128).

Effective communication requires a good understanding and identifying of the target audience, their needs and expectations and the types of communication approaches and attitudes that should be applied in order for the audience to interpret and understand the signals and meanings intended.

Figure 4. Advanced web communication model

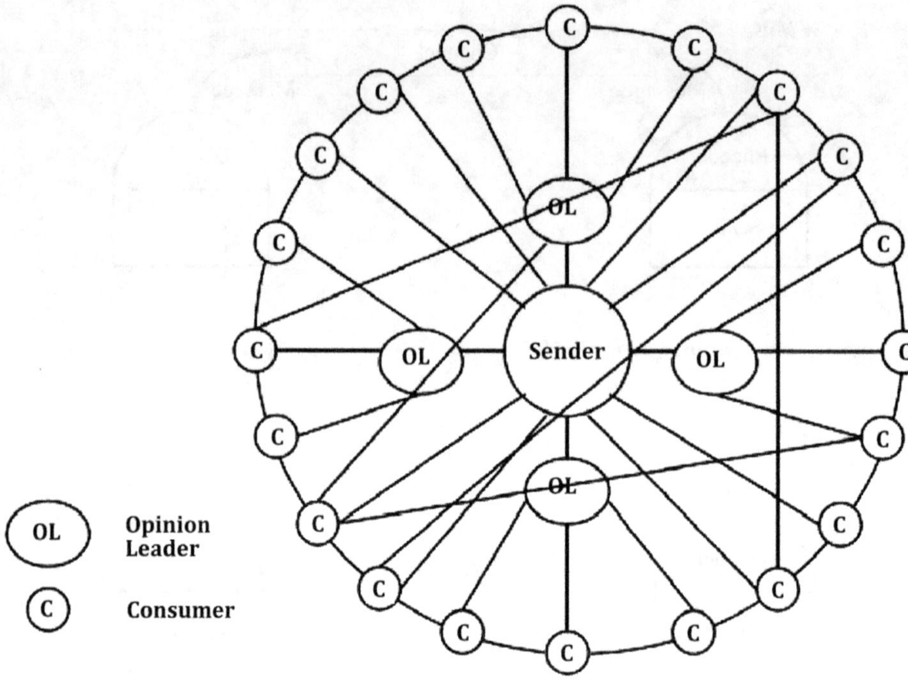

Communication Channels

Communication becomes possible by exchanging messages through a channel; therefore communication channels provide opportunities for interacting with each other and understanding the intentions, emotions and needs of each other. Communication channels exist in different forms and are referred to as traditional and new communication channels. Traditional communication channels are still popular and effective in maintaining contact with each other and transmitting information and knowledge, for instance face to face communication, telephone, team meetings and letters are considered traditional communication channels.

The current extensive range of new communication technologies, referred to as new communication channels, are revolutionizing the process of communication, connectivity and interaction. The availability of new communication tools, websites and software are improving and managing a good quality of communication; examples of new communication channels are cited as mobile phones, the Internet, social networking websites and instant messaging. The selection process of a communication channel depends on the location, time, subject and the importance of the content being in question (Modern types of communication, Erica Starks).

The Internet as a Communication Channel

The emergence of new Internet-based communication channels has provided people with access to new communication possibilities to remain connected and interactive with each other. Internet-based communication capabilities such as websites, social media and discussion forums provide alternatives to the traditional communication media channels e.g. television, newspapers, letters, telephone, thus contributing to the diminishing use and popularity of traditional media channels. The Internet, being a pull medium, allows users the freedom of choosing and accepting the types of content that interest them. The current use of Internet-based communication channels such as social media for communication and promotion is quite substantial and the increasing involvement of people on social media websites is encouraging the organizations to reevaluate the benefits of these communication channels and start launching their own social media pages (Online communication; Weber 2009, 5, 33-36).

The Internet-based communication and promotion capabilities enable the audience to be a part of the discussion and contribute to it; therefore organizations are also forced to react to the user-generated content (UGC) and start monitoring those discussions. Nevertheless, the introduction of social networking technologies in their numerous forms has facilitated real-time interactions between organizations and the potential target groups, thus resulting in rapid dissemination of information and knowledge familiarity (Weber 2009, 39-40).

Social Media Websites as Communication and Promotion Channels

According to Halligan and Shah (2010, 85), social media comprises of online websites that facilitate possibilities for launching profiles and becoming able to generate own content, referred to as user-generated content (UGC), create communities of friends, interact and share ideas, content, thoughts and relationships. Nevertheless, social media is defined as social networking and microblogging websites designed for social interaction which consist of group creation, message boards, blogs (online journals), video blogs, podcasts (distribution of multimedia files over the internet for playback), sharing pictures, videos and music, bookmarking (a link to a web site address saved electronically in a browser to facilitate quick access to the web page), instant messaging and other forms of commercial usages for marketing, public relations and customer service (Halligan & Shah 2010, 85; Scott 2010, 38-39).

Social media is a different media in terms of being designed with viral communication services for conversations, discussions, tagging, commenting and establishing connection with large audiences, which is motivating different generations to become active social media users from which are emerging opinion formers and opinion leaders. Social networking websites allow organizations a combination of a chargeable professional and non-chargeable user-generated content on their pages, that develop a balancing sense to the thoughts and comments which the dialog is afterwards continued by the user-generated content. Through social media, communication is less based on contained and controlled messages and more established on creating irresistible and democratized environments to which users are attracted (Evans 2010, 16, 26, 54; Weber 2009, 39, 40).

According to Smith & Zook (2011, 9), understanding digital communities helps organizations to improve and maintain their presence. Organizations need to understand that their target audiences have transferred from the outbound model of direct mails to the inbound model of social networking websites, thus controlling the flow of conversation and dissemination of information. Therefore, organizations are recommended to join the conversation and contribute to it rather than avoiding it and failing to communicate with the target group.

Different types of social media websites such as Facebook, LinkedIn, Twitter, YouTube, Flicker and Myspace are tailored with unique and functional features for purposes of communication and promotion, which are adding to the variability of communication media. The increasing promotional use of social networking websites indicates that social media is an ideal medium for organizations to transfer from regular websites to viral information dissemination and promotion. Nevertheless, word of mouth, even though both positive and negative, is an important characteristic of social media that might result in broad awareness of a brand, content as well as experiences which prompts the need for constant monitoring and interaction (Weber 2009, 41).

Social media is also popular in Finland and it's usage is still growing (Valtari, 2015). In 2014, around 56 percent of the population aged 16 to 75 were registered into social networks and are using e.g. the services of Facebook and Twitter for personal and professional communication and connectivity. The multiple benefits of social media such as reaching large audiences are expected to encourage more Finnish organizations to integrate social media into their communication strategies.

According to a research based on corporate spending on digital media, the corporate usage of social networking websites is increasing which is supported by the fact that 80 percent of the companies plan to focus their investments on social media technologies and corporate websites. Thus, a large quantity of the investments, 69 percent, is allocated to social networks and applications, 43 percent to social media campaigns and 35 percent to blogs (MarketingProfs, 2011).

The meaning conveyed by social media promotion, is referring to the communication being established through the social media websites for reaching and engaging with potential target groups and prospects. Nevertheless, a primary reason for using social media websites is to generate traffic on a site, increase awareness of a particular brand and receive feedback. According to Answer Lab's research on the utilization approaches of social media channels, brand promoters and agencies cite outbound communications as their principal reasons for applying social media channels which is accounting for 77 percent and 81 percent of the respective respondents. However, it is specified in the research that agencies are more active users of social media channels for outbound communications than brand promoters in terms of better understanding their target audience (MarketingProfs, 2011).

Being transparent in social media is critical for developing trust in the audience and engaging them in dialogues and conversations. Representatives of organizations in social media are expected to operate with real names and publish content that is consistent and relevant to their brand. Users of social networking websites need to remember that they have interdependent profiles, therefore representing and interacting in an open and implicit way is the most appropriate to be able to manage social media leverage and maintain reputation (Facebook marketing for dummies 2011, 25; Weber 2009, 17-18).

Social media is designed for conversations, meaning that the users' primary approach for becoming interactive and noticed is participating in conversations, contributing and be influential. Through social media different forms of conversations and interactions are possible to occur through e.g. videos, podcasts, photos and messages provided that the audience is motivated enough. However, organizations need to understand that the audience is not interested in being approached through advertisement but they rather expect to be able to share ideas and experiences, interact and establish relationships (Evans 2010, 35).

Through social networking websites the audience is provided with freedom of communication to engage in conversations that are important to them, thus organizations need to know that the prerequisite for the audience to become interactive in conversations on their social networking websites is creating quality and value with content. Nevertheless, conversations continue online regardless of the presence and input of an organization's monitoring team, therefore conversations need to be observed, listened to and replied to in order to be able in the long run to establish trusted relationships (Evans 2010, 10-11).

Social networking technologies are revolutionizing the processes of communication, interaction and promotion. Even though social networking websites are still approached as rather new media, their influential and cost-effective possibilities of connecting and reaching broad audiences have resulted in substantial popularity. The current trend is expected to continue as the use of social networking websites becomes an integrated part of the socialization, communication, face to face interaction, information sharing and promotion as shown in Figure 5 (Weinberg, 2012).

According to social media experts, there might be an evolution of social commerce in future as organizations profit, from the large audiences' shared interests, by building stores. Nevertheless, the massive share of information is believed to lead to the contraction of social media into more private segments, therefore granting more control to the users to express their opinions. The social networking websites of Facebook and Twitter are expected to be used as channels through which new technologies and business are developed (Smiciklas, 2010; Weinberg, 2012).

The current information collection process of organizations is expected, in an age of Web 3.0, to remove the need for searching on the web as information finds the users based on the data collected by the organizations, thus facilitating the right information to the right people which saves time and effort. The content that is displayed on the social web is also expected to be more customized to the needs of the audience, ensuring that the information is targeted to their interests. Moreover, in terms of better measuring the progress of return on investment (RoI) of social networking websites, organizations need to understand that the amount of engagement on their websites are more valuable than the number of member in their communities. Nevertheless, trust and transparency between the organizations and the audience is expected to be recognized to develop valuable information networks and physical communities (Smiciklas, 2010; Developments in social networks, 2012).

Towards a Social Media Communication Plan

The application of social networking websites as communication channels is becoming mainstream, the cost-effective methods and approaches of communicating, promoting and reaching large audiences are encouraging organizations to invest more in social media. However, social media facilitate wide

Figure 5. Future of social media

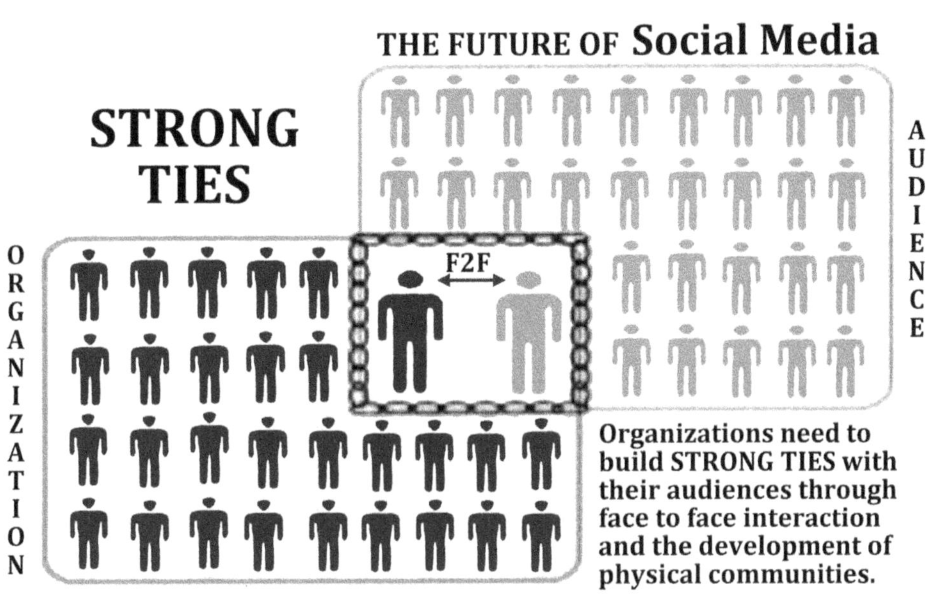

alternatives of profile pages with different content and purposes that maintaining interest and support of the audience towards profiles requires strategies to preserve diversity and consistent updating of a profile. Therefore, promoting teams e.g. promoting team of the Quicker Steps project needs to operate in alignment with communication and promotional staregies to better manage and leverage the communication and promotional capabilities of social media websites. Regardless of the size of e.g. a project and brand, there is the necessity of considering and understanding the needs, the dynamics of interests and motivations of the target audience in social media(Evans 2010, 15; Dunay & Krueger 2011, 37).

Furthermore, a communication plan is defined as a written document that includes an organization's communication objectives and the strategies to achieve those goals. A social media communication plan is essential in determining communication goals, promotional goals and resources, recognizing and understanding target audience, developing content strategy, approaching the right channels of communication and monitoring and measuring page activities. Nevertheless, structuring these general steps is important in aligning the objectives with the strategies and being assisted in consistent evaluation of the process (Dunay & Krueger 2011, 38).

However, a promoting team should be aware that the potential audience in social media does not want to be exposed to direct promotional messages and that instead the audience prefers being conversed with and listened to, thus generating a purpose for researching the audience and their motivations for interaction in order to use time and resources better in attaining predefined goals (Evans 2010, 2, 10; Dunay & Krueger 2011, 37-38).

According to Smith & Zook (2011, 226), different approaches exist for building promotional communication plans and social media plans, however there are essential elements that should be incorporated into each plan. The key elements of a promotional communication plan consist of situation analysis, objectives, strategy, tactics, action and control (SOSTAC) (Smith & Zook 2011, 226). SOSTAC provides a simple and logical structure which is applied in different situations and is possible to be changed and tailored to specific purposes. Thus, in order to build a comprehensive and functional social media communication plan based on SOSTAC, more detailed analysis regarding the target audience and the current situation should be performed. Furthermore, in the following section the author attempts to determine and describe the essential and specific elements of developing a social media communication plan for the Quicker Steps project (Smith & Zook 2011, 226).

Situation Analysis

The situation analysis comprises of a review of the recent functions and processes performed and experienced, a review that includes comparisons of previous trends and performances as well as a short description of the strengths and weaknesses. In this case, the case of the Quicker Steps project, the focus is on the functionality of the current Facebook and LinkedIn profiles of the project including the conversation-, interaction- and promotion-relevant performances. Considering the situation analysis of the Quicker Steps project, an analysis of the target audience, the motivations, interests and expectations of the potential audience, as well as conversation progress, the types of communication approaches and the number of users joining and contributing to the online content should be accomplished (Smith & Zook 2011, 229).

Furthermore, a situation analysis process might also consist of the PEST (Political, Economic, Social and Technological) analysis that is relevant to communications, thus identifying political regulations, economic fluctuations, social trends and technological innovations that might influence the usage of social media communications tools and the behaviors of the audience in the social media websites. To further support the planning process, an evaluation of the current decision-making processes, the allocation of resources and their effectiveness should be performed (Smith & Zook 2011, 229; Dunay & Krueger 2011, 38).

Developing Value Proposition

The development of a social media communication plan, in the case of the Quicker Steps project, should be initiated by considering the value proposition of the concepts and solutions that are communicated and promoted to the audience. The audience expects a description of the value proposition to perceive the unique values, benefits and improvement qualifications delivered through concepts and solutions as well as the capability of tailoring the solutions to their unmet needs. Thus understanding the value provided is essential in developing the communication messages and strategies necessary to develop a communication plan and acquiring the support of the stakeholders in for future ideas and plans (Dunay & Krueger 2011, 39).

Furthermore, setting clear goals is an important part of understanding the value proposition and certain goals are more obvious than others. However in this case, increasing awareness and interaction regrading the Quicker Steps project through the Facebook and LinkedIn profiles of the project are the current and primary objectives. Thus creating an effective value proposition assists in providing reasons to induce the reaction of the audience to the promoted solutions and adjusting communication messages to the goals determined (Dunay & Krueger 2011, 39; Developing a value proposition).

Researching and Understanding the Target Audience

An important part of forming a social media communication plan is performing a thorough research of the target audience, their reasons for engagement on the social media websites and their interests in participating in conversations. Even though there might be a predefined target group receptive of the current messages, in order to reach new audiences, further researching of the audience is needed; thus in implementing social media communication and promotional strategies, valuable time and effort are saved.

The process of researching large audiences is considered demanding, therefore segmenting social media users based on their activity and interest in numerous social media websites might result in a better understanding of the location of the audience. According to different sources, social media users are segmented into six different groups of Creators, Critics, Collectors, Joiners, Spectators and Inactives as shown in Figure 6 (Evans 2010, 42-43).

This classification might serve as guidance in better understanding these distinct groups and applying certain survey tools to understand which demographic among these groups represents the target audience. The utilization of survey tools e.g. Google and other survey software enable search for e.g. age groups and information regarding social media classification of a demographic which leads to identifying the types of users within each demographic. Furthermore, the search engines of social media websites facilitate fast access to extensive information of potential audience to determine psychographics, which is valuable in the communication and promotion process. However, social media websites and demographics are in constant change that relying only on surveys might be misleading; therefore regular research with supplementary survey tools are prerequisite for acquiring results (Finding target audience on social media, 2011; Evans 2010, 45).

Figure 6. User groups in social media

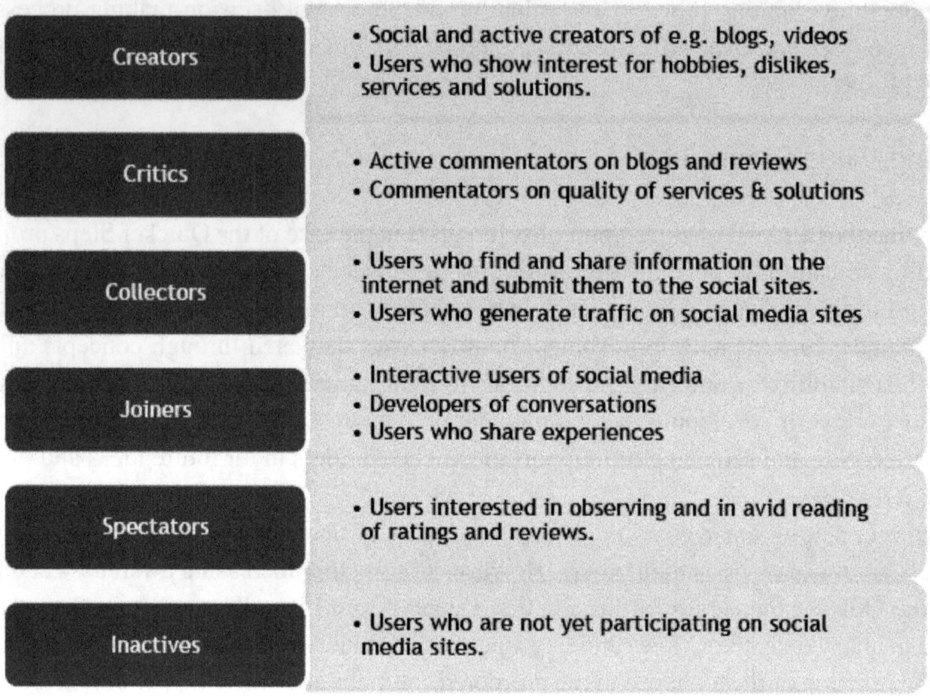

Defining Objectives

Effective communication and promotion on social media websites are implemented in accordance with certain objectives which should be predefined. Regardless of the type and importance of a plan, defined and clear objectives assist in better and easier managing tasks as well as in later knowing the successfulness of the strategy and the possibility of having approached other alternative routes. Specified objectives facilitate prioritization in terms of requirements and the feasibility of the goals, thus enabling analysis of the goals and measurement of performance which is based on the SMART criteria that objectives should be specific, measurable, actionable, realistic and time specific (Evans 2010, 24; Smith & Zook 2011, 233).

After acquiring knowledge of the demographics and psychographics of the audience, a social media communication plan should include certain objectives such as building brand awareness, generating traffic on social media profiles, forming community of members who share the same values and being attentive to feedback and updates. In the case of the Quicker Steps project, a primary source of project awareness being the social media profiles of Facebook and LinkedIn, the current communication objectives might consist of applying approaches that function in generating and increasing awareness, exposure, attitudes, support and interest as well as attracting audience towards interaction and conversation (Smith & Zook 2011, 234; Dunay & Krueger 2011, 42).

As an important objective of a social media communication plan, attending to feedback regarding a brand is essential in becoming aware of the discussions of the audience and their favorite searches on the social media websites. Different types of social media require different types of objectives, in this case the focus being on social media profiles, the goals defined should consider certain metrics that are applied to social media websites such as the number of fans acquired, the number of discussions started on fan and group page, the number of comments, photos and videos posted and tagged in, as well as the number of responses to topics received, the level of traffic generated and the number of pages visited (Dunay & Krueger 2011, 45-47; Evans 2010, 27).

Defining Strategic Communication Approaches

Strategic communication approaches are stated as integration of actions and resources to achieve certain objectives; to acquire strategy outcome, suitable tactics should be followed. Communications strategies facilitate harmonization of tactical communications tools such as approaching potential target audience, positioning of brand, selecting communications channels and prioritizing (Smith & Zook 2011, 235).

Furthermore, developing functional communication strategies for social networking websites are demanding, therefore knowing the audience and understanding factors for motivation and participation of the audience is considered a starting point for developing strategies and tactics (Smith & Zook 2011, 235-236).

As multiple forms of interactions and conversations increase on social media, the need for incorporating social media communication tactics in communication plans to induce attention, maximize awareness and maintain conversations also increases. In the case of the Quicker Steps project, the primary source of project awareness being the social media profiles of Facebook and LinkedIn, potential strategic communication approaches might consist of approaches such as informative messages with broader search engine supported links, controversial video feeds, locating and joining with communities who share same interests, seminars as well as events which assist in creating exposure, awareness, viral attraction, traffic and attracting audience towards interaction (Dunay & Krueger 2011, 14,43-45; Essential social media communication strategies for 2012).

As strategic responsibilities, project promoters should dedicate time and effort to building relationships with the audience, providing methods to help the audience, contributing and showing interest in contribution of the audience, appearing likeable to the audience by being sincere and authentic, focusing on value and quality, forming smaller and connected communities and incentivizing fans by treating them and reaching influencers. Furthermore, other strategic approaches would be applying social media applications that connect for instance with Facebook and LinkedIn to encourage fans to tell their friends regarding the project and purpose, distributing invitations that hold value to the fans and audience and launching the search engine optimization (SEO) which ensures finding of key words, content analysis and phrases regarding the project through search engines such as Google (Dunay & Krueger 2011, 16).

However, effective planning and maintaining strategic approaches for social media websites might require assistance of a professional social media host who is aware of social media communication approaches, techniques, trends and server infrastructure as well as social media monitoring desktop on a website. Active and efficient hosting might result in proper representation of the project brand, more interactive communities, dialogues and sharing of experiences between the brand representatives and the audience. Nevertheless, active hosting also consists of observing changes in social media websites in terms of application updates, new communication approaches and methods to extend reach in social media and maximize exposure (Weber 2009, 206).

Developing Content Strategy

Value is a central component of developing a content that is interactive, useful and inspiring to the audience to participate in social media conversations. Understanding the type of content that the audience finds valuable and tailoring that content based on that value might invoke interest in the potential audience, thus the social media audience perceives that they are being listened to and respected. Furthermore, creating valuable and appealing links facilitate quick dissemination of content on social media websites (Evans 2010, 225).

Moreover, delivering valuable and relevant content to the audience in order to enhance a project brand requires assessing current and available assets e.g. video materials, contributions and interests of the present audience. Different channels of communications e.g. web websites, Facebook and LinkedIn profiles should be observed and monitored while developing a content strategy, thus becoming able to determine the right content for the right communication channel. Nevertheless, promoters need to be aware that in order to be noticed on social media, content should be optimized for search and available on various topics (Dunay & Krueger 2011, 47).

In the case of the Quicker Steps project, content strategies might consist of dedicating high quality content that are purposeful to the target audience e.g. project relevant news, current employment issues and experts' input on the matter as well as corporate actions for attracting and encouraging students to become employed in early stages of studies which indicate the support of the project for important causes thus resulting in more awareness of the purpose of the project. Furthermore, promoting teams are able to build online groups and launch promotional campaigns based on causes relevant to the a project brand to spread information regarding e.g. government measures to handle students' unemployment and certain barriers to their progress in working life which might develop interest in the audience to become interactive.

Nevertheless, developing content based on assumptions regarding the interests of the audience might result in misleading, therefore creating content with value is essential to be based on conducted research. The culture of social media is built on digital fluency and inspiring content which implies that contents should be used to motivate participation and not to be used in abundance to confuse the audience. However, maintaining a consistent approach of communication and creating valuable content is determinant in engaging the potential audience to become interactive with a project brand for the long term (Halligan & Shah 2010, 30-31; Dunay & Krueger 2011, 48).

Action and Implementation of Content Strategy

At this stage, details of the strategic approaches are required to implement the tactics planned. There is a need for active attention and consideration to details, proper communication planning skills, time management, management skills, prioritizing and the ability to manage with pressure and ensuring that tasks are performed. Furthermore, implementing a coherent content strategy requires knowing the audience and understanding their content of value and interest, acquiring content creators and determining sufficient resources (Smith & Zook 2011, 237; Dunay & Krueger 2011, 79-80).

Engaging through dialogues and discussions are basic methods of establishing relationships and promoting a project brand, therefore the more relevant, creative and valuable information that matter to the audience shared the more activity and traffic is generated on a site. Nevertheless, social media audience constitutes of social and conversation-oriented users who expect from a promoting team to be interactive, understanding and appreciative of the knowledge and experiences being shared. In this case, sharing insights and research materials in connection with the solutions being promoted might help the audience in better perceiving the advantages and possibilities in question. Facilitating relevant links to researches, articles, videos, resources, interviews and statements on the social media websites is effective in establishing credibility as a content aggregator (Dunay & Krueger 2011 83-84).

Furthermore, maintaining a common theme while posting updates on the social media websites assures pursuing and achieving of objectives. Therefore, there is a need for using proper conversation tone based on the audience and content type, thus managing in delivering both more conversational and research-oriented content. However, during the implementation of the tactics, project organizers should deliberate on potential problems regarding the consistency and functionality of the content tactics being used e.g. whether the content inspires the audience, addresses their needs, influences their decisions and exposes brand awareness (Dunay & Krueger 2011, 81-82).

Nevertheless, providing interesting applications on the profiles and delivering accessible content in different formats e.g. blog articles, webinars, videos, podcasts and webcasts is necessary to attract participation in conversations and maintain continuing interaction. According to numerous social media experts, the audience needs to be offered incentives to join communities and find reasons for regular interaction; thus a promoting team needs to consider a professional method of responding to the comments and conversations to manage quick and tailored responses and maintain coherent streams of materials and content on a page (Dunay & Krueger 2011, 89-90).

Monitoring and Measuring Page Activity

Applying analytic techniques and sophisticated measurement tools to monitor activities and traffic on social media websites is recommended to achieve effective and reliable results. Measuring and analyzing quantity and intensity of conversations, interests, interactions, visits and traffic on a page determine the functionality and effectiveness of the selected communication approaches and content strategies. Monitoring search optimization and identifying trends and resonant contents allow a promoting team to adapt to a content strategy that the audience prefers (Dunay & Krueger 2011, 147).

Social media websites are designed with measuring and monitoring pages e.g. Insights that assist in observing progress of both users and interactions. However, depending on the necessity of the promoting team, access to additional information e.g. the types of keywords that are applied to find a page and the average length of visiting on a site as well as integrating certain chargeable analytics services that provide detailed data on page activities facilitate more efficient measurement and tracking of progress. Regular management of these analytic processes helps project promoters to attain new experiences and knowledge and incorporate them into improving communication and content strategies (Dunay & Krueger 2011, 147).

Summary of the Theoretical Discussion

The theoretical background provides readers with discussions regarding the theory and models of communication, the Internet as a new communication channel and introduction to social media as communication and promotion channels as well as the elements of developing a social media communication plan. We emphasized the importance of understanding communication process in the social media, understanding the audience of social media, acquiring content strategies and communication approaches that motivate and attract the audience to engage conversations via social media profiles of the Quicker Steps project. We also assessed the need for determining objectives, resources and the audience while developing a communication plan to manage effective leverage of social media websites.

THE QUICKER STEPS CASE

The purpose of the Quicker Steps project is to disseminate knowledge and best practices of the diverse cooperation and partnership solutions between higher education institutions and working life in Finland, Luxemburg, Austria and the United Kingdom.

Background

The aging population in Finland is growing and the proportion of working age population is quite small, therefore young professionals are expected to start their working careers earlier. Nevertheless, the country is experiencing a labor shortage when simultaneously the number of people unemployed is quite high. There is a need for managing projects with the objective of promoting ways to quicker involve the young professionals in working life (Project presentation, 2011).

With the management of the Quicker Steps project, the objective is to disseminate information of best practices and action models that lead to the quick employment of students of higher education. Nevertheless, the purpose is to respond to the labor shortage in certain fields and the employment challenges of the current labor force reserve as well as increase young people's attachment and attention to working life already during their studies. Moreover, the improvement of employment possibilities for the immigrants is also sought by considering their special needs. These challenges are expected to be managed by organizing new forms of education and employment (The Quicker Steps project website).

Target groups

The target audiences of the Quicker Steps project consist of teaching staff of secondary schools, universities of applied sciences and universities, organizations, associations as well as different working life companies. Nevertheless, in addition to the afore mentioned primary target groups, other indirect target audience of the Quicker Steps project are education planners, students, district authorities as well as immigrant organizations and immigrants (Materials of the Quicker Steps project).

Partners of the Quicker Steps project

The partners of the Quicker Steps project are JAMK university of Applied Scienecs (Finland, coordinators of the project), HAAGA-HELIA University of Applied Sciences (Finland), Laurea University of Applied Sciences (Finland), University of Luxembourg (Luxembourg), University of Education-Upper Austria (Austria) and Coventry University (UK).

RESEARCH APPROACH

The research approach of this study comprises of primary and secondary sources. The primary research method is quantitative and is conducted in form of a structured online questionnaire and the secondary research is based on different literature, Internet sources and accessible study materials of the case study. The respondents of the questionnaire, who have participated in the seminar of the Quicker Steps project, constitute of teaching staff of secondary schools, universities of applied sciences and universities, associations and different working life companies. Regarding the purpose of the Quicker Steps project, the background and expertise of the respondents are considered beneficial to the value and significance of the feedback. The purpose of the research is to determine possible effective communication and content approaches to support in managing more interactive and attractive Facebook and LinkedIn profiles for the Quicker Steps project.

The study was planned and implemented in cooperation with the project coordinators of the Quicker Steps project. Data collection was conducted in the form a self-completion questionnaire designed with structured, multiple response and open-ended questions which supports precise and multiple responses as well as the opinions of the respondents in their own words. The questions were tailored to the needs of a specific sample of the population, consisting of teaching staff, associations and different working life companies, who were approached based on their awareness, background and expertise which might be effective in improving the communication and promotion of the purpose of the project. The research was conducted in the middle of April till late in May during which respondents were approached with online questionnaires through e-mail, social media websites and printed questionnaires by the project coordinators of the Quicker Steps project and the author of the chapter.

The research questionnaire was developed in accordance with the theoretical section and the research problems of the Quicker Steps project. The questions were structured to apply to the target audience of the Quicker Steps project and to acquire opinions regarding the level of awareness of the project, social media content and communication approaches and the need for acquiring a social media communication plan for the Quicker Steps project. Nevertheless, the questionnaire was proceeded with questions regarding the channels of familiarization with the Quicker Steps project, the social media accounts being used, the number of friends the audience have in social media which was asked for promotion and communication purposes, the members of the project in different social media websites, the types of communication and content approaches that would attract the audience, the possible suggestions of other social media websites for communicating current issues in addition to Facebook and LinkedIn websites and the requirement for a social media communication plan to have an active social media profile for the Quicker Steps project.

Questions regarding the communication and content approaches were designed with numbers of (1= not important and 5= very important) to indicate the rate of importance of the suggested alternatives. The questionnaire consists of questions with open space for additional thoughts and opinions regarding communication and promotion channels that might provide additional insights.

Respondents

A total of 80 respondents were approached, from which 45 valid responses were collected. Given the size of the sample, the number of responses collected and the presence of multiple response questions the reliability of the results is rather challenged. However, considering the communication and promotional challenges of the Quicker Steps project and the requirement of developing effective social media communication and promotion approaches as well as acquiring knowledge of the level of awareness of the audience, the results are deemed valuable for the promoters of the Quicker Steps project (Brace & Adams 2006, 48).

The responses were processed and analyzed by using the SPSS statistics software.

RESULTS

The results of the research are processed with the SPSS statistics software and presented in forms of tables and figures, the analysis is based on a total of 45 responses that were considered valid to be analyzed.

Awareness of the Quicker Steps project

As shown in Table 1, the majority of respondents acquired awareness of the project through Facebook, which is accounting for 27,3 percent of the responses. However, as this result is based on a multiple response question, the frequency ofc the responses has occurred more often therefore leading to an imbalance in the total of frequencies and the total of the responses of the questionnaire. The second most popular channel of gaining knowledge and awareness appears to be friends with 24,2 percent, followed by seminar which is 19,7 percent. Other popular channels of project awareness are Emails 9, 1 percent, the social media website of LinkedIn 6,1 percent, the Internet and Colleague each 4,5 percent, Project team members 3,0 percent and the Metropolian tuubi 1,5 percent.

As the questionnaire was designed with open-ended questions for submission of suggestions, the respondents also expressed their opinions about acquiring information regarding the Quicker Steps project through colleagues, members of project teams and last but not least the Metropolian tuubi which is an information announcement portal of Metropolia University of Applied Sciences. The results indicate that Facebook is considered as an effective medium for communication and promotion of current issues of the Quicker Steps project.

Table 1. Channels of acquiring awareness of the Quicker Steps project

Multiple Response Question	Frequency of Responses	Percent	Cumulative Percent
Facebook	18	27,3	27,3
LinkedIn	4	6,1	33,3
Internet	3	4,5	37,9
Friend	16	24,2	62,1
Seminar	13	19,7	81,8
Email	6	9,1	90,9
Colleague	3	4,5	95,5
Metropolitan tuubi	1	1,5	97,0
Member of the project team	2	3,0	100,0
Total	66	100,0	

Usage of Social Media Websites

In terms of popularity of using social media websites as shown in Table 2, Facebook is quite popular amongst the audience comprising of 69,1 percent followed by 18,2 percent of the audience using LinkedIn which is substantial. As the result is acquired through multiple response question, the frequency of responses has occurred more often due to the fact that the respondents are using several social media profiles and the possibility of including own suggestions. Nevertheless, the usage of Twitter and blogs is also noticeable among the audience of the Quicker Steps project for communicating and expressing opinions which is depicted as corresponding 1,8 percent for each. However, 5,5 percent of the audience has announced that they are not active social media users, suggesting preference to other media alternatives e.g. emails for connectivity and interaction. Moreover, 3,6 percent of the audience has suggested that they are not using social media accounts which stresses on the need of providing and maintaining alternative media for communicating and promoting the purpose of the Quicker Steps project.

Members of the Quicker Steps Project in Facebook and LinkedIn

In this case as shown in Table 3, since the respondents appear to be members of the Quicker Steps project on Facebook and LinkedIn, therefore the frequency of responses have occurred more often and has led to an imbalance between the total of frequencies and the total of responses of the questionnaire. Nevertheless, the membership percentage of the audience of the Quicker Steps project in Facebook is quite close to the audience membership in LinkedIn with respective numbers of 26,4 and 24,5.

The number of potential audience of the Quicker Steps project not yet acquiring membership of the project's profiles in Facebook and LinkedIn is accounting for 49,1 percent which is quite substantial. As presented in Table 3, the number of audience who are not members of the Quicker Steps project in Facebook and LinkedIn is rather high which might be indicative of absence of motivation and encouragement of the audience to acquire membership and that in case of providing more diversity and reasons for engagement and communication via the profiles of the Quicker Steps project in Facebook and LinkedIn, the situation might be different.

Table 2. Usage of different social media

Multiple Response Question	Frequency of Responses	Percent	Cumulative Percent
Facebook	38	69,1	69,1
LinkedIn	10	18,2	87,3
Twitter	1	1,8	89,1
Not an active social media user	3	5,5	94,5
Not using social media	2	3,6	98,2
Blog	1	1,8	100,0
Total	55	100,0	

Table 3. Members of the Quicker Steps project in Facebook and LinkedIn

Multiple Response Question	Frequency of Responses	Percent	Cumulative Percent
Facebook	14	26,4	26,4
LinkedIn	13	24,5	50,9
Not a member	26	49,1	100,0
Total	53	100,0	

Attractive Communication Approaches

In this case as shown in Table 4, since the respondents were able to select several alternatives, the frequency of responses has occurred more often therefore leading to an imbalance between the total of the frequencies and the responses received through the questionnaire. Furthermore, the majority of the audience has selected "Short informative messages" and "Email messages" as the most attractive approaches which are both indicated as 20,5 percent. Moreover, "Video and graphical messages" and "Podcasts" are the second most preferred alternatives by the audience with 20,0 percent for each respective approach, which might be due to the interest and motivation of the audience in observing and listening rather than conversing and writing.

Also "Events and seminars" are attractive approaches for spreading knowledge of the purpose of the Quicker Steps project, constituting of 19,1 percent of the responses. This percentage is suggestive of interest of the audience in events and seminars and a relative preference in becoming aware of current issues in person and in connection with others which is worth managing and maintaining.

Attractive Content Approaches

As in the case of the question regarding attractive content approaches for the Facebook and LinkedIn profiles of the Quicker Steps project, as shown in Table 5, the respondents were able to select several responses therefore leading to the frequent occurrence of responses and causing an imbalance between the total of the frequencies and the total of the responses received from the questionnaire. Moreover as presented in Table 5, equal percentages of responses are acquired which might be indicative of competitiveness of the approach alternatives. Nevertheless, the audience suggest that "New cooperation models

Table 4. Attractive communication approaches

Multiple Response Question	Frequency of Responses	Percent	Cumulative Percent
Short informative messages	44	20,5	20,5
Events and seminars	41	19,1	39,5
Video and graphical messages	43	20,0	59,5
Podcasts	43	20,0	79,5
Email messages	44	20,5	100,0
Total	215	100,0	

Table 5. Attractive content approaches

Multiple Response Question	Frequency of Responses	Percent	Cumulative Percent
Project relevant news	43	14,2	14,2
New cooperation models between working life representatives and educational institutions	44	14,5	28,7
Relevant research articles	44	14,5	43,2
Relevant political news	41	13,5	56,8
Expert's interview feed	44	14,5	71,3
Student interviews	44	14,5	85,8
Openings for discussions	43	14,2	100,0
Total	303	100,0	

between working life representatives and education institutions", "Relevant research articles", "Expert interview feed" and "Student interviews" are the most attractive and useful content approaches, each accounting for 14,5 percent of the responses.

In addition to the afore mentioned approaches, the respondents are also agreeing that "Project-relevant news" and "Openings for discussion", each constituting of 14,2 percent of the responses, are important content approaches for motivating and attracting the audience towards developing interest and appreciation for the purpose of the Quicker Steps project and becoming involved in conversations and discussions on the Facebook and LinkedIn pages of the Quicker Steps project. Social media audience consists of influencers who are quick in taking initiative to become involved in discussion openings and express opinions.

Nevertheless, the audience suggests that the least favorite content approach is "Relevant political news" comprising of 13,5 percent of the responses which is yet quite approximate to the rest of the percentage numbers. The results represent the interest and confidence of the audience in the effectiveness of these content approaches which are expected to be considered and leveraged in communication and promotional functions.

Other Useful Social Media Channels for the Quicker Steps Project

The questionnaire was also designed with a question regarding the possibility of using other social media websites for communicating and promoting the purpose of the Quicker Steps project. As shown in Table 6, a dominant 20,0 percent of the audience has suggested that the social media microblogging website of Twitter is useful for communicating and promoting the purpose of the Quicker Steps project. This substantial percentage could be due to the current usage and popularity of the services of Twitter in Finland and the possibility of posting quick and short messages to large numbers of the audience. Moreover, the second most suggested social media channel is Google+, which is accounting for 4,4 percent of the responses. The introduction of Google+ might be indicative of the increasing usage of Google+ and the impact of Google as world's largest search engine.

Table 6. Other useful social media channels for the Quicker Steps project

Multiple Response Question	Frequency of Responses	Percent	Cumulative Percent
Twitter	9	20,0	20,0
Google+	2	4,4	24,4
Blog	1	2,2	26,7
YouTube	1	2,2	28,9
Live Journal	1	2,2	31,1
Not sure	31	68,9	100,0
Total	45	100,0	

As shown in Table 5, the results are also indicative of the possibility of using other social media channel alternatives of Blog, YouTube and Live Journal, each comprising of 2,2 percent of the responses. The audience might be considering the substantial usage and popularity of YouTube and blogs as well as the increasing public awareness of Live Journal. However, the majority of the respondents suggests that they are "Not sure" which other social media channel alternatives would be useful for communicating and promoting the purpose of the Quicker Steps project. This conclusion might be due to the availability of numerous unfamiliar social media channels and uncertainty towards social media capabilities and applications.

CONCLUSION

Based on reviewing the results of the research, the author attempts to conclude on the primary aspects of the aforementioned results of developing communication and content approaches, audience awareness as well as discussing possible recommendations.

The results of the research indicate that the current level of audience awareness of the Quicker Steps project is yet moderate considering the consistent efforts of communicating and promoting of the purpose and current issues of the project. The social media websites of Facebook and LinkedIn are considered as effective channels for increasing awareness and interest of the audience in the values of the Quicker Steps project; however the audience still appears to be careful and uncertain towards supporting the cause of the project.

As discussed in the results section, the questionnaire was designed with multiple response questions in which the frequency of the responses has occurred more often therefore leading to unclarity in the total of frequencies and the total of responses of the questionnaire. Moreover, the results suggest that the majority of the audience has acquired awareness of the Quicker Steps project through Facebook, friends and the seminar meaning that the Facebook profile is quite useful for the project and that word of mouth as well as inviting potential audience to seminars and gatherings are also effective methods of maximizing awareness of the project. As presented in the results analysis, a substantial number of the respondents are members of the Quicker Steps project on Facebook and LinkedIn which is indicative of the willingness of the audience to support the project and participate more in interactions and conversations relevant to the project. However, the number of non-members of the Quicker Steps project in Facebook and LinkedIn is exceeding the number of members which might be speculated to be due to lack of familiarity and motivation of the audience towards the project as well as due to the high communication, promotion and motivation expectations of the audience from the promoting team of the Quicker Steps project.

In terms of the researched results of communication approaches, the audience appears to prefer approaching different communication approaches e.g. short, informative, graphical and email messages which are assumed to maintain diversity and interest. Furthermore, regarding the selected content approaches, the audience is supporting facilitation of contents relevant to research, cooperation models, experts' and students' interviews that might reinforce the value and awareness of the purpose of the Quicker Steps project.

In terms of suggestions of suitability and functionality of other social media channels for communicating and promoting the purpose of the Quicker Steps project, the audience seems to be in accordance with launching e.g. Twitter, Google, YouTube, Live Journal and Blog profiles. However, the majority of the audience is expressing uncertainty regarding the suitability of other social media channels which might be connected to the level of popularity and application features of the social media channels in question.

Nevertheless, regarding the need for developing a social media communication plan for the Quicker Steps project, 66, 7 percent of the audience favors acquiring of a social media communication plan for the project. The results are indicative of the suggestions and agreement of the audience towards proceeding with a communication plan to manage more active and interesting social media profiles for the Quicker Steps project.

Recommendation

Considering the earlier stated conclusions, there is a need for focusing more on increasing awareness and strengthening of the purpose of the Quicker Steps project. The audience of the Quicker Steps project is expecting more communication and promotional initiatives to become encouraged and willing to be a part of the process of acknowledging the purpose of the project. The social media websites of Facebook and LinkedIn are effective channels for communicating and promoting the purpose of the Quicker Steps project; however as suggested during the research, other social media channels should also be studied and leveraged for maximizing audience reach and awareness as well as acquiring access to different channel alternatives.

The social media channels of Facebook and LinkedIn are leveraged for various communication and promotional purposes by small, medium and large projects, thus generating a situation in which motivating the audience to be interactive and interested in particular project profiles becomes a struggle.

Therefore, the Facebook and LinkedIn profiles of the Quicker Steps project should be designed with innovative communication approaches and elaborated and inspiring content approaches as well as attractive features that enable the audience to differentiate the profile of the Quicker Steps project from other similar profiles. Nevertheless, promotional activities e.g. interesting applications and debate discussions could be also regarded as motivating and interesting for the audience to join the community of the Quicker Steps project and become interactive.

Furthermore, adapting to a social media communication plan might enable the promoting team of the Quicker Steps project to execute communication and promotional strategies in more consistent and continuous ways. Applying strategies of a social media communication plan facilitate more tailored and elaborated communication and content approaches which might better meet the needs of the audience. New methods of increasing awareness and interest regarding the purpose of the Quicker Steps project should be developed by holding seminars and launching new channels of delivering information as well as promotional campaigns.

Nevertheless, the current popularity of social media channels is inciting organizations to instate professional hosts to manage their social media profiles, a task which is also recommendable for the Quicker Steps project. Social media professionals are aware of the current popular websites, trends, features, new applications and methods of locating audience and motivating them towards activity and interaction.

FUTURE RESEARCH DIRECTIONS

In this chapter we developed a framework for a social media communication plan and studied the effectiveness and attractiveness of several social media channels for the Quicker Steps project. Following up on these two contributions of our work, we suggest the following directions for further research.

- Regarding the framework of a social media communication plan, it would be beneficiary to populate the framework with proven 'best practices' of communication messages, (social) media channels and effects. This would further enhance the understanding of project management professionals on how to develop and deploy specific communication activities, related to the goal of the project and the needs of the stakeholders.
- Regarding the effectiveness of social media channels we suggest that more research is done on this, especially in the light of the rapidly changing social media landscape and the different usage patterns of different stakeholders.

REFERENCES

Brace, I., & Adams, K. (2006). *Introduction to Market and Social Research*. London: Kogan.

Carter, B. (2012). Is content more important than conversation? Retrieved from http://www.ragan.com/Main/Articles/Is_content_more_important_than_conversation_44362.aspx

Dunay, P., & Krueger, R. (2011). *Marketing for dummies*. Indianapolis: Wiley.

Evans, L. (2010). *Social media marketing*. Que publishing.

Halligan, B., & Shah, D. (2010). *Inbound marketing: Get found using Google, social media and blogs*. New Jersey: John Wiley & Sons.

MarketingProfs. (2011). Marketers Up Spending on Digital, Social in 2011. Retrieved from <http://www.marketingprofs.com/charts/2011/4471/marketers-up-spending-on-digital-social-in-2011>

The Quicker Steps project. (2011). Retrieved from http://www.quickersteps.net/project-presentation

Scott, D. M. (2010). *The new rules of marketing and PR*. New Jersey: John Wiley & sons.

Smith, P., & Zook, Z. (2011). *Marketing communications*. London: Kogan.

Smiciklas, M. (2010). Malcolm Gladwell & The Future of Social Media. Retrieved from http://www.intersectionconsulting.com/2010/malcolm-gladwell-the-future-of-social-media/

Valtari, M. (2015). Social Media Statistics from Finland. Retrieved from http://en.someco.fi/blog/social-media-statistics-from-finland/

Weinberg, J. (2012). The future of social networks. Retrieved from http://uk.news.yahoo.com/where-social-networks-are-going-next.html

Chapter 13
Projects without Email, Is that Possible?

Peter Wijngaard
Atos Consulting, The Netherlands

Anne Basten
Atos Consulting, The Netherlands

Ina Wensveen
Atos Consulting, The Netherlands

Tim de Vries
MSD, The Netherlands

ABSTRACT

Email is standard way of communication in our daily life and in projects. But email traffic becomes more and more cumbersome. More than 25 percent of a working day is spend on email related tasks. Email is misused, and can create crisis in project teams. Nowadays the current generation of project team members is more used to using social media and social collaboration to communicate. To take advantage of that and to limit the use of email, the Zero email program was introduced within Atos. Limiting the use of emails with project teams can be achieved by introducing the right set of tools, a thorough management of change program, using early adaptors, starting small and acting – as a project manager – as a good example. Completely get rid of all email is still not possible; only when all parties are working with the same social media and collaboration tooling, a 80% result can be achieved. But in the current global world of project management with all its different stakeholders and parties, there is still a long way to go.

INTRODUCTION

In the 1970s, email was revolutionary. It became a unique tool, allowing people to exchange information, manage documents, tasks, and workflow. It has replaced phone calls and face-to-face meetings. But, for all its strengths, email is also a source of immense frustration. Project team members can receive hundreds of emails a day, some of which are important; most of which probably don't. Just dealing with the daily overload is a huge problem.

It can cause backlog – simply working through your emails after being away from your desk can take days. And it can cause error – missing the most recent message means you might waste time working on the wrong version of a document (Atos, 2012b).

DOI: 10.4018/978-1-4666-9867-3.ch013

Some figures (Galaxy Research, 2010; Jackson & Dawson, 2003; Star survey, 2010; The Radiciti group, 2009):

- One in five UK workers spend 32 days a year managing email.
- 25 percent of the average corporate worker's day is spent on email related tasks.
- 48 percent of managers find the need to constantly reply to emails stressful.
- It takes a minute to recover one's train of thought after interruption by email, meaning that people who check their email every five minutes waste 8.5 hours a week figuring out what they were doing moments before.

Project teams – and specifically international or virtual project teams – are heavily dependent on email. At least, that is what they think they are. And therefore, they encounter the same burden of too many emails a day which impact their work and their results. For the project manager, it is even worse. As a spider in the web, he or she will receive all communication of the team (and the stakeholders). It is easy to send all email as a CC to the project manager; in this case the team member believes the project manager is informed and sometimes he even believes it is not his problem anymore. At the end of the day, this will impact project results in a negative way.

A solution is to aim for a project environment with as less email as possible (Atos, 2012b, 2012c). This is possible by introducing more collaborative, social media-based communications tools (Atos, 2012a; Singh, 2012; Silic et al, 2015). This has as results that email is becoming redundant – and can be eradicated – as other solutions outperform it. Calling on these other technologies – social collaboration, social media, chatting tools – dramatically enhances the way the team share knowledge and can hone each other's skills while safeguarding the collective project knowledge base. In fact, it:

- Increases productivity.
- Introduces better collaboration for greater agility.
- Meets the expectations of the new 'social' generation.
- And there is less information loss, due to better version management.

This does not mean that email will be abandoned completely. It is very likely the project will still need to use email to communicate with customers or suppliers (stakeholders outside your direct project environment), but it shouldn't be used as it has been in the past. Adopting a basic set of behaviors will help reduce the number of emails exchanged within the project. Keep in mind that for every action, there is a reaction: The more email sent, the more received, and CC-ing is like spamming.

This chapter will describe the requirements for projects with less email, how to introduce and implement collaborative, social media-based communications tools, and how to encourage your project team members to change from old to new ways of working. Although future research is still needed to identify the real quantitative effect on the project results, some preliminary results of this new way of working will be shown.

THE USE OF EMAIL IN PROJECT TEAMS

If you are team member of a project the amount of team-emails is probably cluttering your email box. All kind of emails about specifications, regulations, requirements, (standard) procedures, etc... All the email looks the same and all the priority of the emails looks the same. Some people created some rules in their email box (e.g. the email of the project manager is flagged with a green flag) to filter some of the important emails. But most of the email will have to be filtered by the reader him- or herself. Followed by the judgment of which email do require a reaction or an activity. The usage of email is now even so popular that colleagues sitting next to each other are communicating via the email to request a cup of coffee.

Collaboration needs a process or a way that fits the needs of the project team and will ensure that communication can be done (Bradley & McDonald, 2011). In the 1970s collaboration was completely based on face-to-face communication and the more formal external communication via letters. No email was available back then. The current generation would not even be able to understand what a world would be without email. So collaboration back then was completely different, or not? Of course not, the communication channels were different, but the way people still have to work together has not changed. Only technology changed, which has for instance impact on the global and more international approach of the most companies. Collaboration between two different continents is now more and more a day-to-day activity of a lot of employees, which requires technical solutions to avoid waiting for days on your response.

The Way of Working

More and more projects are confronted with other ways of working like Agile or Scrum. This is gaining a lot of popularity, all this kind of methods promote especially the closure of the gap between the customer and the supplier. The customer is becoming more involved in the way the organization develops its new capabilities (Ollus et al, 2009).

Some of the organizations decided to improve communication by changing the way this communication is organized within the team and within the organization. More face-to-face meetings are organized instead of communication and status updates via email. Another example of the way people are communicating within organizations is the usage of all kind of collaboration platforms. Platforms used to share documents, thoughts and information as starting to get more and more common within the organizations.

Organizations need a new way of communicating. Many organizations are already convinced that letters are no longer the solution for internal communication, and most of the organizations are also moving the external communication (with customers and suppliers) to a more digital way (Bradley & McDonald, 2011).

The Intruder

Email became your number one intruder of projects, project member are spending more than a quarter of their time on sending or responding to any incoming email (Star survey, 2010). Email is intruding a normal day of working at the project; the activities are dominated to ensure everything is validated via the right channels and discussed via emails and the attachments. Instead of communicating, people use email to manage the communication. Not walking to the colleague at the other side of the office, but just communicating one way via the email channel. In complex or big projects, the current behavior of the team member seems to be focused on communicating as less as possible via the phone of a face-to-face meeting.

Every project manager would agree that communication and collaboration are the key drivers for success in any project. If you do not ensure the collaboration within the team, the chance of delivering the requirements up to quality standard, is reduced right away. If people do not communicate within the project team, the project is at risk. But why would communication not work via email? Email is a very simple way of communication without boundaries. Therefore a very flexible solution that will have all requirements covered for the project, no difficult platform requirements since every employee has email these days. A quick fix for the communication seems to be the enrollment of standard email procedures within the project team. But would this be the best way of working for a project team? And cover the project (team) needs? Or would this solution only be a quick fix to ensure that the work can be done within the team?

Team members should be collaborating in the project, with or without email (Ollus et al, 2009). What would be the best way to communicate nowadays within the project team? Would the more or less one way communication solution work or is the two way communication the best solution. Two-way, short lines of communication and alignment within the project team, amongst the stakeholders and in the organization are main goals of the project manager. Every project management method will discuss the collaboration, communication and related responsibilities of the project manager. The project method will require that you are in control and will ensure the team to be aligned with this necessity. Would one way communication be the solution considering this responsibility? Can a project manager be in control if his email box is cluttered with copies of all team members?

Email forces the project manager to react on the situation based on the copies he or she receives of the team emails. At the same time the rest of the project team is not aware of this communication is taking place. The team could have handled the question itself, without direct involvement of the project manager. If two team members can solve their own issues, would it not improve the project quality and ensure that the whole of the project team takes responsibility in the collaboration requirements of the project? The project manager role will be changed and will require a new approach, not the expert being involved in any (detailed) communication, but the responsible manager of the project and the team.

More Efficient Teams

So what can you do to improve the quality of collaboration? Sending emails to all the members of the team, e.g. via the reply to all button? Or do you decide to provide a communication platform that ensures that group emails are no longer required? Most employees and project members already have access to other way of communicating in their personal life like collaboration platforms, social media, message apps and smart phones. Despite these developments in the personal life of the project team member, the project seems to be stuck in the old way of working: one-way communication, no direct interaction between team member and no issue solving between two team members (Grit, 2015). If your environment of project is changing, e.g. teams not on the same location, why would you not adopt the way of working? The answer seems to be simple: the project manager is not willing to adapt to new ways of communication because the risk of losing control over the project, the communication and the collaboration within the team. The quality of the project is improved as the collaboration is improved and the team starts working together taking his own responsibility. The project manager will shift his role to accountable on this subject.

The Success of Taking Responsibility by the Team

In the end, the project manager wants to create a perfect project team, with or without the usage of social collaboration. If the responsibility of collaboration and communication is addressed directly to team, it will result in some other dynamics within the project. The team members will become not only responsible for the communication between the teams, but they will also become responsible for their own communication. To achieve this, a more democratic way of selecting the right way of communication is required which can be different depending on the type of project (Thamhain, 2009).

The way the communication within the organization is designed will also have influence on the possibilities of the project manager. If the organization is used to top-down communication, the social collaboration may result in discussions and changing behavior. It might conflict with the standard procedures or the official documents that are required. It is good to realize that those requirements are related to the content of the requirement, not the channel that is required to be used. If you see the content as something different, it will create the possibilities to communicate in a different way without changing the content (Bradley & McDonald, 2011).

If the whole team decides to change the channel and the way of working, you can change the channels used in the project. Using shared documents or social collaboration creates a new way of how the collaboration is performed within the team (Kerzner, 2015). Sending notification (e.g. on a mobile device) creates a link with the source itself, so some copy spread through the organization. They can start working in the same source and not to copy locally (not synchronized). For a project manager it has a lot of advantages if you use platforms that will combine content, since it will ensure the configuration management is done within the project by the team members. Changes of any kind within the project can be stored and filed right away by the team. One of the positive advantages of this kind of collaboration is the fact that any file will be available for every team member, without sending any email around to inform people that they will have to update their locally stored files.

Teams will need to get used to this new way of working and this new way of communication within the project team. In order to ensure collaboration it is important that team member are able to use the platform to the full extent and that the team member do know what is expected from them. If the technique becomes a hurdle, it will limit the advantages of the platform and will result in team members that want go back to older methods of communication, e.g. email (Kerzner, 2015).

If you start with social collaboration it is very import to ensure that the team members know and trust each other (Grit, 2015; Silic, 2015). And that they can rely on the information shared in the team. If information is shared that is not seen as reliable it would influence the effectiveness of the collaboration within the team. The email has for some reason less problems with reliability, although it is one way communication the quality of the communication is ensuring by sending the email to specific persons or copy specific persons into the communication.

The Role of the Project Manager

Is it logic for the project manager to be the early adaptor or is adopting two years later early enough? Just waiting for the rest of the company seems to be the easiest solution. But does waiting for the rest of the organization bring you your collaborating project team? Of course the timelines depend on the skills of the project manager. Some project managers will be able to adapt to this new way of working easier than other project managers. It will depend on the knowledge and skill of the platform, but also the skills and the capabilities related to this new way of communicating.

The selection of the project manager might require a different process if you going to work with this kind of collaboration platforms, especially if the role of the project manager is changing from responsible to facilitator.

DESIGNING A LANDSCAPE OF PROJECT COMMUNICATION

Projects rarely start at a blank canvas: most of the time we are doing our best to reach our project goals within an organization already in place, and often even with multiple organizations: Customers and suppliers, each with its own habits, ways of working, and tools that have a major impact on the way we manage our projects (Kerzner, 2015).

Therefore, just throwing all of these habits and tools out of the window and announcing that we will introduce a brand new way of working by forbidding any emails, will most probably only lead to an annoyed customer. Instead, we need to identify the drivers behind this behavior change, and guide the email overload into more suitable channels.

The main driver is the communication habits of the team members and stakeholders of the project. While some people are accustomed to working on a document "in the cloud", there are also still people who edit documents by printing them and scribbling in the margins. And while instant messaging may be the main way of communication for one project team, there are also those who prefer a phone call. Most of these habits come from personal preferences and previous experience ("this worked best in my previous project so I'll introduce it in my new team as well"). So if the communication habits in the team need developing, a tooling training or demo may be needed to get a deeper understanding of the available tools and their capabilities.

However, communication habits can also highly influenced by conformity; either to written or unwritten norms, or by conforming to behavior of other people, either in the project or in its environment: Once someone sends you a question by email, people tend to reply to it using email again, and will also increase the chances of people using email in future similar situations.

A second driver is the communication need: What are the major communication and collaboration needs in the project, for who is the message meant, what is expected from the receiver, and what is the urgency?

And to conclude, there is one major enabler; tooling. In our current climate the amount of available tools is huge, and a lot of it is just a mouse click away (Kerzner, 2015). At the same time, our project environments can have many restrictions; secret or confidential information, customer regulations and legislation (like the Patriot Act in the US) often influence the tools we have available, since some just do not fulfill the requirements on information safety and integrity. In an ideal social collaboration work environment, the following tools should be available:

1. A direct communications client
2. A content/document management application
3. An enterprise Social Network application
4. An email / calendar application

In order to make optimal use of these tools, access for customers or suppliers can also be important.

IMPLEMENTING THE LANDSCAPE

The Use of a Basic Toolset

To implement the landscape as described in the previous section, a basic toolset for communication and collaboration will be used in order to create smarter ways of working. Specific project management tools can be added to the toolset. This toolset (see Figure 1) has the following elements:

- **Unified Communications:** Direct communication: phone, chat, webinars, screen sharing/presenting, electronic whiteboard and sending files, show availability. When it's clear who is available, you will save a lot of time related to waiting for answers.
- **Enterprise Social Network:** Communication and collaboration, sharing, creating, connecting knowledge, people and groups. Open communication providing direct access to relevant experts and solutions.
- **Enterprise Content Management:** Storage of final versions of documents, large amounts of documents, co-creation in documents. An ECM provides more possibilities for fine tuning access rights in case certain documents are secure or secret.

Figure 1. A basic toolset for communication and collaboration

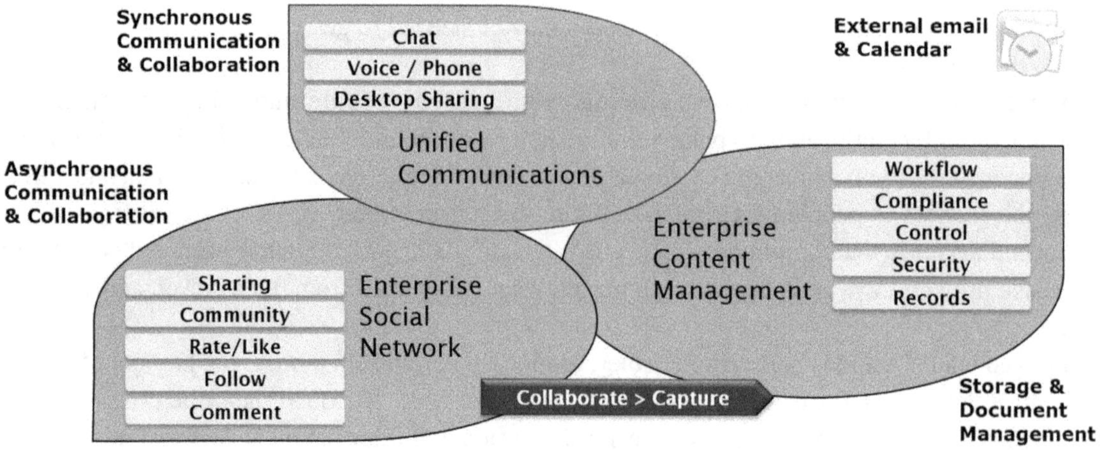

- **Email:** Email communication to external addresses, personal calendar and organizing meetings. Email is often inefficient for collaboration internally by creating information silos and thus preventing access to information. Of course there will always be situations where email is fine to use, like confidential info about HR or in situations with legal requirements enforcing the use of email.

How to Implement this Landscape in your Projects

In a Single Project?

If it is your idea to start with a smarter way of working in your project you do need some kind of formal (project manager) or informal leadership to be credible to your team. If you are working in an agile / scrum environment continuous improvement is more usually and you may expect your team members to be open to suggestions for smarter ways of working.

The existing culture in your organization determines whether it can become a success or not. Is there already a culture of more or less transparency and openness? Or do you work in a very hierarchical structured organization where 'knowledge is power'? In the last case it will be a tough job. Although it can be successful in a single project when you are able to lead by example.

For your new of working you need tools to work with. Most companies do have a lot of communication and collaboration tools which are not optimally combined or not known to everyone. See the previous sections for a basic toolset. Cloud tools are recommended to enable working from home or during traveling. Of course if your project is dealing with security requirements or confidential information you have to carefully check if authorization settings are sufficient. If no suitable tools are available in your organization consider using internet tools. User reviews and best practices are present in abundance on the internet.

Find your first followers in your project. For example "digital natives", the project management officer or the product owner and try to experience the tools together if you are not yet familiar with them. Define the most common and recognizable uses cases of your project. This could be team meeting minutes, progress reports, working on tasks, reviewing deliverables, team discussions (examples of the use cases being used during the implementation of Zero email within Atos can be found in Appendix 1).

Organize sessions with all team members to explain the benefits of the new way of working, facilitate tool training, discuss the use cases you want to start with. Depending on the complexity of the tools and the maturity of your team you need more sessions. Agree with the team when and how to start.

The first steps are always difficult. You have to lead by example and encourage your team members as much as possible. Make it a regular item at your team meeting and retrospectives to improve the way of working and experience new, more complicated, use cases. When your team is getting more mature next steps can be made to onboard steering committee, suppliers and end-users. New uses cases like formal approvals and communication with your end-users are now applying. Communication with end-users can easily evolve into the concept of a "social helpdesk" (Norton, 2013).

In Your Organization?

It you want to harvest the benefits of zero email and smarter ways of working using it only in a single project is not very sustainable. It can even be counterproductive if projects are using their own toolset and way of working. As long as there is no corporate policy for communication and collaboration every department, team, initiative will find its own solution. You will be surprised about the number of tools in your organization! People manage to get licenses with or without the IT department. Besides that it is very easy to access (free of charge) internet tools with all kinds of risks of losing information etc.

The real benefits are not realized in single projects but in transforming the whole organization. Finding peers to exchange experiences and discuss though issues, enable discovery of re-useable materials from other projects/units are for example typically cross project and cross organizational unit benefits.

How to proceed? First start to connect all digital natives, early adopters, social media addicts and empower them to support in formulating an inspiring communication and collaboration vision for your organization. Choose, test and pilot the toolset that best fits and meets the requirements of your organization.

Now that you have an inspiring vision, an appropriate toolset and a group of enthusiastic early adopters it is time to meet the rest of the organization!

From our experiences of the implementation and use of Zero email within Atos (Singh, 2012, Silic et al, 2015), we like to share some lessons learned that worked best in onboarding large numbers of people.

1. *Start a movement with the first early adopters.*

They are your ambassadors, change heroes, and they deserve an awesome name like “zero heroes”, “new workers”, “next generation”. Let them work on use cases for all kind of tasks and problem solving. Use elements of gamification to spread the news and enlarge the group. Reward people for recruiting new members and sharing their personal success stories.

2. *Learn people how to use “the four rooms of change” model.*

This model (see Figure 2) helps to understand that people need time to move from one stage (“room”) to another. It also helps to see that people are in different phases and that every phase has its own approach. Some people can change in one day; other people never get out of “Denial & excuses”.

- **Contentment & Complacency Room:** Coaching someone who is in the contentment & complacency room consists in trying to “wake up” this person by delivering a symbolic shock - for example telling what is going to happen if someone doesn’t change. For example: “I would fear that, when everybody will be using the enterprise social network, you would be isolated and unable to perform your job in a proper way”. When the individual realizes that his performance is in danger, he will start looking for excuses, which leads us to the next room.
- **Denial & Excuses Room:** Coaching someone who’s in this room requires several steps:
    - Reinforcing the feeling of uncertainty, using symbolic shocks again.
    - Then creating awareness of the gap, using facts & figures.
    - Finally, demonstrating that the problem is intrinsic, and not coming from other factors

This process is accelerated when the individual can be mixed with people who are in the renewal & revitalization room. This makes the gap more obvious, and inspires the individual by providing examples of how it looks in the bright side. When the individual is ready for change, he moves into the next room.

Figure 2. The four rooms of change model (Janssen, 1996)

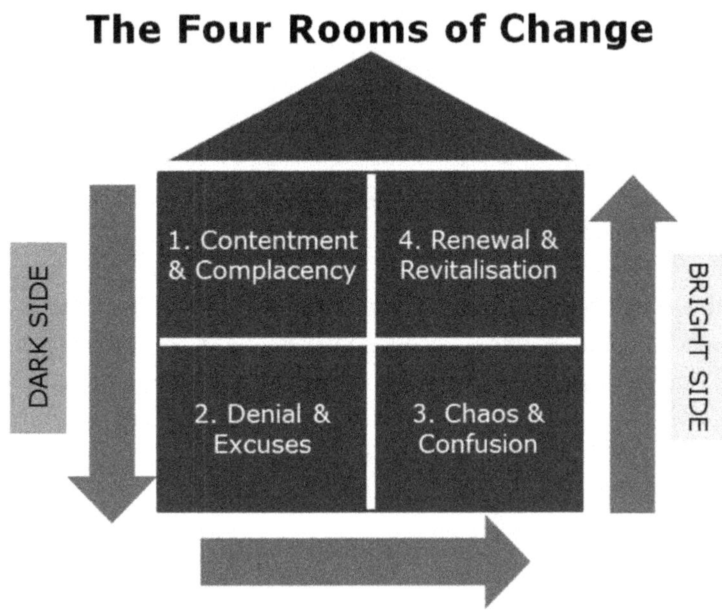

- **Chaos & Confusion Room:** Individuals in chaos & confusion are ready and motivated for change, but they need to be guided to succeed. A stepped approach is also recommended to achieve incremental progress and increasing confidence.
    - Create a compelling vision by showing what success looks like
    - Provide clarity on how to achieve this vision by defining a roadmap
    - Remove hurdles and blockers by identifying and addressing fears of the individual
    - Monitor progress and give feedback along the change journey

When the individual has completed the change process and performs autonomously at the expected level, he needs to stay with the renewal & revitalization room.

- **Renewal & Revitalization Room:** The risk for individuals in this room is to move back to contentment & complacency. Coaching actions to keep them in this room are:
    - Identifying new green fields of potential progress.
    - Provide new challenges and responsibilities that are in the individual's sphere of capabilities.
    - Give regular feedback, in particular, recognize and reward successes.
    - Move achievements into business as usual by setting them as new standards.

USER EXPERIENCES

The use of email is a commodity in business and personal life. People cannot work and even think without the use of email. And therefore, to change into a different way of working is difficult and cumbersome. It took Atos about three to four years to get a certain Zero email status (Silic et al, 2015). And even now, continued focus is needed or else people slowly start to use email again.

Predicting anything to do with technology is difficult, and it becomes even more difficult when everyone can contribute their ideas about this new way of working. As an example of how difficult is to predict to the future, we only have to look at the fax machine. Email was supposed to wipe out fax use completely, but this didn't happen. Even though using a fax machine is more expensive and time consuming. The fax machine will certainly become obsolete, but it is extremely difficult to predict the timing of technology change (Moore, 2010). The same applies to email.

The experience of users in social media and the use – or better the lack of use – of email in projects will be described related to the topics below (Harrin, 2010).

The Use of Tooling in Projects

More and more, traditional project management tools take on the features and functionality provided by social media tools, in fact to improve productivity and effective collaboration. Project management software will include social media suites on a more routine basis. And therefore, the strict need to use email to collaborate will diminish. The additional functionality will make it easier to manage various data and communication streams. And therefore make it easier to connect with stakeholders coming from different organizations (with their own domains). We will see more and more project management software in use as a portal, consolidating all behind-the-scenes social media tools to present one common interface.

In average, tools are distinctive and therefore lack the power of synergy. Project managers will have to use several different tools like MS Project, spreadsheets, office packages, etc.., different email packages (even in the same project), different social media environments like LinkedIn, Facebook, chat software, etc.. Working for one company makes it possible to choose one set of tools commonly used by this company. But even that one set of tools is in most cases a combination. And at the moment the project managers understood the full complexity and makes use of the advantages of this (combination) package, he or she will shift to another company or client with a different set of tools. The whole learning experience starts all over again. Business is still far away from one solution that fits all.

The great results will only come if the tools being applied meet a business need. IT-dominated social media initiatives will fail. Backing from a business unit who will be using the project or program management suite, or social media tool, is crucial for the implementation of this suite or tool. Very important is the role of the project manager itself. Project-based social media initiatives championed by interested and enthusiastic project managers and sponsors will be far more successful, than something made available by the IT department. Social media use through projects needs a business need (Harrin, 2010).

Do not underestimate the habit of project managers and team members to use the tools they have always used. Although most project managers are flexible and quickly adapt – asked by different clients

– to use different project management tooling, they commonly use the same kind of tooling for many many years. It took Atos a long time to convince their employees and – even more difficult – their clients to restrain from use of email. And use social media instead. Proper and carefully planned management of change is important to achieve this new way of thinking.

A New Generation of Team Members

Another growing trend is the next-generation of team members in project teams. This "young" generation has grown up with social media tools, chatting and extremely short and fast communication lines. Email does not fit in there and is not used anymore. This group sees social media as being vital for communication and collaboration and has never known a world without them (Thamhain, 2009). For this group, these tools are not gadgets; they are a way of life. There is by the way a risk that this generation will choose their projects based on the availability of social media tools. And therefore, it is important that certain social media tools should not be blocked during office hours.

Mobility is Growing

Although project teams and stakeholders are already mobile, the current existing toolset do not support sufficiently mobile working. The current ordinary phones, smart phones and iPad's are more and more able to cope with the requirements of social media, but still need development to support this new way of executing projects.

Social media and enterprise collaboration tools will make more of the notion of presence. Giving a user the possibility to show that he or she is willing to be interrupted by instant messages, but also to set their contact preferences to "none" (if he or she does not want to be disturbed). Presence technology will evolve from relying on the user to update their notification settings into picking up clues from the user's location or activity and update status directly (Harrin, 2010).

Implementation of Social Media and Collaboration

It is not easy to predict the pace of change, but we can assume it will be quick. Consider how much is changed in the last ten years. Along with the tremendous rate of change, it is important to consider the rate of adoption. The adoption of this new technology will increase, and being able to operate in a social media workplace will be a key skill for distributed and co-located project teams. Individuals who are early adopters of new tools and technology are likely to blaze a trail and use these tools in their personal lives before they make it into their projects.

Nevertheless, careful implementation of social media and collaboration tooling is important to achieve a higher level of acceptance (Bradley & McDonald, 2011). One of the main rules to start with is: start little. Do not change complete large projects and underlying organization at once. Start with small projects, with a small team, to get experienced and use the lessons learned for the next size of projects. Start "close to home". Although social media and collaboration has explicitly its benefits in multi-national projects, it is better to start with a national, even in-company project, with a few team members and a few stakeholders. The project manager plays an important role. He or she is the figurehead of this new way of working. And therefore should be the role model and gives good example on how to use social media and collaboration, and to restrain from using old-fashioned email.

Although project teams contain more and more "next-generation" members, do not expect that everyone in the team is fully aware of the pros and cons of social media and collaboration. And certainly not fully experienced in using this kind of tooling. Training by using blogs, vodcast, or other computer based trainings will expedite the experience of the project team members in using social media tooling.

Be aware that – although a carefully planned and monitored implementation – the following can still happen:

- **Too Much Spam:** In the same way as with email traffic, there is a risk that the user of social media is overloaded with spam. Meaning getting too much information not related to the current work or project. Spam filters are not common good in social media, so therefore it is the sender's responsibility not to overload the network and tools with non-relevant information. Data overload is in fact a common issue in social media. Still a lot of research has to be carried out to find (technical) solutions for data overload.
- **Mix of Private and Project Matters:** Project team members use in most cases social media already at home. For all kind of private matters. There is a risk that this behavior will be copied to social media used at work. The project – driven by the project manager – should agree on procedures and rules to avoid mixture of private and project matters.
- **Project Manager not in Control:** The project manager becomes more and more a facilitator. The team accepts a certain level of self-management. Executing the project on its own. The risk exists that the project manager does not know what exactly is happening within the project. Constant monitoring and direct contact with the project team members (one-to-one or via project meetings) will mitigate this risk. Self-controlling teams does not release the project manager from maintaining his or her control administration like RAID logs.
- **Actions Directed to Groups of People and Not Specific Persons:** Social media and collaboration can work with user groups, or collaboration groups. Projects do have their own groups, in which all communication and tuning will take place. The risk of using these groups is that specific actions – given to the group – are not picked up and executed because no one in the group sees him- or herself as the owner. RAID logs can mitigate this. Also connecting an action directly to a team member – even in the collaboration group – can also mitigate this. Standard project management rules still apply, also in this way of working.
- **Nobody Knows what to do Exactly:** This can be a final result of what is discussed above. The self-management team is out of control, there is no clear plan anymore, and the project manager takes his role as facilitator too serious forgetting to manage the project. Social media and collaboration tools must support the project, not taken over completely the management of the project. The project manager should remain in control.
- **People Will Still Use Email:** The pace of change can be slow, and the level of acceptance also. Therefore, team members will continue to use email. Also communication with suppliers or different clients can force the team member to use email at a certain level. This is a common fact and will not change immediately. Management of change is needed to convince the supplier or third parties to use the same social media or collaboration tooling as the project team. The advantage of social media, and cloud technologies make that rather easy; it is a matter of new way of thinking (which will result in new way of working).
- **Risk of Unsecure Environment:** Cloud technology, social media tooling has the bad image of being unsecure. Everything you post will be visible to the whole world and will remain on the

internet forever. At least, that is common thinking, and this fear is intensified by news in the media on leakages of different common social media. But more and more attention from IT-industry is given to security aspects of – among others – social media. Specific business related social media tooling can only be used by the project or the business, and has therefore an acceptable level of security. The project must not use public tooling, and stick to those tooling specifically installed per business or per project.

Lessons Learnt from the Atos Case

As already mentioned, it took Atos a long time to change the culture of the organization and the mindset of her employees. But the results are promising because the organization is has now (see also Silic et al, 2015):

- Smarter and better ways of collaborating.
- Opportunities to create new ideas, products and services and advance innovation with crowd-innovation communities.
- Higher competitiveness and productivity where knowledge is the key to succeed and will remain organizational best asset but only when shared.
- Fulfillment of employees' needs through online communities and by sharing knowledge and best practices.
    - Better work-life balance could be achieved.
    - Empowering employees by giving them roles and responsibilities.
    - Higher recognition of high performing individuals.

For Atos, "Social Collaboration implementation is a marathon, not a sprint. Its transformation begins in the inside of our organization and gradually grows out to become a real social business ecosystem with employees, partners and customers" (Silic et al, 2015; Atos, 2012c).

FURTHER RESEARCH DIRECTIONS

Projects without email, or using less email in daily business, is implemented within Atos, and a few businesses (clients). It took a long time to get Atos partly email free (Silic et al, 2015). But it is still being used and the risk that it will be used more again is apparently there. How to avoid that is unclear.

Running projects working with different parties using different communication systems or methodologies is difficult: systems often do not communicate and also people from different parties are sometimes refusing to use other systems or even an overall system or methodology.

Research is needed to identify the approach how to keep an organization email-free (or zero email compliant). Further research is needed to – especially in large, multi-company, international projects – define the way to harmonize different systems and methodologies of different companies working in the same project. A result can be set of clear processes and procedures, but it is evidently that management of change to convince the team members is also necessary.

Furthermore, the real effect of zero email on project results is still to be investigated, not only quantitative – effect on time and budget – but also qualitative. Does it really help?

CONCLUSION

Although the use of email can be reduced by more and more use of other tooling like social media, chats, social collaboration tooling, it is still not possible to get rid of it completely. But, the use of social media is growing; not only in personal life but also in business. And therefore in projects. Social collaboration tooling is becoming more mature, and is able to fulfill a lot of communication and collaboration requirements of projects.

A lot of units in the Atos organization have the Zero email certificate. But it took them more than 3 years to achieve that certificate. And – especially in communication with external stakeholders and parties – it is not possible to move away completely from the use of email.

Humans are social beings and we still are not able to interact completely by using the internet and email, although we are trying. How people are working online in a project environment is not perfect, and we should anticipate that more evolutions and innovations will come in the next coming years to change that, hopefully in an improving way.

It is difficult to predict the pace of change, but looking at the near past, this will be fast. Not only technology will change fast, but also the rate of adoption. This will increase, and project team members have to develop themselves in the use of social media and collaboration tools.

Nevertheless, email is not abandoned completely. And future research is still needed to identify the real quantitative impact of the move from email to social media and collaboration on project results.

REFERENCES

Bradley, A. J., & McDonald, M. P. (2011). *The Social Organization: How to Use Social Media to Tap the Collective Genius of Your Customers and Employees. Gartner Inc.* Harvard Business Review Press.

Enterprise social collaboration for a better way of working. (2012a). *Atos*. Retrieved from https://atos.net/content/dam/global/we-do/atos-Social-collaboration-brochure.pdf

Study Reveals Australian Office Workers Stressed by Irrelevant Email Overload. (2010). *Galaxy Research for IBM*. Retrieved from http://www-03.ibm.com/press/au/en/pressrelease/32913.wss

Grit, R. (2015). *Project Management, A Practical approach*. Netherlands: Noordhoff Publishers.

Harrin, E. (2010). *Social media for Project Managers*. Newton Square, PA: Project Management Institute.

Jackson, Th. W., & Dawson, R. (2003). *Breaking Bad Habits: The Negative Effect of Email and Instant Messaging on the Workplace*. UK: Loughborough University.

Janssen, C. F. (1996). *The Four Rooms of Change, Förändringens fyra rum*. Wahlström & Widstrand.

Kerzner, R. (2015). *Project Management 2.0*. Hoboken, NJ: Wiley.

Moore, S. (2010). *Strategic project portfolio management*. Hoboken, NJ: Wiley.

Norton, R. (2013). *Social Helpdesk – A new era of support – or is it?* Atos Ascent Blog (blog.atos.net)

Ollus, M., Jansson, K., & Karvonen, I. (2006). On the management of collaborative networked organizations. In P. Cunningham, & M. Cunningham (Eds.), *Conference Proceedings from IST-Africa 2006*. IIMC International Information Management Corporation.

Ollus, M., Jansson, K., Karvonen, I., Uoti, M., & Riikonen, H. (2009). On Services for Collaborative Project Management. In L. M. Camarinha-Matos, I. Paraskakis, & H. Afsarmanesh (Eds.), *Leveraging Knowledge for Innovation in Collaborative Networks* (Vol. 307, pp. 451–462). IFIP Advances in Information and Communication Technology.

Silic, M., Back, A., & Silic, D. (2015). Atos – Towards a Zero email company, Teaching Case. *Proceedings of Twenty-Third European Conference on Information Systems (ECIS)*, Germany.

Singh, S. (2012). *New Mega Trends: Implications for Our Future Lives*. UK: Palgrave MacMillan. doi:10.1057/9781137008091

Smarter working with zero email. (2012b). *Atos*. Retrieved from https://atos.net/content/dam/global/we-do/atos-zero-email-brochure-lores.pdf

1 in 5 UK workers spend 32 days a year managing email. (2010). Star survey. Retrieved from http://www.prlog.org/11109396-1-in-5-uk-workers-spend-32-days-year-managing-email.html

Thamhain, H. (2009). The future of team leadership in complex project environments. In D. I. Cleveland & B. Bidanda (Eds.), *Project management circa 2025*. Newton Square, PA: Project Management Institute.

Email Statistics Report, 2009-2013. (2009). *The Radiciti group*.

The zero email company (White paper). (2012c). Atos. Retrieved from http://at.atos.net/content/dam/de/documents/atos-whitepaper-zeroemailcompany.pdf

KEY TERMS AND DEFINITIONS

Social Media: Websites and applications that enable users to create and share content or to participate in social networking.

Tooling: The process of equipping project team members with specific tools for a particular project or activity.

Virtual Project Teams: Groups of geographically, organizationally and/or time dispersed project team members brought together by information and telecommunication technologies to accomplish one or more project task.

Way of Working: The operation or mode of operation of something.

Zero Email: Ambition to communicate and collaborate with as less email traffic as possible. Collaboration: The action of working with someone to produce something.

APPENDIX

Introduction of Zero Email within Atos – Use Cases

During the introduction of the Zero email approach in Atos several personas with use cases have been created to increase understanding and acceptance of the new way of working. A persona is an archetype, characterization of a particular type of user. Recognizable examples are: contract manager, consultant, engineer, sales manager and of course project manager. We will limit ourselves to the project manager. For this manager key elements are described like pain points with traditional way of working, benefits from new way of working, list of most common use cases. We will introduce you to our international project manager, Mathias (Figure 3), who is currently managing the launch of a new banking product called StashUp.

In the traditional way of working Mathias is facing a lot of emails and a lot of pain points. For example: difficult to share experiences, managing geographically spread teams, aligns project team on key knowledge and project news. In the new way of working he can use the toolset in Figure 1. Benefits for Mathias from the new way of working are: collaborate with all team members in the most effective and efficient way, enable fast knowledge transfer and handover of activities by centralizing and structuring knowledge, find peers to exchange experiences and discuss though project issues, enable discovery of re-useable materials from other projects.

For the first benefit "collaborate with all team members in the most effective and efficient way" a number of use cases are made which can be used depending on the main characteristics of a project. We will elaborate on 4 use cases which causes regularly "email storms" in a traditional way of working (see Table 1).

Figure 3. Our project manager, Mathias Plan

Table 1. Use cases which causes regularly "email storms" in a traditional way of working

Use Case	Traditional Way	Zero Email Way
Reviewing deliverables and team discussions	Mathias sends an email with the new StashUp promotion materials to all the members of the marketing team and asks for feedback.	Mathias posts the promotion materials in the project team environment and asks for feedback.
	Some members reply only to him with their remarks, others edit the logo and reply to all. Some of them forward his email to others for new input with or without a cc to Mathias.	All remarks are visible to all members involved; all information is in one place. New members can easily be added to join the discussion. Issues can be solved between members involved.
	Some of the remarks are double or contrary, and some need explanation while Mathias can't find out who made them. It takes a lot of time for Mathias to filter all remarks out of his inbox and decide what and how to change.	All remarks are in one place. Contrary remarks can be discussed directly and are already solved by the team.
Progress control and actions	Mathias emails the agenda of the team meeting and a list of open actions. During the team meeting he asks the action holders what the status of their action is and then edits the statuses in the meeting.	The agenda and action list are on the project team environment. All team members look into the actions before the meeting and can edit the status themselves. Mathias only mentions actions that are still open during the meeting.
	Mathias needs to know whether the StashUp website is ready before the promotion campaign is planned to start. He emails a list with all the agreed deliverables to the team manager of the webcare team and asks for an update of the planning. The team manager goes to the scrum board and types all deliverable statuses into the excel sheet.	Mathias goes to the virtual scrum board in the project team environment, and sees that all deliverables are on schedule.
Formal management approvals	Mathias, together with the marketing team, has decided in the morning team meeting on Monday that to increase traffic to the newly created StashUp website, the launch of the product should be accompanied by a new TV commercial. They are in a hurry but do need approval before they can start filming. Adhering to company policy he emails his request for approval to the Marketing Director that same afternoon. Only after his approval, he can send it to the Contracts Manager and the CEO.	On Monday afternoon Mathias posts his plan, together with a request for approval, on the offerings environment. He adds a sequential work flow cycle with the Marketing Director, the contracts manager and the CEO as approvers.
	On Tuesday morning, Mathias finds out that the Marketing Director has emailed him back with his approval. He forwards the message to the Contracts Manager and starts his meetings. During his lunch break he sees the approval of the contracts manager and sends it on to the CEO. His approval email returns on Wednesday morning.	When checking the offerings environment on Tuesday morning, he sees that his plan has already been approved by the Marketing Director and the Contracts Manager, and is now waiting for approval by the CEO. He contacts him via instant messaging that he is urgently waiting for his approval, which he receives 10 minutes later.
Communication with users	The only thing blocking the launch of the new StashUp banking solution is to make sure the direct sales employees know how to explain the product to the customers. Mathias emails a few explanatory documents and opens an email box to which the employees at the direct sales department can send any questions.	Mathias organizes a web conference to explain the concept of StashUp, the benefits for customers, and the impact it is expected to have for the direct sales department. He creates a virtual StashUp-rollout environment where the direct sales employees can post questions and he also places links to work instructions and his presentation during the web conference there.
	On the first day of the launch, Laura from second line support lets him know that she really needs more help answering the emails coming into the StashUp email box. A lot of the direct sales employees have the same kind of questions but it takes a lot of time to answer all of them.	Laura from second line support opens up the virtual StashUp-rollout environment and starts answering questions. If someone asks a question that has already been asked, she only links to the correct answer. And because the environment is easily searchable and contains all relevant documentation, there aren't even that many questions. Some of the direct sales employees even start answering their colleagues' questions!

Chapter 14
From Reactive to Proactive Use of Social Media in Emergency Response:
A Critical Discussion of the Twitcident Project

Kees Boersma
VU University, The Netherlands

Julie Ferguson
VU University, The Netherlands

Dominique Diks
Hiemstra en De Vries, The Netherlands

Jeroen Wolbers
VU University, The Netherlands

ABSTRACT

This chapter examines the introduction and implementation of the pilot project Twitcident in an emergency response room setting. Twitcident is a web-based system for filtering, searching and analyzing data on real-world incidents or crises. Social media data is seen as important for emergency response operations: it can be used as an 'early warning monitoring system' to detect social unrest, and for improving common operational pictures (COPs). This chapter shows that the expectations on the functioning of the tool were not fully met: first it was hard for the response room professionals to make sense of the data and second, the management did not develop a proper project planning. The recommendations are twofold. On the one hand, the professionals who work with Twitcident must invest in developing new information management routines. On the other hand, the response room management needs to create a much more inclusive project learning strategy.

INTRODUCTION

Over the last five years, the use of social media and social networks such as Twitter, Facebook, Yammer and Instagram by citizens at times of crisis has gained the attention of professionals operating in crisis response organizations, such as the police, fire service and medical teams (Palen, 2008; Merchant, Elmer, & Lurie, 2011). In the crisis management literature it has been recognized for decades that citizens are

DOI: 10.4018/978-1-4666-9867-3.ch014

self-reliant when there is social disruption and in crisis situations, whether those are incidents, emergencies or large-scale disasters (Helsloot & Ruitenberg, 2004). Nowadays, social media platforms provide a new opportunity for people to keep each other informed, adding a bottom-up information network that provides a platform for online communication (Machjzrack & More, 2010). In addition, they can potentially provide welcome additional resources for professionals in crisis response organizations. The promise is that, by using social media data, the first responders can enlarge their *common operational picture* (COP) (Yin, Lampert, Cameron, Robinson, & Power, 2012).

Yet, although the response organizations have started to recognize the importance of social media data during times of crisis, *how* this data actually can be made sense of, interpreted, validated and used is still an issue that requires further research. Therefore, professional crisis response organizations have also carried out (pilot) information management projects to understand how social media platforms actually work and how they can include social media data in their operations, both day-to-day and during crises. Over the years, many pilot projects have been implemented to test social media platforms as early warning systems, and to provide professionals with data that predicts upcoming social disruptions (Goolsby, 2010). In particular, the police have undertaken projects to determine how they could use social media data in their surveillance activities (Crump, 2011). Whereas for a long time social media data was regarded merely as 'noise' or, at best, not validated data[1], these projects indicate that crisis response managers and professionals are starting to take social media and Web 2.0 platforms seriously. Their problem, however, is how to incorporate these new information flows properly into existing information architectures in order to build a coherent crisis information system and, eventually, make the emergency response more reliable.

In this chapter we will present a project management case from the physical safety in the Netherlands, where 25 safety regions were established in 2007 to cover the crisis response across the whole country (Boersma, Groenewegen, & Wagenaar, 2010; Boersma, Wagenaar, & Wolbers, 2012). The safety regions have various functions. First, they facilitate integration between the two main first response disciplines: the fire service and the ambulance service medical teams. They work closely together with the police, who are organized at the national level in the Netherlands. Second, each safety region has had to establish a bureau responsible for developing emergency response plans and strategies and for how their professionals communicate with those in other emergency services, with policymakers and with citizens. Third, the safety region bureau is responsible for undertaking a specific risk analysis and assessment for the region. Finally, the safety region must ensure that there is a dispatch center, or *emergency response room* function, available. In the response room all three of the first response disciplines or services (police, fire and ambulance) are represented. The response room can be shared with other safety regions, on condition that the on condition that they are still able to respond adequately to incoming calls from citizens from across their own region.

Since 2012, those responsible for managing the safety regions have started to improve their crisis information management by implementing social media projects. For the various professionals working in the safety regions, however, it is still difficult to include social media data in their information management at times of emergency. The case we will present in this chapter is a pilot project from one of the 25 Dutch safety regions. In this region a project called *Twitcident* has been put in place to see how social media data – and in particular data from Twitter – could be used in the response room setting. It is a web-based system for filtering, searching and analyzing data on real-world incidents or crises. The project started in April 2014 and has been used by the region. We studied the implementation of the project and interviewed the professionals who were directly and indirectly involved in the introduction and in the actual use of Twitcident. We studied the aims and goals of the project, the expectations of the professionals involved, how Twitcident was *used*, and the first results. Our research question is:

How did Twitcident affect the developing of a common operational picture between different professional disciplines in an emergency control room setting?

The sub-questions are:

Why did the management of the safety region initiate the Twitcident pilot project?
How was Twitcident implemented?
How did Twitcident affect the work of the emergency response room professionals?

We collected our data through observations and interviews during the first half of 2014. Our main concern was to understand both the expectations of the management and the experience of actually using Twitcident, a framework and web-based system for filtering, searching and analyzing data on real-world incidents or crises (Abel, Hauff, Houben, Stronkman, & Tao, 2012). In both of these areas, *sensemaking* in crisis situations (Weick, 1988) was a central issue for us: we were curious to know how those involved made sense of the complex coordination and information-sharing practices in emergency and crisis situations. Sensemaking is seen by Weick as a cognitive activity and ability of framing experienced situations as meaningful. Collective sensemaking is the collaborative process in which different individuals start to create *shared* awareness and understanding of the situation.

We conducted a total of 17 interviews with managers, information system engineers (who were responsible for the actual implementation of the project), professionals from the region's emergency response room, and police officers. Our most important sources of information were the centralists and generalists working in the response room. The *centralists* who do the intake (i.e., receive the incoming emergency calls), validate and, where possible, enrich the data and pass it on to the first responders in the field. The *generalists* who work with additional information sources such as social media platforms and applications that can enrich social media data – the Twitcident project being one example – to provide the centralists with additional information.

Over a period of two months, we observed how the interaction between the generalists and centralists took place, and how Twitcident added to the quality of the information exchange, if at all. We selected this style of ethnographic research and in-situ research in order to gain a fuller picture of the context of the response room and the background to the routines of the generalists and centralists (Alvesson & Sköldberg, 2009). The generalists wrote daily diaries or logbooks, which were very useful in helping us to understand their actions and see what kind of data analysis they undertook with Twitcident. We were also able to get access to formal documents about the pilot project and to the work manuals and standard operational procedures used by the generalists and centralists.

The objectives of this chapter are first of all to understand how pilot projects function as a 'protected space' for introducing and testing new, contested information technologies. Second, we would like to present an actual case in the context of a demanding environment, i.e., the emergency response room, where the time pressures constrain a smooth introduction of new technologies.

BACKGROUND

In the literature on emergency management, adopting a COP is proposed as the solution to poor communication and information-sharing practices in and between response organizations (Wolbers & Boersma, 2013). The idea is that a COP is an integrated part of an information system and used to overcome problems such as information overload, or insufficient evaluation and validation of the information. A COP is defined as the display of relevant information shared by more than one command or unit. Potentially, COPs contribute to a better *situational awareness*, which is the perception of environmental elements during incidents, emergencies and crises with respect to time, space and meaning, critical to the decision-making processes of professional first responders (Sarter & Woods, 1991; Bosse, Majdanik, Boersma, & Ingibergsdóttir, 2013). Adequate information management is seen as a precondition for creating a high-quality COP. Technical solutions are seen as the answer to failing information management. Over the years emergency response rooms information systems have been 'enriched' by a myriad of tools to enable and improve information management and thus the creation of COPs. The newest generation of tools that have been added to emergency response rooms are meant to make social media data suitable for use in emergency response information management.

Social media sites, and Twitter in particular, are seen as an important (additional) source of information in emergency and crisis situations (Mendoza, Poblete, & Castillo, 2010; Schultz, Utz, & Göritz, 2011; Hughes & Palen, 2009; Cassa, Chunara, Mandl, & Brownstein, 2013). With applications such as Twitcident the centralists in the emergency response rooms can actually follow what citizens post on social media and how citizens' information networks come into being. Twitcident can be seen as part of a larger trend in crisis management and practice to enlarge the number of sources for creation of relevant information. In particular, during actual crises and emergencies, information needs to be up-to-date and dynamic (Treurniet, Messemaker, Wolbers and Boersma, 2015). Since the crisis or emergency is constantly changing, the centralists demand sources that can deal with the speed of change. Social media sources have the potential to provide a greater quantity of information and more up-to-date information than other, more static, sources such as databases and information from incoming emergency calls.

The use of social media data in crisis and emergency situations is promising, but not without problems. There are serious concerns relating to the quality of the data from social media platforms, the validation of social media data (Yates & Paquette, 2011), the filtering of relevant information from messy social media data sources (Abel et al., 2012; Oh, Agrawal, & Rao, 2013), and the process of combining social media data with relevant data from other sources (Vieweg, Hughes, Starbird, & Palen, 2010). There are also more fundamental problems such as legal issues and questions to do with privacy and surveillance (Van de Walle, Turoff, & Hiltz, 2009; Fuchs, Boersma, Albrechtslund, & Sandoval, 2011).

Besides the more practical problems relating to the use of social media in emergency and crisis situations, we see that the expectations can be sky-high. The idea that social media data is useful for crisis situations can be seen as information technology *hype* (Meijer, Boersma, & Wagenaar, 2009). A hype can be agenda-setting, but in instances where promises cannot be met, users start to be very disappointed. Through a lack of planning or thoughtless introduction and implementation people will no longer buy in to the hype at all in particular when the claims are exaggerated (Ruef & Markard, 2010). In addition, projects always run the risk of becoming dysfunctional in different project phases, particularly in situations in which there is no common understanding of the project (Van Marrewijk, 2007; Veenswijk,

Van Marrewijk, & Boersma, 2010). Crucial for the success or failure of a project such as Twitcident is a careful and thoughtful plan for its introduction, monitoring and evaluation (Edmondson, Bohmer, & Pisano, 2001).

In order to be successful, Twitcident must be seen as a social, organizational project and not solely as a technical project (Barley, 1986; Orlikowski, & Barley, 2001). However, it has already been known for decades that IT innovation projects are often based on a relatively naïve picture of organizational change. Events, features, and behaviors that are important to the project's success or failure tend to be overlooked (Markus & Robey, 1988; Ciborra & Lanzara, 1994; Boersma & Kingma, 2005; Mirvis, Sales, & Hackett 2006). In this chapter, therefore, we will reflect upon Twitcident not only as a useful additional source of information in crisis management, but we will also consider the particular characteristics of the project, and the way it has been introduced and implemented in the organization.

THE INTRODUCTION AND USE OF TWITCIDENT IN THE EMERGENCY CONTROL ROOM SETTING

In 2012 the Dutch safety regions took an important step in optimizing their information management and information processes. This involved the establishment of *real-time intelligence centers* (RTICs) (Inspectorate of Safety and Justice, 2013). The information technologies used in the RTICs were primarily meant to support police work, but since the centers were housed next to the response rooms, they also started to collect and share information with the fire and ambulance service. The idea behind the RTICs is mainly to create an 'early warning monitoring system'. Centralists are supposed to consult the RTIC information to evaluate and monitor the atmosphere and the behavior of citizens in town centers.

Monitoring citizens' behavior became an issue for the safety regions' bureau after the so-called *project X* incident, during which social media platforms were used to mobilize people to come together for partying. In 2012 a project X party in the Netherlands got out of hand, because the police could not prevent serious rioting during the party (Van Dijck & Poell, 2013). Second, the information from the RTIC is supposed to enable centralists, and eventually officers in the field, to create an *improved COP* of the emergency situation and of the actions and interactions taking place on the ground.

The management of the safety region considered the RTIC the perfect place in which to implement the Twitcident pilot project. Before the introduction of the RTICs to the emergency response rooms, centralist only looked incidentally into social media data, and they had no analytical tools like Twitcident at their disposal.

Setting the Scene: Centralists and Generalists

In order to understand the relative value of Twitcident (and, in a broader sense, social media data), we will describe the organization of the emergency response rooms and their role in the safety region.

The emergency response room and RTIC featured in our study are housed in two rooms next to each other, separated by a glass wall. The rooms are connected by a door that is always open, so that the professionals working there can easily walk from one room to the other, to ask for feedback, exchange information in person, or request validation of decisions or actions. For the generalists it is important to be able to see what is going on in the emergency response room so that they can respond instantly to the 'body language' of their colleagues asking for additional information. The workstations of the centralists and the generalists are very similar.

The centralists in the response room are the dispatchers; they operate the response information systems, take the incoming calls, evaluate the relevance and quality of the information received, and are responsible for disseminating the information to the appropriate first responders on the streets. The centralists have sophisticated communication and information systems at their disposal (Wagenaar, Boersma, Groenewegen, & Niemandsverdriet, 2009). About ten years ago, a new integrated information system was introduced for the response rooms, which used the software *GMS*, the Dutch abbreviation for an Integrated Emergency Room System. This system integrates various services and systems such as the 1-1-2 phone number (the Dutch equivalent of the 9-1-1 emergency number in North America), communication, radio and telephone systems used by first responders, and important databases related to the information needs of the three services, police, fire service and ambulance. One of the GMS screens is a data-entry screen where new information can be added into the database. The other screen shows geographical information about the position of the first responders (e.g., police cars), and the location of the incident. Of course, the centralists use telecommunication devices such as phones, radios and pagers to communicate with citizens and with first responders. The phones are integrated into a system that gives the centralists instant access to the most important numbers (landlines) such as those for hospitals, doctors, police stations and other organizations that are part of the critical infrastructure.

Data entered into GMS by the centralists is visible to those in the three first response services, except for data that are filtered, for example, because of confidential information. The data within GMS can also be consulted by the RTIC generalists. They know which background information will be critical to the first responders, and how to create a COP on the basis of the messages coming in. Their job description includes the need for search skills that enable them to access additional information, and the ability to filter relevant information from social media. This is in contrast to the work of a centralist, who responds to the incoming data in a reactive manner (i.e., after the call has come in, or after an incident has happened). The generalists, however, can enrich data by adding background information such as information on locations, persons, the social environment, and historical detail. This information is entered into GMS using separate files. The generalists can send it to the first responders.

The RTIC's function can be seen as that of an *intelligence service* – it collects, analyses, and exploits information to support the response room and ultimately the actual response operations (Inspectorate of Safety and Justice, 2013, pp. 33-34). The generalists also have access to additional systems such as MobiPol, a database with police information, vehicle tracking systems, specific databases, and enterprise resource systems. They can also access *Blueview*, which contains over 55 million documents with information about criminals and past crimes. And finally, of course, they can consult open information sources such as those on the Internet.

The Introduction of the Twitcident Project

The management of the safety region started to implement the Twitcident project on 1st April 2014. Their main concern was how the professionals in the response room could use social media data proactively. Our interviews with the centralists revealed that they heard about the project only two days before it was introduced. The manager responsible for the instruction used a PowerPoint presentation to explain the technical functionalities of the project. He also drew attention to the way in which the centralists and generalists should use the tool as an addition to the systems already in use. Since the introduction was done with an emphasis on the technical aspects of the tool, the centralists and the generalists – considered to be the end-users – did not directly understand the main goal of the project and how Twitcident could be integrated into their daily routines and information management practices.

According to the managers that we interviewed some weeks after the introduction, however, the goal of Twitcident was clear: using social media websites as an 'antenna', the centralists were supposed to capture important information from citizens. Social media data could provide an answer, at least in part, to the question 'what is going on in society'. At the same time, for them Twitcident was an important project to see whether and how they could align ideas and practices about the use of social media at times of crisis at a local and national level. Twitcident was for them also a tool for organizational change. Both the centralists and the generalists were provided with a personal account (including login and password) to access Twitcident. This way, the managers coordinating the pilot could check who was using the tool, and what kind of (search) actions were taking place.

The centralists, however, interpreted the tool first and foremost as an enabling instrument that would help enlarge the *common operational picture* when incidents were taking place. In other words, for them it became an extra sensor that could be used to provide first responders in the field with relevant information about a particular incident. Also, they saw the introduction of the pilot as an attempt by the management to take initiative: with the introduction of Twitcident they could show sensitivity to the hype surrounding social media.

The rather inadequate 'management of expectations' resulted in different and at times conflicting ideas about how Twitcident could be used. The managers could fall back on a mutual feeling that social media data was potentially useful for the centralists' work, but there was no consensus about *how* that potential could be fully exploited. The centralists doubted from the start whether the Twitcident information would really be helpful to them in their daily operations and at times of crisis. To them it was unclear how they could link the information to other sources of information that they could already access. Also, the centralists had many questions about the way they could *make sense* of the additional information. While this objection could easily be interpreted as resulting from unfamiliarity with the system, there was another aspect of Twitcident that bothered them a lot. Their concern was that implementing and using Twitcident would be very time-consuming in a situation in which they were already experiencing a heavy workload.

Twitcident in Use

The Twitcident interface contains a set of filters (i.e., search options) that capture and categorize incoming information. The most important filters are tweets and retweets. Retweets are the messages on Twitter that show content that was initially posted ('tweeted') by another user. The format is RT @username where username is the Twitter name of the person one is retweeting. Within Twitcident, the tweets are categorized on the basis of predefined search terms and city names. The search terms represent the *types* of incident. Table 1 shows the Twitcident interface: the first column contains the city names, and the top row represents the types of incident.

The table shows the number of tweets per city and per incident. The city names and types of incident are not only categories but also hyperlinks. The generalist can use the links to add details *of a particular incident*, historical data, and the like. Since the software automatically generates data on the basis

Table 1. The Twitcident interface with the categories City Names and Types of Incident

City Name	Burglary	Robbery	Hacked ATM Machine	Physical Violence	Public Order	Guns	Fire
aaa	11			13	2		12
bbb	12	132	1	171	1	4	18
ccc	4	30		7	1		5
ddd	9	23		5	7	1	86
eee	9	6		24		67	154
fff	21	34	2	25	2	5	276
ggg				6	1	5	
hhh	25	55		22	4	16	13
iii	14	19		32	6	9	13
jjj	2			2			9

of the retweets, the generalist's most important task is to enrich the data with background information and details about the location and environment. The generalist can consult the content of the tweets and retweets by clicking on the numbers that pop up in the table. He or she then can decide on the relative urgency of a tweet or retweet and, if needed, delete those hits that simply cause *noise* in the information stream (e.g., because they contain false or irrelevant information). The generalist also can mark an account as spam, so that Twitcident no longer accepts incoming information from that particular account.

Twitcident also has an archival storage or preservation function because digital information – the tweets and retweets – is easily lost or corrupted. This storage function can help the generalists when they are writing after-action reports or looking at patterns of information.

Analysis and Discussion

The added value of Twitcident for the daily response room practices was disappointing. In the first eight weeks after the introduction of the tool (the same period in which we did our observations), there was no proactive use of the social media data. In other words, the expectations of the management that the tool could be used as an antenna, or 'early warning monitoring' system, were not met. Furthermore, although the generalists and centralists started to work together in the weeks after Twitcident was introduced, the centralists told us that the work of the generalists had little effect on their work routines. From our observations and interviews with centralists and generalists we could discern three main practical problems in the actual implementation and use of Twitcident.

First, the generalists complained about the constraining effect of the pre-defined search terms. The search terms are based on the categories set up by the generalists. For example, they have to categorize incoming calls under terms such as Public Order, Robbery, Fire, etc. Social media data, however, is messy and full of contradictions. Citizens who post a tweet about a burglary use terms such as 'we've had a break-in', 'theft', 'break-in', 'someone's broken in' and the like. In other words, citizens use a variety of terms, including more colloquial language. For the generalists it was challenging, if not impossible, to use the search terms systematically in order 'filter' the social media data. The predefined search terms stopped them from making flexible choices and interpretations of the raw data. The Twitcident software allowed them to add new search terms, but it was very difficult for the generalists to come to a consensus about more adequate categories.

Second, the generalists were confronted with different uses and interpretations of the terms by the different first response disciplines. In particular the police have their own terminology, and since most of the Twitter data has to do with public order and safety, they started to dominate the discussion about terms and categories (as is also reflected in the table). The generalists started to adjust the terms, which led to an instant increase in the number of Twitcident hits. The main problem still remained: the search terms turned out to be too specific for the generic use and analysis of social media data.

Third, for the generalists geo-information is crucial for validating tweets and for linking the information to other sources and informing first responders on the ground. Therefore a tweet or retweet is only recognized in Twitcident if it contains geo-information on the sender. Tweets without a geo-location and/or a city name are filtered out. However, since most people who use Twitter do not add geo-information, most of the data from Twitter turned out to add no value to the information that was already available. Potentially, a lot of valuable data was missed or filtered out.

Alongside these practical issues, we see two more fundamental problems with Twitcident and the way that the social media is, or could be, used in the daily practices and routines of the emergency response room.

First, the generalists and centralists became demotivated in the weeks following the introduction of Twitcident. Social media, and in the case of Twitcident *Twitter*, was supposed to enrich their job, but in reality the data that came out of Twitcident appeared to be rather poor. On top of that, not a single incident or emergency was filtered out from the social media data that was not already known by the centralists as a result of the 1-1-2 calls. It meant that Twitcident could not meet the management's expectations of being an 'early warning monitoring system' or an antenna for social unrest. During our observations we noticed that some days after it was introduced, the generalists stopped using Twitcident as part of their standard procedure, but instead used it only occasionally and on a relatively ad-hoc basis. They did not invest time in establishing stable routines for using Twitcident. For the centralists it meant that they were not really able to rely on this additional source of information. What made the integration of the Twitcident data even more problematic is that no interconnection (or, in technical terms, interoperability) was possible with GMS or with other systems in use. Instead of being a help to them, Twitcident turned out to be yet another thing they had to deal with. This made it all too easy for them to ignore Twitcident completely. As they told us during the interviews, centralists still believe that Twitcident could be useful, but, given their experiences, they see its added value as being for writing after-action reports, for example.

Second, it was really hard for the centralists to fully appreciate the tool since they were not involved in its design, nor in the implementation process. They saw Twitcident as a management initiative. In the absence of an adequate monitoring process, the result was a significant mismatch between expectations and actual experiences, a problem that is commonly reported in the information technology implementation literature (Fleck et al., 1990). Twitcident was introduced in a top-down fashion and the management had high expectations, but the professionals who actually had to work with the tool felt a lack of ownership. The work of a centralist can be stressful, particularly during incidents and emergencies. Information overload and time pressures are serious concerns for them, and paradoxically this is especially the case at times when the potential of social media data is at its greatest.

SOLUTIONS AND RECOMMENDATIONS

We have shown in this chapter that the management of the emergency response room and coordinators of the tool had high expectations of the pilot project. In particular they expected Twitcident to be a rich source of instant data not just at times of crisis, but also for day-to-day operations. However, the first results turned out to be disappointing. Not only was the social media data hard to validate (i.e., it was difficult to verify the trustworthiness of the content), but it was also almost impossible to keep up with the amount of data provided by Twitcident. When the centralists tried to use Twitcident to improve their operational picture, they had a difficult time interpreting and validating social media data and linking it to other sources of information. In addition, looking through social media content for 'monitoring' purposes turned out to be useless. This does not mean, however, that the use of social media data has to be abandoned completely by the safety region response rooms.

What needs to happen is first of all that, the generalists and centralists must create a shared understanding of the intended and unintended consequences of social media data for their work. Having a more realistic view of how Twitter, and other social media, could be used in their work will help them to develop new work routines (Feldman & Pentland, 2003) in which the use of this additional information source can be embedded. Twitcident can only be a valuable extra source of information for the centralists if they are clear about why and how they should use it. The dual nature of Twitcident – an early warning monitoring system on the one hand, and a system to enlarge COPs on the other – made that it fell between two stools. Early warning systems need a different type of organizational routine (i.e., scanning big data with broad search terms) than COP development (i.e., a precise and channeled search for adequate additional information about a particular incident). Thinking through the routines in use (Orlikowski, 1992) needed for Twitcident is crucial for organizations to use the tool effectively.

Second, Twitcident was seen as yet another information source that could be easily accessed and consulted by centralists. In other words, it was seen as an 'information warehouse' where users could select information that was relevant to them in performing their tasks. Unconsciously, they assumed that they could simply select information from the warehouse database to help them in executing their task because (as with any other information database) the information was supposed to be stored in an easy and accessible form (Davenport, 1998). However, to regard Twitcident as a warehouse dataset will lead to a failure of the tool. Instead, the use of Twitcident data must be based on a collective *sense-making* perspective. Centralists and generalists have to realize that they (knowingly or unknowingly) give meaning to information and that their sensemaking can differ from that of other people because there are differences in routines, beliefs and assumptions that can potentially lead to misinterpretation of information (Wolbers & Boersma, 2013). Upfront there is no guarantee that social media data can contribute to creating COPs or help organizations to monitor behavior. If Twitcident is to contribute to the control room information management, the stakeholders involved (the response room's management, generalists, centralists, and first responders) all have to reflect upon their sensemaking process. In other words, simply sending data from Twitcident from the RTIC room to the emergency response room and on to the first responders is useless. It has to have *meaning* attached, and the only way to do that is to talk about the information (Weick, 1988) so that people can then understand the constraints, and start to appreciate the relative value of the data source.

Finally, the Twitcident project lacked a proper project *plan* – there was no thoughtful introduction or implementation strategy, let alone a monitoring process. For Twitcident to be successful, the management needs to invest far more in 'managing expectations'. Earlier studies of new technology implementation have shown that top-down introduction of new technologies in organizations can have a disruptive effect. Those who implemented such technologies successfully underwent a qualitatively different *learning process* than those who were unsuccessful. Important steps in this process are: enrollment, preparation, trials, and reflection (Edmonson et al., 2001). In the Twitcident case it means that the users – generalists and centralists – have to be involved in the further use of the tool, and develop the motivation needed to use it. Being more reflective about their work would encourage a learning process to begin, and would allow them to develop new routines for using social media data. From our interviews it is clear that it is not too late for this, since the centralists still believe that there is value to be gained from using social media data, but only if they can embed this in their information management routines.

FUTURE RESEARCH DIRECTIONS

Twitcident was introduced, implemented and used in an emergency response room setting as part of a *pilot* project. For further research it would be interesting to study the subsequent development of Twitcident, and to analyze the pros and cons of using social media data for emergency response in a more systematic manner. For example, one could look at the use of social media data by first responders in major crisis situations or disasters. It might be that disruptions of this kind would also make the generalists' searching of social media sites more targeted.

It is also known that the hectic environment in the emergency response room – with time pressure on the centralists – influences the way that information streams are managed. Therefore, it might be useful to look at how projects using similar applications are used in other settings where the time pressures are not so great – for example, in marketing or consumer insight activity. (Evans, 2012; Tuton & Solomon, 2014).

Clearly, projects such as Twitcident can only succeed if they are carefully embedded in an organization's information management. A future research direction might therefore be to study social media as part of the wider and more complex information architecture of an organization (Koltay, 2011) to understand the conditions in which the social media data can become part of the structural design of shared information environments.

Finally, we need to research and understand how people make sense of social media data in complex organizational settings. This chapter has shown that in order to use social media data successfully, we have to take seriously the sensemaking processes of who are trying to interpret that data. This would require us to look at the social aspects of social media implementation and use. In times of uncertainty, people try to make sense of the situation and the incoming information. It is important that we start to understand how people in organizational (in our case centralists and generalists) take cues from social media data that help them decide which information is relevant for their work. In other words, we need to explore creatively the way in which meaning is attached to social media (see, for example, Bechmann & Lomborg, 2013).

CONCLUSION

The emergency control room's management had high expectations of the pilot project Twitcident, as they expected it to be a rich source of instant data not just at times of crisis, but also for monitoring processes in daily situations. This dual nature, however, was never adequately explained to the professionals who had to work with it - the centralists and generalist. In fact, the implementation process has been done in a top-down fashion. Therefore, the generalists and centralists never developed a full understanding of the meaning and potential usefulness of Twitcident for their work, which had eventually a negative effect on the success of the tool.

Perhaps the most important outcome of our study into the Twitcident project is that professional response organizations have to think in advance what to do with social media data and how they want to use it. Social media data is not clean; it is messy, full of contradictions, and therefore difficult to integrate into the daily operations of the centralists. The professionals have to develop the skills to actually *make sense* of social media data. They have to ask themselves the question: what does this data actually mean? What does it mean for my operations, for my information management, and how does it interfere, complement or align with other information sources that we are already using?

Our study makes clear that social media data and information are not very useful if the organization does not know how to link this additional source of information to its other information streams. In other words, social media has to be strategically *integrated* into the overall information management of the crisis response organization in order to be of use. Our case has clearly shown that the introduction of social media (i.e., here the Twitcident project) to the emergency response room must be treated as part of a careful learning process that includes enrolment, preparation, trial and testing out. This is the only way for such projects to be successful.

REFERENCES

Abel, F., Hauff, C., Houben, G. J., Stronkman, R., & Tao, K. (2012). Twitcident: fighting fire with information from social web streams. *Proceedings of the 21st International Conference Companion on World Wide Web* (pp. 305-308). doi:10.1145/2187980.2188035

Alvesson, M., & Sköldberg, K. (2009). *Reflexive methodology: New vistas for qualitative research.* London: Sage.

Barley, S. R. (1986). Technology as an occasion for structuring: Evidence from observations of CT scanners and the social order of radiology departments. *Administrative Science Quarterly*, *31*(1), 78–108. doi:10.2307/2392767 PMID:10281188

Bechmann, A., & Lomborg, S. (2013). Mapping actor roles in social media: Different perspectives on value creation in theories of user participation. *New Media & Society*, *15*(5), 765–781. doi:10.1177/1461444812462853

Boersma, F. K. Groenewegen, & P. Wagenaar, P. (2010). The information management of co-located Emergency Response Rooms in the Netherlands. In H. Rahman (Ed.), Cases on Adoption, Diffusion and Evaluation of Global E-Governance Systems (pp. 107-116). Hershey USA: IGI Publishing.

Boersma, F. K., & Kingma, S. F. (2005). From Means to Ends: The Transformation of ERP in a Manufacturing Company. *The Journal of Strategic Information Systems*, *14*(2), 197–219. doi:10.1016/j.jsis.2005.04.003

Boersma, F.K., Wagenaar, P., & Wolbers, J. (2012). Negotiating the 'Trading Zone'. Creating a Shared Information Infrastructure in the Dutch Public Safety Sector. *Journal of Homeland Security and Emergency Management, 9*(2).

Bosse, T., Majdanik, K., Boersma, F. K., & Ingibergsdóttir, K. (2013). Studying Shared Situation Awareness by Agent-Based Simulation, *Web Intelligence (WI) and Intelligent Agent Technologies (IAT)*, Atlanta, USA. *Proceedings of the 2013 IEEE/WIC/ACM International Joint Conference* (Vol. 2, pp. 201-208).

Cassa, C. A., Chunara, R., Mandl, K., & Brownstein, J. S. (2013). Twitter as a sentinel in emergency situations: Lessons from the Boston marathon explosions. *PLoS Currents*, July. PMID:23852273

Ciborra, C. U., & Lanzara, G. F. (1994). Formative contexts and information technology: Understanding the dynamics of innovation in organizations. *Accounting, Management and Information Technologies, 4*(2), 61–86. doi:10.1016/0959-8022(94)90005-1

Crump, J. (2011). What are the police doing on Twitter? Social media, the police and the public. *Policy & Internet, 3*(4), 1–27. doi:10.2202/1944-2866.1130

Davenport, T. H. (1998). Putting the enterprise into the enterprise system. *Harvard Business Review, 76*, 121–131. PMID:10181586

Edmondson, A. C., Bohmer, R. M., & Pisano, G. P. (2001). Disrupted routines: Team learning and new technology implementation in hospitals. *Administrative Science Quarterly, 46*(4), 685–716. doi:10.2307/3094828

Evans, D. (2012). *Social media marketing: An hour a day*. Indianapolis: John Wiley & Sons.

Feldman, M. S., & Pentland, B. T. (2003). Reconceptualizing organizational routines as a source of flexibility and change. *Administrative Science Quarterly, 48*(1), 94–118. doi:10.2307/3556620

Fleck, J., Webster, J., & Williams, R. (1990). Dynamics of information technology implementation: A reassessment of paradigms and trajectories of development. *Futures, 22*(6), 618–640. doi:10.1016/0016-3287(90)90131-Z

Fuchs, C., Boersma, F. K., Albrechtslund, A., & Sandoval, M. (2011). Internet & Surveillance. Introduction. In C. Fuchs, F. K. Boersma, A. Albrechtslund, & M. Sandoval (Eds.), *Internet and Surveillance* (pp. 1–29). London: Routledge.

Goolsby, R. (2010). Social media as crisis platform: The future of community maps/crisis maps. *ACM Transactions on Intelligent Systems and Technology, 7*(1), 1–11. doi:10.1145/1858948.1858955

Helsloot, I., & Ruitenberg, A. (2004). Citizen response to disasters: A survey of literature and some practical implications. *Journal of Contingencies and Crisis Management, 12*(3), 98–111. doi:10.1111/j.0966-0879.2004.00440.x

Hughes, A. L., & Palen, L. (2009). Twitter adoption and use in mass convergence and emergency events. *International Journal of Emergency Management, 6*(3), 248–260. doi:10.1504/IJEM.2009.031564

Inspectie Veiligheid en Justitie. (2013). *Nationale Politie op Koers?* Den Haag: IVJ.

Koltay, T. (2011). Information overload, information architecture and digital literacy. *Bulletin of the American Society for Information Science and Technology*, *38*(1), 33–35. doi:10.1002/bult.2011.1720380111

Markus, M. L., & Robey, D. (1988). Information technology and organizational change: Causal structure in theory and research. *Management Science*, *34*(5), 583–598. doi:10.1287/mnsc.34.5.583

Meijer, A., Boersma, F. K., & Wagenaar, P. (Eds.), (2009). *ICTs, Citizens & Governance: After the Hype!* Amsterdam: IOS Press.

Mendoza, M., Poblete, B., & Castillo, C. (2010). Twitter Under Crisis: Can we trust what we RT? *Proceedings of the first workshop on social media analytics* (pp. 71-79). doi:10.1145/1964858.1964869

Merchant, R. M., Elmer, S., & Lurie, N. (2011). Integrating social media into emergency-preparedness efforts. *The New England Journal of Medicine*, *365*(4), 289–291. doi:10.1056/NEJMp1103591 PMID:21793742

Mirvis, P., Sales, A., & Hackett, E. (2006). The implementation and adoption of new technology in organizations: The impact on work, people, and culture. *Human Resource Management*, *30*(1), 113–139. doi:10.1002/hrm.3930300107

Oh, O., Agrawal, M., & Rao, H. R. (2013). Community intelligence and social media services: A rumor theoretic analysis of tweets during social crises. *Management Information Systems Quarterly*, *37*(2), 407–426.

Orlikowski, W. J. (1992). The duality of technology: Rethinking the concept of technology in organizations. *Organization Science*, *3*(3), 398–427. doi:10.1287/orsc.3.3.398

Orlikowski, W. J., & Barley, S. R. (2001). Technology and institutions: What can research on information technology and research on organizations learn from each other? *Management Information Systems Quarterly*, *25*(2), 145–165. doi:10.2307/3250927

Palen, L. (2008). Online social media in crisis events. *EDUCAUSE Quarterly*, *31*(3), 12.

Ruef, A., & Markard, J. (2010). What happens after a hype? *Technology Analysis and Strategic Management*, *22*(3), 317–338. doi:10.1080/09537321003647354

Sarter, N. B., & Woods, D. D. (1991). Situation Awareness: A Critical but Ill-Defined Phenomenon. *The International Journal of Aviation Psychology*, *1*(1), 45–57. doi:10.1207/s15327108ijap0101_4

Schultz, F., Utz, S., & Göritz, A. (2011). Is the medium the message? Perceptions of and reactions to crisis communication via twitter, blogs and traditional media. *Public Relations Review*, *37*(1), 20–27. doi:10.1016/j.pubrev.2010.12.001

Treurniet, W., Messemaker, M., Wolbers, J., & Boersma, F. K. (2015). Shaping the societal impact of emergencies: Striking a balance between Control and Cooperation. *International Journal of Emergency Services*, 4(1), 129-151. http://dx.doi.org/10.1108/IJES-06-2014-0007

Tuten, T. L., & Solomon, M. R. (2014). *Social media marketing*. London: Sage.

Van de Walle, B., Turoff, M., & Hiltz, S. R. (Eds.), (2009). *Information systems for emergency management*. New York: ME Sharpe.

Van Dijck, J., & Poell, T. (2013). Understanding social media logic. *Media and Communication*, *1*(1), 2–14. doi:10.17645/mac.v1i1.70

Van Marrewijk, A. (2007). Managing project culture: The case of Environ Megaproject. *International Journal of Project Management*, *25*(3), 290–299. doi:10.1016/j.ijproman.2006.11.004

Veenswijk, M., Marrewijk, A., & Boersma, K. (2010). Developing New Knowledge in Collaborative Relationships in Megaproject Alliances: Organising Reflection in the Dutch Construction Sector. *International Journal of Knowledge Management Studies*, *4*(2), 216–232. doi:10.1504/IJKMS.2010.030793

Vieweg, S., Hughes, A. L., Starbird, K., & Palen, L. (2010). Microblogging during two natural hazards events: what twitter may contribute to situational awareness. *Proceedings of the SIGCHI conference on human factors in computing systems* (pp. 1079-1088). doi:10.1145/1753326.1753486

Wagenaar, P., Boersma, F. K., Groenewegen, P., & Niemandsverdriet, P. (2009). Implementing C2000 in the Dutch police region 'Hollands-Midden.' In A. Meijer, F.K. Boersma, & P. Wagenaar, (Eds.), ICTs, Citizens & Governance: After the Hype! (pp. 119-134). Amsterdam: IOS Press.

Weick, K. E. (1988). Enacted Sensemaking in Crisis Situations. *Journal of Management Studies*, *25*(4), 305–317. doi:10.1111/j.1467-6486.1988.tb00039.x

Wolbers, J. J., & Boersma, F. K. (2013). The Common Operational Picture As Collective Sensemaking. *Journal of Contingencies and Crisis Management*, *21*(4), 186–199. doi:10.1111/1468-5973.12027

Yates, D., & Paquette, S. (2011). Emergency knowledge management and social media technologies: A case study of the 2010 Haitian earthquake. *International Journal of Information Management*, *31*(1), 6–13. doi:10.1016/j.ijinfomgt.2010.10.001

Yin, J., Lampert, A., Cameron, M., Robinson, B., & Power, R. (2012). Using social media to enhance emergency situation awareness. *IEEE Intelligent Systems*, *27*(6), 52–59. doi:10.1109/MIS.2012.6

ADDITIONAL READING

Coombs, W. T. (2014). *Ongoing crisis communication: Planning, managing, and responding*. London: Sage Publications.

Kietzmann, J. H., Hermkens, K., McCarthy, I. P., & Silvestre, B. S. (2011). Social media? Get serious! Understanding the functional building blocks of social media. *Business Horizons*, *54*(3), 241–251. doi:10.1016/j.bushor.2011.01.005

Latonero, M., & Shklovski, I. (2011). Emergency management, Twitter, and social media evangelism. *International Journal of Information Systems for Crisis Response and Management*, *3*(4), 67–86.

Reuter, C., Marx, A., & Pipek, V. (2012). Crisis management 2.0: Towards a systematization of social software use in crisis situations. *International Journal of Information Systems for Crisis Response and Management*, *4*(1), 1–16. doi:10.4018/jiscrm.2012010101

Veil, S. R., Buehner, T., & Palenchar, M. J. (2011). A Work-In-Process Literature Review: Incorporating Social Media in Risk and Crisis Communication. *Journal of Contingencies and Crisis Management*, *19*(2), 110–122. doi:10.1111/j.1468-5973.2011.00639.x

White, C. M. (2011). *Social media, crisis communication, and emergency management: Leveraging Web 2.0 technologies. Tailor & Francis Group*. CRC press. doi:10.1201/b11251

Artman, H., & Wærn, Y. (1999). Distributed cognition in an emergency co-ordination center. *Cognition Technology and Work*, *1*(4), 237–246. doi:10.1007/s101110050020

Furniss, D., & Blandford, A. (2006). Understanding emergency medical dispatch in terms of distributed cognition: A case study. *Ergonomics*, *49*(12-13), 1174–1203. doi:10.1080/00140130600612663 PMID:17008252

Heath, C., & Luff, P. (1992). Collaboration and control. Crisis management and multimedia technology in London Underground Line Control Rooms. [CSCW]. *Computer Supported Cooperative Work*, *1*(1-2), 69–94. doi:10.1007/BF00752451

Suchman, L. A. (1987). *Plans and situated actions: the problem of human-machine communication.* Cambridge: Cambridge University Press.

Boersma, K., & Kingma, S. F. (2005). Developing a cultural perspective on ERP. *Business Process Management Journal*, *11*(2), 123–136. doi:10.1108/14637150510591138

Joshi, K. (1991). A model of users' perspective on change: The case of information systems technology implementation. *Management Information Systems Quarterly*, *15*(2), 229–242. doi:10.2307/249384

Lapointe, L., & Rivard, S. (2005). A multilevel model of resistance to information technology implementation. *Management Information Systems Quarterly*, *29*(3), 461–491.

Moore, G. C., & Benbasat, I. (1991). Development of an instrument to measure the perceptions of adopting an information technology innovation. *Information Systems Research*, *2*(3), 192–222. doi:10.1287/isre.2.3.192

Orlikowski, W. J., & Gash, D. C. (1994). Technological frames: Making sense of information technology in organizations. *ACM Transactions on Information Systems*, *12*(2), 174–207. doi:10.1145/196734.196745

Taylor, S., & Todd, P. A. (1995). Understanding information technology usage: A test of competing models. *Information Systems Research*, *6*(2), 144–176. doi:10.1287/isre.6.2.144

Venkatesh, V., Morris, M. G., Davis, G. B., & Davis, F. D. (2003). User acceptance of information technology: Toward a unified view. *Management Information Systems Quarterly*, *27*(3), 425–478.

KEY TERMS AND DEFINITIONS

Common Operational Picture (COP): The display of relevant information shared by more than one command or unit, facilitation situation awareness.

Crisis Management: The organization function that deals with expected and unexpected, disruptive situations, such as incidents, emergencies and (natural) disasters.

Emergency Response Rooms: Dispatch centers occupied by the first response organizations (i.e. the police, fire and ambulance service) for the intake of emergency calls, the 'cleaning' of the information and for the dissemination of the information to first responders.

GMS: Integrated Emergency Room System.

Information Technology Implementation: The process through which new information technologies are introduced and enrolled in organizational settings.

RTIC: Real-time intelligence center.

Sense-Making: The process by which people give meaning to information and experiences. The sense-making becomes evident through written and spoken narratives.

Social Media: Computer-mediated platforms that enable people to create, share or exchange information, ideas, and pictures/videos in virtual communities.

Trading Zone: The notion that data from (social media) information sources is something to talk about, that is, actors must give meaning to the data in order to be able to link it to other information sources.

Twitcident: A web-based system for filtering, searching and analyzing data on real-world incidents or crises.

ENDNOTES

1. We define social media *data* as the raw data from social media platforms to which no meaning is (as yet) attached. Only after professionals have attached meaning to data can we speak of *information*.

Chapter 15
Using Twitter for Collaborative Student and Project Manager Learning:
Reflections from a UK Pilot Project

Kate Barnett-Richards
Coventry University, UK

Marie Sams
Coventry University, UK

ABSTRACT

This chapter presents an insight into a pilot project which took place at a UK higher education institution which used Twitter as a social media tool for engaging industry managers and students in sharing knowledge and collaborating on problem solving in the field of project management. Project management education and team formation literature is discussed, as well as reflections from the authors on the advantages and challenges for project teams on using Twitter as a social media tool. The wider implications for Project Managers adopting social media is considered more broadly, and important factors are recommended when making decisions whether to use social media to encourage teamwork and co-operation.

INTRODUCTION

In recent years, there have been an increasing number of ways for people to connect using social media tools such as Facebook, Twitter, LinkedIn, YouTube and Yammer, amongst many others. Adopting social media as a way of linking with like-minded individuals has now become an everyday regular mode of communication, being instantly available on mobile phones, tablets and laptops which can be used at any time across the globe.

The reasons for using social media as a method for communicating within teams, specifically project teams are abundant. As project management increases as a profession, the need to involve a wide base

DOI: 10.4018/978-1-4666-9867-3.ch015

of stakeholders is fundamental to project success (Assundani et al 2010). Furthermore, communication across different countries is becoming less expensive and more efficient with the integration of technology on international projects. Additionally, the notion that projects are a central part of organizations has seen the escalation of collaborative project software being introduced in teams. It remains to be seen how effective communication can truly be when using social media as the dominant mode of exchange in preference to face-to-face. There are questions to be asked when deciding if, how, and when, social media should be used to encourage the exchange of ideas and enhance teamwork. Regardless, it is clear that social media is here to stay as a means of communication both socially and professionally, and therefore it is imperative that organizations understand how to harness the full use and potential of these tools.

The basis of this chapter focusses on the use of Twitter as a method of engagement, learning, and sharing of ideas using a case study from the United Kingdom (UK), which took place at a Higher Education Institution. The authors initiated a project to enable students and industry professionals to discuss project management issues and challenges in a collaborative team based environment. The objective of this social media project was to enhance student involvement in debate and discourse with employers in creating an informal community of practice where project management was the main focus.

This chapter will discuss the evolving nature of project management education and the need for both industry professionals and project management students to engage in collaborative learning in order to enhance both the employability of students, and enabling managers to reflect on their own practice and understanding. The make-up of how teams collaborate on projects is changing at pace, and the literature regarding how project teams come together, communicate and learn from each other using technology is also presented. The authors reflections and perspectives of the value and challenges in using Twitter for this type of endeavor are discussed in detail. Finally, the future implications for adopting the use of a) Twitter, and b) social media more broadly for project teams are presented. This chapter will be of interest to project management professionals who are considering using Twitter or other social media tools as a method of communication to encourage dialogue in project teams.

BACKGROUND

Project Management Learning

Traditional project management education, focusing on the development of technical skills, is seen by many as the best way to educate and train future project managers (Pant & Baroudi 2008, Schultz 2008) and is often facilitated by the use of established project management approaches such as Agile, PMBoK and PRINCE2. Many in the industry have gained their understanding of project management either as part of a degree programme, which included project management units or modules, or during intensive week long training and professional development programmes within, or outside of their organizations. Whilst these sessions provide plenty of technical knowledge they allow little opportunity for reflection and application to real world scenarios and issues. For example, project management taught as part of an undergraduate degree involves a high proportion of students who have never worked with project management. Those on intensive week long training and development programmes, who often do have experience within the field are given little time to reflect upon theories being taught and apply them to their practice until after the training has occurred.

When education and training is provided in the intense and focused nature that is often observed in project management, frequently the development of knowledge silos are created meaning that those undertaking or progressing through this type of education are lacking in awareness of how project management fits within and around the rest of the business.

Traditional models of education, which focus heavily on the development of technical skills, often do so at the expense of creating a more holistic and integrated method of working with others, something which is essential to achieving project success. Students will often be exposed to technical skills and theories related only to one particular subject area in any given module or unit. It is this approach to education that encourages a continuing cycle of silo based education, training, working and practice. Wee, Kek and Kelley (2003) have suggested that educational silos are seen across the disciplines; additionally they support the view that the subject based curriculum of traditional forms of education encourages and supports an individualistic mentality.

It can therefore be inferred that the traditional design of project management education encourages practitioners to work in this silo based manner leading to a vicious cycle of poor communication across various teams and disciplines within projects. Ashleigh et al (2012) suggest that the lack of skill development during project management education and training have had a marked impact on the overall rate of project failures across the world. It is also suggested that this traditional style of education and training does not allow for the development of soft skills such as interpersonal working, communications skills, or team development; all of which are considered to be essential skills for the successful project manager. Communication skills are considered to be particularly vital, especially when project teams can now be spread across a number of countries and cultures, therefore requiring more diverse and effective forms of communication to ensure project success. In focusing on technical silos as opposed to soft skill development students are lacking in skills required by employers that can contribute to successful project teams.

The Chartered Management Institute (2014) suggests that one of the ways to improve this is to involve employers in shaping the educational experience for the student, and to provide means for students to communicate with the managers of today. In addition there is a growing body of literature which suggests that project management education is becoming outdated and may need to develop in order to keep pace with the ever changing field of project management (Koskela & Howell 2002, Thomas & Mengel 2008, Winter et al 2006). With this is mind it is important to consider the need to break down both the barriers between the related disciplines in order to encourage better levels of communication and understanding as well as the barriers between industry and education to foster a cycle of continuous learning and development for all.

As the industry expects project managers to work in high performing cross-functional teams, it should be feasible that the training they receive prepares them for all aspects of the role, as opposed to focusing solely on the technical skills. It is therefore particularly important for project management education to change and develop as the industry does in order to produce project managers with the required skills. Authors such as Thomas and Mengel (2008) have suggested that it would be beneficial for project management education to involve the use of live projects in order for students to have a greater understanding and appreciation for the subject area. There are potential issues with the level of integration that is possible, particularly when time limitations of education and training are considered. However in adopting the use of a live project students would be able to gain additional skills and knowledge only possible once they have been exposed to an ever changing and realistic project. It is particularly important to consider the use and engagement of industry in initiatives such as this in order for the employers to have an influence on the education of future project managers.

Córdoba and Piki (2012) have also suggested ways of making project management education more reflective of practice, mainly focusing on group facilitation in order to provide the realistic simulation of real life project management. It is initiatives such as this that would encourage the development of softer skills, particularly communication and team working skills. It should also be consider how to best reflect the dynamics and make up of project teams, perhaps including students from other disciplines and industry partners in order to provide a valuable learning experience.

It is clear that the lines between education and industry need to be distorted in order to better prepare students and allow employers to have the necessary input into the educational process in order to see future project managers coming through with the required skills. Additionally it is evident that there is a great deal of value placed on the experiential learning that takes place once a project manager actually takes their first post or role within the industry and can see how theories and methodologies can be applied in real and challenging environments. The idea of 'on-the-job' training can provide both educators and industry professionals with an opportunity to learn and develop, irrespective of the stage of their career, and should be utilized for the benefit of all.

Project Team Development

How project teams are formed, relationships built and the methods for communication are all fundamental to project success. It is suggested by Hollingshead et al (1993) that teams can be genuinely successful only when face-to-face interaction has taken place and the team has gone through development stages. One model which has been successfully used in practice is Tuckman's (1965) four stages of group development, forming (when groups are formed), storming (when roles and responsibilities and clarification of aims and objectives are debated), norming (when the team settles down into day to day activities), performing (when teams start to achieve objectives). This was adapted to add a fifth stage of adjournment (when teams disperse), which could suggest that this model is particularly relevant to project teams when moving through the closure phase of the project lifecycle. (Tuckman & Jensen 1977). Although this model was predominantly used in face-to-face environments, there is some evidence that this model could be transferable to support the development of virtual teams. Johnson et al (2002) in their study of learning in an online environment suggests that virtual teams may skip out certain stages of this model, instead progressing through the model differently to those in a face-to-face environment, with successful results.

More recently, Gilly Salmon developed and tested a model which highlighted the journey participants take within online learning communities (Salmon 2000). The model, presented in fig. 1, demonstrates the various stages that online learners will progress through in order to become truly engaged with the team, as well as building their ability to reflect on their own practice. The model takes the learner through a journey of online socialization with group members before information exchange and learning can start to take place, which is a similar concept to Tuckman's model. Additionally, she emphasized the need for online facilitation, in prompting discussion and asking questions in order to see information being transferred between participants and knowledge being created successfully.

Figure 1. Gilly Salmon's five stages model (Source: Salmon, 2015)

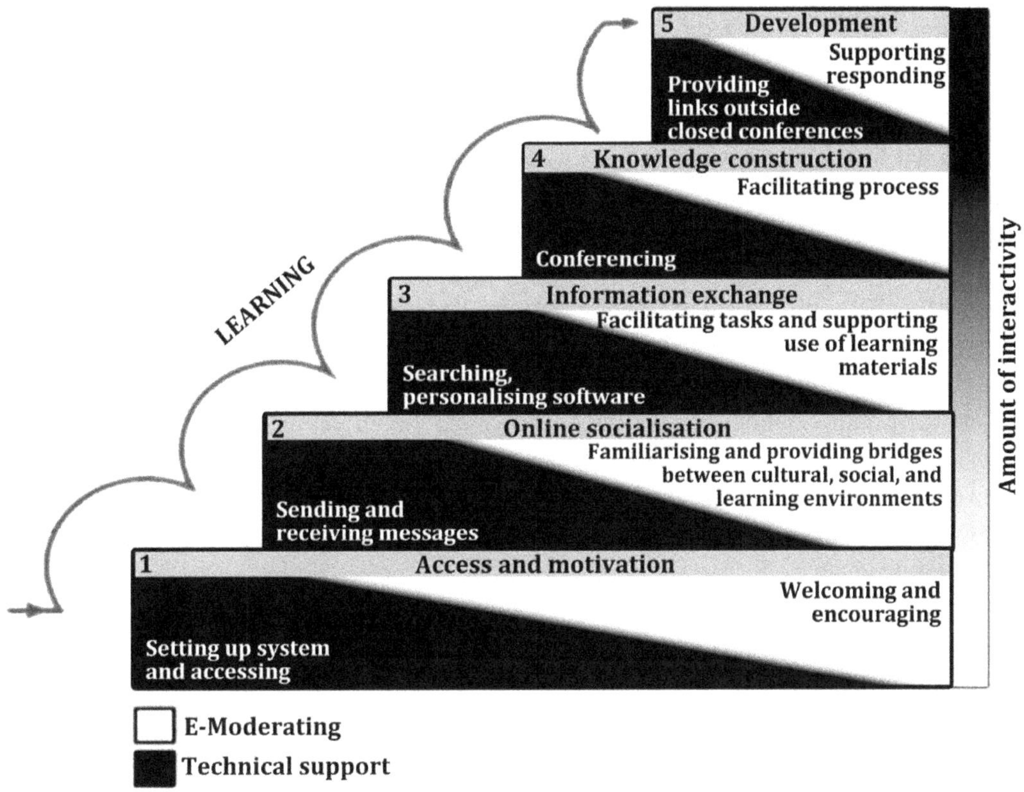

Allen (1977) suggests that the level of communication between team members decreases when spatial distance between them is vast. However, more recent evidence shows that the online and virtual environments can provide an effective substitution for more traditional face-to-face communication if successfully utilized. One of the apparent success factors in the effective use of the virtual environment is that of trust. Charles Handy (1995) suggests that in order to build trust within the virtual team there needs to be at least some face-to-face communication in order to cement the ideas and direction of the team. Javenpaa and Leidner (2006) suggest that if virtual teams are made up of individuals that are highly motivated and enthusiastic towards the task in hand, trust can be built very quickly and therefore lead to the high performance of the team. Furthermore, Meyerson et al. (1995) suggest that it is the tight deadlines that teams, such as those seen within project management, have to adhere to that encourage trust to develop quickly in order to begin working effectively. Conversely, DiStefano and Maznevski (2000) suggest that in practice virtual global teams often do not create the level of value expected of them. Grosse (2002) however suggests that learning how to deal with the technology in hand, as well as the diverse nature of virtual teams is one of the biggest challenges to any organization.

The Use of Social Media

Considering the historical nature of team development is important to understand what is required to enhance team collaboration on projects. However since the introduction of social media tools it is only natural that organizations are now moving towards the adoption of these technologies (McKinsey 2011, Office, 2015). The advantages of organizations adopting a social media strategy (which can be a common occurrence) can be summarized as follows:

- **Speed**: Adopting a social media tool within project teams enables communication to be fast paced, asynchronous, timely and allows for clarification and feedback that the message has been understood.
- **Flexibility**: Social media can be accessed via mobile phones at any time, in most places
- **Cost**: Although there may be a cost to some organisations in the buying, setting up and training on social media tools, most are freely available. The cost savings to the organisation are clearly apparent in reduced meeting and travel times.
- **Crossing Boundaries**: The introduction of social media has clearly enabled projects to reach beyond their traditional boundaries, such as overseas collaborations, translation of languages and accessing stakeholders which may have been previously challenging to access.
- **Crowdsourcing**: The ability to gain views of multiple social media users on an idea, posting updates to the project, or even winning additional resources is invaluable in shaping project plans and initiating change.

Twitter is one of the main social media tools used across the world and since its launch in 2007 has seen its users grow to more than 100 million users a day (Twitter 2015). Twitter is used by organizations predominantly as an information sharing tool, however it has been used more recently as a method for sharing information online and encouraging professionals to engage in discussions on shared interested topics. At only 140 characters per tweet, the principle of this social media platform is to be able to get your point across in a succinct and clear manner.

Clearly, the success of Twitter has demonstrated the benefits that social media can bring to large audiences and smaller group of individuals alike. However, there is a gap in the literature field on how project teams can share, learn and obtain knowledge from using Twitter as a social media tool.

THE COVENTRY CASE STUDY

Purpose

The grounds of the pilot study presented within this chapter was based on an intention to increase the dialogue between students and industry managers in a project management context. This was in order to give students an authentic insight into what project management is like in practice and how it relates to the theoretical frameworks and models that they are exposed to whilst at University.

The project was also intended as a starting point for testing out an idea of replacing the traditional guest lecture by an industry speaker with a more dynamic communication flow and exchange of ideas between project managers and students on genuine challenges presented in the workplace. Once tested and evaluated, the aim was to learn lessons from the project and adapt it in order to scale the project up in future.

Student learning was not the only factor involved in testing this pilot, but also the value that the managers placed upon on the discussions. Involving managers on a continuous basis in business education poses questions around how to motivate and incentivize engagement from such a busy and demanding profession.

Project Outline

The project was set up to take place over a two week period, using Twitter as the platform for discussion. The choice of social media was based on a number of recent studies which had explored the use of Twitter within a learning environment with some degree of success (Evans 2014, Wright et al 2014).

Additionally, Twitter is also used by a number of project management professionals to discuss and debate current issues within the field such as the Association for Project Management, Project Management Institute and various recruitment specialists. The types of social media considered along with their advantages and disadvantages are presented in table 1. The main rationale for using Twitter was in order to limit the length of postings (for which the managers would not have time to read), and to choose a social media platform that most of the participants felt comfortable with using, with minimum training required.

Two managers from industry were sourced from existing networks and agreed to participate in the project to share specific issues and challenges that they were currently facing as managers, to generate discussion, ideas and to encourage students to develop proposed solutions on these specific issues. Both managers had a significant amount of experience in the retail and technical facilities management sectors spanning over 15 years experience between them.

Additionally, fifteen students volunteered to participate after the project was advertised on the course web site. All either already had Twitter accounts or found the technology fairly intuitive and therefore there was little training required as part of the initial setting up other than a drop in session for students who wanted any clarification on how the project would be run. As a public dialogue would be taking place, a number of ethical ground rules were set up to ensure that participants respected the authenticity of discussions taking place which could be publically viewed.

Table 1. Social Media considered with advantages and disadvantages (Source: Authors own construction)

Social Media Considered	Advantages	Disadvantages
Facebook	• Most will have an account • Easy to create discussion groups	Students indicated they wanted to keep their Facebook for personal use only.
Linkedin	• Most will have an account • Easy to create discussion groups • - No restriction on postings	• Manager profiles will be easily accessed making it more difficult to present real issues and challenges • High risk • No restriction on postings
Twitter	• Most will have an account • Can use with a certain level of privacy • Character restriction	Character restriction
Yammer	Accounts fairly easy to set up	• Used more frequently within organisations • Students unfamiliar with the media

The decision was made to not include a face-to-face initiation meeting as part of the project as it was felt that this contradicted the ideas and principle of the pilot study, such as bringing the managers physically into the University. Additionally, there was a requirement for the authors to observe the developing online community and dialogue, that reflected the changing nature of diverse project teams.

The Twitter discussions were intended to take place in the public domain using the hash tag PSCMChat. The option to keep the discussions public were purely due to the logistical issue of not being able to request every user to make their profile private (some used Twitter accounts for personal use). However, it was clear that there was a risk of commercially sensitive issues being disclosed in a public arena which needed to be addressed. Therefore, before the online discussions started, the two managers involved were asked to develop a short biography for students which gave them an indication of their role, responsibilities and the sector that they worked in, without disclosing the company name.

Each day for the first week, both managers would present a specific issue for the students to respond to. An example of this is presented in figure 2. In this particular example, a common challenge that faces project managers was presented in increasing project expectations without an increase in budget.

All issues presented were realistic and students were asked to reflect on their project management learning to present solutions on what they might do. Examples of the responses given in figure 2 are presented in figures 3 and 4 respectively.

The objective for this approach on Twitter was to try and encourage a dialogue that was not only two-way, but so that those involved would post, share and read others ideas, so that students would be able to enhance their problem solving skills by considering a number of different approaches to dealing with a certain work-based issues. Additionally it was hoped that this project would encourage students to look for answers outside of project management and become more aware of the wider environment, hence breaking down some of the silos seen within traditional education. Both academic staff involved did not engage in responding to the issues but acted as facilitators only, in prompting students with further questions or in clarifying the meaning of several points made.

In the second week of the project, the students then had the opportunity to ask managers questions about what it was like to work in that specialist area. The intention was that students could gain an insight

Figure 2. Example of manager issue (Source: Twitter, 2015)

Figure 3. Example student answer (a) (Source: Twitter, 2015)

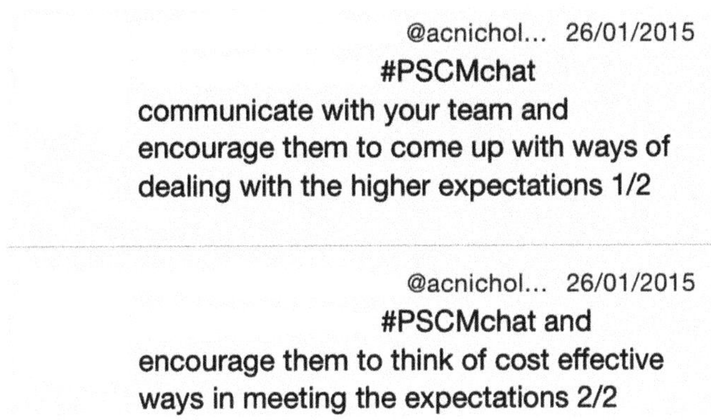

Figure 4. Example student answer (b) (Source: Twitter, 2015)

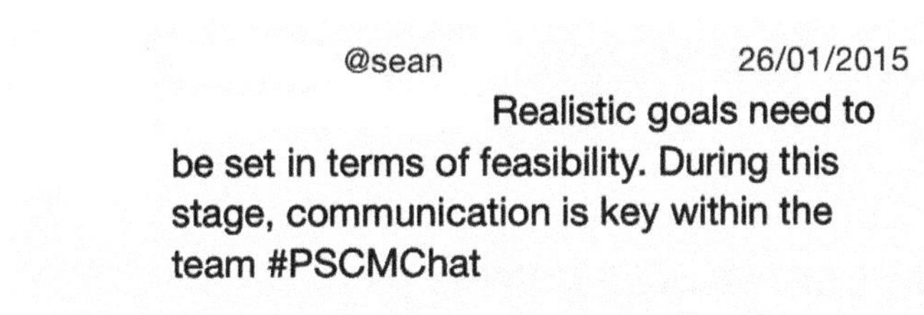

into the specific skills they would need to focus on to work in that area, or to understand the opportunities and challenges that a particular role may present. An example of a typical question and answer is presented in figure 5.

After the two week period had been completed, the managers and students were asked for their perceptions on how well the project had worked.

Approach

Surveys and interviews were conducted for this pilot study, and the analysis which took place focused particularly on the project management learning that students had obtained throughout the two weeks (Sams & Mottram 2015), as this was an original focus of the study. However, it was clear from the original project that there was additional learning to embrace in relation to how useful Twitter is as a platform for enhancing learning and developing teams in a virtual format. Therefore, it is the author's main reflections and observations taken from the pilot study that are used to analyse the success of the project from this particular perspective.

Figure 5. Example question and answer session posting

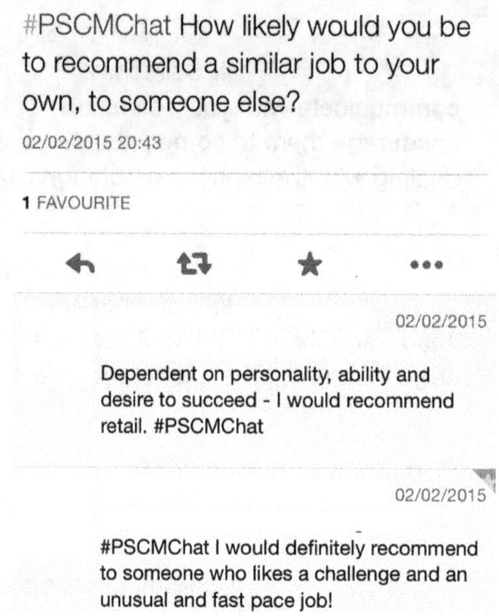

REFLECTIONS AND LESSONS LEARNED

Motivation and Engagement

Before the project started, and as outlined in the case study information, the authors gave each student involved a short biographical account of each manager that would be participating to give some information on the sector and size of the business that they were involved with. All participants were asked to follow the managers (and vice versa) to provide confirmation of participation and the authors posted a welcome message to officially launch the discussions (see figure 6). It was felt approaching the project in this way would allow all of the participants to be eased into the online learning environment. It was considered especially important to ensure that everyone felt supported in using Twitter as a professional communication tool as opposed to a social communication tool, hence the need for the authors to facilitate the project virtually.

The authors motivation for facilitating this project stemmed around a desire to engage a wider and more diverse group in discussions around project management that could take place outside of a traditional classroom environment. It was hoped that richer discussions would take place using Twitter as opposed

Figure 6. Example of welcome message (Source: Twitter, 2015)

to within a traditional guest lecture session within the university. During the first week of the project the authors were required to facilitate the discussions during its initial stages, once responses and discussions began to flow it was possible to step back from the role of facilitator and observe the interactions instead. Once the team became self-facilitating it was clear to see the benefits that all participants, but especially the students, in engaging in discussions with current project managers.

In terms of incentives and motivation for involvement, there was no assessment or payment linked with this exercise, yet students and managers still engaged. During the project one student put forward an idea on Twitter that there could be a prize for the 'best' solution to a problem. This was implemented and both managers were asked to retweet their favourite solution to an issue at the end of the project. This suggests that the participants involved were 'self-motivated' in putting this idea forward, and having some fun with their postings in the process. In putting forward ideas for incentives, this suggests that Salmon's model as discussed earlier in the chapter is not necessarily linear, and motivation for engagement can be revisited at any stage during the learning process where required.

Online Learning

Reflections on the initial days of the project highlighted some apprehension with those involved to engage in conversation and discussion. It was observed that a number of team members held back from posting to the Twitter discussion until they had seen the engagement of others. It is important to note that as Twitter allows for asynchronous communication it is possible that participants were instead waiting to join the conversations until they had more free time, however as discussion later in the project took place throughout the day it can be inferred that participants were wary of the project initially, which was as to be expected given that we were asking all team members to use social media in a way that they had not done so before.

Over the course of the first week of the pilot project the authors observed the industry managers beginning to engage in greater levels of discussion with the rest of the team members. Post project discussion with the two managers highlighted that it was once this greater depth of discussion started to take place that they felt that they were able to learn from the project via Twitter.

It was clear throughout the project that students were confident in their ideas and could provide further clarification when asked, often reflecting upon theoretical models taught within the classroom to enhance their discussion. It was however the students immediate ideas to the problems presented that contained the most originality, once the students had time to think about their answers before posting a response they became more guarded in their approach. It can therefore be inferred that when using Twitter for faster paced interaction and learning, richer and more original ideas and responses can be gathered to problems presented.

Despite the clear indications from the literature of a need to go through some form of online socialisation (Salmon 2000), the authors observed little in the way of social interaction between participants within Twitter. It could be suggested that team members felt as though there was a line of professional respect which therefore did not allow for socialisation, however if this project had been extended for a greater period of time or included members which all perceived themselves to be equal within the group this outcome may have been different. As more and more people are used to engaging with social media as part of their daily lives it can be questioned whether online introductions and socialisation is required prior to functioning as a performing team.

Outside of the pilot project the authors could see through the use of the Twitter feed function that a number of the team members were continuing to use Twitter as a learning and debate platform once the project had come to an end. Students fed back that they were also actively seeking to follow more professionally based Twitter accounts, as well as seeing an increased level of interest from recruitment agencies for their own Twitter accounts.

Technical Advantages and Challenges

The first and most significant challenge overall was the character restriction from the student perspective, and quite often those involved would label their postings (1/3, 2/3, 3/3) to try and get around the 140 character restriction. However, this defeats the principle of using Twitter. Managers fed back that they found using the platform advantageous at times, as in reality if discussion forums were used they would simply not have the time to be able to read and respond to what they described as 'mini essays'.

The second challenge emerged in relation to the use of the hashtag. On attempting to search for the discussion thread using #PSCMChat, it appeared that although the majority of respondents were using this in their posts as instructed, that some participants had forgotten to insert it. This caused an access issue when attempting to search for a thread and instead having to look at each individual student profile to see if they were posting. This was a vital consideration in terms of future use for the authors, as scaling this up to larger teams would mean a logistical problem in checking those involved were using the correct hash tag; a key fundamental of the Twitter platform.

Not surprisingly, the biggest advantage of using Twitter as a medium for discussion was its access and flexibility for use. Both students and managers could use the technology at any given point during the day or night, and particularly for the managers was an easy app that they were able to access whilst 'on the go' at work. This has implications for teams in practice as the social media choice needs to be easy enough for team members to access, use and do so whilst working on other aspects of their daily jobs. However, the authors considered the frequency of the issues and challenges presented (one per day, per manager) and the response levels to each. Not every student responded to every issue, and whilst it may be argued that this approach was okay for the objective of the task, this may not transfer to fast paced projects where anything and everything to do with the project may be up for discussion using social media. It was clear that the social media worked well whilst task boundaries were set, however how this would work once those boundaries were lifted is questionable.

Role of the Facilitator

The role of the facilitator online is not necessarily to engage and put forward ideas and feedback to postings but to encourage discussion, link discussions with course design, prompt for further ideas and deal with any technical issues which might arise (Merril 2003).

From the outset of the project, it was clear that the managers were clearly engaged from a task perspective in posting up their daily issues, but also took on the role of the facilitator from the outset in prompting students for ideas and further clarification on points.

The authors (as facilitators) posted several prompts to students who were not initially engaging, however this was only over the first couple of days. Once the team was starting to exchange ideas and communicate with each other the authors were able to step back as facilitators.

On reflecting on the project, one of the biggest challenges for the facilitator is how to encourage and generate debate within some of the challenges discussed. As previously stated, students may see it as controversial to challenge the managers involved in the study due to the level of respect they are maintaining in a virtual setting. However, in relation to project management it is the diversity of ideas and challenging thinking that is to be encouraged to generate new and innovative thinking.

It was implied earlier that students had missed out the 'online socialisation' stage of Salmon's model, and could be further suggested that Tuckman's stage of 'storming' was also skipped. It is difficult to assess how much facilitation or guidance is required in an online setting to ensure team members feel comfortable enough to challenge, when indeed it is something which is testing enough in a face-to-face environment. However, without this taking place, the discussions may generate ideas, but never actually reach any conclusions if the ideas are not debated.

Development of a Virtual Learning Community

The fundamental objective of the pilot was to assess if participants had had actually developed any new ways of thinking about project management whether from a problem solving perspective or in relation to new insights about the professional itself.

From the student perspective, it was clear that value had been added to what they had learned in the 'traditional' format of project management education which they had been used to undertaking. Particularly of interest was the recognition that they identified with different approaches to solving problems rather than just taking a logical step approach, and the value of insight into how the theory they had been exposed to linked with practice (Sams & Mottram 2015).

Furthermore, managers felt that the Twitter project had enabled them to revisit and reflect on their own practice and the models that could be useful to them. They placed value on the fresh insights that students were providing on problems that they were facing, suggesting that it was a good way of enabling them to think more critically about the role that they undertake within the organisation (Sams & Mottram 2015).

IMPLICATION FOR USING SOCIAL MEDIA IN PROJECT TEAMS

It is clear that there are benefits to using Twitter as a social media platform for sparking discussions between professionals and students, however there are also some challenges which need to be addressed by organisations wishing to use Twitter as a mode of information sharing and exchange.

Use of Twitter

The pilot project indicated that students and managers had found the interactions very useful indeed, and learning had clearly taken place in relation to knowledge exchange and idea generation, which in turn helped to develop the students problem solving skills. However in evaluating the impact of scaling this up to a larger team, it may not be as effective.

It is questionable from the project whether Twitter would be an effective platform for project team members to engage in, and depends very much on the purpose of the discussions. Whilst the benefits of being a free, easily accessible tool with little training required are clear advantages, the reasons for using Twitter as a social media tool needs to be considered in greater depth. Issues of commercial sensitivity and length of postings need to be carefully thought about before embarking on developing a community of learning.

Wider Considerations

This chapter has highlighted the observations and reflections of the authors, and from this key themes have emerged which should be considered when looking to implement the use of social media within project teams which have been illustrated in in Figure 7. Ideally, this model should be considered by a project manager before considering the likes of Salmon's five step model or Tuckman's team formation in considering the essential ingredients for bringing teams together in a virtual format.

Stage 1: Scoping

It can be seen from the above model that considerations need to be made by project managers seeking to utilize Twitter or other social media platforms within their project teams. Initially it is paramount to fully understand the aim and objectives for adopting the use of social media for use in teams. For example, when the need arises to engage with stakeholders from different countries, or an organization is seeking ideas on which project management methodology to use and wants to consult with its team, this is a clearly set out requirement. Without this the project team will tend to lack engagement with its use and therefore it is of little value to them.

The team should also be made aware how frequently they are required to engage with the social media platform, as well as making it clear what the benefits are for them in return. This may simply be a more efficient way of communication (rather than face-to-face meetings), or a one off session to discuss a new project initiation document. The frequency of engagement may need to be increased or

Figure 7. Three stage model of social media integration in project teams (Source: Authors' own creation)

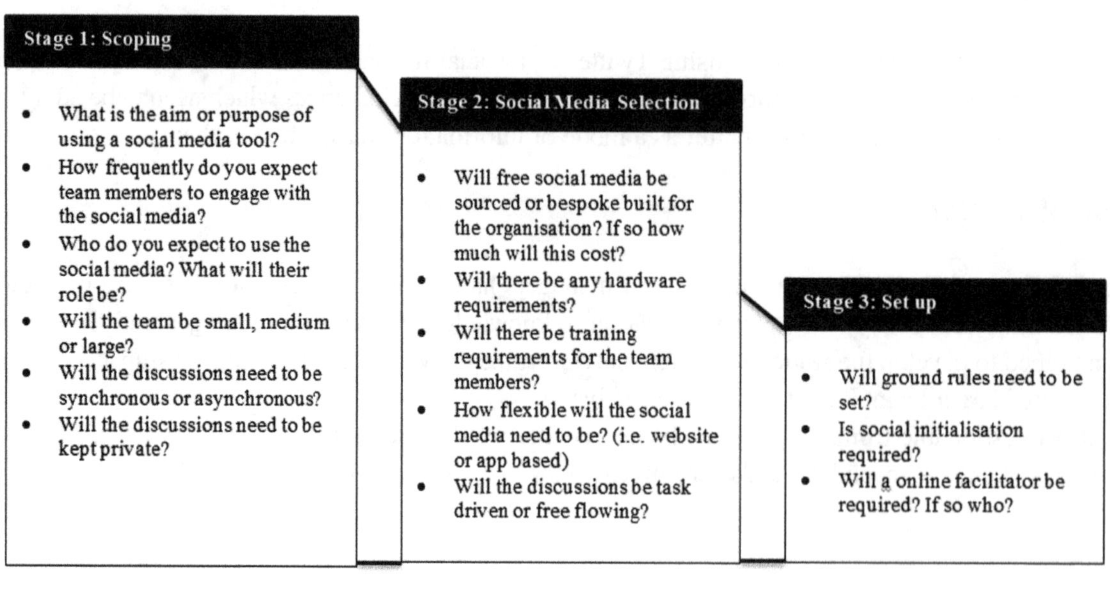

decreased as time moves on to suit the changing nature of discussions however some guidance at the outset will help team members to define how often they should engage. What is missing from this, and should also be considered is why those particular team members should be engaging in the first place. In project management teams, theory indicates that one of the major success factors is in carefully defining roles and responsibilities of team members and what they will be contributing. This is no different for a team coming together using social media. When implementing this type of initiative, the project manager should be very clear on who should be involved and why, questioning what each team member will bring to the discussion. The size of the team using the media is a vital consideration. This chapter has clearly seen the benefits of using Twitter in a small group as learning was evident and knowledge shared; however the challenges of using Twitter if scaled up in size are clear. Considering these factors early on will help to reduce the risk of problems occurring later.

Other considerations to be made before deciding on social media type will be whether the discussions are intended to take place in a synchronous or asynchronous manner. It may be more beneficial for some teams to have scheduled discussions in place of face-to-face interactions, or in some instances it may be preferable to have an ongoing dialogue. The project manager should decide which approach if preferable as this will help in the process of selecting the most appropriate social media.

Finally, the project manager must consider the nature of the potential discussions to be had in terms of their confidentiality as this will also influence the choice of social media to be used.

Stage 2: Social Media Selection

Once the above questions have been considered, the project manager should then be able to make a shortlist of the most appropriate social media tools to use. An obvious influencing factor for any organization is that of cost. If the organization chooses to use a freely available social media tool for discussion, then this may decrease the requirement for training team members on how to use the software. If a tool is selected which is bespoke to the organization, this will obviously be higher cost however clearly the benefits are in acquiring a tool which is tailored to the requirements of all projects across an organization. Associated with this is the training consideration of project team members. If team members are widely dispersed this can become problematic unless guidance manuals or the likes of webinar training is provided, which could be a possibility.

The social media choice should also consider the flexibility of the tools available. For example, the majority of free social media tools are available as downloadable apps which can be used in a more intuitive way than those where users may have to physically log into a website. The flexible nature of these tools and how they are set up will impact heavily on how likely team members are to engage with them. Likewise, if social media is imposed upon a project team member for use in collaboration on the go, the organization may need to consider whether the appropriate hardware to access the media is supplied through the organization or expected that personal mobile phones, laptops or tablets will be used.

Finally, within the social media selection stage, the pace of use once again needs to be considered. The aim of a project team using social media as a method for collaboration should be re-visited at this point, to assess whether the discussions taking place are intended to be task driven by a facilitator or free-flowing. Indeed, it could be suggested that idea stimulation online may be hindered when the boundaries of a question or task are presented to the group, however in contrast to this, if free flowing communication is encouraged the pace may become too fast to be able to obtain any value from the exchanges. The nature of the project and what is to be achieved will help in evaluating this.

Stage 3: Implementation

Once a social media tool has been decided upon, the project manager can then start to initiate the set-up of the virtual team. It may be appropriate (depending on the public nature or the roles involved in the discussion), to present a set of ground rules in relation to what members can and should post as well as what should be avoided. It was clear from this pilot project that social initialization was omitted, and arguments have been made both for and against this. It could be suggested that society today is so used to using technology that 'socialization' is just no longer required; however the authors have demonstrated that there was also a lack of challenging debate online. To try and combat the problems of a team being overly cohesive, the social initiation should perhaps not only focus on getting to know each other (and the technology), but to also encourage and stimulate an online area where team members are able to constructively criticize ideas and plans in a respectful manner without fear of negative repercussions.

The role of the facilitator needs to be agreed at this stage. Should there be one? This very much depends on the project and the purpose of communications online. If an online facilitator is decided as something which will provide value (especially when using new technologies), it should be questioned whether the project manager is the right person to do this. An online facilitator as has been discussed, should prompt engagement, seek clarification on points and deal with any technical issues that emerge, therefore perhaps the project manager is not the most suitable person for this role.

This model is not intended to provide a prescriptive menu for social media implementation, however should be used as a guide to ensuring the most successful and productive use of these exciting technologies, as a precursor for discussion in project teams.

FUTURE RESEARCH DIRECTIONS

Whilst this contribution presents some useful insights into the use of Twitter on a small scale project management student and manager engagement project, there is a clear need to further evaluate the impact of the learning which is generated when engaging with social media to encourage teamwork and collaboration. The project presented in this chapter was constrained to the UK project management industry, and the sample of students who participated would need to increase to provide further insight into the usefulness of using Twitter as a delivery mode for problem solving and knowledge exchange.

Additionally, there is a limited amount of research on the impact that virtual teams have on the overall success of projects and whether there is a direct correlation with online discussions and the performance of the teams. This is a field for further exploration once social media is a more established norm within teams in organizations.

CONCLUSION

This chapter has discussed the use of Twitter both within a UK Higher Education case study pilot project and within project teams. It is clear from the rapid and sustained growth of various social media tools that this alternative method of communication is here to stay.

It is useful to embrace the use of social media platforms such as Twitter, not only on a social level but also as a professional communication and collaboration tool. The need for team working and collaboration across continents and times zones within project teams should encourage professionals to look towards these types of tools which can provide low cost, flexible options of bringing people and thoughts together in order to share and create ideas and knowledge.

Social media tools such as Twitter have the potential be utilized as a space for learning, both within formal educational settings and in later employment. When used in small scale project teams or groups Twitter allows learning to take place between the team members as well as the creation new knowledge. On the larger scale when Twitter is used as a wider community it becomes far more useful as an information sharing tool rather than a problem solving tool.

It is understood that Twitter, or other social media platforms, will not be suitable for use within every project and that project managers will need to take the time to consider why they would consider the use of social media and for what purpose. Unless this is clear and rationale it is expected that the use of social media will not contribute to project success.

REFERENCES

Allen, T. J. (1977). *Managing the flow of technology*. Cambridge, MA: The MIT Press.

Ashleigh, M., Ojiako, U., Chipulu, M., & Wang, J. K. (2012). Critical learning themes in project management education: Implications for blended learning. *International Journal of Project Management*, *30*(2), 153–161. doi:10.1016/j.ijproman.2011.05.002

Assudani, R., & Kloppenborg, T. J. (2010). Managing stakeholder for project management success: An emergent model of stakeholders.(Report). *Journal of General Management*, *35*(3), 67–80.

Chartered Management Institute. (2014). *21st Century Leaders: Building practice into the curriculum to boost employability*. Retrieved from http://www.managers.org.uk/Insights/Research/Current-research/2014/June/21st-Century-Leaders.aspx

Córdoba, J., & Piki, A. (2012). Facilitating project management education through groups as systems. *International Journal of Project Management*, *30*(1), 83–93. doi:10.1016/j.ijproman.2011.02.011

DiStefano, J. J., & Maznevski, M. L. (2000). Creating value with diverse teams in global management. *Organizational Dynamics*, 29(1), 45-63.

Evans, C. (2014). Twitter for teaching: Can social media be used to enhance the process of learning? *British Journal of Educational Technology*, *45*(5), 902–915. doi:10.1111/bjet.12099

Grosse, C. U. (2002). Managing Communication within Virtual Intercultural Teams, Business and Professional. *Communication Quarterly*, *65*(4), 22–38.

Handy, C. (1995). Trust and the virtual organization. *Harvard Business Review*, *73*(3), 40–50.

Hollingshead, J., McGrath, K., & O'Connor, K. M. (1993). Group task performance and communication technology: A longitudinal study of computer-mediated versus face-to-face work groups. *Small Group Research*, *24*(3), 307–333. doi:10.1177/1046496493243003

Jarvenpaa, S. L., & Leidner, D. E. (1998). Communication and Trust un Global Virtual Teams. *Journal of Computer-Mediated Communication, 3*(4), 0. doi:10.1111/j.1083-6101.1998.tb00080.x

Johnson, S. D., Suriya, C., Yoon, S. W., Berret, J. V., & La Fleur, J. (2000). Team Development and group processes of virtual learning teams. *Computers & Education, 39*, 393–397.

Koskela, L. J., & Howell, G. (2002). The Underlying Theory of Project Management is Obsolete. *Proceedings of the PMI Research Conference*, Seattle, Washington.

McKinsey. (2011). *How social technologies are extending the organization.* Retrieved from http://www.mckinsey.com/insights/high_tech_telecoms_internet/how_social_technologies_are_extending_the_organization

Merrill, H. S. (2003). Best practices for online facilitation. *Adult Learning, 14*(2), 13.

Meyerson, D., Weick, K. E., & Kramer, R. M. (1996). Swift trust and temporary groups. In R. M. Kramer, T. R. Tyler (Eds.), Trust in Organizations (pp. 166-195). Thousand Oaks, CA: Sage. doi:10.4135/9781452243610.n9

Pant, I., & Baroudi, B. (2008). Project management education: The human skills imperative. *International Journal of Project Management, 26*(2), 124–128. doi:10.1016/j.ijproman.2007.05.010

Salmon, G. (2011). *E-moderating: The key to teaching and learning online* (3rd ed.). New York: Routledge.

Salmon, G. K. (2000). *E-moderating: the key to teaching and learning online.* London, New York: Routledge Falmer. doi:10.4324/9780203465424

Salmon, G. K. (2015). *The Five Stage Model.* Retrieved from http://www.gillysalmon.com/five-stage-model.html

Sams, M., & Mottram, K. (2015). Using twitter as a project management learning intervention #PSCMCHAT. Project Management Development – Practice and Perspectives (pp. 328-339). Riga, University of Latvia.

Schulz, B. (2008). The Importance of Soft Skills: Education beyond academic knowledge. *NAWA Journal of Language and Communication,* 2(1), 146-154

Thomas, J., & Mengel, T. (2008). Preparing project managers to deal with complexity – Advanced project management education. *International Journal of Project Management, 26*(3), 304–315. doi:10.1016/j.ijproman.2008.01.001

Tuckman, B. W. (1965). Developmental sequence in small groups. *Psychological Bulletin, 63*(6), 384–399. doi:10.1037/h0022100 PMID:14314073

Tuckman, B. W., & Jensen, M. A. C. (1977). Stages of Small-Group Development Revisited. *Group and Organization Studies, 2*(4), 419–427. doi:10.1177/105960117700200404

Use Twitter, Facebook and other social media to help manage projects and teams. (2015). Office. Retrieved from https://support.office.com/en-gb/article/Use-Twitter-Facebook-and-other-social-media-to-help-manage-projects-and-teams-1c9b9c86-e417-4763-91ed-35a5f6e86208

Wee, L. K.-N., Alexandria, M., Kek, Y.-C., & Kelley, C. A. (2003). Transforming the marketing curriculum using problem-based learning: A case study. *Journal of Marketing Education*, *25*(2), 150–162. doi:10.1177/0273475303254016

Winter, M., Smith, C., Morris, P., & Cicmil, S. (2006). Directions for future research in project management: The main findings of a UK government-funded research network. *International Journal of Project Management*, *24*(8), 638–649. doi:10.1016/j.ijproman.2006.08.009

Wright, K., Frame, T., & Hartzler, M. (2014). Student perceptions of a Self-Care course taught exclusively by team-based learning and utilizing Twitter. *Currents in Pharmacy and Teaching*, *6*(6), 842–848. doi:10.1016/j.cptl.2014.07.003

KEY TERMS AND DEFINITIONS

App: An application with a specific purpose usually access via a smart mobile phone or tablet device.

Learning Community: A group with common learning goals that aim to work together in order to collaborate and build knowledge.

Online Socialisation: The acquisition of knowledge, norms and values using an online medium required in order to integrate as part of the online group.

Project Team: A team of people who are brought together for a defined period of time in order to work on a particular project or task.

Social Media: Websites (or applications) that allow people to share content with an online network

Twitter: An online social media platform which restricts users' posts to 140 characters.

Virtual Teams: Teams of people that have a specific end goal yet do not meet on a face-to-face basis and instead communicate and conduct activities by other means.

Chapter 16
Social Media Applications Promote Constituent Involvement in Government Management

Gerald A. Merwin Jr.
Valdosta State University, USA

John R. Bennett Jr.
Valdosta State University, USA

J. Scott McDonald
University of Texas El Paso, USA

Keith A. Merwin
Merwin Associates, USA

ABSTRACT

This chapter explores the use of social media applications by local governments to communicate with constituents and promote involvement in policy and project management activities. Although public and private sector organizations make different uses of social media (Halverson, Hauknes, Miles, & Røste, 2005), there are many ways for government and nonprofit entities to make use of Web 2.0 applications. The focus in this chapter is on local government and a variety of examples will be provided. Some local government agencies primarily provide information to constituents through the social media apps, while others solicit the input from citizens to expand involvement. Finally, suggestions for future research and uses will be discussed.

INTRODUCTION

Local governments use social media applications in a variety of ways to involve citizens in policy and project management activities. Citizen involvement or engagement is advocated by a number of authors (Hollingsworth and Cooper, 2011; Hui & Hayllar, 2010; Linders, 2012; McNutt, 2012). This chapter explores some examples of the use of Web 2.0 to connect governments with their constituents and provides some suggestions for other applications.

Numerous local governments have elicited citizen reports of potholes or street lights that are out of order to facilitate repairs. This can be done in a variety of ways, but the obvious advantages of social

DOI: 10.4018/978-1-4666-9867-3.ch016

media greatly increase the appeal to the citizens and also speed up the response time of the government agencies. Another evolving use of social media is communication between residents and either police or fire department officials. Crime, accident, or fire reporting can be easily accomplished through online methods. Additionally, use of Web 2.0 technologies is applied to disaster response and recovery efforts.

The communications can be done in either direction. In many cases social media will allow the local government agency to inform residents of the latest news or reports on crime, street repairs, or other developments. Also, announcements of meetings of special interest can be spread online and could result in many more constituents being involved.

This chapter explores a variety of ways that local government actors are using social media to improve relations with citizens, involve citizens in improving the community, and otherwise building linkages with neighborhood groups. Successful innovations are identified to serve as best-practices for other local governments that hope to make similar efforts as the technology becomes simpler to use.

DISRUPTIVE TECHNOLOGIES IMPACT ON PUBLIC SECTOR POLICY IMPLEMENTATION AND PROJECT MANAGEMENT

Disruptive technologies and their ramifications are on the minds of government managers at all levels. In the private sector the impacts of disruptive technology are notable for displacing an earlier technology and the creation of new markets (Oram, 2001; Denning, 2014). In the public sector, one is more likely to see technologies coexist as market forces are less prevalent and the profit motive has far less impact. Nevertheless, disruptive technologies clearly impact how governments do business as well as what business governments might act to undertake (Bent, Østergaard, & Villumsen, 2002).

It is not difficult to identify some prior disruptive technologies and their impacts on how government transacts its business. For example finger printing, the automobile, and two-way radios yielded much of today's modern law enforcement. More recently, the personal video camera and GIS are yielding significant changes in local law enforcement (Bellis, n.d.). These technology shifts impacted law enforcement while leaving much of the rest of government unimpacted. A more macro disruptive innovation has been and continues to impact all governments (with the possible exception of North Korea), at all levels, in innumerable ways -- the use of social media. Over the past decade or so, local governments have grappled with both the potentials and applications of this disruptive technology (Dixon & Keyes, 2013).

The Web is the root of numerous disruptions in the ways local governments operate, and no change has presented more potential than the use of social media to promote constituent involvement. Before proceeding it is essential to disaggregate citizen involvement into its two basic components: participation via political avenues; and participation by way of administrative government, the focus of this chapter. Briefly, political impacts of electronic media are well documented for at least two decades (Mayrowitz, 1995). The importance of contemporary social media in politics is evidenced in recent uprisings in the Arab world (Tufkei & Wilson, 2012).

Returning to the focus of this chapter, social media and administrative government warrant continued research. While scholars and practitioners have researched and experimented with various aspects of social media, the technology (hardware and software) continues to evolve and at times revolutionize, while understanding of the capabilities of social media similarly continue to evolve (Zeider, 2007; Lee & Kwak, 2012; Rudnick, Wootton, & Wyatt, 2009; Wright, 2009).

The motivation for private sector use of social media centers of course around profit, even when the rationale given is media or public relations (Pettigrew & Reber, 2010; Dunn, 2010; Evans, Twomey, & Talan, 2011; Minton-Eversole, 2010). There are notable differences between public and private sector uses of social media (Halverson, Hauknes, Miles, & Røste, 2005). The wide range of public sector usage of social media is impressive. This diversity is evident in at least two dimensions, geographical scope of authority and diversity of applications. First and foremost, the importance of social media to effective and participatory government is being recognized in the U.S. (Kavanaugh, Fox, Sheetz, Yang, Li, Shoemaker, Natsev, & Xie, 2012; Ellcessor, 2010) and other national governments (E-Petitions, 2009; Hinsberg, 2009; Faria & Peixoto, 2009; Rooksby & Sommerville, 2012). In the U.S., states have adopted social media applications (Deamer, 2011), e.g. Georgia (Streib & Navarro, 2006), Ohio (Ohio, 2015), and Nebraska (Nebraska, 2015) to name a few. At a local level, counties such as Orange County, California (Orange County), Oakland County, Michigan (Oakland County), and Roanoke County, Virginia (Roanoke County) and cities of all sizes from large cities such as New York (New York City, 2014), Chicago (Chicago, 2015), and Arlington, Texas (Arlington, 2015) to a wide variety of smaller cities (Kingsley, 2010).

In the public sector, social media has been applied to a wide array of governmental programs and policy areas including emergency management (Huang, Chan, & Hyder, 2010; Majchrzak & More, 2011; Kavanaugh et al., 2012), access to public records and data (Shark, 2010; Chun, Shulman, Sandoval, & Hovy, 2010), planning (Salkin, 2011; Kingsley, 2010), social policy and programs (Henman, 2013), libraries (Burkhardt, 2010), education (Moran, Seaman, & Tinti-Kane, 2011; Ferriter, 2010), public health (Thackery, Neiger, Smith, & Van Wagenen, 2012), and public services (Hootsuite, n.d.), among others. On a broader front, social media is contributing to increased levels of government transparency (Bertot, Jaeger, & Grimes, 2010; Bonson, Torres, Royo, & Flores; Nath, 2011), accessibility (Bricout & Baker, 2010), citizen engagement (MacNamara, Sakinofsky, & Beattie, 2012; Barnes & Mann, 2011; Smith, 2013; McNutt, 2014; Lee & Kwak, 2012), collaboration (Szkuta, 2014; Nath, 2011; Poje, 2011; Hui & Hayllar, 2010), and coproduction between citizens and government (Linders, 2012).

It is difficult to imagine a disruptive technology having broader impacts on government than social media, but it could be that after more than a decade of experiments and experiences with social media, governments are just scratching the surface in terms of applications and understanding. Coleman (2013) argues that in the near future there will be three new challenges involving social media: smart city proliferation, vehicles becoming technology platforms, and expansion of the content economy. Smart city proliferation will involve smarter use of all technologies including a wide array of social media (Komninos, Schaffer, & Pallot, 2011). Drivers (vehicles) are already using a variety of apps to find and pay for parking, plan trips around traffic congestion, construction, and even traffic cops, and this is just the beginning. Finally, the content economy is exploding and governments are currently responsible for a large share of potential content, i.e., big data.

Social Media: Critical to Success

"Project communication is the exchange of project-specific information with the emphasis on creating understanding between the sender and the receiver. Effective communication is one of the most important factors contributing to the success of a project" (Office of Project Management Process Improvement, 2007, p. 6). Successful project management requires timely and effective communication, there can be no doubt. Some authors go so far as to classify communication as a set of rights, the rights to be informed, to have access to information, and the opportunity to express opinion to influence decision making (Biocca, 2005). Project communication is broad-reaching, both within an organization and between an organization and its outside stakeholders. Project communication is two-way, for example, between a project team and impacted communities as the team informs communities of project issues and as the community expresses their perspectives on the project.

Both public and private organizations face the same critical issues with regard to project management (Hamilton, 2004). Successful project development including planning, implementation, and evaluation requires communication throughout the process. The necessity of successful communication is heightened in the public sector, as policy is translated into action (Stewart, 2013). However, this in no way diminishes the critical role communication plays with private sector projects. Possibly the most complex communication situation may be found in projects involving public and private partnerships, (Hamilton, 2004) especially in situations with compressed time frames like fast-track design-build projects (Cho, Hyun, Koo, & Hong, 2010).

More than anything else, effective communication, especially in the case of complex projects and/or complex organizational structures (like public-private partnerships), decreases risk (Biocca, 2015). Every manager likes to see risk decreased, because risk may yield higher costs, time delays, and greater unpredictability of outcomes (Krauss, 2014; Biocca, 2015; Wang, 2011).

All stages of project development are impacted by social media, from determining demand to gaining customer input regarding project design, to communicating within and between implementing organizations, to assessing success (Treem, J., Dailey, S. Pierce, C, & Leonardi, P., 2015; Calloway, J., 2011; Lipton, E. & Davenport, C., 2015; Connelly, P., 2009; Trees, L., 2015). As projects and programs become larger, more complex, and/or more controversial, the role of communication and thereby the role of social media becomes more critical.

The above challenges are entering the picture in today's environment where practitioners and scholars still attempt to make sense of how to best use social media. We might even take a step back; it is not just social media that governments are struggling with, some public organizations continue to struggle with the more basic avenues of communication including hearings and other public meetings, phone services, and websites. That said, it is important that we build case studies to seek lessons, both positive and negative, to inform practitioners of pitfalls to avoid and to develop best practices for application in other communities.

LOCAL GOVERNMENTS RECOGNIZED FOR SOCIAL MEDIA PROJECT MANAGEMENT ACCOMPLISHMENTS

There are a variety of ways for local governments to gain recognition for their efforts to communicate with constituents. One such source of recognition is Public Technology Institute annual awards (2013). Boston, Massachusetts, won an award for Boston City Connect app, which is a comprehensive method for exchanging messages with citizens living in Boston (2015). To give some indication of the success of this operation, the Boston City Connect Reports (2015) site shows nearly a half million reports processed from citizens. Examples of reports include neighborhood parking violations, snow/ice piles creating driving hazards, traffic signal pole down, refuse violation, potholes, and litter. A review of the app as presently applied, shows some items closed, while other items are clearly in process or being reviewed.

Boston has received recognition previously for providing excellence in the area of economic development resources available on the Web (Merwin, McDonald, & Odera, 2008). In that review, a combination of data, mapping, and site selection resources that would make recruiting or developing a new business or industry much easier. The economic development site also provided information for citizens about job training and educational opportunities useful in getting a job. For most local governments, this type of assistance is also important in recruiting new businesses or building existing operations.

Likewise, the Boston Career Center (2015) has links to both training and job opportunities with city departments and units such as Emergency Medical Services, Fire and Police Departments, the Public Health Commission, Public Library, School System, Redevelopment Authority, and Water and Sewer Commission. The Career Center also provides access to information on internships and volunteering opportunities, plus adult basic education and skills training. The Adult Services unit provides career coaching, job placement, and follow-up services.

The Public Technology Institute annual awards (2013) also honored the City of New York, New York, for the TXT–2–Work program. According to the City of New York site, Job Training and Placement Services for Public Assistance Recipients (2015), "TXT-2-Work: Allows Cash Assistance and Food Stamp recipients to receive text messages about new job openings." As a service to citizens, the City establishes linkages with employers who have openings and facilitates the search process. The site also has links to information about job training and placement services.

Santa Monica, CA, Be Excited! Be Prepared (2015) won recognition from Public Technology Institute (2013) for a site that gives citizens direct information about construction projects, such as streets, light rail, parking structures, public buildings, and a traffic management system. The site provides a map that is interactive and also has postings of road closures.

While these are but a few examples of innovations using social media to link local government agencies and their constituents, they do represent some varied methods of using the available methods. It is likely that many more will be explored by local governments in the coming years. We turn now to one more detailed example of this approach.

Case Study: Savannah Chatham Metropolitan Police Department Precinct 2, Savannah, Georgia

The Savannah Chatham County Metropolitan Police Department (SCMPD) was created by a merger of the Savannah Police Department and Chatham County Police Department in 1995.

Precinct 2 is unique among others in the SCMPD jurisdiction because of the contrasts that reside within it. It is home to luxury hotels and weekly-rate boarding houses, multi-million dollar historic mansions and public housing projects. Within its boundaries are portions of the fourth-largest seaport in the nation and the Savannah College of Art and Design, which has classroom, administrative and dormitory buildings arrayed throughout the precinct. In addition to students and full-time residents, more than 13 million people visited the city in 2013, with most of them spending their visits within precinct boundaries. In 2014, mall developer Ben Carter Enterprises announced a $100 million plan to redevelop Broughton Street, the precinct's main commercial corridor.

Precinct 2 Commander Capt. Ben Herron (2015) is a Savannah native who joined the force in 1988. In 2014 he began using Nextdoor.com to interact with citizens and particularly with members of the Downtown Neighborhood Association and the Victorian Neighborhood Association. Herron was not directed to begin using the platform, rather he took note of the precinct's crime prevention officer using the social media network and began using it himself, because he believed it could be beneficial in improving communication between his department and the citizens it serves.

"When I started using it, I was new to dealing with social media," he said. "However, I realized early on that it was a good method to get the vibe of the community. It allows me to empathize with residents' positions and hear what they are saying. It helps me to engage different neighborhoods."

Herron's description of communication with residents about his department's projects and using social media to gauge their opinion is "two-way" and "between a project team and impacted communities as the team informs communities of project issues and as the community expresses their perspectives on the project" (Biocca).

Herron stated monitoring Nextdoor.com has helped him learn about the issues, which he had not identified as being critical, but were major concerns to people within the neighborhoods.

"You see a variety of information and it gives you perspective on what's important to people. In our profession, we may look at something and think, that's not a big deal, but it is a big deal to them. And because it's a big deal to them, we need to be interested in it, too," he said.

Herron said he reads residents' opinions, then asks himself if he would feel the same way. "The answer to that question is usually yes," he said.

Herron said Nextdoor.com has also helped him identify issues that may not have been brought forward otherwise and respond quickly to them. For example, he described seeing a post about a suspicious vehicle. He quickly relayed it to a shift manager, who then dispatched an officer.

In cases in which a resident may not have felt the situation merited a 911 call, social media posts allow information that might not have been reported by other means, to flow to the police. Herron has also been able to share with other commanders information found on Nextdoor.com. This indicates the potential of social media in collaborative project management across precinct boundaries. In addition, he uses the department's analysis software to compare reports on Nextdoor.com to actual activity.

Amy Brock (2015) is the communications director for the Downtown Neighborhood Association (DNA). As a lead in the Nextdoor.com online community for the Savannah Historic District, she often acts as a liaison in the online community and encourages conversations between residents, and between residents and Herron. She also communicates public safety information regularly to the DNA membership via Facebook, email and the organization's website, SavannahDNA.org.

Brock agrees that social media has increased the willingness of residents to report crimes and can increase the effectiveness of projects designed to improve public safety.

"I think the more open lines of communication that we've developed have empowered neighbors to speak up, to report crimes no matter how insignificant they may seem," she said. "Neighbors are also able to play a role in identifying suspects because they have description information available through the social media channels they have subscribed to."

Brock's statement seems to demonstrate that using social media in this way, allows project stakeholders the "opportunity to express opinion to influence decision making," as Biocca suggests.

In addition to improving communication between stakeholders to aid in the management of the overall crime reduction projects, social media has been vital to smaller projects that support them, including one aimed at building a database of residential video surveillance camera installation locations. By creating of an inventory of private surveillance cameras, the project aims to fill gaps in coverage, as city cameras are installed primarily in parks and in other public spaces. This network of cameras, installed by residents, can expand the police department's field of vision.

Social media are used not only to encourage residents to volunteer their cameras to be listed in the database inventory project, but also used by the police to communicate descriptions of suspects to camera owners.

"By having suspect descriptions, neighbors are able to assist in trying to identify and/or keeping an eye out for suspect," Brock said. "With more and more neighbors investing in home video surveillance cameras, there is a greater chance of capturing a crime on video. Overall, the community is strengthened."

A resident's camera mounted on a front porch might capture footage of a suspect fleeing a crime scene. Theft from vehicles is also a major concern of residents and the network of cameras assembled by the project could be used in the management of programs aimed at reducing these crimes. The network could be used not just to identify individuals, with information being exchanged via social media, but also to document the travel patterns of people who move through neighborhoods pulling on door handles in search of unlocked cars.

According to Herron, residents often complain that they do not see police patrols in their neighborhoods often enough. He said his interactions via Nextdoor.com produce a kind of virtual police presence that reassures citizens and justifies their continued participation in public safety projects.

"Because we are responding and being attentive to what's going on, I think they feel heard," he said. "When you respond quickly to things, it lets them know that you are paying attention." He said that other city departments, including the Mobility and Parking Services and the citizen liaison office are also using social media to identify issues and concerns before they become larger problems and to reinforce the idea that city officials are listening and responding. Use of social media can also demonstrate that officials are actively seeking citizen input to improve project management.

"We can impact the overall perception of city services," he said.

Herron said some of his colleagues are resistant to social media because they are unfamiliar with their use. He suggested there is also a cultural shift that will need to occur before more adopt social media as a tool.

"In police work I think we sometimes get caught up in the idea that we respond only when someone makes a complaint or calls 911," Herron said. Actively using social media requires officers to respond before situations reach that level, something they may not feel comfortable doing.

Herron said SCMPD Chief Joseph Lumpkin, who joined the department in November 2014 from the Athens-Clarke County (GA) Police Department, has been supportive of his efforts as he believes it leads to greater transparency. Herron shares this belief and said that working with residents through Nextdoor.com has allowed them a better understanding of how his department works and the challenges it faces.

"They are getting a good look into our organization," he said.

Brock agreed the communication has been helpful in encouraging cooperation with police and improving the success of crime reduction projects, even if the look into the police department gained through greater access to incident reports, crime statistics, and alerts transmitted through social media can be alarming for some residents.

"I think the interactions between Capt. Herron and the Downtown Neighborhood Association have created a greater sense of awareness of the incidents impacting the residential and commercial areas of downtown Savannah," she said. "I don't want to say it's necessarily comforting to learn of these incidents, but do think the more frequent communication from Capt. Herron has been mutually beneficial for residents and the SCMPD."

"Effective communication is one of the most important factors contributing to the success of a project." (Office of Project Management Process Improvement, 2007, p. 6), and Brock said she feels communication through social media has aided in the management of public safety projects and improved their rates of success.

"It is imperative that we (the DNA/neighborhood) continue to communicate regularly with SCMPD to inform and engage our neighbors as we work together to improve public safety and reduce crime in downtown Savannah," she said.

Apps and Government-Constituent Interactions for Project Management

Government planning and project management organizations are beginning to realize the value of real-time data available from users of social media. The planners of the 2014 World Cup in Rio de Janeiro used information from both drivers and pedestrians gathered through Waze navigation app and Moovit public transportation app. In Florida, the Department of Transportation (FDOT) has partnered with Waze, a mobile mapping app that uses social media to gather and disseminate real time traffic information (Olson, 2014). As users run Waze, it automatically gathers GPS location and speed information and sends them back to the server. Users can also enter location specific data on traffic congestion, accidents, and weather related hazards. The FDOT will receive this information from Waze and, in return, provide that app with information on road construction, road closures and special events that affect traffic. This exchange of information will allow project managers to determine the changes to detours and schedules necessary to meet traffic requirements.

MacMillan (2013) reported that SeeClickFix is another social media app working to connect constituents to local government to solve problems. This mobile app and website allows users to report infrastructure problems to local government and the media. Started as a website, it has grown to include mobile apps that provide the user with the ability to photograph a problem and associate its GPS coordinates as part of the report. For many of the over 160 cities SeeClickFix is partnered with, it is the primary tool used by them for non-emergency service requests (MacMillan, 2013). This type of information makes it possible for managers to schedule work efficiently. It also creates a method of constituent feedback that increases the chance a problem will be detected and handled faster.

CitySourced is a similar app that integrates directly into a local government's workflow (Greene, 2010). Users provide geographically tagged pictures of a problem that include a time and date stamp and category of issue along with a note. This information is fed directly to the computer system of the correct department in that local government. A unique feature of CitySourced is a crowd sourcing option to fund needs suggested by citizens that are not covered by a current budget.

SOLUTIONS AND RECOMMENDATIONS

We recommend that public organizations find niches in their units that are interested in utilizing social media to communicate with constituents and then identify best practices for that type of function. While the examples in this chapter might be limited, they are wide enough to provide some good starting points for government agencies that might find Web 2.0 beneficial. Locating those examples and then seeking contacts who might have experience with using an application will often help with directions. In some cases, users groups or mailing lists will be available to help link the newcomers to those already using an application. Professional groups in most states might also provide connections for this type of expertise.

FUTURE RESEARCH DIRECTIONS

As with most new technologies, it is difficult to imagine how the use of social media apps will evolve. While many of these have been around for some time, it seems very likely that as local government agencies find useful apps, they will promote them to enhance communication with citizens. Now, more than ever, it is also likely that activists in many jurisdictions will be finding the apps and putting them to use in hopes that the local government agencies will follow suit and work with them in applying the data provided through the apps. It is easy to imagine that these opportunities will multiply rapidly, because both the constituents and local governments are likely to benefit. Future research will hopefully track these trends reporting on them in a qualitative manner as did the examples discussed herein. In the future, there is need to find ways to quantify the effectiveness and efficiencies that might result from social media apps.

CONCLUSION

Overall this chapter has covered the current status of uses found by local governments to apply social media apps to involve citizens in project management and other policy development activities. While most local agencies are in the early stages of establishing these practices, it seems likely that the viability of the apps will result in many further uses and a major expansion of the efforts to build and use more. Many of the examples here have shown that the benefits are clear, while they do require some learning curve for the local government people responsible for the use of the apps. In the long run, agencies and citizens will both gain from this effort.

REFERENCES

(2015). Boston Career Center. City of Boston. Retrieved from http://www.cityofboston.gov/ohr/career-center/

Barnes, W., & Mann, B. (2011). Making local democracy work: Municipal officials' views about public engagement. *National Civic Review*, *100*(3), 58–62. doi:10.1002/ncr.20063

Bellis, M. (n. d.). Police technology and forensic science: Timeline of police technology 1850 – 1960. Retrieved from http://inventors.about.com/od/fstartinventions/a/forensic_4.htm

Bent, D., Østergaard, C., & Villumsen, G. (2002). Technological life cycles: Regional clusters facing disruption. Aalborg, Aalborg University (DRUID Working Paper, No. 10).

Berlot, J., Jaeger, P., & Grimes, J. (2010). Using ICTs to create a culture of transparency: E-government and social media as openness and anti-corruption tools for societies. *Government Information Quarterly*, *27*(3), 264–271. doi:10.1016/j.giq.2010.03.001

Biocca, M. (2005). Risk communication and the precautionary principle. *Human and Ecological Risk Assessment*, *11*(1), 261–266. doi:10.1080/10807030590920097

Bonson, E., Torres, L., Royo, S., & Flores, F. (2012). Local e-government 2.0: Social media and corporate transparency in municipalities. *Government Information Quarterly*, *29*(2), 123–132. doi:10.1016/j.giq.2011.10.001

Boston Citizens Connect Reports. (2015). City of Boston. Retrieved from https://mayors24.cityofboston.gov:4443/

Boston City Connect. (2015). City of Boston. Retrieved from http://www.cityofboston.gov/doit/apps/citizensconnect.asp

Bricout, J., & Baker, P. (2010). Leveraging online social networks for people with disabilities in emergency communications and recovery. *International Journal of Emergency Management*, *7*(1), 59–74. doi:10.1504/IJEM.2010.032045

Burkhardt, A. (2010). Social media: A guide for college and university libraries. *College & Research Libraries*, *71*(1), 10–24.

Calloway, J. (2011). Social media management tools. *GPSolo*, *28*(4), 54–55.

Cho, K., Hyun, C., Koo, K., & Hong, T. (2010). Partnering process model for public sector fast-track design-build projects in Korea. *Journal of Management Engineering*, *26*(1), 19–29. doi:10.1061/(ASCE)0742-597X(2010)26:1(19)

Chun, S., Shulman, S., Sandoval, R., & Hovy, E. (2010). Government 2.0: Making connections between citizens, data, and government. *Information Policy*, *15*, 1–9.

Coleman, K. (2013, July 24). 3 disruptive technologies gaining speed. *Information Week*. Retrieved from http://www.informationweek.com/regulations/3-disruptive-technologies-gaining-speed/d/d-id/1110899?

Connect with the City of Chicago via social media. (2015). City of Chicago. Retrieved from http://www.cityofchicago.org/city/en/narr/misc/social_media.html

Connect with us on social media. (2015). City of Arlington. Retrieved from http://www.arlington-tx.gov/departments/social-media/

Connelly, P. (2009). Push comes to. GOV. *The American Prospect*, *20*(10), 8–11.

Deamer, K. (2011). States get social: Government use of social media is popular, but is it following state laws? *The News Media & the Law*, (Winter) 24.

Denning, S. (2014, January 7). Business's worst nightmare: Big Bang Disruption. *Forbes*. Retrieved from http://www.forbes.com/sites/stevedenning/2014/01/07/businesss-worst-nightmare-big-bang-disruption/

Dixon, J., & Keyes, D. (2013). The permanent disruption of social media. *Stanford Social Innovation Review*, *11*(1), 24–29.

Dunn, B. (2010). How I did it…: Best Buy's CEO on learning to love social media. *Harvard Business Review*, *88*(12), 43–48.

E-Petitions preserves old British tradition (2009). *Intergovernmental Solutions Newsletter,* (Fall), 18-19.

Ellcessor, E. (2010). Bridging Disability Divides. *Information Communication and Society*, *13*(3), 289–308. doi:10.1080/13691180903456546

Evans, A., Twomey, J., & Talan, S. (2011). Twitter as a public relations tool. *The Public Relations Journal*, *5*(1), 1–20.

Faria, C. & Peixoto, T. (2009). Participatory lawmaking in Brazil. *Intergovernmental Solutions Newsletter,* (Fall), 22-23.

Ferriter, W. (2010). Digitally speaking / Using social media to reach your community. *Educational Leadership*, *68*(4), 87–88.

Greene, K. (2010). An App with a Direct Line to City Hall. *MIT Technology Review*. Retrieved from http://www.technologyreview.com/news/421770/an-app-with-a-direct-line-to-city-hall/

Halverson, T., Hauknes, J., Miles, I., & Røste, R. (2005). *On the differences between public and private sector innovation*. Oslo: NIFU STEP.

Hamilton, A. (2004). Project management reform: A public body case study. *Proceedings of the Institution of Civil Engineers. Municipal Engineer*, *157*(3), 199–207. doi:10.1680/muen.2004.157.3.199

Help Avoid Traffic Congestion with the Waze App. (2015). State of Florida, Department of Transportation. *SunPassages Newsletter*. Retrieved from http://www.floridasturnpike.com/sunpassages/14.fall/waze-app.html

Henman, P. (2013). Governmentalities of Gov 2.0. *Information Communication and Society*, *16*(9), 1397–1418. doi:10.1080/1369118X.2012.706314

Hinsberg, H. (2009). My better Estonia. *Intergovernmental Solutions Newsletter,* Fall, 20-21.

Hollingworth, A., & Cooper, T. (2011). Why Government Must Do Better With Web 2.0. *Public Management*, *40*(3), 30–34.

Huang, C., & Chan, E., & Hyder, A. (2010). Web 2.0 and internet social networking?: A new tool for disaster management? – Lessons from Taiwan. *BMC Medical Informatics and Decision Making*, *10*(57), 1–5. PMID:20925944

Hui, G., & Hayllar, M. (2010). Creating public value in e-government: A public-private-citizen collaboration framework in Web 2.0. *Australian Journal of Public Administration*, *69*(S1), S120–S131. doi:10.1111/j.1467-8500.2009.00662.x

Kavanaugh, A., Fox, E., Sheetz, S., Yang, S., Li, L., Shoemaker, D., & Xie, L. et al. (2012). Social media use by government: From the routine to the critical. *Government Information Quarterly*, *29*(4), 480–491. doi:10.1016/j.giq.2012.06.002

Kingsley, C. (2010). *Making the most of social media: 7 lessons from successful cities*. Philadelphia, PA: Fels Institute of Government.

Komninos, N., Schaffers, H., & Pallot, M. (2011). Developing a policy roadmap for smart cities and the future Internet. In P. Cunningham & M. Cunningham (Eds.), *Proceedings of the eChallenges e-2011 Conference*. Dublin: IIMC.

Krauss, E. (2014). How does operational readiness assist in asset management: It surely is an operations function? *Australian Journal of Multi-disciplinary Engineering*, *11*(1), 1–11. doi:10.7158/N13-AM10.2014.11.1

Lee, G., & Kwak, Y. (2012). An open government maturity model for social media-based public engagement. *Government Information Quarterly*, *29*(4), 492–503. doi:10.1016/j.giq.2012.06.001

Linders, D. (2012). From e-government to we-government: Defining a typology for citizen coproduction in the age of social media. *Government Information Quarterly*, *29*(4), 446–454. doi:10.1016/j.giq.2012.06.003

Lipton, E., & Davenport, C. (2015, May 19). Critics hear EPA's voice in 'Public Comments'. *New York Times, 164*(56871) A1-A18.

MacMillan, T. (2013). 6 Years On, SeeClickFix Has Changed New Haven, *New Haven Independent*. Retrieved from http://www.newhavenindependent.org/index.php/archives/entry/seeclickfix_6_years/

MacNamara, J., Sakinofsky, P., & Beattie, J. (2012). E-electoral engagement: How governments use social media to engage voters. *Australian Journal of Political Science*, *47*(4), 623–639. doi:10.1080/10361146.2012.731491

Majchrzak, A., & More, P. (2011). Emergency! Web 2.0 to the rescue! *Communications of the ACM*, *54*(4), 125–132. doi:10.1145/1924421.1924449

McNutt, K. (2014). Public engagement in the Web 2.0 era: Social Collaborative technologies in a public sector context. *Canadian Public Administration / Administration Publique du Canada, 57*(1), 49-70.

Merwin, G., McDonald, J., & Odera, L. (2008). Economic Development: Governments' Cutting Edge in IT. In M. S. Raisinghani (Ed.), *Handbook of Research on Global Information Technology Management in the Digital Economy* (pp. 1–37). Hershey, PA: Information Science Reference. doi:10.4018/978-1-59904-875-8.ch001

Meyrowitz, J. (1985). *No sense of place: The impact of electronic media on social behavior*. Oxford: Oxford University Press.

Minton-Eversole, T. (2010). *Social media tools redefining learning in organizations*. Retrieved from http://www.shrm.org/hrdisciplines/staffingmanagement/Articles/Pages/ToolsRedefineLearning

Morgan, M., Seaman, J., & Tinti-Kane, H. (2011). *Teaching, learning, and sharing: How today's higher education faculty use social media*. Boston: Pearson.

Nath, J. (2011). Reimagining government in the digital age. *National Civic Review*, *100*(3), 19–23. doi:10.1002/ncr.20070

Nebraska Statewide Social Media. (2015). State of Nebraska. Retrieved from http://www.nebraska.gov/social-media.html

New York. City of (2014). *Welcome to NYC.gov*. Retrieved from http://www1.nyc.gov/

New York. City of (2015). Job Training and Placement Services for Public Assistance Recipients. Retrieved from http://www1.nyc.gov/nyc-resources/service/2982/job-training-and-placement-services-for-public-assistance-recipients

Ohio, State of. (2015). *Ohio.gov: State Agencies on Social Media.* Retrieved from http://www.ohio.gov/social/

Olson, P. (2014). Why Google's Waze Is Trading User Data With Local Governments. *Forbes*. Retrieved from http://www.forbes.com/sites/parmyolson/2014/07/07/why-google-waze-helps-local-governments-track-its-users/

Oram, A. (2001). *Harnessing the power of disruptive technologies*. Sebastopol, California: O'Reilly Media.

My OC: Social Media Hub. (2015). Orange County, California. Retrieved from http://ocgov.com/contact/connect

Pettigrew, J., & Reber, B. (2010). The new dynamic in corporate media relations: How Fortune 500 companies are using virtual press rooms to engage the press. *Journal of Public Relations Research*, *22*(4), 404–428. doi:10.1080/10627261003801412

Poje, J. (2011). Gov 2.0: Interaction, innovation, and collaboration. *Public Law*, *19*(1), 2–11.

*Project Communication Handbook (*2nd ed.*)*. (2007). Project Management Process Improvement. Sacramento, CA: Caltrans.

PTI Names 2013 Web 2.0 Winning Jurisdictions. (2013). Public Technology Institute. Retrieved from http://www.pti.org/index.php/t1/more/161

Roanoke County's Official Social Media Channels. (2015). Roanoke County, Virginia. Retrieved from http://www.roanokecountyva.gov/index.aspx?NID=816

Rooksby, J., & Sommerville, I. (2012). The management and use of social network sites in a government department. *Computer Supported Cooperative Work*, *21*(4-5), 397–415. doi:10.1007/s10606-011-9150-2

Rudnick, M., Wootton, A., & Wyatt, W. (2009). *Trends in employee self-service and manager self-service.* Retrieved from http://www.shrm.org/multimedia/webcasts/Pages/509essmss.aspx

Salkin, P. (2011). Social networking and land use planning and regulation: Practical benefits, pitfalls, and ethical considerations. *Pace Law Review*, *31*(1), 54–94.

Be Excited! Be Prepared. (2015). *City of Santa Monica*. Retrieved from http://www.smgov.net/bebp/

Shark, A. (2010). Behind the curve. *American City and County*, *125*(7), 48–51.

Smith, A. (2013). *Civic engagement in the digital age*. Washington, D.C.: Pew Research Center.

Social Media in Government: 5 Key Considerations (Whitepaper). (n. d.). *Hootsuite*. Vancouver.

Socialize. (2015). Oakland County, Michigan. Retrieved from http://www.oakgov.com/social/Pages/default.aspx

Stewart, J. (2013). Public policy as information. *Prometheus*, *31*(1), 3–19. doi:10.1080/08109028.2013.763630

Streib, G., & Navarro, I. (2006). Citizen demand for interactive e-government: The case of Georgia Consumer services. *American Review of Public Administration*, *36*(3), 288–300. doi:10.1177/0275074005283371

Szkuta, K., Pizzicannella, R., & Osimo, D. (2014). Collaborative approaches to public sector innovation: A scoping study. *Telecommunications Policy*, *38*(5/6), 558–567. doi:10.1016/j.telpol.2014.04.002

Thackeray, R., Neiger, B., Smith, A., & Van Wagenen, S. (2012). Adoption and use of social media among public health departments. *BMC Public Health*, *12*(242). doi:10.1186/1471-2458-12-242 PMID:22449137

Treem, J., Dailey, S., Pierce, C., & Leonardi, P. (2015). Bringing technological frames to work: How previous experience with social media shapes the technology's meaning in an organization. *Journal of Communication*, *65*(2), 296–422. doi:10.1111/jcom.12149

Trees, L. (2015). Putting enterprise content where people work: Best-practice organization use process maps, team sites and mobile apps to get content in front of the right people at the right time. *KM World*, *24*(4), 8–9.

Tufekci, Z., & Wilson, C. (2012). Social media and the decision to participate in political protest: Observations from Tahrir Square. *Journal of Communication*, *62*(2), 363–379. doi:10.1111/j.1460-2466.2012.01629.x

Wang, N. (2011). Risk allocation in the operational stage of private finance initiative projects. *Journal of Performance of Constructed Facilities*, *25*(6), 598–605. doi:10.1061/(ASCE)CF.1943-5509.0000194

Wright, A. (2009). Why getting a twitter coach is a smart idea. Retrieved from http://www.shrm.org/hrdisciplines/technology/Articles/Pages/GettingaTwitterCoach.aspx

Zeider, R. (2007). *Internet provides disciplinary challenges for employers*. Retrieved from http://www.shrm.org/hrdisciplines/technology/Articles/Pages/InternetDisciplinaryChallenges

ADDITIONAL READING

A Roadmap for Successful Adoption of Social Computing in the Enterprise. (2009). *Newsgator Technologies*.

Addison, C. (2006). Web 2.0: A new chapter in development in practice? *Development in Practice*, *16*(6), 623–627. doi:10.1080/09614520600958348

Aikins, S. (2009). Designing web sites for internet-based citizen participation. *The Ideas Quarterly Report*, (Spring). Retrieved from http://icma.org/en/Article/100035/Designing_Web_Sites_for_InternetBased_Citizen_Participation

Bahl, R. (2004). *Local government expenditures and revenues. Aronson, J. & Schwartz, E. Management Policies in Local Government Finance* (pp. 79–99). Washington, D.C.: ICMA.

Banovetz, J. (1984). *Small Cities and Counties: A Guide to Managing Services*. Washington, D.C.: ICMA.

Batorski, M., & Hadden, D. (2010). *Embracing Government 2.0: Leading Transformative Change in the Public Sector*. Alexandria, VA: Grant Thornton.

Baumgarten, J. & Chui, M. (2009). E-government 2.0. *McKinsey on Government, 4*(Sum.) 26-31.

Bertolini, P. (2009). Increasing Citizen Engagement in Government. *Intergovernmental Solutions Newsletter: Engaging Citizens in Government,* Fall, 27-28.

Bowley, S., & Keidan, G. (2012). *A Local Official's Guide to Online Public Engagement*. Sacramento, California: Institute for Local Government.

Clark, S. (n. d.). *Broadening Public Participation Using Online Engagement Tools: Choosing and Using Online Tools to Expand Public Participation in Local Decision-Making*. Sacramento, California. *Institute for Local Government.*

Coleman, C. (2009). *Web 2.0 Tools Encourage Public Debate: Remarks by Casey Coleman, Chief Information Officer, U.S. General Services Administration. CRM Evolution 2009, New York, New York, August 25*. Washington, D.C.: General Services Administration.

Combs, S. Texas (2009). Websites improve accountability. *Intergovernmental Solutions Newsletter: Transparency and Open Government,* Spring.

Cordis News. (2009, November 20). *Why social networking will change society.* Luxembourg: European Commission Publications Office.

Cormode, G., & Krishnamurthy, B. (2008). *Key differences between Web1.0 and Web 2.0*. Florham Park, NJ: AT&T Labs.

County Social Media Use Policy and Procedure. (2010, March 30). Orange County, California.

Customer Case Study – National Health Service Orkney. (n.d.a). *Newsgator Technologies.*

Dadashzadeh, M. (2010). Social media in government: From egovernment to egovernance. *Journal of Business and Economics Research*, *8*(11), 81–86.

The Promise of Web 2.0. (2006). Deloitte Touche Tohmatsu.

DotGov Spotlight. (2009).Dave McClure, Associate Administrator, GSA Office or Citizen Services and Communications. *The dotgovbuzz, 4*(10) 3-5.

E-gov and E-policy. (n. d.). *Pew*. Washington, D.C.

E-petitions preserves old British tradition. (2009). *Intergovernmental Solutions Newsletter: Engaging Citizens in Government.* Fall, 18-19.

Eggers, W. (2006). *Technology impact of Web 2.0 on government. N.p.* Deloitte Touche Tohmatsu.

Fisk, J. (2009). Web 2.0: The next step in citizen engagement? *Kansas Government Journal*, August, 234-236.

Franzel, J. (2010). The great recession, U.S. local governments and e-government solutions. *PM Magazine, 92*(8).

Godwin, B. (2008). *USA.gov and best practices.* Washington, D.C.: GSA Office of Citizen Services.

Grant Thornton. (2010). Three new leadership skills for implementing Government 2.0.: Embracing Government 2.0. 13-18 Alexandria, Virginia: Grant Thornton LLP.

Grzeskowiak, J. (2008). Taking on technology. *American City and County*, (December): 32–37.

Gummesson, E. (2000). *Qualitative Methods in Management Research (2nd).* Thousand Oaks, California: Sage.

Hinsberg, H. (2009). My better Estonia. Increasing Citizen Engagement in Government, The Intergovernmental Solutions Newsletter, Fall 2009: 20-21. Washington, D.C.: Center for Intergovernmental Solutions, U.S. General Services Administration, Office of Citizens Services and Communications.

Hof, R. (2006). Web 2.0 has corporate America spinning: What every CEO needs to know about the array of new tools that foster online collaboration – and could revolutionize business. *Bloomberg Businessweek* (June 5).

Hood, J. (2010). Washington borrows, Raleigh spends. *Carolina Journal Online,* 6 October.

How Web 2.0 is changing the way we work: An interview with MIT's Andrew McAfee (2009). *McKinsey Quarterly,* November.

International City/County Management Association. (2012). *Playbook: Social Media and Local Government (e-document).* Washington, D.C.: ICMA.

International City/County Management Association. (2013). *ICMA's Digital Use Survey Results – 2013.* Washington, D.C.: ICMA.

International City/County Management Association. (2014, 13-14 September). *Community Technology Profiles: Learn What Local Governments Want from Apps, Dashboards and Other Tools Helping Their Communities.* At Charlotte Convention Center.

International City/County Management Association. (n. d.). *Learn about Code for America at ICMA's 96th Annual Conference.* Washington, D.C.: ICMA.

Jowaisas, B. (2010). *Public library funding & technology access study results released. Library Developments: Program News & Information from the Texas State Library & Archives Commission.* Austin: Texas State Library & Archives Commission.

Kobzo, K. (2009). Emerging themes for effective on-line engagement. *Intergovernmental Solutions Newsletter: Engaging Citizens in Government,* Fall, 40-41.

Kundra, V. (2009). *Memorandum for chief information officers on update on the trusted internet connections initiative.* Washington, D.C.: Office of Management and Budget.

Lal, K. (2009). *How U.S. government agencies are using social publishing to interact with citizens.* Woburn, MA: Acquina, Inc.

Lemley, T., & Brunham, J. (2009). Web 2.0 tools in medical and nursing school curricula. *Journal of the Medical Library Association: JMLA, 97*(1), 50–52. doi:10.3163/1536-5050.97.1.010 PMID:19159003

Local governments and public school systems by type and state: 2007. (2008). U.S. Census Bureau. Washington, D.C.

Madden, M. & Fox, S. (2006). *Riding the waves of "Web 2.0": More than a buzzword, but still not easily defined.* Washington, D. C.: Pew.

Martini, P. (2007). *Web 2.0 in Brazil: The Overmundo case.* London: iCommone.org.

McCartney, J. (2009). *Web 2.0: New rules of communication.* Colorado Municipalities 8-10.

McDonald, J., Merwin, G., Merwin, K., Morris, R., & Brannen (2010). Serving constituents with Limited English Proficiency (LEP) in the U.S.: Challenges and implications for local government websites. In E. Downey, C. Ekstrom, & M. Jones (eds.), *E-Government Website Development: Future Trends and Strategic Models.* Hershey, NY: Information Science Research.

Merwin, G., McDonald, J., Merwin, K., McDonald, M. & Bennett (2012). Local governments and social networking: Do you speak our language? In E. Downey & M. Jones (eds.) *Public Service Governance and Web 2.0 Technologies: Future Trends in Social Media.* Hershey, NY: Information Science Research.

Minnesota Department of Transportation (2011). *Use of Social Media by Minnesota Cities and Counties.* St. Paul.

Moe, T. (2004). Bridging the "Digital Divide" in Colorado libraries. Survey results from the Colorado Public Libraries & the "Digital Divide" 2002 study. *Public Libraries, 43*(4), 227–232.

NASBO. (2002). *Budget Shortfalls: Strategies for Closing Spending and Revenue Gaps, 3rd.* Washington, D.C.: National Association of State Budget Officers.

Newsgator for Federal Government: Enabling Government to Build Social Communities that Drive Efficiencies, Effectiveness and Mission Execution. (n.d.b). *Newsgator Technologies.*

North Carolina Department of Cultural Resources. (2010). Raleigh: Best Practices for Local Government Social Media Usage in North Carolina.

O'Reilly, T. (2005a) *Design patterns and business models for the next generation of software.* O'Reilly Network.

O'Reilly, T. (2005b). *What is Web 2.0?* O'Reilly Network.

Obama, B. (2009, January 26). Memorandum for the heads of executive departments and agencies on transparency and open government. *Federal Register, 74*(15), 4685-4686.

Office of Ohio Secretary of State Jennifer Brunner (2009). *Ohio redistricting competition Intergovernmental Solutions Newsletter: Engaging Citizens in Government*, Fall.

Osimo, D. (2008a). Benchmarking eGovernment in the Web 2.0 era: What to measure and how. *European Journal of ePractice, 4*(August), 1-11.

Osimo, D. (2008b). *Web 2.0 in Government: Why and How? JRC Scientific and Technical Reports.* Luxembourg: European Commission.

Ostergaard, S., & Hvass, M. (2008). eGovernment 2.0 – How can government benefit from web 2.0? *Journal of Systemics. Cybernetics and Informatics, 6*(6), 13–18.

Paus-Hasebrink, I., Wijnen, C., & Jadin, T. (2010). Opportunities for Web 2.0: Potentials of learning. *International Journal of Media and Cultural Politics, 6*(1), 45–62. doi:10.1386/macp.6.1.45/1

Phoenix, AZ launches free droid application for residents to report blight. (2010). *Alliance for Innovation: Transforming Local Government*, August 25.

Rainie, L. & Larsen, E. (2002). *Digital Town Hall.* Washington, D.C., Pew.

Riley, D. (2007). America: The growing digital divide. *TechCrunch* (6 May).

Sander, T. (2008). Government 2.0: Building communities with Web 2.0 and social networking. Folsom, CA: e.Republic, Inc.

Schrier, B. (n. d.). *How Web 2.0 will transform local government.* Retrieved from www.govtech.com

Section 10-1: Social Media Policy. (2009, August). City of Arlington, Texas.

Smith, A., Achlozman, K., Verba, S., & Brady, H. (2009). *The Internet and Civic Engagement.* Washington, D.C.: Pew Internet and American Life Project.

Stanton, K. (2009). By the people, for the people. *Intergovernmental Solutions Newsletter: Engaging Citizens in Government.* Fall, 4.

Sternberg, N. (2009). *Engaging citizens: Open government is about people, not technology.* Retrieved from http://www.federaltimes.com/article/20091116/ADOP06/911160303/1040/ADOP06

Stott, A. (2009). Citizen engagement. *Intergovernmental Solutions Newsletter: Engaging Citizens in Government*, Fall, 5-6.

Streib, G., & Navarro, I. (2006). Citizen demand for interactive e-government: The case of Georgia Consumer services. *American Review of Public Administration, 36*(3), 288–300. doi:10.1177/0275074005283371

Technology Excellence Award Goes to Fairfax County. (2010, May 17). Fairfax County, Virginia.

The adoption of the internet in cities. (2010). *Pew.* Washington, D.C.

Thoreson, K. (2009). Connecting with your community. *The Ideas Quarterly Report,* Spring.

Troiano, N. & Golden, C. (2009). A millennial model of civic engagement. *Intergovernmental Solutions Newsletter: Engaging Citizens in Government*, Fall, 38-39.

Trudeau, L. (2009). National dialogues build communities. *Intergovernmental Solutions Newsletter: Engaging Citizens in Government*. Fall, 7-8.

U.S. Government, DHS Privacy Office. (2009). *Government 2.0: Privacy and Best Practices; Report on the DHS Privacy Office Public Workshop, June 22 and 23, 2009*. Washington, D.C.: Homeland Security.

Van den Broek, T., Frissen, V., Huijboom, N., & Punie, Y. (2009). The impact of social computing on public services: A rationale for government 2.0. *European Journal of ePractice*, 9(March), 1-15.

Van Leuven, L. (n. d.). *Optimizing Citizen Engagement During Emergencies Through Use of Web 2.0 Technologies* [Thesis]. Monterey, California: Naval Postgraduate School.

Vogel, P. (2010, May 11). *Impact of Social Media on Open Government: Statement to the Texas Senate Committee on State Affairs*. State of Texas, Senate.

Vogel, R. (2009). Public comments on the Web: An inclusive approach to citizen involvement. *The Ideas Quarterly Report* (Spring). Retrieved from http://icma.org/en/Article/100032/Public_Comments_on_the_Web_An_Inclusive_Approach_to_Citizen_Involvement

Webb, L., & Pollack, A. (n.d.). Reaching citizens thru 2.0. n.p. *Webb Consulting*.

Welfley, J. (2009, June 29). City CIOs tackle 4G network: Web 2.0 as part of roundtable discussion. *U.S. Mayor Newspaper*.

Williams, M. (2010, October 6). Half the public sector embracing Gov 2.0, survey finds. *Government Technology*.

Yin, R. (2003). *Case Study Research: Design and Methods (3rd)*. Thousand Oaks, California: Sage.

KEY TERMS AND DEFINITIONS

App: Short for application, particularly those computer or smartphone or mobile applications used for social media and communications.

GIS: Geographic Information Systems used to gather, analyze, and manipulate information about the earth's surface, particularly related to mapping functions.

Mobile: Phones, tablets, and other small devices widely used through either cellular or Wi-Fi networks for portable communications and computing.

Nextdoor.com: Private social network for neighborhoods, limiting group membership to those living in the area nextdoor.com.

Social Media: The technology, tools and services utilized to facilitate social interaction. From http://multibrain.net/about/social-media-defined.

Web: World Wide Web, commonly known as the Internet.

Web 2.0: Sites that feature two-way communication with users, as the second generation of the Web, focusing on input from those who visit the site.

Waze: An application for mapping (GIS) and transportation navigation that merges highway data with social media through input from users https://www.waze.com/.

Section 5
Conclusion

Chapter 17
Social Project Management?

Gilbert Silvius
LOI University of Applied Sciences, The Netherlands & University of Johannesburg, South Africa

ABSTRACT

This conclusion aims to reflect upon and summarize the lessons that may be learned from this book. In three concise paragraphs, it discusses the common ground amongst the different contributions, the 'takeaways' from the book and the concept of 'social project management' as the future outlook on social media in project management.

INTRODUCTION

This conclusion aims to reflect upon and summarize the lessons that may be learned from this book. In order to do so, the next paragraph will discuss the common ground amongst the authors. What statements may summarize the different experiences and contributions? Elaborating on this, we will summarize what the reader may or should 'take away' from the book. What can be learned from social media and applied to project communication? In the final paragraph of this conclusion, we will take these lessons further and ask ourselves what 'social project management' could look like.

COMMON GROUND

When reflecting upon the contributions in this book, some common ground can be discovered amongst the different contributions.

Efficient and Effective Team Communication

First of all, social media provides an opportunity for supporting efficient and effective team communication in project teams. Many contributions in this book, most notably chapters 1, 2, 3, 4, 5, 6, 9, 10 and 13, highlight the opportunities that social media offer for supporting efficient and effective communication within project teams.

DOI: 10.4018/978-1-4666-9867-3.ch017

Understand Differences

While recognizing the opportunities of social media, chapter 8 highlights the fact that the social media landscape is not unified. By discussing differences between regions, countries and generations, this contribution makes us aware that a social media communication strategy needs to be carefully planned, especially in the case of international projects with geographically dispersed teams.

Develop a Plan

Plan the project's social media communication strategy is also the conclusion that comes from chapter 11, the analysis of project management apps. An example of the development of such a social media communication strategy is contributed in chapter 12. The step-for-step approach described here may provide project managers with a practical process description for the development of their communication strategy.

There is a Learning Curve

The cases reported in chapters 14 and 15 show us that there will be a learning curve in the effective use of social media. Just as any new technology requires some 'getting used to', this may also be the case in the application of social media in the professional setting of projects.

And there May be Barriers

Chapters 2 and 7 help us to understand that the adoption of social media in projects may also experience barriers. Some of these barriers may have to do with individual concerns of team members, for example loss of privacy and blurring of lines between professional and personal online presence, whereas other barriers may be caused by the organization's engaged in the project. For example concerns about data security or compliancy with the organization's policies.

Social Media in Stakeholder Engagement is Lagging Behind

A final reflection should be that the 'external' use of social media, the use of social media in stakeholder engagement, is lagging behind the 'internal' use, the use of social media within the project team. In the 'opportunity' section of the book, chapters 1 to 4, do identify stakeholder management as an application area of social media in projects, however, the use of social media with the project team is more prominent in these contributions. This bias towards the internal use of social media is even stronger within the sections 'human factor' and 'tools and technologies', where only chapter 11 explicitly discusses the use of social media for stakeholder engagement. In the 'cases and applications' section, chapters 12 and 16 report cases in which the use of social media was specifically aimed at engaging with external stakeholders.

Should it be concluded that in the external use of social media in projects the actual use of social media is ahead of our conceptual understanding of this use?

WHAT SHOULD YOU TAKE AWAY?

What should you take away from this book? Well, first of all some questions. Questions on how social media are used in your project and on how they may be used in your project. The following paragraph discusses these questions.

However, you should also take some encouragement away from this book. Encouragement to take the plunge and simply start. The integration of social media in projects and project management is still a developing topic. Clear rules and absolute truths are not available. A step-by step 'trial and learn' approach may therefore be the best way forward.

Questions

Is your Project Social?

For many professionals working in projects, social media is part of their everyday life. Some may use it mainly in their personal life, whereas others also engage professionally on social media. How is this in your project? How do you use social media to support team communication? Can team members ask questions and seek information within the team? Are social media used to share updates and inform each other? Can team members 'show' themselves in profiles? Is the way social media are used deliberate or accidental? Is it clear for everyone in the team what the boundaries of social media use are? Is there a 'code of social media conduct' with regards to the project?

And also in the communication with stakeholders outside the management team, social media provide a powerful tool. Is social media part of the project marketing mix? Are social media used to create stakeholder engagement? Is the project sponsor involved in the communication on social media?

In today's world, it is not a question whether social media are used in projects, but how they are used. Communication is a key aspect of project management and social media are part of this. The project manager should therefore deliberately integrate social media in the communication strategy of the project.

What Can You Learn from Social Media?

Social media differ from traditional communication in many ways. This paragraph addresses some of these differences and discusses what we can learn from social media.

Fast and Unforgiving

Social media are fast and unforgiving. Fast in the sense that social media are perfectly fit for spreading information quickly to a large group of direct and indirect stakeholders. This quality offers tremendous opportunities. However, social media are also unforgiving. Messages that are inaccurate, inadequate or sent by mistake are 'out there' forever. Corrections are hard to make and carefully developed reputations can be destroyed in seconds. Be careful! is a meager, but oh so true advice.

Top-Down and Bottom-Up

By nature, social media allow for both top-down and bottom-up communication. This is a great quality if we want to support team collaboration or engage with stakeholders. However, this openness also has a flipside. The traditional control that the project manager had over the communication with the project sponsor and (external) stakeholders decreases. Team members may post updates on their work in the project on twitter, Facebook or LinkedIn, as part of their personal profiling or online socializing. Project managers should be aware of this and set guidelines and boundaries for how team members can express themselves with regards to the project. A general ban on social media is probably not the best solution. Paying attention in the team on what is sensible on social media and what is not, may make more sense.

Create a Community

Social media provide the opportunity to build a community within or around your project. And as humans are social beings, communities are a great good. Communities create involvement, engagement and, sometimes, loyalty. Use the opportunities that social media offer to find interested individuals, understand interests, keep stakeholders informed and create a fan-base. Do not neglect the 'social' in social media.

Entertaining

Effective communication through social media requires more than a text based newsletter or press release. Make content rich, attractive and entertaining. 'A picture is worth a thousand words' and social media are very well suited for sharing photos and videos. Include this visual aspect in your project communication.

Engage

Social media provide unprecedented opportunities for two-way communication with stakeholders. The traditional approach to stakeholder management, 'sending' information to stakeholders in order to hope to win their support, can therefore evolve to stakeholder engagement. An approach to stakeholder relations that builds upon a two-way communication with stakeholders in order to create a 'better' project for all stakeholders involved.

Encouragement

This book should be seen as an encouragement. An encouragement to apply social media in projects, both within project teams and in stakeholder engagement. Engaging on social media is fun! And it makes us more aware of news, fun facts and interesting events that may be worth sharing. Social media increase the intensity of communication and thereby the engagement of the ones communicating. All of which are desirable effects in projects.

Social media are here to stay, so go out there and 'play'. Make a plan, but do it. Try and learn.

TOWARDS SOCIAL PROJECT MANAGEMENT?

Projects have never been easy, but project managers today face high pressure to perform. Rapidly developing technologies and changing markets force organizations to anticipate, respond and change constantly. Projects are more than ever at the heart of every organizations survival and success.

In this highly volatile environment, the execution of projects also is dynamic. Project teams are international, intercultural, geographically dispersed and increasingly self-organizing. Project managers are faced the question how to increase collaborative capabilities and maximize performance of the team, while maintaining control and oversight?

Social media and Web 2.0 technologies provide great opportunities to enable teams, especially virtual teams, to collaborate and share information, thereby enhancing project collaboration and coordination.

However, social media also allows project managers to take this development even further and to make project management truly social. 'Social Project Management' recognizing that project teams are part of a broader project community, which is both formal and informal, and that engaging with that community is the key to getting things done ("Social Project Management," 2012). In social project management, the core business processes of the project and project's management are brought online. Social project management makes the project process visible to everyone, both inside and outside the team. Thereby creating transparency and giving the internal and external project community visibility into the events of the project, in order to enable smarter, quicker and more efficient collaboration. Social project management allows for anyone who is interested, to engage socially with the team to assist in accomplishing the project and organization's goals ("Social Project Management," 2012).

REFERENCES

Social Project Management. (2012). *Engaging the Social Network to Deliver Project Success*. Triolog Group.

Chapter 18
Inside the Project Management Institute
Setting up Change Makers for Success Based on Social Connection

Deborah Walker
Project Management Institute, USA

Dave Garrett
Project Management Institute, USA

ABSTRACT

PMI is the world's leading not-for-profit professional membership association for the project, program, and portfolio management profession. Now in its 46th year, the association provides global advocacy, collaboration, education, and research to more than 2.9 million professionals working in nearly every country in the world. To better support project practitioners in their role as "change agents," PMI utilizes popular social media platforms, as well as a robust virtual community. Through social media, PMI creates an environment in which project practitioners create, curate, and share strong value-added content, take part in well-informed discussions, and collaborate to seek effective solutions.

INTRODUCTION

Project management may very well be the world's loneliest job. Project managers are often the only person in their organization responsible for the type of project they run, facing unique issues that no one around them understands. They may have more in common with a project manager on the other side of the world than with a colleague on the other side of the cubicle wall.

And the project manager is nearly always a "change agent," driving unprecedented and unfamiliar initiatives. This can work to isolate project managers from their coworkers, leaving them yearning for relevant discussion or a sympathetic ear. Recognizing these unique challenges, the Project Management Institute (PMI) reaches out to project practitioners through popular social media platforms, as well as through a robust virtual community known as ProjectManagement.com.

DOI: 10.4018/978-1-4666-9867-3.ch018

PMI has learned that connecting project practitioners who work on similar projects can mean bridging more than geographical boundaries. Cultures, experiences, and involvement levels must also be considered. PMI's global outreach is as diverse as it is far-flung, including PMI members and certification holders, volunteers, and professionals loosely affiliated with PMI who seek assistance.

Since 1969, PMI has been meeting the challenge of keeping this multi-faceted audience connected and engaged by hosting face-to-face meetings, including annual global congresses in the North America and EMEA regions and localized PMI chapter events, as well as by offering networking-rich opportunities for volunteers. But social media has offered an even greater opportunity for PMI to easily connect its members and reach an extended audience of project practitioners.

HOW PMI USES POPULAR SOCIAL MEDIA CHANNELS

PMI currently employs LinkedIn, Twitter, Facebook, Google+, YouTube, and its own virtual community at ProjectManagement.com to connect with aspiring and practicing project practitioners and to facilitate knowledge sharing among them. Approximately 1.4 million people engage with PMI through social media and the community on ProjectManagement.com.

PMI specifically uses social media to:

Connect Project Practitioners

PMI's LinkedIn discussion group, now approaching 200,000 members, is managed day to day by a small group of volunteer moderators who are also experienced project managers. Many members participate in group discussions, showcasing their expertise and building their personal brand on the world's most popular professional network. Discussions often tackle difficult issues, such as working with disengaged executive sponsors, transitioning a company from a waterfall to an agile approach or managing remote project teams spanning various locations, languages, and cultures.

In addition, aspiring project managers frequently visit PMI's LinkedIn forum to seek advice on studying for their certification exams or getting their first project management job. Writers for *PM Network*®, PMI's flagship magazine, also initiate discussions and feature responses in each issue of the magazine, giving group members the opportunity to appear in a prominent, project management–focused publication.

Stay in Touch and Get Feedback

From discussions of complex topics to lighter interactions, project practitioners respond to thought-provoking content on all PMI social channels by sharing their rich personal experiences. Members and chapters often reach out to PMI, typically on Twitter, to share pictures and updates from their regional events, exhibiting the diverse industries and locations where project practitioners work, as well as volunteer work such as community improvement projects.

Provide Encouragement

Within its social media channels, PMI frequently hears from project practitioners seeking to achieve their Project Management Professional (PMP)®, PMI Agile Certified Practitioner (PMI-ACP)® or other

PMI certifications. Practitioners who want details on certifications or the application process are put in touch with a customer care representative for appropriate support.

PMI even receives photos of certification study sessions, often with creative shots of the aspiring PMP® certification holder's constant companion, *A Guide to the Project Management Body of Knowledge (PMBOK® Guide)*. (One long-time PMI member even made a YouTube music video called *Rock the PMBOK®*.) And many hard-working applicants ultimately tweet pictures of themselves displaying their well-earned certification!

Enhance the Member Experience

In PMI's case, social media does not replace events or volunteer activities; rather, it is used to enhance and encourage volunteerism, community, and engagement. The importance of technology-based community interaction is acknowledged in PMI's Strategic Plan, which empowers staff to use social media and virtual communities to forge stronger, faster, and better connections between project practitioners.

Disseminate Knowledge

PMI spreads knowledge and news about project management to project practitioners, reaching users via their preferred, popular social media platforms.

Most content is of general interest to project practitioners, such as new research, profiles of project practitioners and projects, case studies and tools, tips, and templates that can be put to immediate use. Articles and blog posts cover topics key to the profession, such as project, program, and portfolio management; stakeholder management; change management; requirements management; benefits realization; executive sponsorship; team communication; career advancement; leadership and more. PMI members and certification holders can find additional news about exam changes, certification changes, or volunteer opportunities through these updates.

Share the Best of PMI Events

PMI members are very active tweeters, bloggers, and podcasters at events such as the PMI global congress (#pmicongress). Via social media, attendees share live event updates and earn the appreciation and attention of global colleagues who could not be in attendance.

Leverage Volunteers

PMI leverages a special group of volunteers, known as the Social Media Advisory Group, who recommend ways in which PMI can better serve the project management community. Annually, the group reviews and revises PMI's social media guidelines for volunteers, assuring that the guidelines help project practitioners use social media effectively, responsibly, and ethically. To view the guidelines, visit pmi.org/en/About-Us/Governance.aspx

TAKING SOCIAL MEDIA TO THE NEXT LEVEL

PMI also offers ProjectManagement.com, an internationally recognized online community of 740,000 peer connections that acts as a one-stop shop for project practitioners in information technology and other industries. Originally launched as *gantthead* in 2000, ProjectManagement.com provides over 12,000 how-to articles and 1,000 templates and the opportunity to intensively network with peers. If a project practitioner cannot find an answer to his or her question by searching existing content, the site makes it easy to reach out to like-minded professionals who might provide a solution.

ProjectManagement.com complements PMI's career-shaping value-adds in membership, certification, jobs/career help, and professional volunteering. It offers the sort of robust help project practitioners seek every day, from best practices and templates, to peer access and rapid discussion of urgent questions and issues.

Some comments from members:

You can read a textbook, but seeing opinions from others who have experienced the problems is a better way to grow and learn. Let them take the path less travelled and I can hitch a ride.

Readable relevant information. Not just heavy turgid theory.

The wealth of experience and information ProjectManagement.com provides gives me the chance to check in whenever I have a question or issue I need to address. Having a place to gather with other PMs, going through some of the same things makes it not so lonely out here!

Member profiles on ProjectManagement.com offer a deep look into members as project practitioners—who they are, what they believe in, and how they help others. Members' profiles are effectively their online "body of work," where they can showcase their own unique knowledge and expertise.

Recently, PMI added an influence score, on a scale from 1 to 100, to each member's profile, indicating how much influence that individual carries within the ProjectManagement.com community. Each member also carries influence scores within over 40 popular project management practice areas, such as agile or requirements management. Someone considering a potential connection can use a member's profile and influence score to learn a lot about that connection's past interactions and influence on the community. Recruiters also find this information useful to identify strong, skilled job candidates.

The influence score not only raises the voices of members that the community respects, it also rewards a principle common across all social media: *Influence is measured not by how much someone talks, but by how much people respond.* Posting 1,000 times and getting zero responses is not as valuable as posting once and receiving 1,000 responses.

GETTING SOCIAL: TIPS FOR PROJECT PRACTITIONERS

For those who are new to the professional use of social media and not sure where to begin, one of the most effective places to begin is LinkedIn. Founded as a social networking site for business in 2003, it is now the world's largest professional network with hundreds of millions of members.

Start by creating an account and LinkedIn profile—or, if you already have one, be sure it's up to date. Then begin to build a network of connections.

Next, to encourage industry peers to spend their valuable time reading your content, become a trusted curator of information. Find pieces of online content related to work issues you face, and share some of the best with your connections each week. Twitter works well for this too. To build your own Twitter following, follow others, retweet others, and include appropriate hashtags such as #projectmanagement or #pmot when you tweet.

When sharing a link, provide a comment of your own, so your connections know your perspective. It's a way to associate yourself—and your personal brand—with powerful content, without having to write it yourself. It also provides value to your connections, by sharing content they might not otherwise see. You can easily find relevant content by setting up searches in a tool like Google Alerts or by subscribing to industry newsletters.

Next, join some groups. The ProjectManagement.com community and PMI's LinkedIn Project, Program and Portfolio Management Group are great places to start. Ask and answer questions, stay engaged in discussions you initiate and thank those who participate.

Once you've built a foundation of professional connections, consider blogging—ProjectManagement.com is a very relevant channel for bloggers and comes with an engaged, built-in audience. You might also try vlogging or podcasting. Because effective social media is a conversation, not a monologue, remember to use your network to promote the work of others, as well as your own.

Kiron's Story: Social Media for Career Advancement

Kiron Bondale, PMI-RMP, PMP has managed multiple change management projects, and has worked in both internal and professional services project management capacities. He has provided project portfolio management and project management consulting services to more than 100 clients across multiple industries. The authors asked Kiron how he uses social media to build his career and personal brand.

I have been an active user of LinkedIn, Twitter, and WordPress for over five years. These sites give me the opportunity to easily share my perspective on the benefits of taking a pragmatic approach to organizational change. I'm able to reach an even broader community beyond those I reach by presenting at conferences or publishing in print media. The weekly articles I publish on my personal blog and other project management blogs are often mentioned by hiring managers...or by candidates when I'm the hiring manager. The LinkedIn recommendations I've requested from colleagues in my past roles have also helped to differentiate me from the competition. I am an avid online reader, and Twitter enables me to quickly curate and share useful content with my followers. Finally, by taking an active role to answer questions and participate in forums such as LinkedIn discussion groups, social media gives me yet another method to give back to the project management community—a responsibility that all project management professionals share. (Kiron Bondale, 2015)

THE END OF THE LONELY PROJECT MANAGER

Through effective use of social media, PMI has been able to connect a large international project management community across industries, geographies, and cultures, with all participants speaking "the language of project management." The association has built an environment in which project practitioners create, curate, and share strong value-added content, take part in well-informed discussions, and collaborate to seek effective solutions.

PMI believes that, by engaging actively with social media, no one ever needs to play the role of "the lonely project manager."

Appendix

MODEL PROJECT SOCIAL MEDIA POLICY

These guidelines apply to team members of project [Project name], being either employees of company [Company name] or contracted, who create or contribute to blogs, wikis, social networks, virtual worlds, or any other kind of social media during work-hours. Media addressed with this guideline are: Twitter, Facebook, Tumblr, Google+, Wikipedia, Pinterest, Instagram, YouTube, Foursquare, LinkedIn, Snapchat, Wordpress, Vimeo, and media or websites that provide similar functionalities as the listed media.

This policy does not apply to employees' personal use of social media platforms outside of work-hours where the employee makes no reference to company related topics.

Take time to read, understand and follow these simple but important guidelines. Our overall goal is simple: to enable employees and contractors to participate online in a respectful, relevant way that contributes to the goal of the project and the participating organizations, is respecting individual values and reputations, and follows the letter and spirit of the law.

Internet/Intranet Usage

1. Internet access is to be used primarily for business purposes. Any personal social media use must not interfere with normal business activities, must not involve solicitations, must not be associated with any for-profit outside business activity, and must not potentially embarrass, damage the reputation or tarnish the image of the project or any of its stakeholders.
2. The project or the participating companies, at its sole discretion, reserves the right to block access to any Internet site.
3. Never represent yourself, the project or the participating companies in a false or misleading way. All statements must be true and not misleading; all claims must be substantiated.
4. Post meaningful, respectful comments - in other words, please no Spam and no remarks that are off-topic or offensive.
5. Stick to your area of expertise and feel free to provide unique, individual perspectives on non-confidential activities at the project.
6. Be smart about protecting yourself, your privacy, and the company's confidential information. What you publish is widely accessible and will be around for a long time, so consider the content carefully, Google has a long memory.

Team Members Should Not

7. Comment on any topic related to legal matters, litigation or any stakeholders the project, or any of the participating companies, may be in litigation with.
8. Participate in Social Media when the topic being discussed may be considered a crisis situation. Even anonymous comments may be traced back to your or the company's IP address. Refer all Social Media activity around crisis topics to the communications officer.
9. Create project specific Social Media profiles on their own. Doing so dilutes the follower-base and creates situations where the profiles are individually-owned instead of project-owned or corporate-owned. The project's Social Media platforms/profiles are created by the project's communications officer.

Consequences of Violation

Please be informed that employee and contractor's engagement in Social Media while at work will be monitored. There should be no expectation of privacy while using Social Media during working hours.

In the event of the company's Social Media policy violation, the project's management will report unlawful activity to the authorities. Inappropriate activity that is in conflict with this document's guidelines will be reported to the company the team member is employed with and may result in termination of the cooperation in the project.

Signing

Please confirm that you have read and understand the guidelines.

____

Team member
Name Signature Date

Compilation of References

1 in 5 UK workers spend 32 days a year managing email. (2010). Star survey. Retrieved from http://www.prlog.org/11109396-1-in-5-uk-workers-spend-32-days-year-managing-email.html

Abel, F., Hauff, C., Houben, G. J., Stronkman, R., & Tao, K. (2012). Twitcident: fighting fire with information from social web streams.*Proceedings of the 21st International Conference Companion on World Wide Web* (pp. 305-308). doi:10.1145/2187980.2188035

Aizen, I. (2010). *TPB.* Retrieved Jan 13, 2011, from http://www.people.umass.edu/aizen/: http://www.people.umass.edu/aizen/tpb.diag.html#null-link

Allcott, G. (2014). *How To Be A Productivity Ninja*. London: Icon Books.

Allen, T. J. (1977). *Managing the flow of technology*. Cambridge, MA: The MIT Press.

Alvesson, M., & Sköldberg, K. (2009). *Reflexive methodology: New vistas for qualitative research*. London: Sage.

Anbari, F. T. (1985). A systems approach to project evaluation. *Project Management Journal, 16*(3), 21–26.

Andriole, S. J. (2010). Business impact of Web 2.0 technologies. *Communications of the ACM, 53*(12), 67–79. doi:10.1145/1859204.1859225

Angel, H. C., & Ignacio, R. (2010). The influence of the commercial features of the Internet on the adoption of e-commerce by consumers.Find More Like This. *Electronic Commerce Research and Applications, 9*(6), 562–657. doi:10.1016/j.elerap.2010.04.006

App Store (IOS) page. (2015, March 14). Wikipedia. Retrieved from http://en.wikipedia.org/wiki/App_Store_(iOS)

Ashleigh, M., Ojiako, U., Chipulu, M., & Wang, J. K. (2012). Critical learning themes in project management education: Implications for blended learning. *International Journal of Project Management, 30*(2), 153–161. doi:10.1016/j.ijproman.2011.05.002

Assudani, R., & Kloppenborg, T. J. (2010). Managing stakeholder for project management success: An emergent model of stakeholders.(Report). *Journal of General Management, 35*(3), 67–80.

Augar, N., & Zeleznikow, J. (2013). 'I just saw this on Facebook, I need it now': Exploring Small Business use of Facebook.*Proceedings of 24th Australasian Conference on Information Systems.*

Azhar, S., & Abeln, J. (2014). Investigating social media applications for the construction industry. *Procedia - social and behavioral sciences*, 85, 42-51.

Baaz, A., Holmberg, L., Nilsson, A., Olsson, H. H., & Sandberg, A. B. (2010). Appreciating Lessons Learned. *Software, IEEE, 27*(4), 72–79. doi:10.1109/MS.2009.198

Badea, M. (2014). Social media and organizational communication. *Procedia - social and behavioral sciences*, 149, 70-75.

Baker, D.P., Horvath, L., Campion, M., Offermann, L., Salas, E. (n. d.). *Measuring Adult Literacy and Life skills.* The ALL Teamwork Framework. Statistics Canada – Catalogue no. 89-552-MIE, no. 13.

Banes, S. (2009). Social Media: lessons or the enterprise. *Orange Business.com.* Retrieved from http://www.orange-business.com/en/blogs/connecting-technology/social-media/social-media-lessons-for-the-enterprise

Barley, S. R. (1986). Technology as an occasion for structuring: Evidence from observations of CT scanners and the social order of radiology departments. *Administrative Science Quarterly*, *31*(1), 78–108. doi:10.2307/2392767 PMID:10281188

Barnes, W., & Mann, B. (2011). Making local democracy work: Municipal officials' views about public engagement. *National Civic Review*, *100*(3), 58–62. doi:10.1002/ncr.20063

Barroso, A., Ricciardi, R., & Azevedo, J. (2013). Web 2.0 and project management: reviewing the change path and discussing a Few Cases. In I. R. Management Association (Ed.), Enterprise Resource Planning: Concepts, Methodologies, Tools, and Applications. IGI Global.

Basagila, S., Caporarello, M., & Pennarola, F. (2007). Individual Adoption of Convergent Mobile Technologies in Italy. In A. D'Atri, & M. De Marco (Ed.), *Interdisciplinary Aspects of Information Systems Studies: The Italian Association for Information systems: Italian Association for Information Systems (ItAIS)Annual Conference* (pp. 63 - 68). San Servolo: Springer.

Basten, D., Pankratz, O., & Joosten, D., (2013). Assessing the assessors - an overview and evaluation of IT project success reports. ECIS 2013 Completed Research.

Baum, A. (1997). *Cambridge handbook of psychology, health, and medicine.* Cambridge: Cambridge University Press.

Be Excited! Be Prepared. (2015). *City ofSanta Monica.* Retrieved from http://www.smgov.net/bebp/

Bean, L., & Hott, D. D. (2005). Wiki: A speedy new tool to manage projects. *Journal of Corporate Accounting & Finance*, *16*(5), 3–8. doi:10.1002/jcaf.20128

Bechmann, A., & Lomborg, S. (2013). Mapping actor roles in social media: Different perspectives on value creation in theories of user participation. *New Media & Society*, *15*(5), 765–781. doi:10.1177/1461444812462853

Belassi, W., & Tukel, O. I. (1996). A new framework for determining critical success/failure factors in projects. *International Journal of Project Management*, *14*(3), 141–151. doi:10.1016/0263-7863(95)00064-X

Bellis, M. (n. d.). Police technology and forensic science: Timeline of police technology 1850 – 1960. Retrieved from http://inventors.about.com/od/fstartinventions/a/forensic_4.htm

Bent, D., Østergaard, C., & Villumsen, G. (2002). Technological life cycles: Regional clusters facing disruption. Aalborg, Aalborg University (DRUID Working Paper, No. 10).

Bentley, C. (2010). *PRINCE2: a practical handbook.* Amsterdam: Elsevier/Butterworth-Heinemann.

Berlot, J., Jaeger, P., & Grimes, J. (2010). Using ICTs to create a culture of transparency: E-government and social media as openness and anti-corruption tools for societies. *Government Information Quarterly*, *27*(3), 264–271. doi:10.1016/j.giq.2010.03.001

Berman, S., et al. (2008). *Making Change Work.* IBM Global Business Services. Retrieved from http://www-935.ibm.com/services/us/gbs/bus/pdf/gbe03100-usen-03-making-change-work.pdf

Berthon, P., Pitt, L., & Campbell, C. (2008). Ad lib: When customers create the ad. *California Management Review*, *50*(4), 6–30. doi:10.2307/41166454

Beyerlein, M. M., Johnson, D. A., & Beyerlein, S. T. (2001). *Virtual Teams*. Emerald Group.

Bharadwaj, A., El Sawy, O., Pavlou, P., & Venkatraman, N. (2013). Digital business strategy: Toward a next generation of insights. *Management Information Systems Quarterly*, *37*(2), 471–482.

Bilandzic, M., & Weckermann, D. (2008). Technology Acceptance Research – current development and concerns. *Proceedings of the 2nd Workshop on Information Systems and Services Sciences 2008 (2nd WISSS 08)* (pp. 57-65). Technische Universität München: Garching. Retrieved from www.winfobase.de

Binder, J. C. (2007). *Global project management: communication, collaboration and management across borders*. Gower Publishing.

Biocca, M. (2005). Risk communication and the precautionary principle. *Human and Ecological Risk Assessment*, *11*(1), 261–266. doi:10.1080/10807030590920097

Boersma, F. K. Groenewegen, & P. Wagenaar, P. (2010). The information management of co-located Emergency Response Rooms in the Netherlands. In H. Rahman (Ed.), Cases on Adoption, Diffusion and Evaluation of Global E-Governance Systems (pp. 107-116). Hershey USA: IGI Publishing.

Boersma, F.K., Wagenaar, P., & Wolbers, J. (2012). Negotiating the 'Trading Zone'. Creating a Shared Information Infrastructure in the Dutch Public Safety Sector. *Journal of Homeland Security and Emergency Management, 9*(2).

Boersma, F. K., & Kingma, S. F. (2005). From Means to Ends: The Transformation of ERP in a Manufacturing Company. *The Journal of Strategic Information Systems*, *14*(2), 197–219. doi:10.1016/j.jsis.2005.04.003

Bohm, D. (1999). *On Dialogue NY*. NY: Lee Nichol.

Bohringer, M., & Richter, A. (2009). Adopting social software to the intranet: A case study on enterprise microblogging. *Proceedings Mensch und Computer*, *2009*, 1–10.

Bonson, E., Torres, L., Royo, S., & Flores, F. (2012). Local e-government 2.0: Social media and corporate transparency in municipalities. *Government Information Quarterly*, *29*(2), 123–132. doi:10.1016/j.giq.2011.10.001

Bosse, T., Majdanik, K., Boersma, F. K., & Ingibergsdóttir, K. (2013). Studying Shared Situation Awareness by Agent-Based Simulation, *Web Intelligence (WI) and Intelligent Agent Technologies (IAT)*, Atlanta, USA. *Proceedings of the 2013 IEEE/WIC/ACM International Joint Conference* (Vol. 2, pp. 201-208).

Boston Career Center. (2015). City of Boston. Retrieved from http://www.cityofboston.gov/ohr/careercenter/

Boston Citizens Connect Reports. (2015). City of Boston. Retrieved from https://mayors24.cityofboston.gov:4443/

Boston City Connect. (2015). City of Boston. Retrieved from http://www.cityofboston.gov/doit/apps/citizensconnect.asp

Boyd, M. D., & Ellison, N. B. (2008). Social Network Sites: Definition, History, and Scholarship. *Journal of Computer-Mediated Communication.*

Brace, I., & Adams, K. (2006). *Introduction to Market and Social Research*. London: Kogan.

Bradley, A. J., & McDonald, M. P. (2011). *The Social Organization: How to Use Social Media to Tap the Collective Genius of Your Customers and Employees. Gartner Inc.* Harvard Business Review Press.

Bradley, A., & McDonald, M. (2013). *The Social Organization: How to Use Social Media to Tap the Collective Genius of Your Customers and Employees*. Harvard Business Press.

Brady, R. (2009). *Growth in Outsourcing, Like it or Not.* Retrieved from www.businessweek.com

Brannick, M. T., Salas, E., & Prince, C. (1997). *Team Performance: Assessment and Measurement: Theory, Methods and Applications*. Lawrence Erlbaum Associates Inc.

Bredillet, C. (2006a). Investigating the future of project management: a co-word analysis approach. *International Research Network for Organizing by Projects-IRNOP 7.*

Bredillet, C. (2006b). The future of project management: mapping the dynamics of project management field in action. In D.I. Cleland & R. Gareis (Eds.), *Global Project Management Handbook: Planning, Organizing and Controlling International Projects* (2nd ed.). Planning, Organizing, and Controlling International Projects.

Bricout, J., & Baker, P. (2010). Leveraging online social networks for people with disabilities in emergency communications and recovery. *International Journal of Emergency Management*, *7*(1), 59–74. doi:10.1504/IJEM.2010.032045

Brookes, N. J., Morton, S. C., Dainty, A. R. J., & Burns, N. D. (2006). Social processes, patterns and practices and project knowledge management: A theoretical framework and an empirical investigation. *International Journal of Project Management*, *24*(6), 474–482. doi:10.1016/j.ijproman.2006.03.005

Brown, B., & Chalmers, M. (2003). Tourism and Mobile Technology. *Proceedings of the European Conference of Computer Supported Cooperative Work (ECSCW)*, Helsinki (pp. 335-354).

Bryman, A., & Bell, E. (2007). *Business research methods*. Oxford university press.

Bughin, J., & Chui, M. (2010). *The rise of the networked enterprise: Web 2.0 finds its payday*. Retrieved from http://www.mckinsey.com/insights/high_tech_telecoms_internet/the_rise_of_the_networked_enterprise_web_20_finds_its_payday

Burkhardt, A. (2010). Social media: A guide for college and university libraries. *College & Research Libraries*, *71*(1), 10–24.

Busby, J. S. (1999). An assessment of post-project reviews. *Project Management Journal*, *30*(3), 23–29.

Bushey, R. (2013). The 15 Most Pupola3 Free iPhone Apps of 2013. *Business Insider*. Retrieved from http://www.businessinsider.com/popular-free-iphone-apps-2013-12?op=1

Calloway, J. (2011). Social media management tools. *GPSolo*, *28*(4), 54–55.

Camarinha, M., Paraskakis, L., & Afsarmanesh, I. (2009). Leveraging Knowledge for Innovation in Collaborative Networks. *Proceedings of the 10th IFIP WG 5.5 Working Conference on Virtual Enterprises, PRO-VE,* Thessaloniki (p. 457). Springer.

Carlson, N. (2014). Pinterest CEO: Here's How We Became The Web's Next Big Thing. *Business Insider.com*. Retrieved from http://www.businessinsider.com/pinterest-founding-story-2012-4?op=1#ixzz3SPFYLzP6

Carrillo, P. M., & Anumba, C. J. (2002). Knowledge management in the AEC sector: An exploration of the mergers and acquisition context. *Knowledge and Process Management*, *9*(3), 149–161. doi:10.1002/kpm.146

Carter, B. (2012). Is content more important than conversation? Retrieved from http://www.ragan.com/Main/Articles/Is_content_more_important_than_conversation_44362.aspx

Cassa, C. A., Chunara, R., Mandl, K., & Brownstein, J. S. (2013). Twitter as a sentinel in emergency situations: Lessons from the Boston marathon explosions. *PLoS Currents*, July. PMID:23852273

Castka, P., Bamber, C.J., Sharp, J.M. (2003) Measuring teamwork culture: The use of a modified EFQM model. The Journal of Management Development, 22(1/2), 149.

Catlin, T., Scanlan, J., & Willmott, P. (2015). *Raising Your Digital Quotient.* Retrieved from http://www.mckinsey.com/insights/strategy/raising_your_digital_quotient

Cearley, D. W. (2014). *The Top 10 Strategic Technology Trends for 2014.* Gartner. Retrieved from https://www.gartner.com/doc/2667526?ref=clientFriendlyURL

Center, U. A. C. A. (1993). *A leader's guide to after-action reviews (Training Circular 25-20).* KS: Fort Leavenworth.

Chai, S., & Kim, M. (2010). What makes bloggers share knowledge? An investigation on the role of trust. *International Journal of Information Management, 30*(5), 408–415. doi:10.1016/j.ijinfomgt.2010.02.005

Chartered Management Institute. (2014). *21st Century Leaders: Building practice into the curriculum to boost employability.* Retrieved from http://www.managers.org.uk/Insights/Research/Current-research/2014/June/21st-Century-Leaders.aspx

Chasalow, L. (2008). What makes agile development different?: A case study of agile in practice. *Proceedings of SAIS 2008.*

Chaves, M. S., & Veronese, G. (2014). A Proposal to Manage Lessons Learned in Projects: Web 2.0 Technologies to Promote Innovation. *International Journal of Innovation, 2*(1), 1–17.

Cheah, Y., Khoh, S. B., & Ooi, G. B. (2011). An ontological approach for Program Management Lessons Learned: Case study at Motorola Penang Design Centre. *Proceedings of the IEEE International* Conference on *Industrial Engineering and Engineering Management IEEM* (pp. 1612-1616).

Chen, J., & Tsou, H. (2007). *Information technology adoption for service innovation practices and competitive advantage: the case of financial firms.* Retrieved from http://informationr.net/ir/12-3/paper314.html

Chen, Y., & Lou, H. (2000). Toward an Understanding of Behavioural Intention to Use a Groupware Application. *Challenges of information technology management in the 21st century:2000 Information Resources Management Association International Conference* (pp. 419 - 421). Alaska: Idea Group (IGI).

Chiu, M., Manyika, J., Bughin, J., Dobbs, R., Roxburgh, C., ..., Westergren, M. (2012). *The social economy: Unlocking value and productivity through social technologies.* McKinsey Global Institute. Retrieved from http://www.mckinsey.com/~/media/McKinsey/dotcom/Insights%20and%20pubs/MGI/Research/Technology%20and%20Innovation/The%20social%20economy/MGI_The_social_economy_Full_report.ashx

Cho, K., Hyun, C., Koo, K., & Hong, T. (2010). Partnering process model for public sector fast-track design-build projects in Korea. *Journal of Management Engineering, 26*(1), 19–29. doi:10.1061/(ASCE)0742-597X(2010)26:1(19)

Chun, S., Shulman, S., Sandoval, R., & Hovy, E. (2010). Government 2.0: Making connections between citizens, data, and government. *Information Policy, 15*, 1–9.

Chutter, M. Y. (2009). Overview of the Technology Acceptance Model: Origins, Developments and Future Directions. *Sprouts: Working Papers on Information Systems, 9*, pp. 9-37.

Chuttur, m. (2009). *Overview of the Technology Acceptance Model: Origins, Developments and Future Directions.* Retrieved from http://sprouts.aisnet.org

Ciborra, C. U., & Lanzara, G. F. (1994). Formative contexts and information technology: Understanding the dynamics of innovation in organizations. *Accounting, Management and Information Technologies, 4*(2), 61–86. doi:10.1016/0959-8022(94)90005-1

Clarke, R. (1999, September 26). *A Primer in Diffusion of Innovations Theory*. Retrieved from http://www.rogerclarke.com

Cleland, D. I., & Gareis, R. (2006). *Global project management handbook: planning, organizing, and controlling international projects*. McGraw-Hill Professional.

Cleland, D. I., & King, W. R. (1983). *Systems Analysis and Project Management*. New York: McGraw Hill.

Cohen, S. G., & Bailey, D. E. (1997). What Makes Teams Work: Group Effectiveness Research from the shop floor to the Executive Suite. *Journal of Management*, *23*(3), 239–290. doi:10.1177/014920639702300303

Coleman, D. (2008). Social Project Management *Agile Product & Project Management Executive Reports, 8*(5).

Coleman, K. (2013, July 24). 3 disruptive technologies gaining speed. *Information Week*. Retrieved from http://www.informationweek.com/regulations/3-disruptive-technologies-gaining-speed/d/d-id/1110899?

Collier, B., DeMarco, T., Fearey, P., (1996). A defined process for project postmortem review. *IEEE Software Journal*, 65–71.

Conforto, E. C., Salum, F., Amaral, D. C., da Silva, S. L., & de Almeida, L. F. M. (2014). Can Agile Project Management Be Adopted by Industries Other than Software Development? *Project Management Journal*, *45*(3), 21–34. doi:10.1002/pmj.21410

Connect with the City of Chicago via social media. (2015). City of Chicago. Retrieved from http://www.cityofchicago.org/city/en/narr/misc/social_media.html

Connect with us on social media. (2015). City of Arlington. Retrieved from http://www.arlington-tx.gov/departments/social-media/

Connelly, P. (2009). Push comes to. GOV. *The American Prospect*, *20*(10), 8–11.

Córdoba, J., & Piki, A. (2012). Facilitating project management education through groups as systems. *International Journal of Project Management*, *30*(1), 83–93. doi:10.1016/j.ijproman.2011.02.011

Cross, M (2014). The Social Media Security: Leveraging Social Networking While Mitigating Risk. Syngress – Elsevier.

Crump, J. (2011). What are the police doing on Twitter? Social media, the police and the public. *Policy & Internet*, *3*(4), 1–27. doi:10.2202/1944-2866.1130

Culnan, M. J., Mchugh, P. J., & Zubillaga, J. I. (2010). How large U.S. companies can use twitter and other social media to gain business value. *MIS Quarterly Executive*, *9*(4), 243–260.

Daft, R. L., & Lengel, R. H. (1986). Organizational information requirements, media richness, and structural design. *Management Science*, *32*(5), 554–571. doi:10.1287/mnsc.32.5.554

Dahnil, M., Marzuki, K., Langgat, J., & Fabeil, N. (2014). Factors influencing SMEs adoption of social media marketing. *Procedia - social and behavioral sciences*, 148, 119-126.

Darrow, R. (2007, October 30). *Diffusion of Innovations research*. Retrieved from http://docjourney.wordpress.com

Dasgupta, S. (2006). Virtual Reality User Acceptance. In Encyclopedia of virtual communities and technologies (p. 567). Idea Group (IGI).

Davenport, T. H. (1998). Putting the enterprise into the enterprise system. *Harvard Business Review*, *76*, 121–131. PMID:10181586

Deamer, K. (2011). States get social: Government use of social media is popular, but is it following state laws? *The News Media & the Law*, (Winter) 24.

Dearing, J. W. (2009, September). *Applying Diffusion of Innovation Theory to Intervention Development.* Retrieved from http://rsw.sagepub.com/content/19/5/503.short

Deloitte Consulting. (2011). *Social Computing. Tech Trends 2011 – The natural convergence of business and IT.*

Denning, S. (2014, January 7). Business's worst nightmare: Big Bang Disruption. *Forbes.* Retrieved from http://www.forbes.com/sites/stevedenning/2014/01/07/businesss-worst-nightmare-big-bang-disruption/

Dietrich, P., Eskerod, P., & Sandhawalia, B. (2010, September). The Dynamics of Collaboration in Multipartner Projects. *Project Management Journal, 41*(4), 59–78. doi:10.1002/pmj.20194

Digital Information World. (2015). Fascinating Social Media Stats 2015. Retrieved from http://www.digitalinformationworld.com/2015/02/fascinating-social-networking-stats-2015.html

Dillard, J. P., & Pfau, M. (2002). The Persuasion Handbook. *Sage (Atlanta, Ga.).*

Dinsmore, P. C., & Cabanis-Brewin, J. (2010). *The AMA Handbook of Project Management.* AMACOM Div American Mgmt Assn.

Dishaw, M. T., Strong, D. M., & Brandy, B. D. (2004). The Impact of Task-Technology Fit in Technology Acceptance and Utilization Models. *Proceedings of theTenth Americas Conference on Information Systems* (p. Paper 416). New York: AMCIS.

DiStefano, J. J., & Maznevski, M. L. (2000). Creating value with diverse teams in global management. *Organizational Dynamics*, 29(1), 45-63.

Dixon, J., & Keyes, D. (2013). The permanent disruption of social media. *Stanford Social Innovation Review, 11*(1), 24–29.

Dourish, P., & Bellotti, V. (1992). Awareness and coordination in shared workspaces. *CSCW, 92*, 107–114.

Duggan, M., Ellison, N. B., Lampe, C., Lenhart, A., & Madden, M. (2015). Social Media Update 2014. *PewResearch-Centre*, Retrieved from http://www.pewinternet.org/2015/01/09/social-media-update-2014/

Dunay, P., & Krueger, R. (2011). *Marketing for dummies.* Indianapolis: Wiley.

Dunbar, R. I. M. (1992). Neocortex size as a constraint on group size in primates. *Journal of Human Evolution, 22*(6), 469–493. doi:10.1016/0047-2484(92)90081-J

Dunn, B. (2010). How I did it…: Best Buy's CEO on learning to love social media. *Harvard Business Review, 88*(12), 43–48.

Edmondson, A. C., Bohmer, R. M., & Pisano, G. P. (2001). Disrupted routines: Team learning and new technology implementation in hospitals. *Administrative Science Quarterly, 46*(4), 685–716. doi:10.2307/3094828

Ellcessor, E. (2010). Bridging Disability Divides. *Information Communication and Society, 13*(3), 289–308. doi:10.1080/13691180903456546

Email Statistics Report, 2009-2013. (2009). *The Radiciti group.*

Engeström, Y. (2001). Expansive learning at work: Toward an activity-theoretical reconceptualization. *Journal of Education and Work, 14*(1), 133–156. doi:10.1080/13639080020028747

Enterprise Apps Today. (2012, August 21). Social Media Meets Project Management. Retrieved from http://www.enterpriseappstoday.com/social-media/social-media-meets-project-management.html

Enterprise social collaboration for a better way of working. (2012a). *Atos*. Retrieved from https://atos.net/content/dam/global/we-do/atos-Social-collaboration-brochure.pdf

E-Petitions preserves old British tradition (2009). *Intergovernmental Solutions Newsletter,* (Fall), 18-19.

Evans, A., Twomey, J., & Talan, S. (2011). Twitter as a public relations tool. *The Public Relations Journal*, *5*(1), 1–20.

Evans, C. (2014). Twitter for teaching: Can social media be used to enhance the process of learning? *British Journal of Educational Technology*, *45*(5), 902–915. doi:10.1111/bjet.12099

Evans, D. (2008). *Social Media Marketing: An hour a day*. Indianapolis: Wiley Publishing Inc.

Evans, D. (2012). *Social media marketing: An hour a day*. Indianapolis: John Wiley & Sons.

Evans, L. (2010). *Social media marketing*. Que publishing.

Everett, R. M. (1962). *Diffusion of Innovations*. Glencoe: Free Press.

Faas, R. C. (1977). *Decision making in project review: processes, participation, and performance in Michigan multi county comprehensive health planning*. Agric Econ Rep Dep Agric Econ Mich State Univ.

Faria, C. & Peixoto, T. (2009). Participatory lawmaking in Brazil. *Intergovernmental Solutions Newsletter,* (Fall), 22-23.

Feldman, M. S., & Pentland, B. T. (2003). Reconceptualizing organizational routines as a source of flexibility and change. *Administrative Science Quarterly*, *48*(1), 94–118. doi:10.2307/3556620

Ferriter, W. (2010). Digitally speaking / Using social media to reach your community. *Educational Leadership*, *68*(4), 87–88.

Filve, A. (2008). Discovering the benefits of project management 2.0. *Cutter IT Journal*, *21*(5), 40–45.

First Round Review. (2015). Adam Pisoni explains how a culture shift toward transparency, experimentation and empowerment can make companies more successful. Retrieved from http://www.fastcompany.com/3042221/hit-the-ground-running/how-yammers-cofounder-impressed-bill-gates-with-a-story-about-a-burger

Fleck, J., Webster, J., & Williams, R. (1990). Dynamics of information technology implementation: A reassessment of paradigms and trajectories of development. *Futures*, *22*(6), 618–640. doi:10.1016/0016-3287(90)90131-Z

Flinders, K. (2014). Social media for communication inside the enterprise. Retrieved from http://www.computerweekly.com/feature/Social-media-for-communication-inside-the-enterprise

Flynn, N. (2009). *2009 Electronic Business Communication Policies and Procedures Survey*. Retrieved from http://www.epolicyinstitute.com/2009-electronic-business-communication-policies-procedures-survey-results

Fricker, R. D. (2006). *Sampling Methods for Web and E-mail Surveys*. Retrieved from http://www.nps.navy.mil

Fuchs, C., Boersma, F. K., Albrechtslund, A., & Sandoval, M. (2011). Internet & Surveillance. Introduction. In C. Fuchs, F. K. Boersma, A. Albrechtslund, & M. Sandoval (Eds.), *Internet and Surveillance* (pp. 1–29). London: Routledge.

Furneaux b, B. (2005, September 30). *Theories Used in IS Research: Unified Theory of Acceptance and Use of Technology.* Retrieved from www.istheory.yorku.ca

Furneaux, B. (2006). *Theories Used in IS Research.* Retrieved from www.istheory.yorku.ca

Furumo, K., & Pearson, M. J. (2007). Gender-Based Communication Styles, Trust, and. *Journal of Information, Information Technology, and Organizations, 2*, 1–14. Retrieved from www.jiito.org

Galegher, J., Kraut, R. E., & Egido, C. (2014). *Intellectual Teamwork: Social and Technological Foundations of Cooperative Work.* Psychology Press.

Garson, D. G. (2011). *Partial Least Squares Regression.* Retrieved from http://faculty.chass.ncsu.edu

Garton, C., & McCulloch, E. (2012). Fundamentals of Technology Project Management (2nd ed.). The Use of Social Media in Project Management. Canada: MC Press.

Gassler, G., Hug, T., & Glahn, C. (2004). Integrated Micro Learning – An outline of the basic method and first results. *Interactive Computer Aided Learning, 4.*

Gholami, B., & Murugesan, S. (2011). Global IT Project Management Using Web 2.0. *International Journal of Information Technology Project Management, 2*(3), 30–52. doi:10.4018/jitpm.2011070103

Girlsguidetopm. (2012). Social Media in a Project Environment: 2011 Survey Results. Retrieved from http://www.girlsguidetopm.com/social-media-in-a-project-environment-2011-survey-results/

Godwin-Jones, R. (2011). Emerging Technologies; Mobile Apps for Language Learning. *Language Learning & Technology, 15*(2), 2–11.

Goffman, E. (1959). *The presentation of self in everyday life.* New York: Doubleday Anchor Books.

Google Play page. (2015b, March 14). Wikipedia. Retrieved from http://en.wikipedia.org/wiki/Google_Play_Store#Play_Store_.28Android_app.29

Goolsby, R. (2010). Social media as crisis platform: The future of community maps/crisis maps. *ACM Transactions on Intelligent Systems and Technology, 7*(1), 1–11. doi:10.1145/1858948.1858955

Gossart, H. (2013, September 16). Communication- The single biggest problem with communication is the illusion that it has taken place (George Bernard Shaw). Retrieved from http://www.ncea.org/department-news/communication-single-biggest-problem-communication-illusion-it-has-taken-place

Grace, T. P. L. (2009). Wikis as a knowledge management tool. *Journal of Knowledge Management, 13*(4), 64–74. doi:10.1108/13673270910971833

Green, S., & Higgins, J. (2005). Glossary. Cochrane handbook for systematic reviews of interventions 4.2.5. The Cochrane Collaboration. Retrieved from http://www.cochrane.org/resources/glossary.htm

Green, B. (2010). Realizing returns on collaboration in an IP-enabled world. *NetworkWorld Asia, 6*(1), 24–26.

Greene, K. (2010). An App with a Direct Line to City Hall. *MIT Technology Review.* Retrieved from http://www.technologyreview.com/news/421770/an-app-with-a-direct-line-to-city-hall/

Greenhow, C., Peppler, K. A., & Solomou, M. (2011). Building creativity: Collaborative learning and creativity in social media environments. *On the Horizon, 19*(1), 13–23. doi:10.1108/10748121111107672

Grit, R. (2015). *Project Management, A Practical approach.* Netherlands: Noordhoff Publishers.

Grosse, C. U. (2002). Managing Communication within Virtual Intercultural Teams, Business and Professional. *Communication Quarterly, 65*(4), 22–38.

Gross, N., & Martin, W. E. (1952). On group cohesiveness. *American Journal of Sociology*, *57*(6), 546–554. doi:10.1086/221041

Grudin, J. (2006). Enterprise Knowledge Management and Emerging Technologies.*Proceedings of the 39th Hawaii International Conference on System Sciences* (p. 57a). IEEE.

Guarino, J. (2012). Social media for project managers. Evolutionary IT. Retrieved from http://www.evolutionaryit.com/presentations/social_media_for_project_managers.pdf

Guliciuc, V. (2014). Complexity and social media. *Procedia - social and behavioral sciences*, 149, 371-371.

Gulliver, F. R. (1987). Post-project appraisals pay. *Harvard Business Review*, *65*(2), 128.

Gunter, O., Riehle, D., Krasnova, H., & Schondienst, V. (2009). Modelings microblogging adoption in the enterprise. *Proceedings of the fifteenth Americas conference in information systems* (pp. 1-10).

Günther, O., Krasnova, H., Riehle, D., & Schoendienst, V. (2009). Modeling Microblogging Adoption in the Enterprise. Proceedings of AMCIS 2009.

Hachman, M. (2013). Windows Phone Store passes 200,000 apps, so let's make them better, Microsoft! *PC World*. Retrieved from: http://www.pcworld.com/article/2080804/windows-phone-store-passes-200-000-apps-so-lets-make-them-better-microsoft.html

Hagel, J., Seely-Brown, J., Samoylova, T., & Frost, M. (2013). *2013 Shift Index metrics: The burdens of the past.* Deloitte Center for the Edge, Deloitte University Press. Retrieved from http://dupress.com/articles/the-burdens-of-the-past

Halligan, B., & Shah, D. (2010). *Inbound marketing: Get found using Google, social media and blogs*. New Jersey: John Wiley & Sons.

Halverson, T., Hauknes, J., Miles, I., & Røste, R. (2005). *On the differences between public and private sector innovation*. Oslo: NIFU STEP.

Hamilton, M. B. (2009). Online survey response rates and times: background and guidance for an industry SuperSurvey.

Hamilton, A. (2004). Project management reform: A public body case study. *Proceedings of the Institution of Civil Engineers. Municipal Engineer*, *157*(3), 199–207. doi:10.1680/muen.2004.157.3.199

Handy, C. (1995). Trust and the virtual organization. *Harvard Business Review*, *73*(3), 40–50.

Harell, G., & Daim, T. U. (2009). Virtual Teams and the Importance of Building Trust. *IT Professional Magazine*, *11*(6), 46–49. doi:10.1109/MITP.2009.135

Harrin, E. (2011). *Social Media in A Project Environment: Survey Results*. Retrieved from http://www.pm4girls.elizabeth-harrin.com/social-media-in-a-project-environment-2011-survey-results/

Harrin, E. (2010). *Social media for Project Managers*. Newton Square, PA: Project Management Institute.

Harrin, E. (2010a). *Social Media for Project Managers*. PMI.

Harrin, E. (2011). *Get started using social media on your projects* (3rd ed.). Newtown Square, PA: Project Management Institute Press.

Harrin, H. (2010). *Social media for project managers*. Project Management Institute.

Hayden, B., & Tomal, R. (2012). A History of Social Media. *CopyBlogger.com*. Retrieved from http://www.copyblogger.com/history-of-social-media/

Hearing, G., & Ussery, B. (2012a). The times they are changin' the impact of technology and social media on the public workspace, part I. *The Florida Bar Journal*, 86(3), 35–39.

Hearing, G., & Ussery, B. (2012b). The times they are a changin': The impact of technology and social media on the public workplace, part II. *The Florida Bar Journal*, 86(4), 20–24.

Heivadi, T., Khajeheian, D. (2013). Construction of Social Identity in Social Media: An investigation of Iranian Users' Appearance in Facebook. *Interdisciplinary Journal of Contemporary Research in Business,* 4(12).

Help Avoid Traffic Congestion with the Waze App. (2015). State of Florida, Department of Transportation. *SunPassages Newsletter*. Retrieved from http://www.floridasturnpike.com/sunpassages/14.fall/waze-app.html

Helsloot, I., & Ruitenberg, A. (2004). Citizen response to disasters: A survey of literature and some practical implications. *Journal of Contingencies and Crisis Management, 12*(3), 98–111. doi:10.1111/j.0966-0879.2004.00440.x

Henman, P. (2013). Governmentalities of Gov 2.0. *Information Communication and Society, 16*(9), 1397–1418. doi:10.1080/1369118X.2012.706314

Herrin, E. (2010). *Social Media for Project Managers.* PMI.

Hevner, A. R., March, S. T., Park, J., & Ram, S. (2004). Design science in information systems research. *Management Information Systems Quarterly, 28*(1), 75–105.

Highsmith, J. (2001). History: The Agile Manifesto. Retrieved from http://www.agilemanifesto.org/history.html

Hinchcliffe, D. (2012). Enterprise 2.0 success: BASF. Retrieved from: http://www.zdnet.com/article/enterprise-2-0-success-basf/

Hinsberg, H. (2009). My better Estonia. *Intergovernmental Solutions Newsletter,* Fall, 20-21.

Hoegl, M., & Gemuenden, H. G. (2001). Teamwork Quality and the Success of Innovative Projects: A Theoretical Concept and Empirical Evidence. *Organization Science, 12*(4), 435–449. doi:10.1287/orsc.12.4.435.10635

Hollaway, A. (2005). *IT Project Failures, Accountancy Age*. KPMG Highlights.

Hollingshead, J., McGrath, K., & O'Connor, K. M. (1993). Group task performance and communication technology: A longitudinal study of computer-mediated versus face-to-face work groups. *Small Group Research, 24*(3), 307–333. doi:10.1177/1046496493243003

Hollingsworth, C. (2010). PMPs on FB? OMG. *PM NETWORK, 24*(3), 40–46.

Hollingworth, A., & Cooper, T. (2011). Why Government Must Do Better With Web 2.0. *Public Management, 40*(3), 30–34.

Hong, J. F., & Vai, S. (2009). Knowledge-sharing in cross-functional virtual teams. *Journal of General Management, 34*(2), 21–37.

Hornby, A. S., & Turnbull, J. (2010). *Oxford advanced learner's dictionary of current English.* Oxford: Oxford University Press.

Hout, R., Vrancken, J., & Schrijnen, P. (2010). Wiki-Based Knowledge Management in a Transport Consultancy, a Case Study. *The Electronic Journal Information Systems Evaluation, 13*(2), 133–142.

Howard, C., Natis, Y. F., Harris-Ferrante, K., Proctor, P. E., Cain, M. W., ..., Anderson, E. (2014). *Transform your business with the Nexus of Forces*. Retrieved from https://www.gartner.com/doc/267381528

Hsu, C.-L., & Lin, J. C.-C. (2008). Acceptance of blog usage: The roles of technology acceptance, social influence and knowledge sharing motivation. *Information & Management*, *45*(1), 65–74. doi:10.1016/j.im.2007.11.001

Huang, C., & Chan, E., & Hyder, A. (2010). Web 2.0 and internet social networking?: A new tool for disaster management? – Lessons from Taiwan. *BMC Medical Informatics and Decision Making*, *10*(57), 1–5. PMID:20925944

Huemann, M. (2006). *Project management personnel in the project-oriented company*. Global Project Management Handbook.

Hughes, A. L., & Palen, L. (2009). Twitter adoption and use in mass convergence and emergency events. *International Journal of Emergency Management*, *6*(3), 248–260. doi:10.1504/IJEM.2009.031564

Hui, G., & Hayllar, M. (2010). Creating public value in e-government: A public-private-citizen collaboration framework in Web 2.0. *Australian Journal of Public Administration*, *69*(S1), S120–S131. doi:10.1111/j.1467-8500.2009.00662.x

IFIP. (2004). Virtual enterprises and collaborative networks. *Proceedings of the IFIP 18th World Computer Congress: TC5/WG5.5 - 5th Working Conference on Virtual Enterprises*, Toulouse, France (p. 255a).

Ilieva, J., Baron, S., & Healy, N. M. (2002). *Online surveys: Pros and cons*. Retrieved from www.serprofessoruniversitario.pro.br/

Inspectie Veiligheid en Justitie. (2013). *Nationale Politie op Koers?* Den Haag: IVJ.

Internetworldstats.com. (2012). Internet Usage in the European Union - EU27 Retrieved from http://www.internetworldstats.com/stats9.htm#eu

IPMA (2006). *International Competence Baseline Version 3.0*. Nijkerk.

Isaacs, W. (1999). *Dialogue and the art of thinking together*. NY, NY: Doubleday.

ISO. (2012). ISO 21500: Guidance on Project Management. Geneva, Switzerland.

Jackson, Th. W., & Dawson, R. (2003). *Breaking Bad Habits: The Negative Effect of Email and Instant Messaging on the Workplace*. UK: Loughborough University.

James, V., Rosenhead, R., & Taylor, P. (2013). *Strategies for Project Sponsorship*. Tysons Corner: Management Concepts Press.

Janssen, C. F. (1996). *The Four Rooms of Change, Förändringens fyra rum*. Wahlström & Widstrand.

Jarvenpaa, S. L., & Leidner, D. E. (1998). Communication and Trust un Global Virtual Teams. *Journal of Computer-Mediated Communication*, *3*(4), 0. doi:10.1111/j.1083-6101.1998.tb00080.x

Jensen, J. 2012. Social media for project management. Retrieved from http://www.slideshare.net/jonniejensen/social-media-for-project-management

Johnson, S. (2010). Where good ideas come from. *TED*. Retrieved from http://www.ted.com/talks/steven_johnson_where_good_ideas_come_from?language=en

Johnson, S. D., Suriya, C., Yoon, S. W., Berret, J. V., & La Fleur, J. (2000). Team Development and group processes of virtual learning teams. *Computers & Education*, *39*, 393–397.

Jordan, P. W., Thomas, B., Weerdmeester, B. A., & McClelland, I.L. (Eds), (1996). Usability Evaluation in Industry. London: Taylor & Francis Ltd.

Jugdev, K. (2012). Learning from Lessons Learned: Project Management Research Program. *American Journal of Economics and Business Administration*, *4*(1), 13–22. doi:10.3844/ajebasp.2012.13.22

Jugdev, K., & Wishart, P. (2014). Mutual Caring—Resolving Habituation Through Awareness: Supporting Meaningful Learning From Projects. *Project Management Journal*, *45*(2), 66–82. doi:10.1002/pmj.21406

Kaewkitipong, L., Chen, C., & Ractham, P. (2012). Lessons learned from the use of social media in combating a crisis: A case study of 2011 Thailand flooding disaster. *Proceedings of the 33rd international conference on information systems*, Orlando, FL, USA.

Kangas, P., Toivonen, A. & Back, A. (2008). *Ads by Google and other social media models.* VTT research notes 2384.

Kaplan, A. M., & Haenlein, M. (2010). Users of the world unite! The challenges and opportunities of Social Media. *Business Horizons*, *53*(1), 59–68. doi:10.1016/j.bushor.2009.09.003

Kaplan, A. M., & Haenlein, M. (2010). Users of the world, unite! The challenges and opportunities of Social Media. *Business Horizons*, *53*(1), 59–68.

Kaplan, A., & Haenlein, M. (2011). The early bird catches the news: Nine things you should know about micro-blogging. *Business Horizons*, *54*(2), 105–113. doi:10.1016/j.bushor.2010.09.004

Karaduman, I. (2013). The effect of social media on personal branding efforts of top level executives. *Procedia - social and behavioral sciences*, 99, 465-473.

Kautz, K. (1995). Diffusion and adoption of information technology. *First IFIP WG 8.6 Working Conference on the Diffusion and Adoption of Information Technology* (p. 133). Aslo: Springer.

Kavanaugh, A., Fox, E., Sheetz, S., Yang, S., Li, L., Shoemaker, D., & Xie, L. et al. (2012). Social media use by government: From the routine to the critical. *Government Information Quarterly*, *29*(4), 480–491. doi:10.1016/j.giq.2012.06.002

Kerzner, H. (1998). *Project Management: a systems approach to planning, scheduling, and controlling*. New York: Van Nostrand Reinhold.

Kerzner, R. (2015). *Project Management 2.0.* Wiley.

Keyes, J. (2012). *Enterprise 2.0: Social Networking Tools to Transform Your Organization*. Boca Raton, FL: CRC Press. doi:10.1201/b12532

Kietzmann, J. H., & Angell, I. (2010). Panopticon revisited. *Communications of the ACM*, *53*(6), 135–138. doi:10.1145/1743546.1743582

Kietzmann, J. H., Hermkens, K., McCarthy, I. P., & Silvestre, B. S. (2010). Social Media? Get serious! Understanding the functional building blocks of social media. *Business Horizons*, *2011*(54), 241–251.

Kietzmann, J., Hermkens, K., McCarthy, I., & Silvestre, B. S. (2011). Social media? Get serious! Understanding the functional building blocks of social media. *Business Horizons*, *54*(3), 241–251. doi:10.1016/j.bushor.2011.01.005

Kijsanayotin, B., Pannarunothai, S., & Speedie, S. M. (2009). Factors influencing health information technology adoption in Thailand's community health centers: Applying the UTAUT model. *International Journal of Medical Informatics*, *78*(6), 404–416. doi:10.1016/j.ijmedinf.2008.12.005 PMID:19196548

Kimble, C. (2011, January/February). Building effective virtual teams: How to overcome the problems of trust and identity in virtual teams. *Global Business & Organizational Excellence*, *30*(2), 6–15. doi:10.1002/joe.20364

King (2010). Social Media and Infrastructural projects. Retrieved from http://www.kennisinhetgroot.nl/upload/documents/produkten/King%20social%20Media_totaal.pdf

Kingsley, C. (2010). *Making the most of social media: 7 lessons from successful cities*. Philadelphia, PA: Fels Institute of Government.

Kiron, D., & Palmer, D. Nguyen Phillips, A., & Berkman, R. (2013). *Social Business: Shifting Out of First Gear*. MIT Sloan Management Review/Deloitte University Press. Retrieved from http://cdn.dupress.com/wp-content/uploads/2013/07/DUP446_SB_Report_Final.pdf

Klynstra, M. (2012). Retrieved from http://www.enterpriseappstoday.com/social-media/social-media-meets-project-management.html

Klynstra, M. (2012). Social media applied to project teams. Retrieved from http://www.geneca.com/social-media-meets-project-management/

Klynstra, M. (2012, August 21). Social Media Meets Project Management. Retrieved from http://www.geneca.com/social-media-meets-project-management/

Koltay, T. (2011). Information overload, information architecture and digital literacy. *Bulletin of the American Society for Information Science and Technology*, *38*(1), 33–35. doi:10.1002/bult.2011.1720380111

Komninos, N., Schaffers, H., & Pallot, M. (2011). Developing a policy roadmap for smart cities and the future Internet. In P. Cunningham & M. Cunningham (Eds.), *Proceedings of the eChallenges e-2011 Conference*. Dublin: IIMC.

Koskela, L. J., & Howell, G. (2002). The Underlying Theory of Project Management is Obsolete. *Proceedings of thePMI Research Conference*, Seattle, Washington.

Kotnour, T., & Vergopia, C. (2005). Learning-Based Project Reviews: Observations and Lessons Learned from the Kennedy Space Center. *Engineering Management Journal*, *17*(4), 30–38. doi:10.1080/10429247.2005.11431670

Kozlowski, S. W. J., & Bell, B. S. (2001). Handbook of psychology: Vol. 12. *Work Groups and Teams in Organizations* (pp. 333–375). Industrial and Organizational Psychology.

KPMG. (2013). *Social Media – Het speelkwartier is voorbij: Time to talk business*. Retrieved from http://secure.kpmg.com/NL/nl/IssuesAndInsights/ArticlesPublications/Documents/PDF/Management-Consulting/Social-media-het-speelkwartier-is-voorbij.pdf

Krauss, E. (2014). How does operational readiness assist in asset management: It surely is an operations function? *Australian Journal of Multi-disciplinary Engineering*, *11*(1), 1–11. doi:10.7158/N13-AM10.2014.11.1

Kresimir, J., Vrecko, I. V., & Zlatk, B. (2013). Web 2.0 Technologies Supporting Project Management Needs. *Interdisciplinary Management Research*, *9*, 219–226.

Krüger, N., Brockmann, T., & Stieglitz, S. (2013). A framework for enterprise social media guidelines.*Proceedings of the Nineteenth Americas Conference on Information Systems.*

Laplante, P. A., & Neill, C. J. (2004). The demise of the waterfall model is imminent and other urban myths. *Queue*, *1*(10), 10–15. doi:10.1145/971564.971573

Larcker, D. F. (n. d.). *Social Media Use Among Directors and Senior Managers*. Stanford Graduate School of Business, Center for Leadership Development and Research. Retrieved from https://www.gsb.stanford.edu/sites/default/files/13SocialMedia.pdf

Lave, J., & Wenger, E. (1991). *Situated Learning: Legitimate Peripheral Participation*. Cambridge: Cambridge University Press. doi:10.1017/CBO9780511815355

Lavender, S. (2014). *Management for the Construction Industry*. Routledge.

Lee, G., & Kwak, Y. (2012). An open government maturity model for social media-based public engagement. *Government Information Quarterly*, *29*(4), 492–503. doi:10.1016/j.giq.2012.06.001

Lee-Kelley, L. (2006, April). Locus of control and attitudes to working in virtual teams. *International Journal of Project Management*, *24*(3), 234–243. doi:10.1016/j.ijproman.2006.01.003

Leitch, R. (2014, March 13). Why Project Managers Should Embrace Social Media. Retrieved from http://www.business2community.com/social-media/project-managers-embrace-social-media-0802531

Lepsinger, R., & DeRosa, D. (2010). *Team Success: A Practical Guide for Working and Leading from a Distance*. John Wiley and Sons.

Levine, A. (2014). Social Networking Tools: An Introduction to Their Role in Project Management. In P. Dinsmore & J. Cabanis-brewin (Eds.), The AMA Handbook of Project Management (4th edition ed.): American management Association.

Levitt, R. (2011). Towards project management 2.0. *Engineering Project Organization Journal*, *1-3*(3), 197–210. doi: 10.1080/21573727.2011.609558

Levy, M. (2009). Web 2.0 implications on knowledge management. *Journal of Knowledge Management*, *13*(1), 120–134. doi:10.1108/13673270910931215

Lewis-Beck, M. S., Bryman, A., & Futing Liao, T. (2004). *The Sage encyclopedia of social science research methods* (Vol. 1). Sage. doi:10.4135/9781412950589

Li, M., Chen, G., Zhang, Z., & Fu, Y. (2012). A social collaboration platform for enterprise social networking. *Proceedings of the 2012 IEEE 16th International Conference on Computer Supported Cooperative Work in Design (CSCWD)* (pp. 671–677). IEEE. doi:10.1109/CSCWD.2012.6221890

Likert, R. (1932). A Technique for the Measurement of Attitudes. *Archives de Psychologie*, *140*, 1–55.

Linders, D. (2012). From e-government to we-government: Defining a typology for citizen coproduction in the age of social media. *Government Information Quarterly*, *29*(4), 446–454. doi:10.1016/j.giq.2012.06.003

Lipton, E., & Davenport, C. (2015, May 19). Critics hear EPA's voice in 'Public Comments'. *New York Times*, *164*(56871) A1-A18.

Locke, D. (1984). *Project Management*. New York: St Martin's Press.

Loo, R. (2002). Journaling: A learning tool for project management training and team-building. *Project Management Journal*, *33*(4), 61–66.

Louridas, P. (2006). Using wikis in software development. *IEEE Software*, *23*(2), 88–91. doi:10.1109/MS.2006.62

Lousberg, L., Wamelink, H., Atkin, B., & Borgbrant, J. (2009). *Foundation of a practical theory of project management*. New York: SPON Press Taylor & Francis.

Lundy, V., & Morin, P.-P. (2013). Project leadership influences resistance to change: The case of the Canadian public service. *Project Management Journal*, *44*(4), 45–64. doi:10.1002/pmj.21355

Lykourentzou, I., Dagka, F., Papadaki, K., Lepouras, G., & Vassilakis, C. (2012). Wikis in enterprise settings: A survey. *Enterprise Information Systems*, *6*(1), 1–53. doi:10.1080/17517575.2011.580008

Lynch, C. (2008). Blogs Clean Up Project Management Messes. Retrieved from http://www.cio.com/article/163250

MacMillan, T. (2013). 6 Years On, SeeClickFix Has Changed New Haven, *New Haven Independent*. Retrieved from http://www.newhavenindependent.org/index.php/archives/entry/seeclickfix_6_years/

MacNamara, J., Sakinofsky, P., & Beattie, J. (2012). E-electoral engagement: How governments use social media to engage voters. *Australian Journal of Political Science*, *47*(4), 623–639. doi:10.1080/10361146.2012.731491

Majchrzak, A., & More, P. (2011). Emergency! Web 2.0 to the rescue! *Communications of the ACM*, *54*(4), 125–132. doi:10.1145/1924421.1924449

Majchrzak, A., Wagner, C., & Yates, D. (2006). Corporate wiki users: results of a survey.*Proceedings of the International Symposium on Wikis* (pp. 99–104). Odense, Denmark: ACM Press. doi:10.1145/1149453.1149472

Maltzman, R., & Shirley, D. (2012). *Green Project Management*. CRC Press.

Mancini, D. J. (2010). Building organizational trust in virtual teams. *Journal of Behavioral Studies in Business*, *2*, 1–5.

Mangold, W. G., & Faulds, D. J. (2009). Social media: The new hybrid element of the promotion mix. *Elsevier Business Horizons*, *52*(4), 357–365. doi:10.1016/j.bushor.2009.03.002

Marimuthu, M., & Dean, A. M. (2007). *The Influence of Perceived Service Value on Information System*. Retrieved from http://conferences.anzmac.org/ANZMAC2007/papers/M%20Marimuthu_1a.pdf

MarketingProfs. (2011). Marketers Up Spending on Digital, Social in 2011. Retrieved from <http://www.marketingprofs.com/charts/2011/4471/marketers-up-spending-on-digital-social-in-2011>

Markus, M. L., & Robey, D. (1988). Information technology and organizational change: Causal structure in theory and research. *Management Science*, *34*(5), 583–598. doi:10.1287/mnsc.34.5.583

Martina, E., Oppier, D., Fafie, D., Hoogland, D., Krouwel, L., & Kroef, v.d. (2014). Minor social media & virtual networks. Utrecht: BuDeCo.

Mayfield, A. (2008). What is social media? Retrieved from http://www.icrossing.co.uk/fileadmin/uploads/eBooks/What_is_Social_Media_iCrossing_ebook.pdf

Mayfield, A. (2008). What is Social Media? Retrieved from http://www.icrossing.co.uk/fileadmin/uploads/ebooks/what_is_social_media_icrossing_ebook.pdf

McAfee, A. (2009). *Enterprise 2.0: New Collaborative Tools for Your Organization's Toughest Challenges*. Harvard Business Press.

McKinsey. (2011). *How social technologies are extending the organization*. Retrieved from http://www.mckinsey.com/insights/high_tech_telecoms_internet/how_social_technologies_are_extending_the_organization

McNutt, K. (2014). Public engagement in the Web 2.0 era: Social Collaborative technologies in a public sector context. *Canadian Public Administration / Administration Publique du Canada, 57*(1), 49-70.

Meijer, A., Boersma, F. K., & Wagenaar, P. (Eds.), (2009). *ICTs, Citizens & Governance: After the Hype!* Amsterdam: IOS Press.

Melcrum. (2008). *How to use social media to engage employees*. Retrieved from http://www.melcrum.com

Melendez, L., Wolfson, O., Adjouadi, M., & Rishe, N. (2010). Qualitative Analysis of Commercial Social Neworks Profiles. In B. Furht (Ed.), *Handbook of Social Network Technologies and Applications*. Springer Science & Business Media. doi:10.1007/978-1-4419-7142-5_5

Mendoza, M., Poblete, B., & Castillo, C. (2010). Twitter Under Crisis: Can we trust what we RT?*Proceedings of the first workshop on social media analytics* (pp. 71-79). doi:10.1145/1964858.1964869

Merchant, S. (2007). Exploring the Influence of Cultural Values on the Acceptance of Information Technology: An Application of the Technology Acceptance Model. Journal of Issues in Informing Science and Information, 4, 431.

Merchant, R. M., Elmer, S., & Lurie, N. (2011). Integrating social media into emergency-preparedness efforts. *The New England Journal of Medicine*, *365*(4), 289–291. doi:10.1056/NEJMp1103591 PMID:21793742

Merrill, H. S. (2003). Best practices for online facilitation. *Adult Learning*, *14*(2), 13.

Merwin, G., McDonald, J., & Odera, L. (2008). Economic Development: Governments' Cutting Edge in IT. In M. S. Raisinghani (Ed.), *Handbook of Research on Global Information Technology Management in the Digital Economy* (pp. 1–37). Hershey, PA: Information Science Reference. doi:10.4018/978-1-59904-875-8.ch001

Messieh, N. 2011. How Google+ could become an essential business tool. Retrieved from http://thenextweb.com/google/2011/07/13/how-google-could-become-an-essential-business-tool/

Meyerson, D., Weick, K. E., & Kramer, R. M. (1996). Swift trust and temporary groups. In R. M. Kramer, T. R. Tyler (Eds.), Trust in Organizations (pp. 166-195). Thousand Oaks, CA: Sage. doi:10.4135/9781452243610.n9

Meyrowitz, J. (1985). *No sense of place: The impact of electronic media on social behavior*. Oxford: Oxford University Press.

Microsoft Office Support. (2015). Use Twitter, Facebook and other social media to help manage projects and teams. Retrieved from https://support.office.microsoft.com/en-za/article/Use-Twitter-Facebook-and-other-social-media-to-help-manage-projects-and-teams

Microsoft. (n. d.). Use Twitter, Facebook and other social media to help manage projects and teams. Retrieved from https://support.office.com/en-us/article/Use-Twitter-Facebook-and-other-social-media-to-help-manage-projects-and-teams-1c9b9c86-e417-4763-91ed-35a5f6e86208?CorrelationId=b805fa25-81d5-4793-b446-c4495661dd22&ui=en-US&rs=en-US&ad=US#

Minton-Eversole, T. (2010). *Social media tools redefining learning in organizations*. Retrieved from http://www.shrm.org/hrdisciplines/staffingmanagement/Articles/Pages/ToolsRedefineLearning

Mirvis, P., Sales, A., & Hackett, E. (2006). The implementation and adoption of new technology in organizations: The impact on work, people, and culture. *Human Resource Management*, *30*(1), 113–139. doi:10.1002/hrm.3930300107

Moher, D., Liberati, A., Tetzlaff, J., & Altman, D. G. (2009). Preferred reporting Items for systematic reviews and meta-analyses. The PRISMA Statement. *PLoS Medicine*, *6*(6). PMID:19621072

Moise, D., & Cruceru, A. (2014). An empirical study of promoting different kinds of events trough various social media networks websites. *Procedia: Social and Behavioral Sciences*, *109*, 98–102. doi:10.1016/j.sbspro.2013.12.426

Moore, S. (2010). *Strategic project portfolio management*. Hoboken, NJ: Wiley.

Moqbel, M. (2012, *February 29–March*). Explaining user acceptance of social networking: Employees' Perspective. *Proceedings of the Southwest Decision Science Institute Forty Third Annual Conference* (Vol. 3, pp. 110-118).

Morgan, M., Seaman, J., & Tinti-Kane, H. (2011). *Teaching, learning, and sharing: How today's higher education faculty use social media*. Boston: Pearson.

Moulaert, F., MacCallum, D., & Hillier, J. (2013). Social innovation: intuition, precept, concept. *The International Handbook on Social Innovation: Collective Action, Social Learning and Transdisciplinary Research* (p. 13).

Mullen, B., & Copper, C. (1994). The relation between group cohesiveness and performance: An integration. *Psychological Bulletin, 115*(2), 210–227. doi:10.1037/0033-2909.115.2.210

Muller, J., & Stocker, A. (2011). Enterprise microblogging for advanced knowledge sharing: The references@BT case study. *Journal of Universal Computer Science, 17*(4), 532–547.

Muller, M., Ehrlich, K., Matthews, T., Perer, A., Ronen, I., & Guy, I. (2012). Diversity among enterprise online communities collaborating, teaming, and innovating though social media. *CHI, 12*, 1–10.

Munkvold, B. E. (2003). *Implementing collaboration technologies in industry*. Springer. doi:10.1007/978-1-4471-0073-7

Murugesan, S. (2007). Business uses of Web 2.0, potentials and prospects. *Business-IT Strategies, 10*(1), 1–28.

Murugesan, S. (2009). Web X.0: A Road Map. In M. San (Ed.), *Handbook of Research on Web 2.0, 3.0, and X.0: Technologies, Business, and Social Applications: Technologies, Business, and Social Applications*. IGI Global.

Mustonen, P. (2009). Social Media – a new way to success? *Turku School of Economics. Uniprint, Turku.* Retrieved from http://info.tse.fi/julkaisut/kr/KRe1_2009

My OC: Social Media Hub. (2015). Orange County, California. Retrieved from http://ocgov.com/contact/connect

Nath, J. (2011). Reimagining government in the digital age. *National Civic Review, 100*(3), 19–23. doi:10.1002/ncr.20070

Naumann, J. D., & Jenkins, A. M. (1982). Prototyping: The new paradigm for systems development. *Management Information Systems Quarterly, 6*(3), 29–44. doi:10.2307/248654

Nebraska Statewide Social Media. (2015). State of Nebraska. Retrieved from http://www.nebraska.gov/social-media.html

New York. City of (2014). *Welcome to NYC.gov*. Retrieved from http://www1.nyc.gov/

New York. City of (2015). Job Training and Placement Services for Public Assistance Recipients. Retrieved from http://www1.nyc.gov/nyc-resources/service/2982/job-training-and-placement-services-for-public-assistance-recipients

Nicholls, S. (2011). Social media in business (Ch. 2, p. 84). UK: Bookinars.

Nicol, D. (2013). *Mobile Strategy: How Your Company Can Win by Embracing Mobile Technologies*. IBM Press.

Nicoletti, B. (2012). *Lean and Digitize: An Integrated Approach to Process Improvement*. Gower Publishing, Ltd.

Nielsen. (2014, June 17). Global Consumers are Willing to Put Their Money Where Their Heart is When it Comes to Goods and Services from Companies Committed to Social Responsibility. Retrieved from http://www.nielsen.com/us/en/press-room/2014/global-consumers-are-willing-to-put-their-money-where-their-heart-is.html

Noll, M. G., & Meinel, C. (2007). Web Search Personalization Via Social Bookmarking and Tagging. In K. Aberer, K.-S. Choi, N. Noy, D. Allemang, K.-I. Lee, L. Nixon, … P. Cudré-Mauroux (Eds.), The Semantic Web (Vol. 4825, pp. 367–380). Springer Berlin Heidelberg. doi:10.1007/978-3-540-76298-0_27

Nonaka, I., Toyama, R., & Konno, N. (2000). SECI, *Ba* and Leadership: A Unified Model of Dynamic Knowledge Creation. *Long Range Planning, 33*(1), 5–34. doi:10.1016/S0024-6301(99)00115-6

Norton, R. (2013). *Social Helpdesk – A new era of support – or is it?* Atos Ascent Blog (blog.atos.net)

Noy, E., & Ellis, S. (2003). Risk: A neglected component of strategy formulation. *Journal of Managerial Psychology*, *18*(7), 691–707. doi:10.1108/02683940310502395

NRC. (2014). Facebook buys WhatsApp for 16 billion dollar. Retrieved from http://www.nrc.nl/nieuws/2014/02/19/facebook-koopt-whatsapp-voor-16-miljard-dollar/

Number of apps available in leading app stores as of July 2015. (2015). *Statista.* Retrieved from http://www.statista.com/statistics/276623/number-of-apps-available-in-leading-app-stores/

OECD. (2007). *Participative web and user-created content: Web 2.0, wikis, and social networking*. Paris: Organisation for Economic Co-operation and Development.

Office of Government Commerce. (2009). *Managing Successful Projects with PRINCE 2*. Edition Manual.

Office of the Government Commerce. (2009). *Managing successful projects with PRINCE2*. Norwich.

Ohio, State of. (2015). *Ohio.gov: State Agencies on Social Media.* Retrieved from http://www.ohio.gov/social/

Oh, O., Agrawal, M., & Rao, H. R. (2013). Community intelligence and social media services: A rumor theoretic analysis of tweets during social crises. *Management Information Systems Quarterly*, *37*(2), 407–426.

Ollus, M., Jansson, K., & Karvonen, I. (2006). On the management of collaborative networked organizations. In P. Cunningham, & M. Cunningham (Eds.), *Conference Proceedings from IST-Africa 2006*. IIMC International Information Management Corporation.

Ollus, M., Jansson, K., Karvonen, I., Uoti, M., & Riikonen, H. (2009). On Services for Collaborative Project Management. In L. Camarinha-Matos, I. Paraskakis, & H. Afsarmanesh (Eds.), *Leveraging Knowledge for Innovation in Collaborative Networks* (Vol. 307, pp. 451–462). Springer Berlin Heidelberg. doi:10.1007/978-3-642-04568-4_47

Ollus, M., Jansson, K., Karvonen, I., Uoti, M., & Riikonen, H. (2011). Supporting collaborative project management. *Production Planning and Control*, *22*(5-6), 538–553. doi:10.1080/09537287.2010.536624

Olson, P. (2014). Why Google's Waze Is Trading User Data With Local Governments. *Forbes*. Retrieved from http://www.forbes.com/sites/parmyolson/2014/07/07/why-google-waze-helps-local-governments-track-its-users/

Oram, A. (2001). *Harnessing the power of disruptive technologies*. Sebastopol, California: O'Reilly Media.

Orlikowski, W. J. (1992). The duality of technology: Rethinking the concept of technology in organizations. *Organization Science*, *3*(3), 398–427. doi:10.1287/orsc.3.3.398

Orlikowski, W. J., & Barley, S. R. (2001). Technology and institutions: What can research on information technology and research on organizations learn from each other? *Management Information Systems Quarterly*, *25*(2), 145–165. doi:10.2307/3250927

Oser, R., McCallum, G.A., Salas, E., & Morgan, B.B., Jr. (1989, March). Toward a definition of teamwork: an analysis of critical team behaviours. Human Factors Division Naval Training Systems Center, Orlando, FL.

Paillant, J. (2010). *SPSS Survival Manual* (4th ed.). McGraw-Hill.

Palen, L. (2008). Online social media in crisis events. *EDUCAUSE Quarterly*, *31*(3), 12.

Pant, I., & Baroudi, B. (2008). Project management education: The human skills imperative. *International Journal of Project Management*, *26*(2), 124–128. doi:10.1016/j.ijproman.2007.05.010

Parcells, F. E. (2015). Social Media trends 2015. Retrieved from http://www.slideshare.net/feparcells/social-media-trends-2015-44900830

Parker, K., & Chao, J. (2007). Wiki as a Teaching Tool. *Interdisciplinary Journal of E-Learning and Learning Objects*, *3*(1), 57–72.

Pavlou, P. A., & Fygenson, M. (2006). Understanding and predicting electronic commerce adoption: an extension ofthe theory of planned behavior. *MIS Quaterly*, *30*(1), 115–143.

Petter, S., & Vaishnavi, V. (2008). Facilitating experience reuse among software project managers. *Information Sciences*, *178*(7), 1783–1802. doi:10.1016/j.ins.2007.11.020

Pettigrew, J., & Reber, B. (2010). The new dynamic in corporate media relations: How Fortune 500 companies are using virtual press rooms to engage the press. *Journal of Public Relations Research*, *22*(4), 404–428. doi:10.1080/10627261003801412

Pink, D. H. (2011). *Drive: The surprising truth about what motivates us*. Penguin.

Pinto, J. K. & Slevin, D. P. (1989). Critical success factors in R&D projects. *Research Technology Management*, 32(1), 31-35

Pinto, M. B., & Pinto, J. K. (1990). Project team communication and crossfunctional cooperation in new program development. *Journal of Product Innovation Management*, *7*(3), 200–212. doi:10.1016/0737-6782(90)90004-X

Plummer, D. C., Fiering, L., Dulaney, K., McGuire, M., Da Rold, C. ..., Marian, K. (2014). *Top 10 strategic predictions for 2015 and beyond: Digital business is driving 'big change'*. Retrieved from https://www.gartner.com/doc/2864817?srcId=1-4782295242

PMI. (2014a). *Enabling Organizational Change through Strategic Initiatives*. PMI. Retrieved from http://www.pmi.org/learning/pulse.aspx#

PMI. (2014b). *Executive Sponsor Engagement: Top driver ofproject and program success*. PMI/Boston Consulting Group. Retrieved from http://www.pmi.org/~/media/PDF/learning/tranlations/2015/executive-sponsor-engagement-uk.ashx

Poade, D. (2011). *Sampling and Response: The experience of conducting an online student survey*. Retrieved from www.research.plymouth.ac.uk

Poje, J. (2011). Gov 2.0: Interaction, innovation, and collaboration. *Public Law*, *19*(1), 2–11.

Polanyi, M. (1966). *The Tacit Dimension*. Garden City, N.Y., USA: Doubleday & Co.

Pollack, J., & Adler, D. (2015). Does project management affect business productivity? Evidence from Australian small to medium enterprises. *Project Management Journal*, *45*(6), 17–24. doi:10.1002/pmj.21459

Pritchard, C. (2013). *The Project Management Communications Toolkit* (2nd ed.). USA: Artech House.

Probst, G., & Borzillo, S. (2008). Why communities of practice succeed and why they fail. *European Management Journal*, *26*(5), 335–347. doi:10.1016/j.emj.2008.05.003

Project Communication Handbook (2nd ed.). (2007). Project Management Process Improvement. Sacramento, CA: Caltrans.

Project Management Institute. (2008). *A Guide to the Project Management Body of Knowledge (PMBOK Guide)*. Upper Darby: Project Management Institute Inc.

Project Management Institute. (2013). *A guide to the project management body of knowledge (PMBOK® guide)* (5th ed.). Project Management Institute.

Project Management Institute. a professional membership association (2015). Retrieved from http://www.pmi.org/Learning/podcasts.aspx

Projectplace. (n. d.). Social Project Management - Our Philosophy. Retrieved from https://www.projectplace.com/about-us/social-project-management/

PTI Names 2013 Web 2.0 Winning Jurisdictions. (2013). Public Technology Institute. Retrieved from http://www.pti.org/index.php/t1/more/161

Qingfei, M., Shaobo, J., & Gang, Q. (2008). Mobile Commerce User Acceptance Study in China: A Revised UTAUT Model. *Tsinghua Science and Technology*, *13*(3), 257–264. doi:10.1016/S1007-0214(08)70042-7

Qualman, E. (2013). *Socialnomics: How Social Media Transforms the Way We Live and Do Business*. John Wiley & Sons.

Rai, S. (2012). Engaging young employees (Gen Y) in a social media dominated world – Review and Retrospection. *Procedia: Social and Behavioral Sciences*, *37*, 257–266. doi:10.1016/j.sbspro.2012.03.292

Räkers, M. (2009). A communication efficiency model for ETL projects in financial data warehousing. *Proceedings of ECIS 2009*.

Remidez, R., & Jones, N.B. (2012) Developing a Model for Social Media in Project Management Communications. *International Journal of Business and Social Science*, 3(3), 33-36. Retrieved from http://www.ijbssnet.com/journals/Vol_3_No_3_February_2012/3.pdf

Reusch, P. J., Khushnood, M., Khan, R. A., & Aslam, S. (2010). After the Crisis we need Social Project Management. Proceedings of the International Business Research Conference, University of Northern Florida UNF, Jacksonville.

Richter, A., & Koch, M. (2008). Functions of Social Networking Services. *Proceedings of COOP '08: the 8th International Conference on the Design of Cooperative Systems.*

Riemer, K., & Richter, A. (2010). Tweet inside: microblogging in a corporate context. BLED Proceedings 1-17.

Roanoke County's Official Social Media Channels. (2015). Roanoke County, Virginia. Retrieved from http://www.roanokecountyva.gov/index.aspx?NID=816

Rooksby, J., & Sommerville, I. (2012). The management and use of social network sites in a government department. *Computer Supported Cooperative Work*, *21*(4-5), 397–415. doi:10.1007/s10606-011-9150-2

Rosenberg, D. (2009). *Reducing IT infrastructure costs via outsourcing*. Retrieved from http://news.cnet.com

Roth, G., & Kleiner, A. (1998). Developing organizational memory through learning histories. *Organizational Dynamics*, *27*(2), 43–60. doi:10.1016/S0090-2616(98)90023-7

Rousseau, V., Aubé, C., Savoie, A., (2006) Teamwork Behaviors A Review and an Integration of Frameworks. *Small Group Research*, 37(5), 540-570.

Rudnick, M., Wootton, A., & Wyatt, W. (2009). *Trends in employee self-service and manager self-service*. Retrieved from http://www.shrm.org/multimedia/webcasts/Pages/509essmss.aspx

Ruef, A., & Markard, J. (2010). What happens after a hype? *Technology Analysis and Strategic Management*, *22*(3), 317–338. doi:10.1080/09537321003647354

Salas, E., Sims, D. E., & Burke, C. S. (2005). Is there a "Big Five" in teamwork? *Small Group Research*, *36*(5), 555–599. doi:10.1177/1046496405277134

Salkin, P. (2011). Social networking and land use planning and regulation: Practical benefits, pitfalls, and ethical considerations. *Pace Law Review*, *31*(1), 54–94.

Salmon, G. K. (2015). *The Five Stage Model*. Retrieved from http://www.gillysalmon.com/five-stage-model.html

Salmon, G. (2011). *E-moderating: The key to teaching and learning online* (3rd ed.). New York: Routledge.

Salmon, G. K. (2000). *E-moderating: the key to teaching and learning online*. London, New York: Routledge Falmer. doi:10.4324/9780203465424

Salovaara, A., & Tamminen, S. (2010). *Accept or appropriate? A design-oriented critique on technology*. Retrieved from www.hiit.fi

Sams, M., & Mottram, K. (2015). Using twitter as a project management learning intervention #PSCMCHAT. Project Management Development – Practice and Perspectives (pp. 328-339). Riga, University of Latvia.

Sarter, N. B., & Woods, D. D. (1991). Situation Awareness: A Critical but Ill-Defined Phenomenon. *The International Journal of Aviation Psychology*, *1*(1), 45–57. doi:10.1207/s15327108ijap0101_4

Scarborough, H., Swan, J., & Preston, J. (1999). *Knowledge management: a literature review*. London: Institute of Personnel and Development.

Schau, H. J., & Gilly, M. C. (2003). We are what we post? Selfpresentation in personal web space. *The Journal of Consumer Research*, *30*(3), 385–404. doi:10.1086/378616

Schettini, F., & Weiss, B. (2011, October 3). Social Media: A Growing Factor in Project Success. *CIO Insight*. Retrieved from http://www.cioinsight.com/c/a/Expert-Voices/Social-Media-a-Growing-Factor-in-Project-Success-806642

Schindler, M., & Eppler, M. J. (2003). Harvesting project knowledge: A review of project learning methods and success factors. *International Journal of Project Management*, *21*(3), 219–228. doi:10.1016/S0263-7863(02)00096-0

Schneider, K. (2000). LIDs: a light-weight approach to experience elicitation and reuse. In *Product Focused Software Process Improvement* (pp. 407–424). Springer Berlin Heidelberg.

Schultz, F., Utz, S., & Göritz, A. (2011). Is the medium the message? Perceptions of and reactions to crisis communication via twitter, blogs and traditional media. *Public Relations Review*, *37*(1), 20–27. doi:10.1016/j.pubrev.2010.12.001

Schulz, B. (2008). The Importance of Soft Skills: Education beyond academic knowledge. *NAWA Journal of Language and Communication,* 2(1), 146-154

Schwaber, K. (2004). *Agile Project Management with Scrum (Developer Best Practices)*. Washington: Microsoft Press.

Schwaber, K., & Beedle, M. (2002). *Agile Software Development with Scrum*. Upper Saddle River, NJ: Prentice Hall.

Schwaber, K., & Sutherland, J. (2013). *The Scrum Guide - The Definitive Guide to Scrum: The Rules of the Game*. Scrum Org.

Schwalbe, K. (1999). *Information technology project management* (2nd ed.). Course Technology, Thomson Learning.

Scott, D. M. (2010). *The new rules of marketing and PR*. New Jersey: John Wiley & sons.

Secchi, P., Ciaschi, R., & Spence, D. (1999). A Concept for an ESA Lessons Learned System. In P. Secchi (Ed.), *Proceedings of Alerts and LL: An Effective way to prevent failures and problems (Tech. Rep. WPP-167)*. The Netherlands: ESTEC.

Senge, P. M. (1991). The fifth discipline, the art and practice of the learning organization. *Performance + Instruction, 30*(5), 37–37.

Sense, A. J. (2004). An architecture for learning in projects? *Journal of Workplace Learning*, *16*(3), 123–145. doi:10.1108/13665620410528498

Shang, S. S. C., Li, E. Y., Wu, Y.-L., & Hou, O. C. L. (2011). Understanding Web 2.0 service models: A knowledge-creating perspective. *Information & Management*, *48*(4-5), 178–184. doi:10.1016/j.im.2011.01.005

Shark, A. (2010). Behind the curve. *American City and County*, *125*(7), 48–51.

Shawaludin, A. (2010). *Diffusion of Innovations: Theoretical Perspectives and Future Prospects of Diffusion Studies.* Retrieved from http://www.nmconf.uob.edu.bh: http://www.nmconf.uob.edu.bh/download/english_article/010.pdf

Sheppard, B. H., Hartwick, J., & Warshaw, P. R. (1998, December). The Theory of Reasoned Action: A Meta-Analysis of Past Research with Recommendations for Modifications and Future Research. *The Journal of Consumer Research*, *15*(3), 325–343. doi:10.1086/209170

Shih, Y.-Y., & Fang, K. (2004). The use of a decomposed theory of planned behavior to study Internet banking in Taiwan. *Internet Research*, *14*(3), 213–223. doi:10.1108/10662240410542643

Short, J., Williams, E., & Christie, B. (1976). *The social psychology of telecommunications.* Hoboken, NJ: John Wiley & Sons, Ltd.

Silic, M., Back, A., & Silic, D. (2015). Atos – Towards a Zero email company, Teaching Case.*Proceedings of Twenty-Third European Conference on Information Systems (ECIS)*, Germany.

Silvestre, B.S., Kietzmann, J.H., McCarthy, I.P., Pitt, L. (2012) Unpacking the social media phenomenon: towards a research agenda. *Journal of Public Affairs (Special Issue),* 12(2), 109-119. DOI:10.1002/pa.1412

Silvius, A. J. G., van der Brink, J., & Köhler, A. (2012). *The impact of sustainability on project management, in the project as a social system, Henry Linger and Jill Owen* (pp. 183–200). Victoria: Monash University Publishing.

Singh, S. (2012). *New Mega Trends: Implications for Our Future Lives.* UK: Palgrave MacMillan. doi:10.1057/9781137008091

Skeen, D. R. (1977). User involvement with EDP systems development. In *Proceedings of the fifteenth annual SIGCPR conference* (pp. 62-71). ACM. doi:10.1145/800100.803233

Smarter working with zero email. (2012b). *Atos.* Retrieved from https://atos.net/content/dam/global/we-do/atos-zero-email-brochure-lores.pdf

Smiciklas, M. (2010). Malcolm Gladwell & The Future of Social Media. Retrieved from http://www.intersectionconsulting.com/2010/malcolm-gladwell-the-future-of-social-media/

Smith, A. (2013). *Civic engagement in the digital age.* Washington, D.C.: Pew Research Center.

Smith, P., & Zook, Z. (2011). *Marketing communications.* London: Kogan.

Snowden, S., & Cheah, P-K. (2015). *A Marketplace Without Boundaries? Responding to Disruption.* PwC 18th Annual CEO Survey. Retrieved from http://www.pwc.com/gx/en/ceo-survey/2015/assets/pwc-18th-annual-global-ceo-survey-jan-2015.pdf

Social Media in Government: 5 Key Considerations (Whitepaper). (n. d.). *Hootsuite.* Vancouver.

Social Project Management. (2012). *Engaging the Social Network to Deliver Project Success.* Triolog Group.

Socialize. (2015). Oakland County, Michigan. Retrieved from http://www.oakgov.com/social/Pages/default.aspx

Sponselee, M.G.M., (2014). Social Media & Project Management. The effects of Social Media on Project Management.

Standing, C., & Kiniti, S. (2011). How can organizations use wikis for innovation? *Technovation*, *31*(7), 287–295. doi:10.1016/j.technovation.2011.02.005

Standish Group International. (1999). *Chaos: A recipe for success*. The Standish Group International, Inc.

Statista. (2015). Number of monthly active Facebook users worldwide. *Statista.com*. Retrieved from http://www.statista.com/statistics/264810/number-of-monthly-active-facebook-users-worldwide/\

Statista. (2015). Number of monthly active Twitter users worldwide from 1st quarter 2010 to 4th quarter 2014. *Statista.com*. Retrieved from http://www.statista.com/statistics/282087/number-of-monthly-active-twitter-users/

Stewart, J. (2013). Public policy as information. *Prometheus*, *31*(1), 3–19. doi:10.1080/08109028.2013.763630

Streib, G., & Navarro, I. (2006). Citizen demand for interactive e-government: The case of Georgia Consumer services. *American Review of Public Administration*, *36*(3), 288–300. doi:10.1177/0275074005283371

Study Reveals Australian Office Workers Stressed by Irrelevant Email Overload. (2010). *Galaxy Research for IBM*. Retrieved from http://www-03.ibm.com/press/au/en/pressrelease/32913.wss

Suresh, S. (2006). *Knowledge management in small and medium enterprises in the United Kingdom construction industry* [PhD thesis]. Glasgow Caledonian University, Scotland, UK.

Sutherland, J. V., & Schwaber, K. (1995). Business object design and implementation: OOPSLA '95 workshop proceedings. The University of Michigan.

Swan, J., Scarbrough, H., & Newell, S. (2010). Why don't (or do) organizations learn from projects? *Management Learning*, *41*(3), 325–344. doi:10.1177/1350507609357003

Symonds, M. (2013, July 15). Where does social media fit into project management? *Parallel Project Training*. Retrieved from http://blog.parallelprojecttraining.com/project-management-articles/where-does-social-media-fit-into-project-management/

Symonds, M. 2012. Social Media in the project management arena. Retrieved from Parallel Project Training: http://blog.parallelprojecttraining.com/project-management-articles/social-media-in-the-project-management-arena/

Szkuta, K., Pizzicannella, R., & Osimo, D. (2014). Collaborative approaches to public sector innovation: A scoping study. *Telecommunications Policy*, *38*(5/6), 558–567. doi:10.1016/j.telpol.2014.04.002

Taylor, S., & Todd, P. A. (2001). Understanding Information Technology Usage: A test of Competing Models. *Information Systems Research*, *6*(2), 144–176. doi:10.1287/isre.6.2.144

Thackeray, R., Neiger, B., Smith, A., & Van Wagenen, S. (2012). Adoption and use of social media among public health departments. *BMC Public Health*, *12*(242). doi:10.1186/1471-2458-12-242 PMID:22449137

Thamhain, H. (2009). The future of team leadership in complex project environments. In D. I. Cleveland & B. Bidanda (Eds.), *Project management circa 2025*. Newton Square, PA: Project Management Institute.

The Quicker Steps project. (2011). Retrieved from http://www.quickersteps.net/project-presentation

The Radicati Group. (2013). Email Statistics Report, 2013-2017.

The Standish Group. (2013). *CHAOS Manifesto 2013: Think Big*. Act Small.

The Statistics Portal for Statistics and Studies. (2015). Retrieved from http://www.statista.com

The zero email company (White paper). (2012c). Atos. Retrieved from http://at.atos.net/content/dam/de/documents/atos-whitepaper-zeroemailcompany.pdf

Thomas, J., & Mengel, T. (2008). Preparing project managers to deal with complexity – Advanced project management education. *International Journal of Project Management*, *26*(3), 304–315. doi:10.1016/j.ijproman.2008.01.001

Towers Watson. (2013). *How the fundamentals have evolved and the best adapt: Change and communication ROI study report.* Retrieved from http://www.towerswatson.com/DownloadMedia.aspx?media=9AD1B8E9-813C-4FE8-AED2-0E753B1E098F

Treem, J.W. & Leonardi, P.M. (2012). Social Media Use in Organisations: Exploring the Affordances of Visibility, Editability, Persistence and Association. *Communication Yearbook,* 36.

Treem, J., Dailey, S., Pierce, C., & Leonardi, P. (2015). Bringing technological frames to work: How previous experience with social media shapes the technology's meaning in an organization. *Journal of Communication*, *65*(2), 296–422. doi:10.1111/jcom.12149

Trees, L. (2015). Putting enterprise content where people work: Best-practice organization use process maps, team sites and mobile apps to get content in front of the right people at the right time. *KM World*, *24*(4), 8–9.

Treurniet, W., Messemaker, M., Wolbers, J., & Boersma, F. K. (2015). Shaping the societal impact of emergencies: Striking a balance between Control and Cooperation. *International Journal of Emergency Services*, 4(1), 129-151. http://dx.doi.org/10.1108/IJES-06-2014-0007

Tuckman, B. W. (1965). Developmental sequence in small groups. *Psychological Bulletin*, *63*(6), 384–399. doi:10.1037/h0022100 PMID:14314073

Tuckman, B. W., & Jensen, M. A. C. (1977). Stages of Small-Group Development Revisited. *Group and Organization Studies*, *2*(4), 419–427. doi:10.1177/105960117700200404

Tufekci, Z., & Wilson, C. (2012). Social media and the decision to participate in political protest: Observations from Tahrir Square. *Journal of Communication*, *62*(2), 363–379. doi:10.1111/j.1460-2466.2012.01629.x

Turban, E., & King, D. (2012). *Electronic Commerce 2012: Managerial and Social Networks Perspectives* (7th ed.). Prentice Hall.

Twente, U. o. (2010). *Theory of Planned Behavior/ Reasoned Action.* Retrieved from http://www.utwente.nl

UNData. (2014). Mobile-cellular telephone subscriptions. Retrieved from http://data.un.org/

Use Twitter, Facebook and other social media to help manage projects and teams. (2015). Office. Retrieved from https://support.office.com/en-gb/article/Use-Twitter-Facebook-and-other-social-media-to-help-manage-projects-and-teams-1c9b9c86-e417-4763-91ed-35a5f6e86208

Valtari, M. (2015). Social Media Statistics from Finland. Retrieved from http://en.someco.fi/blog/social-media-statistics-from-finland/

van Aken, T. (1995). *De weg naar projectsucces*. Elsevier/De Tijdstroom.

Van de Walle, B., Turoff, M., & Hiltz, S. R. (Eds.), (2009). *Information systems for emergency management.* New York: ME Sharpe.

Van Dijck, J., & Poell, T. (2013). Understanding social media logic. *Media and Communication*, *1*(1), 2–14. doi:10.17645/mac.v1i1.70

Van Marrewijk, A. (2007). Managing project culture: The case of Environ Megaproject. *International Journal of Project Management*, *25*(3), 290–299. doi:10.1016/j.ijproman.2006.11.004

Veenswijk, M., Marrewijk, A., & Boersma, K. (2010). Developing New Knowledge in Collaborative Relationships in Megaproject Alliances: Organising Reflection in the Dutch Construction Sector. *International Journal of Knowledge Management Studies*, *4*(2), 216–232. doi:10.1504/IJKMS.2010.030793

Venkatesh, V. (2010b). *User Acceptance of Information Technology: Toward a Unified View.* Retrieved from www.vvenkatesh.com

Venkatesh, V., Morris, M., Davis, G., & Davis, F. D. (2003). User Acceptance of Information Technology: Toward a Unified View. *MIS Qquarterly*, *27*(3), 425–478.

Veronese, G. S. (2014). Métodos para Captura de Lições Aprendidas: Em Direção a Melhoria Contínua na Gestão de Projetos. *Revista Gestão e Projetos*, *5*(1), 71–83. doi:10.5585/gep.v5i1.250

Vieweg, S., Hughes, A. L., Starbird, K., & Palen, L. (2010). Microblogging during two natural hazards events: what twitter may contribute to situational awareness.*Proceedings of the SIGCHI conference on human factors in computing systems* (pp. 1079-1088). doi:10.1145/1753326.1753486

Vlietsra, J. (2001). *Dictionary of Acronyms and Technical Abbreviations*. London: Springer London. doi:10.1007/978-1-4471-0263-2

Von Zedtwitz, M. (2002). Organizational learning through post–project reviews in R&D. *R & D Management*, *32*(3), 255–268. doi:10.1111/1467-9310.00258

Wagenaar, P., Boersma, F. K., Groenewegen, P., & Niemandsverdriet, P. (2009). Implementing C2000 in the Dutch police region 'Hollands-Midden.' In A. Meijer, F.K. Boersma, & P. Wagenaar, (Eds.), ICTs, Citizens & Governance: After the Hype! (pp. 119-134). Amsterdam: IOS Press.

Walker, R. (2009). Social-networking tools fuel collaboration. *GCN.com*. Retrieved from http://gcn.com/Articles/2009/06/10/Social-networking-tools-fuel-collaboration.aspx

Walkey, G. (2009, Sep 16). *Guest Blogger – What do Project Managers need to know about Social Media?* Retrieved from www.arraspeople.co.uk

Wang, N. (2011). Risk allocation in the operational stage of private finance initiative projects. *Journal of Performance of Constructed Facilities*, *25*(6), 598–605. doi:10.1061/(ASCE)CF.1943-5509.0000194

Waters, J., & Lester, L. (2010). *The Everything Guide to Social Media: All you need to know about participating in today's most popular online communities*. Karen Cooper.

Weber, R., Aha, D. W., & Becerra-Fernandez, I. (2001). Intelligent lessons learned systems. *Expert Systems with Applications*, *20*(1), 17–34. doi:10.1016/S0957-4174(00)00046-4

Wee, L. K.-N., Alexandria, M., Kek, Y.-C., & Kelley, C. A. (2003). Transforming the marketing curriculum using problem-based learning: A case study. *Journal of Marketing Education*, *25*(2), 150–162. doi:10.1177/0273475303254016

Weick, K. E. (1988). Enacted Sensemaking in Crisis Situations. *Journal of Management Studies*, *25*(4), 305–317. doi:10.1111/j.1467-6486.1988.tb00039.x

Weinberg, J. (2012). The future of social networks. Retrieved from http://uk.news.yahoo.com/where-social-networks-are-going-next.html

Weisbuch, G. (2007). Tackling Complexity in Science: General Integration of the Application of Complexity in Science. Retrieved from http://www.soms.ethz.ch/research/complexityscience/EU_complexity_report.pdf

Wellman, B. (2005). Community: From neighborhood to network. *Communications of the ACM*, *48*(10), 53–55. doi:10.1145/1089107.1089137

Wenger, E., McDermott, R., & Snyder, W. M. (2002). *Cultivating Communities of Practice: A Guide to Managing Knowledge*. Boston: Harvard Business School Press.

Werder, K., Helms, R. W., & Jansen, S. (2014). Social media for success: A strategic framework.*Proceedings of the Pacific Asia Conference on Information Systems*.

Westbrook, R. N. (2012). Online Management System: Wielding Web 2.0 Tools to Collaboratively Manage and Track Projects. *Journal of Library Innovation*, *3*(1), 86–100.

White, D.S. (2010). Social Media growth from 2006 to 2010. Retrieved from http://dstevenwhite.com/2010/08/08/social-media-growth-from-2006-to-2010/

Wiewiora, A., & Murphy, G. (2015). Unpacking 'lessons learned': Investigating failures and considering alternative solutions. *Knowledge Management Research & Practice*, *13*(1), 17–30. doi:10.1057/kmrp.2013.26

Wiewiora, A., Murphy, G., Trigunarsyah, B., & Brown, K. (2014). Interactions between organizational culture, trustworthiness, and mechanisms for inter-project knowledge sharing. *Project Management Journal*, *45*(2), 48–65. doi:10.1002/pmj.21407

Wikipedia. (2011). SixDegrees.com. Retrieved from http://en.wikipedia.org/wiki/SixDegrees.com

Wikipedia. (2012). Catfish: The TV Show. Retrieved from http://en.wikipedia.org/wiki/Catfish:_The_TV_Show

Wikipedia. (2014). United Breaks Guitars Retrieved from http://en.wikipedia.org/wiki/United_Breaks_Guitars

Williams, T. (2003). Learning from projects. *The Journal of the Operational Research Society*, *54*(5), 443–451. doi:10.1057/palgrave.jors.2601549

Willke, H. (1998). *Systemisches Wissensmanagement*. Stuttgart: Lucius & Lucius Verlagsgesellschaft.

Winter, M., Smith, C., Morris, P., & Cicmil, S. (2006). Directions for future research in project management: The main findings of a UK government-funded research network. *International Journal of Project Management*, *24*(8), 638–649. doi:10.1016/j.ijproman.2006.08.009

Wolbers, J. J., & Boersma, F. K. (2013). The Common Operational Picture As Collective Sensemaking. *Journal of Contingencies and Crisis Management*, *21*(4), 186–199. doi:10.1111/1468-5973.12027

Worsley, L. (2015). The LinkedIn effect: a new way of learning – Focus on project management communities. Retrieved from http://www.slideshare.net/PiCubed/the-linkedin-effect-a-new-way-of-learning

Wright, A. (2009). Why getting a twitter coach is a smart idea. Retrieved from http://www.shrm.org/hrdisciplines/technology/Articles/Pages/GettingaTwitterCoach.aspx

Wright, K., Frame, T., & Hartzler, M. (2014). Student perceptions of a Self-Care course taught exclusively by team-based learning and utilizing Twitter. *Currents in Pharmacy and Teaching*, *6*(6), 842–848. doi:10.1016/j.cptl.2014.07.003

Yates, D., & Paquette, S. (2011). Emergency knowledge management and social media technologies: A case study of the 2010 Haitian earthquake. *International Journal of Information Management*, *31*(1), 6–13. doi:10.1016/j.ijinfomgt.2010.10.001

Yin, J., Lampert, A., Cameron, M., Robinson, B., & Power, R. (2012). Using social media to enhance emergency situation awareness. *IEEE Intelligent Systems*, *27*(6), 52–59. doi:10.1109/MIS.2012.6

York University. (2010, Nov 18). *Technology acceptance model.* Retrieved from http://www.fsc.yorku.ca

Young, T. (2013). Four million reasons why you should be on LinkedIn. Retrieved from http://www.smartcompany.com.au/leadership/professional-development/40412-how-linkedin-has-grown-to-be-an-influential-business-network.html#

Zandhuis, A., Legerman, A., & Stellingwerf, R. (2012). *ISO 21500 in practice: A Management Guide: The International Guideline for Project Management.* Van: Haren Publishing.

Zeider, R. (2007). *Internet provides disciplinary challenges for employers.* Retrieved from http://www.shrm.org/hrdisciplines/technology/Articles/Pages/InternetDisciplinaryChallenges

Zeng, B. & Gerritsen, R. (2014). What do we know about social media in tourism? A review. *Tourism Management Perspectives.*

Zhang, J., Qu, Y., Cody, J., & Wu, Y. (2010). A case study of micro-blogging in the enterprise: Use, value and related issues.*Proceedings of the SIGCHI Conference on Human Factors in Computing Systems* (pp. 123–132). ACM Press. doi:10.1145/1753326.1753346

About the Contributors

Gilbert Silvius (1963) is professor of project and programme management at LOI University of Applied Sciences in the Netherlands and senior research associate at the University of Johannesburg in South Africa. He initiated and developed the first MSc in Project Management program in the Netherlands and is considered a leading expert in the field of project management. Gilbert has published over a 100 academic papers and several books. He holds a PhD degree in information sciences from Utrecht University and masters' degrees in economics and business administration. As a practitioner, Gilbert has over 20 years' experience in organizational change and IT projects. He is principal consultant at Van Aetsveld, project and change management, and is a member of the international enable2change network of project management experts.

***

Anne Basten got her Research Master's in Behavioral Science / Psychology in 2010 and has put that to work in various internal and customer projects within Atos since then. As a product of "Generation Y," Anne has been involved in finding smarter ways of working together in projects through enterprise social media and other social collaboration tools.

John R. Bennett Jr. holds a doctorate in public administration and master's degrees in higher education and historic preservation. He is an adjunct professor at Valdosta State University and executive director of a non-profit organization based in Savannah, GA.

Kees (F.K.) Boersma is Associate Professor in the Department of Organization Sciences of the VU University Amsterdam. He completed his (awarded) PhD thesis at the Eindhoven University of Technology. His current research is about organization networks and strategies in the context of safety, crisis management and security. He is the group leader of AREA: Amsterdam Research on Emergency Administration, senior member of the Netherlands Institute of Governance (NIG) and senior editor of the Journal of Contingencies and Crisis Management (guest editor), Organization Management Journal and the International Journal of Emergency Services. He is an active member of the international Information Systems for Crisis Response and Management (ISCRAM) Community, at the 2014 conference on Empowering Citizens and Communities through Information Systems for Crisis Response and Management he is invited to join a panel on crisis, citizens and sensemaking.

Marcirio Silveira Chaves holds a Ph.D. in Computer Science from the University of Lisbon. He is currently Professor at Nove de Julho University (UNINOVE), where he leads the research line Managing of Projects and the research group Managing Web 2.0 Technologies in Projects - TiP 2.0. He is also part of the faculty's Informatics and Knowledge Management Graduate Program. He is Associate Editor of the Journal of Business and Projects, member of the Association for information Systems (AIS) and the editorial board of the Iberoamerican Journal of Project Management – IJoPM and reviewer of papers for several journals and conferences. He has more than 50 papers published in journals and scientific events and has collaborated with more than 50 authors. He has been cited by 250 authors with more than 580 citations to his work.

Dominique Diks (MSc) is currently working as a junior consultant at Hiemstra & de Vries, a Dutch consultancy company that focuses on change processes within public organizations. After succeeding her Organization Sciences Bachelor, she enrolled in the Master's Policy, Communication and Organization. During her Master's, she specialized herself in social issues and corresponding problems. She finds her passion in doing things that have an impact on society and wherein she can achieve crystal clear positive results for the public benefit. Modern technology can help her achieve these results. She spent her Master's thesis researching how social media and (big) data can contribute to the public sector. At the moment she is using this knowledge in her daily job at Hiemstra & de Vries, where she played an important role in organizing the Smart Government Congress.

Esther (S.E.) van Dokkum combines working as inbound marketer and her studies at the HU University of Applied Sciences, Utrecht. And is an active participant in the Top Class program, she has certificates for internet marketing, inbound marketing and PRINCE2®. Esther is an experienced online marketer and regularly organizes both business and cultural events. Esther has done market research for several companies and takes part in the development of the 'Cultuurmonitor' (Cultural monitor) on consumer confidence in the cultural sector in the Netherlands.

Julie (J.E.) Ferguson is Assistant Professor of Organization Sciences, VU University (PhD Economics and Business Administration). Her main research interests are ICT-enabled collaboration in heterogeneous, dispersed knowledge networks, particularly in development cooperation and emergency relief. Julie is a Research Associate of Royal Holloway University of London ICT4D Collective, and member of IFIP Working Group on Social Implications of Computers in Developing Countries. One of her major research projects (based on a Dutch Science Foundation grant, with co-authors Boersma and Wolbers) focuses on humanitarian disaster coordination, in particular the role of social media and citizen participation. Julie has published among others in Journal of Information Technology, Information Systems Journal, World Development, Journal of Knowledge Management, and Knowledge Management for Development Journal.

Dave Garrett is the Director of Digital Presence for PMI and the President of ProjectManagement.com, PMI's Global Knowledge Portal. As the Director of Digital Presence, Dave is responsible for the design and analytics of all of PMI's digital properties. As President of ProjectManagement.com, Dave drives community engagement by delivering extreme value to 51M Project Practitioners globally - regardless of their level of expertise or the standards they follow.

Jerry Giltenane Professional services director with Aspiracon, a consultancy company based in Ireland and regional support director for the Irish Chapter of the PMI. Holds a MBA from Henley /Business School, as well as a bachelor's business degree and graduate diploma in computer science from the University of Limerick. Previously he worked with Dell, IBM, and System Dynamics. Co-Founder of Dell's PM4LIFE program which was a winner at the global PMI professional awards for contribution via project management to the voluntary sector in 2104.

Elizabeth Harrin, MA, FAPM, MBCS is the author of Customer-Centric Project Management, Social Media for Project Managers and others. She is the award-winning blogger behind A Girl's Guide to Project Management. With over 15 years as a practicing project manager, Elizabeth has wide experience in IT and healthcare projects.

Amir Manzoor holds a bachelor's degree in engineering from NED University, Karachi, an MBA from Lahore University of Management Sciences (LUMS), and an MBA from Bangor University, United Kingdom. He has many years of diverse professional and teaching experience working at many renowned national and internal organizations and higher education institutions. His research interests include electronic commerce and technology applications in business. He is a member of Chartered Banker Institute of UK and Project Management Institute, USA.

J. Scott McDonald (Ph.D. – Political Science, Northern Illinois University, M.S. – Geography, Northern Illinois University, BS – Geography, Northern Illinois University) is a Professor of Public Administration at the University of Texas El Paso. He has authored or coauthored more than 50 refereed and governmental publications focused primarily on economic development and community development, leadership, innovation, and quality of life matters. He has conducted projects for a wide range of federal, state, regional, and local entities.

Linky van der Merwe is a certified project management professional (PMP) and Founder of Virtual Project Consulting. She has been a senior project manager at Microsoft Consulting Services South Africa for 6 years and is now a Programme Manager at a major Retailer. Her mission is to provide best practice advice and to recommend resources to aspiring and existing project managers. With 20 years of IT industry experience she has a passion for delivery through projects.

Keith A. Merwin is a principal in Merwin Associates, a consulting firm providing strategic technology analysis, planning, and development and change management services. He has 25 years' experience developing software and providing training for customer service operations in government and for-profit organizations including meeting the needs of multilingual users.

Gerald "Jerry" Merwin, Ph.D., is a Professor of Public Administration, in the Political Science Department at Valdosta State University. His primary research interests relate to information management in the public sector and the role of information technology in economic development. He teaches primarily graduate courses in the Public Administration online programs for MPA and DPA students. Jerry is a member of Georgia Political Science Association and the Council for Adult and Experiential

Learning. In past educational positions, Jerry taught in both technical college and university settings. His teaching included information management and related courses for students in a business administration degree program and he coordinated the program at an off-campus location. He earned the Ph.D. in Industrial/Organizational and Vocational Psychology at North Carolina State University.

Frank Molendijk is a senior consultant with experience in complex IT projects, advice / research reports in which he had a mixed set of roles varying from IT specialist to project manager. His interest is strongly focused on IT in the broadest sense but also the human aspect of IT and the impact this has. In his current role, Frank is working at the Port of Rotterdam Authority as a business consultant and primarily on the possibilities and opportunities that IT trends—such as Internet of Things, Predictive Analytics, etc.—present.

Hamid Nach is professor of Business Technology Management (BTM) at the University of Quebec at Rimouski, Lévis Campus. he has been working in the private sector before he enrolled in academia. He teaches undergraduate and graduate classes in the field of information systems. His research interests concerns generally the study of how people use and transform information and communication technologies (ICT) and how, in return, ICT transform their lives. His teaching covers a wide range of Business-Technology-Management related areas such as, IS strategy, IT management, cloud computing, ecommerce and social media.

Ahdia Nazari is a service consultant at the Omnia Vocational College in Espoo, Finland. She received her BBA degree from the Laurea University of Applied Sciences in Espoo, Finland. In cooperation with Laurea's project management department, she decided to write her thesis based on developing a social media plan featuring a case project that aimed at promoting methods of disseminating knowledge of students' possibilities to quicker step into work life. She has been working as marketing assistant and service consultant. Ahdia Nazari has recently cooperated with an author by contributing a chapter from her thesis.

Pascal Ravesteijn PhD is a Professor of Process Innovation and Information Systems. His main research interest is in Business Process Management (BPM). He is a member of the board of directors at the International Information Management Association (IIMA) and is a board member of the Dutch BPM-Forum. Furthermore, Pascal is editor of the Journal of International Technology Information Management and he is a member of the editorial board of the International Journal of Global Management Studies.

Kate Barnett-Richards is an experienced lecturer at Coventry University, and Fellow of the Higher Education Academy, who specialises in Operations and Supply Chain Management. Prior to entering academia Kate held a number of Operations Management roles in both the retail and healthcare sectors. Her current research focuses on sustainable food supply chains; as well as disruptive and innovation learning practices.

Marie Sams is currently a Senior Lecturer within the School of Strategy and Leadership at Coventry University. Prior to that, she taught part-time at the University while working as a Project Manager on a variety of health and social care related publicly funded projects. Sponsors included Department of

Health, National Health Service and the Higher Education Funding Council for England. Recent research includes evaluating the differences in project management approaches in the private and public sectors, and disruptive learning (using social media to encourage discourse between industry managers and students). She is an active member of the Association for Project Management and a Fellow of the Higher Education Academy.

Céline Silvius (1992) is studying Cultural Events Management MSc at De Montfort University, Leicester. She is a BBA in International Business and Management, as well as a PRINCE2® certified junior project manager with experience in managing both business and cultural events. A few projects in her portfolio include working on the first edition of the China (Shanghai) International Technology Fair, the first edition of BonAppetito Food & Festival Utrecht and several theatrical and musical productions.

Mark Sponselee (30) received a Master's degree in project management in 2014, after completing the Master's Project Management program at the Hogeschool Utrecht. His master's thesis was about the application possibilities of social media in project management. Mark started working as a project management consultant at Van Aetsveld in 2008 and possesses knowledge and experience in portfolio, programme, and project—change management.

Giuliana Veronese holds a Ph.D. in Computer Science from the University of Lisbon. Worked on European research projects developing large-scale distributed algorithms based on new security paradigms aiming to prevent systems against malicious attacks. Responsible for several articles published on international conferences (ACM, IEEE). Currently, she is responsible for managing all LATAM delivery centers located in the following countries: Argentina, Chile, Colombia, Peru and Mexico. Managing 460 professionals creating high performance, multi-cultural and focused teams capable of designing and delivering IT projects aligned with business strategies. Integration of delivery centers using common management processes, methodologies and tools, increasing significantly the customers' satisfaction. She is responsible for successful implementation of world class IT services based on recognized methodologies such as PMBOK, ITIL, CMMI and Agile Methodologies. Solid management of project costs achieving effective financial results.

Tim de Vries is a pragmatic change manager. He has multiple years of experience in managing projects and programs, most of them related to customer communication and social collaboration. With his pro-active approach he is able to help organizations collaborate within the organization and with customers. By communicating in a transparent and straight forward way, he is able to get teams working on the strategic goals.

Deborah Walker is a seasoned marketing communications professional specializing in social media. She holds a Masters of Education from Pennsylvania State University with a focus on Instructional Design. Deborah has spent more than a decade connecting stakeholders through virtual communities and building brand awareness through social media for professional associations including the American Academy of Pediatrics and Project Management Institute.

Ina Wensveen has been working in Information Technology since 1987 in various roles and assignments, particularly in the banking sector. She has many years of professional experience in change management, team development and organizational change. Ina has been actively involved in the Atos Zero email program from the start in 2011. As a social collaboration expert she supports teams and organizations in adopting new, collaborative ways of working to deliver more added value.

Peter Wijngaard (IPMA-B certified, international program manager) has 20 years project management experience in various sectors, including Oil & Gas, ICT, Telecom, Central Government, and Pharmaceuticals. Peter got his PhD at the Agricultural University, and continued his career as management consultant, and project and program manager. He is Thought Leader P3M: active in professionalization of project management by scientific research, solution development, teaching, publishing, reviewer for IJPM, and international assessor for the IPMA Project Excellence Award. He is co-author of the book "De Kloof".

Jeroen (J.J.) Wolbers has written his PhD thesis at the VU Amsterdam Research on Emergency Administration research group (promotion date: January 2016). His PhD thesis is titled 'Drawing the Line: Practicing cross-boundary coordination in emergency response'. Based upon an interpretive analysis he describes how cross-boundary coordination is practiced between heterogeneous response organizations and gives an explanation for how coordination can lead both to integration and fragmentation of response operations. Part of his work is published in leading crisis management journals and he is an active member of the ISCRAM association.

Index

Q

R

S

T

V

W

Y

Z

www.ingramcontent.com/pod-product-compliance
Lightning Source LLC
LaVergne TN
LVHW060416300926
849162LV00006B/1438